Masters, Slaves, & Subjects

This watercolor, "The Old Plantation," was painted by an unknown artist in the last quarter of the eighteenth century, purportedly near Charleston. The image, while obviously idealized, offers fascinating evidence for the intermixture of African and English modes of cultural expression among low-country blacks in this period. The pose of the dancers, their use of a stick and scarves, and the musical instruments are of African derivation, while their clothing (with the important exception of their headdresses) more closely reflects eighteenth-century English ideas of ceremonial costume. In the background a classically Georgian "Great House" lies surrounded by its dependencies, outbuildings, and slave quarters. Meanwhile in the middle distance, Africans (or their descendants) travel upon the river in canoes. Source: Abby Aldrich Rockefeller Folk Art Center, Williamsburg, Virginia.

Masters, Slaves, & Subjects

The Culture of Power in the

South Carolina Low Country,

1740–1790

ROBERT OLWELL

CORNELL UNIVERSITY PRESS

ITHACA AND LONDON

First published 1998 by Cornell University Press
First printing, Cornell Paperbacks, 1998

Printed in the United States of America

Library of Congress Cataloging-in-Publication Data

Olwell, Robert, b. 1960
    Masters, slaves, and subjects : the culture of power in the South Carolina low country, 1740–1790 / Robert Olwell.
        p. cm.
    Includes bibliographical references and index.
    ISBN 0-8014-3488-2 (cloth : alk. paper). — ISBN 0-8014-8491-X (pbk. : alk. paper)
    1. Slavery—South Carolina—History—18th century.   2. Plantation life—South Carolina—History—18th century.   I. Title.
E445.S7046   1998
975.7'02—dc21   97-53061

Cornell University Press strives to use environmentally responsible suppliers and materials to the fullest extent possible in the publishing of its books. Such materials include vegetable-based, low-VOC inks and acid-free papers that are recycled, totally chlorine-free, or partly composed of nonwood fibers. Books that bear the logo of the FSC (Forest Stewardship Council) use paper taken from forests that have been inspected and certified as meeting the highest standards for environmental and social responsibility. For further information, visit our website at www.cornellpress.cornell.edu.

Cloth printing   10 9 8 7 6 5 4 3 2 1
Paperback printing   10 9 8 7 6 5 4 3 2

For Julie

Contents

Maps and Illustrations

Preface

I made my first trip to Charleston in the summer of 1984. I was a first-year graduate student at the University of Wisconsin at Milwaukee, and the purpose of my trip was to conduct research for a master's thesis on the subject of slavery and the American Revolution in South Carolina. (I did not yet know that I had bitten off far more than I could chew, either in a short research expedition or in a master's thesis.) I spent several weeks working in the archives in Columbia. But when I was down to my last few days and last few dollars, I felt compelled to see Charleston for myself. The next morning, I rode a Greyhound bus down to the low country on Interstate 26.

I left the Charleston bus station and started walking south down Meeting Street. It was hot. To a native Midwesterner, it felt like the tropics. As I continued south past Broad Street I was thrilled to find so many eighteenth-century buildings, but even more to discover an eighteenth-century cityscape. The Charleston I found seemed remarkably like the Charles Town I had read of in books. St. Michael's steeple was still the highest point in the city, and the Exchange house still dominated the east end of Broad Street. South of Broad, entire streets appeared to be unchanged from the colonial era. For a moment, I felt that I had traveled not only to another place but also to another time.

Eventually, of course, as I began to notice the BMWs in the gated driveways and to hear the quiet hum of air conditioners, that first impression of Charleston as a place where the past had not passed wore off. I soon realized that the restored homes and churches were like stone monuments whose builders had long since departed, replaced by people like me or by tour guides in "historic" costume. I tried to imagine why these places had been built, the impression they made when they were new, and what the world was like when these buildings were still alive with purpose. In one sense, this book is the product of both that first illusory vision and my subsequent quest to recapture it.

To the extent that they seek to perceive the past on its own terms, all historians might be considered time-travelers. This book marks the end of a very long journey. In the many travels, both literal and intellectual, that have led to the completion of this project, I have received assistance from many people. Now, like a hiker at the end of a long cross-country walk, I am happy to have finished, eager to put down my pack, and grateful to be able to thank all those people whose encouraging words or material support helped to sustain me along the way.

I have had the very good fortune to have excellent teachers. I took my first steps as a professional historian at the University of Wisconsin at Milwaukee, where Reginald Horsman and Carole Shammas guided me through a master's thesis that ended up focusing on slavery during only the first year of the revolution in South Carolina. I next went to the Johns Hopkins University and to Jack P. Greene. From Jack, and from my colleagues in his graduate seminar, I learned what it is to be simultaneously a curious student and an insightful scholar. In Baltimore, William W. Freehling and J. G. A. Pocock offered trenchant critiques of my research design as I headed off to the archives.

Several members of the Greene seminar deserve special thanks. Christine Daniels went well beyond the call of friendship when she gave me her old VW Beetle to take with me to South Carolina. That car did a lot to make the year more fruitful and enjoyable. Jim Sidbury and I have pursued unexpectedly parallel tracks from our first days at Hopkins to our present positions at the University of Texas. Over the past twelve years we have drunk enough coffee to float a battleship while we solved the problems of the early modern world. I know that those conversations (not to mention the coffee) greatly improved this book. Karin Wulf and Steve Lofgren alternately provided analysis of and escape from "the book"; both the advice and the respite were welcome and much needed.

In South Carolina, I was fortunate to be a fellow at the Institute for Southern Studies at the University of South Carolina, where Walter Edgar, Nancy Vance Ashmore, and Tibby Dozier offered both logistical support and a refuge from the documents. Also at USC, David Chesnutt and Peggy Clark of the Henry Laurens Papers office allowed me to peruse the as-yet-unpublished portions of Laurens's letters. The staffs of the South Caroliniana Library at the University of South Carolina, the state Department of Archives and History, and the South Carolina Historical Society were patient and unstintingly helpful. Other South Carolina scholars have been gracious in offering both their time and their knowledge. Robert Weir has steadfastly offered me his support, and Charles Joyner kindly gave me and my wife a memorable tour of his own part of the low country. At an early stage in my research, Peter Wood welcomed me to the subject and provided crucial advice and much-appreciated encouragement.

Many other people helped in small, but significant, ways, and I am glad for the chance finally to thank some of them. Oliver Russell allowed access to the papers of James Grant at Ballindalloch Castle in Scotland. George Terry and G. Melvin Herndon shared with me some of their research into eighteenth-century low-country society. Rosemary Brana-Shute, David Barry Gaspar, Darlene Clark Hine, Larry Hudson, and Randy Sparks invited me to share some of my preliminary work at conferences or in anthologies. These occasions and their critiques helped concentrate my mind and clarify my thoughts. Peter Dorsey undertook a page-by-page reading of my dissertation as I began the long process of revision, a thankless task for which I nonetheless offer thanks. My colleagues at Mount Saint Mary's College and at the University of Texas at Austin, especially Shearer Davis Bowman, Sally Clarke, Richard Graham, Michael Hall, Curt Johnson, Kevin Kenny, Sandra Lauderdale, Martha Newman, Gunther Peck, and Robert Preston, allowed me to sharpen my analytical tools both by reading and listening to my ideas and by sharing their own work with me. At the Cornell University Press, Peter Agree and Grey Osterud, editor and copy editor respectively, were a model of professionalism. Shannon Crum produced the maps.

Small portions of this book have been published elsewhere, and I am grateful to the editors for granting me permission to reprint much-revised extracts from those essays here. Parts of chapter 4 appeared as " 'Loose, Idle and Disorderly': Slave Women in the Eighteenth-Century Charleston Marketplace," in *More Than Chattel: Black Women and Slavery in the Americas*, ed. David Barry Gaspar and Darlene Clark Hine (Bloomington: Indiana University Press, 1996). Parts of chapters 4 and 5 appeared as " 'A Reckoning of Accounts': Patriarchy, Market Relations, and Control on Henry Laurens's Lowcountry Plantations, 1762–1785," in *Working toward Freedom: Slave Society and Domestic Economy in the American South*, ed. Larry E. Hudson (Rochester: University of Rochester Press, 1994). And portions of chapter 6 appeared as " 'Domestick Enemies': Slavery and Political Independence in South Carolina, May 1775–March 1776," *Journal of Southern History* 55 (February 1989), 21–48.

In the course of my research and writing, I received financial assistance from several institutions. As a graduate student, I was helped with a Beveridge research grant from the American Historical Association and by years of research fellowships from the University of Wisconsin at Milwaukee and the Johns Hopkins University. As an assistant professor, I greatly benefited from summer research grants made by Mount Saint Mary's College and the University of Texas at Austin.

I met Julie Hardwick two weeks after I returned from that first trip to Charleston. Since then, our travels have taken us from Wisconsin to Maryland, South Carolina, Pennsylvania, France, England, Scotland, and at last Texas. Along the way, she cheerfully accepted long stays at abysmal motels and my need to read every historic marker we passed. She also helped me conduct research, even while she had her own book to complete, and patiently read and re-read every chapter. Without her support, intelligence, and humor, I suspect that not only would this be a very different book but it would likely not be a book at all.

Our other collaborative project, our daughter Rose, arrived too late to be pressed into service as a research assistant. But her birth did provide me with a deadline that I could not evade. Her first steps closely coincided with the last steps of this figurative long march.

ROBERT OLWELL

Austin, Texas

Abbreviations

BPRO   British Public Record Office, London, England.
DAR   *Documents of the American Revolution, 1770–1783* [Colonial Office
           Series], ed. K. G. Davies, 21 vols. (Dublin, 1972–81).
JCHA   *Journal of the Commons House of Assembly*, ed. J. H. Esterby et al.,
           14 vols. to date (Columbia, S.C., 1951–   ).
JCHA   Journal of Commons House of Assembly.
JGC   Journal of the Governor's Council.
LC   Library of Congress, Washington, D.C.
Loyalists Transcript of the Manuscript Books and Papers of the
           Commission of Enquiry into the Losses and Services of the
           American Loyalists, New York Public Library.
MEL-JHU   Milton Eisenhower Library, Johns Hopkins University, Baltimore,
           Maryland.
PHL   *The Papers of Henry Laurens*, ed. Philip M. Hamer et al., 14 vols. to
           date (Columbia, S.C., 1968–   ).
SCDAH   South Carolina Department of Archives and History, Columbia,
           S.C.
SCHM   *South Carolina Historical Magazine / South Carolina Historical and
           Genealogical Magazine*.
SCHS   South Carolina Historical Society, Charleston, S.C.
SCL-USC   South Caroliniana Library, University of South Carolina,
           Columbia, S.C.
SHC-UNC   Southern Historical Collection, University of North Carolina,
           Chapel Hill, N.C.

SPG   Society for the Propagation of the Gospel.
Statutes   *The Statutes at Large of South Carolina*, ed. Thomas Cooper and
            David J. McCord, 10 vols. (Columbia, 1836–41).
WPL-DU   William Perkins Library, Duke University, Durham, N.C.
WSCRO   West Sussex County Record Office, Chichester, England.

Masters, Slaves, & Subjects

Introduction:
Kings and Slaves

In the early summer of 1765, Henry Laurens, a forty-one-year-old Charles Town merchant turned slave master and rice planter, received word from the overseer of one of his plantations that Bill, a valued slave, had recently died. Laurens sent his regrets but added philosophically that "we must both Kings & Slaves submit to the strokes of death."[1] Laurens's reply at first seems a familiar and timeless cliché. At second glance, however, the remark offers a revealing insight into the world both Laurens and Bill lived in. While Laurens piously opined that in death all men were rendered equal, he took it for granted that in life *inequality* was the rule. Between "Kings & Slaves" lay a hierarchical chain of being in which every person had an assigned place and role. Moreover, Laurens's use of the royal "we" implies that in this particular context he, as master, expected to play the part of the "King" to the unfortunate Bill's "slave." Finally, Laurens's aside recalls a time and place where both "Kings & Slaves" casually coexisted as ideals and realities in the minds and lives of Americans.

The colony of South Carolina in the era between 1740 and the end of the American Revolution was a world in which both kings and slaves were taken for granted. Slaves were present every day not only in the rice and indigo fields but also on the roads and rivers of the countryside, in the streets of Charles Town, in the Anglican church and in the market,

1. Henry Laurens to Peter Horlbeck, 15 May 1765, *PHL*, 4, 624.

The colony of South Carolina, 1775 (with Anglican parish boundaries)

and in gentry dining rooms, kitchens, and stableyards. While the British king never set foot in the colony, his presence was nonetheless felt. The health of the reigning monarch was prayed for every Sunday in the Anglican church, and his name was invoked at every meeting of the Assembly and every sitting of a court. Oaths were taken, toasts made, and land grants, laws, and pardons all issued in the name of "his gracious majesty." On the king's birthday, Charles Town celebrated with bonfires and fireworks. At news of the king's death, people went about dressed in mourning clothes.

In some ways, as Laurens's letter suggests, the king and the slaves were conceptualized as opposites. If the name and image of the king epitomized the colony's close ties to (and appropriation of) British culture and politics, the presence of slaves embodied the colony's adaptation to the new world environment. The figure of the king represented order, authority, and hierarchy, while crowds of slaves threatened disorder, rebellion, and anarchy. Ordinarily, for men like Henry Laurens, the king was to be obeyed, and slaves were to be commanded.

Yet the idea of kingship and the reality of slavery were also closely intertwined. Slaves were tried, executed, and (rarely) pardoned in the king's name. Slaves were among those who prayed for the health of the king in the church. But slaves also prayed that the king would deliver them from their bondage. Masters thought of themselves as the monarchs of their plantations and likened their authority over their slaves to that of a king over his subjects. At the same time, Anglican ministers and political theorists described the rule of the king as analogous to that of the master of a household, and the kingdom as analogous to a large family. When South Carolina's political leaders felt that their liberty was threatened by royal policies and actions, they compared their situation to that of their slaves. After 1775, as low-country masters first defied and then denied the authority of their monarch, they found that their slaves could likewise challenge their "rightful" rulers.

One aim of this book is to illuminate the complex interrelationship between "Kings & Slaves," colonialism and slavery, in one early American slave society: the mid-eighteenth-century South Carolina low country. Through a close examination of the institutions, rituals, and languages within which masters, slaves, and metropolis contested and negotiated, it seeks to reveal how domination was both imposed and resisted and how the social order was constructed and perpetuated in a small corner of the early modern Anglo-American world.

By analyzing the role of the metropolitan state and English culture in a colonial setting, and by examining how colonial conditions and peoples could alter metropolitan institutions and English ideas, this study adopts a perspective on the eighteenth-century Atlantic world that focuses upon issues of cultural exchange, appropriation, and reciprocity. Such an endeavor is in accord with J. G. A. Pocock's "plea" for students of the British empire to trace "the processes by which a diversity of societies, nationalities, and political structures came into being" and to examine discrete elements of empire within "the history of their interactions" with the whole; it is also in keeping with Bernard Bailyn and Philip Morgan's more recent suggestion that colonial constructions of race and ethnicity must be inserted into the imperial mix.[2]

2. J. G. A. Pocock, "British History: A Plea for a New Subject," *Journal of Modern History* 47 (1975), 601–21; and also Pocock, "The Limits and Divisions of British History: In Search of the Unknown Subject," *American Historical Review* 87 (1982), 311–16; Bernard Bailyn and Philip D. Morgan, eds., *Strangers within the Realm: Cultural Margins of the First British Empire* (Chapel Hill, 1991).

Most studies of the southern colonies and of early American slavery have accepted the existence of kings and slaves without question. For the most part, these works have not regarded the coexistence of these two institutions as a significant factor in shaping the culture and character of the societies they examined. Instead, the historiographies of eighteenth-century American slavery and of the colonial South have pursued different questions, tending down quite separate tracks. Thus, while Henry Laurens wrote and thought of "Kings *and* Slaves" as two halves of a whole, most studies have chosen to focus their attention upon either kings *or* slaves, colonialism *or* slavery.

The importance of slavery in the development of the southern colonies of British North America has long been acknowledged. In the past three decades, a number of studies have provided a rich and complex view of the origins and development of slavery in this region.[3] Similarly, a great deal of excellent work has been done on the influence of Britain upon society and culture in the eighteenth-century southern colonies. But few scholars have long considered the degree to which the eighteenth-century plantation South's condition as *colonies* may have affected their development as slave societies or, conversely, how the institution of slavery may have affected the colonies' reception and adaptation of metropolitan forms.[4]

3. Among the important works on slavery in the southern colonies are: Thad W. Tate, *The Negro in Eighteenth-Century Williamsburg* (Charlottesville, 1966); Gerald W. Mullin, *Flight and Rebellion: Slave Resistance in Eighteenth-Century Virginia* (Oxford, 1972); Peter H. Wood, *Black Majority: Slaves in Colonial South Carolina from 1670 to the Stono Rebellion* (New York, 1974); Edmund S. Morgan, *American Slavery, American Freedom: The Ordeal of Colonial Virginia* (New York, 1975); Daniel C. Littlefield, *Rice and Slaves: Ethnicity and the Slave Trade in Colonial South Carolina* (Baton Rouge, 1981); Betty Wood, *Slavery in Colonial Georgia, 1730–1775* (Athens, 1984); Allan Kulikoff, *Tobacco and Slaves: The Development of Southern Cultures in the Chesapeake, 1680–1800* (Chapel Hill, 1986); Mechal Sobel, *The World They Made Together: Black and White Values in Eighteenth-Century Virginia* (Princeton, 1987); Michael Mullin, *Africa in America: Slave Acculturation and Resistance in the American South and the British Caribbean, 1736–1831* (Urbana, 1991); Marvin L. Michael Kay and Lorin Lee Cary, *Slavery in North Carolina, 1748–1775* (Chapel Hill, 1995). A work that appeared too late to be consulted here, but that promises to be a major contribution to the literature on this subject, is Philip D. Morgan, *Slave Counterpoint: Black Culture in the Eighteenth-Century Chesapeake and Lowcountry* (Chapel Hill, 1998).

4. For example, Rhys Isaac's brilliant portrait of mid-eighteenth-century Virginia as a cultural province of England, *The Transformation of Virginia, 1740–1790* (Chapel Hill, 1982), devotes little attention to the fact that over 40 percent of Virginia's population in this period was made up of slaves, despite his insightful handling of master-slave relations in the book's afterword, "Discourse on the Method." Additional recent examples of slaves hiding in plain sight in otherwise subtle works on eighteenth-century American society and politics include M. Eugene Sirmans, *Colonial South Carolina: A Political History, 1663–1763* (Chapel Hill, 1966); David Hackett Fischer, *Albion's Seed: Four British Folkways in America* (New York, 1989); Richard L. Bushman, *The Refinement of America: Persons, Houses and Cities* (New York, 1992); Gordon S. Wood, *The Radicalism of the American Revolution* (New York, 1992). For suggestive

Understanding the social dynamics of the South Carolina low country in the years from 1740 to 1790 requires that these two historiographical traditions be woven together. In the low country in this era, the chains of slavery and the bonds of empire were both particularly strong. Nowhere else in British North America were slaves as numerous and influential. Likewise, perhaps no other colonial elite was so attached to England, or to imitating English ways, as were the slave masters of Charles Town on the eve of the Revolution. The social development and political culture of South Carolina low-country society in this period cannot be understood without giving full consideration to its dual character as both a colonial society and a slave society. Because the South Carolina low country in the mid-eighteenth century was a *slave* society, the domination of slaves was always the main objective of the ministers of state and church and the main public and private concern of the masters. Because South Carolina in this period was a *colonial* society, the forms of both domination and resistance were determined to an important degree by the precedent, standard, and power of the metropolis.

The new world offered European colonists new possibilities for wealth, property, and power, but it also confronted them with unfamiliar plants, peoples, and possibilities. In some ways, early America was a cultural "hothouse" where some English transplants quickly wilted while others adapted to new world realities, mutated in the American environment, and thrived far beyond the dreams (or nightmares) of the old world.

The most significant of these new world realities was the institution of chattel slavery. Slavery was from the start a colonial institution. The first Africans enslaved to Englishmen in English territory arrived in Virginia in 1619. Yet for a long period slavery remained the exception rather than the rule in the English new world. The Caribbean island colony of Barbados, established in 1627, was the first English colonial society to change from a society with slaves into a slave society, a world in which the master-slave relation was the central pivot of the entire social order. Motivated by the enormous profits to be made from sugar cultivation, English settlers in Barbados during the years between 1640 and 1660 imported thousands of Africans and constructed the legal and institutional infrastructure required to control persons who were deemed to be the property of others. In the last quarter of the seventeenth century, the Chesapeake region underwent a similar transformation. South Carolina, established during these same years and settled in part from Barbados, was a slave society from the very first.[5]

---

examples of how slaves might be written into this story, see Philip D. Morgan, "British Encounters with Africans and African-Americans, circa 1600–1780," in Bailyn and Morgan, eds., *Strangers within the Realm*, 157–219.

5. For English attitudes toward slavery and Africans in the age of colonization, see Win-

To describe mid-eighteenth-century South Carolina as a colonial society is to assert that the region was politically, culturally, and economically in the orbit of the British metropole. It should not be taken to imply that the colony was therefore in an early, or transitory, stage of development. Although it is fraught with unresolved tensions, the colonial condition is not necessarily temporary. The colonial South did of course give way to the so-called old South of the nineteenth century, which in turn gave way to a "new South" after 1865. But there was nothing inevitable or natural about this course of events. Like many established social orders, the colonial slave society changed in part through the attempts of its inhabitants to maintain the status quo.

The Culture of Power

Slavery was a system of domination. As such, it relied for its perpetuation upon a continuous, if unequal, dialogue between rulers and ruled, dominators and dominated. Even actions or declarations by the dominant group that did not seem to require, allow for, or permit an immediate reply from the dominated were made in the expectation and anticipation of a response. Domination was continuously and publicly asserted, legitimized, and naturalized as well as resisted, accommodated, and refuted within a specific historical and cultural context—even while the dialectical processes of domination and resistance altered the very historical contexts and cultural structures that created them.[6]

---

throp Jordan, *White over Black: American Attitudes toward the Negro, 1590–1812* (Chapel Hill, 1968); for Barbados see Richard S. Dunn, *Sugar and Slaves: the Rise of the Planter Class in the English West Indies, 1624–1713* (Chapel Hill, 1973); for Virginia, see Oscar and Mary F. Handlin, "Origins of the Southern Labor System," *William and Mary Quarterly*, 3rd series, 6 (1950), 199–222; Carl N. Degler, "Slavery and the Genesis of American Race Prejudice," *Contemporary Studies in Society and History* 2 (1959), 49–66; Morgan, *American Slavery, American Freedom*; Russell R. Menard, "From Servants to Slaves: The Transformation of the Chesapeake Labor System," *Southern Studies* 16 (1977), 355–90; Timothy H. Breen and Stephen Innes, *"Myne Owne Ground": Race and Freedom on Virginia's Eastern Shore, 1640–1676* (New York, 1980); and Kathleen M. Brown, *Good Wives, Nasty Wenches, and Anxious Patriarchs: Gender, Race, and Power in Colonial Virginia* (Chapel Hill, 1996).

6. Although I cannot hope to offer a comprehensive list, the works that have influenced my own thinking on these issues include (in chronological order): M. M. Bakhtin, *Rabelais and His World*, trans. H. Iswolsky (Cambridge, Mass., 1968); Clifford Geertz, *The Interpretation of Cultures* (New York, 1973); Eugene Genovese, *Roll, Jordan, Roll: The World the Slaves Made* (New York, 1974); Michel Foucault, *Discipline and Punish: The Birth of the Prison*, trans. Alan Sheridan (New York, 1977); Pierre Bourdieu, *Outline of a Theory of Practice*, trans. R. Nice (Cambridge, 1977); David Warren Sabean, *Power in the Blood: Popular Culture and Village Discourse in Early Modern Germany* (Cambridge, 1984); Jean Comaroff, *Body of Power, Spirit of Resistance: The Culture and History of a South African People* (Chicago, 1985); Shula Marks, *Ambiguities of Dependence in South Africa: Class, Nationalism, and the State in Twentieth-Century*

Throughout human history, rulers have understood that their dominion rests on more than force alone. Accordingly, dominant groups have always employed public spectacles and cultural metaphors to disguise, symbolize, and enact their rule.[7] In the mid-eighteenth-century South Carolina low country, the public arenas, languages, and rituals within which slaves and masters contested were the transplanted and transformed institutions and discourses of the English law, the established church, the marketplace (and market relations), and the plantation great house (and patriarchy). Taken together, the sites and languages within which domination was exercised and resistance expressed represent what might be termed the "culture of power." I mean culture not only in the ethnographic sense, which Rhys Isaac has described as "the codes by which those who share in the culture convey meanings and significance to each other," but also in the sense of cultivation.[8] In and through the culture of power, the seeds of domination were sown, nurtured, and ultimately harvested.

Another equally important aim of this study is to reveal slaves' agency in the creation and perpetuation of late-colonial South Carolina's social order. By the third quarter of the eighteenth century, Europeans, Africans, and their descendants had been living with and contending against each other in the low-country landscape for over three generations. The growing familiarity between South Carolina's whites and blacks bred a good measure of contempt and hatred, but it also inspired a degree of mutual comprehension, calculation, and negotiation. Relations between masters and slaves more closely resembled an ongoing "tug of war" than open warfare or the slaves' abject submission before an overwhelming power. Slaves were not merely the passive subjects of the slave society but were intelligent agents whose choices and actions, while always shackled by their condition, nonetheless helped to shape the world they lived in.

Of course, historians attempting to recapture the point of view of slaves or other subaltern groups face a number of problems. In the written record, often the only source of information about the past, slaves are almost always in the position of the observed rather than the observer. Even in the rare instances when slaves' own words are recorded in the documents, they are filtered through the mediation of a transcriber

---

Natal (Baltimore, 1986); Jean-Christophe Agnew, *Worlds Apart: The Market and the Theater in Anglo-American Thought, 1550–1750* (Cambridge, 1986); and James C. Scott, *Domination and the Arts of Resistance: Hidden Transcripts* (New Haven, 1990).

7. See Timothy Mitchell, "Everyday Metaphors of Power," *Theory and Society* 19 (1990), 545–77.

8. Isaac, *Transformation of Virginia*, 324–25.

who is often deeply implicated in the process of domination. It is a truism that those instances when slaves appear most prominently in the historic record were precisely those moments in their lives when they were most subject to their masters' scrutiny and power.

Given these caveats, surviving documentary sources are awkward lenses through which to perceive how Africans and their descendants thought and acted when they were free from the gaze of authority. Although they remain largely hidden from the view of researchers, there undoubtedly were times and places where low-country blacks could and did live of and by themselves, according to their own language, culture, and traditions. As early as 1740, for example, the Anglican commissary to South Carolina described low-country blacks as "a Nation within a Nation." In the countryside, he wrote, blacks "labour together and converse almost wholly among themselves."[9] Despite these problems of evidence, several penetrating studies have been written about the low-country black community under slavery. The work of these scholars, while for the most part focusing on the nineteenth century, suggests just how complex and sustaining this African-Carolinian culture may have been.[10]

However, because the focus of this study is on the interstices between slaves, masters, and power (what might be termed the "public" world of blacks), the same characteristics that constitute documentary drawbacks for those seeking to glimpse blacks' private thoughts are, instead, opportunities. The record of individual or collective agency that survives in the archives consists for the most part of people caught in the act of contending with or appealing to their masters or the other authorities of church or state. Thus, the transcripts of these interactions allow us to examine relations of power quite directly. Seeing blacks through the eyes and pens of their rulers in "public" contexts and as "slaves" presents us with good evidence of how blacks accommodated and resisted rule. Despite the obvious constraints of their situation and the problematics of

9. Alexander Garden to the SPG, 6 May 1740, SPG Records, microfilm SCL-USC, Reel 4, 33–35.
10. The documents with which to construct a portrait of the South Carolina slave community in the second half of the eighteenth century are relatively scarce, but the best place to begin is Phillip D. Morgan, "The Development of Slave Culture in Eighteenth-Century Plantation America" (Ph.D. diss., University of London, 1977), and his *Slave Counterpoint*. Other important works on the low-country slave community, which are set primarily in the nineteenth century, include Charles Joyner, *Down by the Riverside: A South Carolina Slave Community* (Urbana, 1982); Margaret Creel, *A Peculiar People: Slave Religion and Community Culture among the Gullahs* (New York, 1988); and Larry E. Hudson, Jr., *To Have and to Hold: Slave Work and Family Life in Antebellum South Carolina* (Athens, 1997). A less sanguine view can be found in William Dusinberre, *Them Dark Days: Slavery in the American Rice Swamps* (Oxford, 1996).

the records' production, blacks' voices, resistance, and agency do come through. In the face of their masters, and despite the consequences, some slaves always dared to speak truth to power.

The culture of power played a vital part in the social order and political economy of the colonial slave society. Low-country masters attended to the cultivation of power with at least as much care as they devoted to the rice that their slaves grew in the low-country swamps. The rituals and discourses of the law, the church, the market, and the great house were analogous in this regard to the ditches, dikes, sluices, and reservoirs that planters drove their slaves to painstakingly build and maintain in order to cultivate the rice crop.

To pursue the analogy a bit further, everyday forms of slave resistance might be seen as akin to the flocks of birds that might consume the rice if not kept in check (although the birds always ate some of the crop), or perhaps to the spring floods that might be turned aside by well-kept dikes (although the floods always claimed some planters' fields). In this vein, rebellions, revolutions, and other violent and collective expressions of popular outrage were like fires or hurricanes that could arise with little warning and suddenly sweep away the plantations and those who lived on them.

Such cataclysmic events were rare. Most slaves and masters went their entire lives without encountering either a rebellion or a hurricane. But when they did occur, these episodes were far beyond the ability of any individual either to predict or to control. As the clouds grew dark, the wind blew strong, and the waters rose, both masters and slaves looked to themselves and their loved ones and prayed for deliverance.

Unlike most studies of early American slavery which have focused primarily on slavery's origins and development or have sought to explain dramatic moments of rebellion, this book seeks to understand the social dynamics of a mature colonial slave society in an era that was largely devoid of collective and violent challenges to the masters' dominion. However, the fact that low-country slaves did not rise up in arms in the years between 1740 and 1775 should not to be taken as evidence of their contentment or acquiescence. As will be shown, slaves' desire for autonomy and their determination to resist their masters' power constituted a constant force. Nor, as the events after 1775 were to prove, were slaves incapable of taking radical action when the opportunity arose.

But in scrutinizing slaves' responses to their masters' power in more ordinary times, this study does suggest how modes and avenues of everyday resistance tended to implicate and entangle slaves within the very institutions and discourses that oppressed them. In order to articulate their grievances, slaves often had to appropriate the languages and metaphors of the dominant culture. Similarly, before a slave could become a member of the church or trade in the market, a degree of accommodation to power was required. It is the irony of everyday resistance that, precisely because it was routine, it could to a large degree be incorporated into the slave society and itself be made a part of the structures of everyday life.

A Place with a Past

The stage for these interactions, and the setting for this study, is the region of South Carolina known as the low country. The low country, or lower coastal plain, extends along South Carolina's Atlantic shore for approximately two hundred miles and inland for fifty miles or so. The term "low country" referred originally to the topography of this region; as one of the original colonists wrote, and as any modern traveler who flies over the area can corroborate, the land is "soe plaine & Levyll that it may be compared to a Bowling ally."[11]

Thirty thousand years ago the low country lay under the sea, and the landscape is still dominated by water. Into "this half-drowned coast country," as one scholar has aptly described it, a series of rivers flow from the Carolina piedmont that lies to the west.[12] As these rivers slowly wind toward the ocean, they widen and meet to form a series of large estuaries interwoven by a web of creeks and sloughs. South of Georgetown, where the Waccamaw and Pee Dee Rivers join and flow into Winyah Bay, the coast is composed of a tapestry of islands. Inland, the low country is a mixture of dry pine land divided by watercourses and interspersed with vast freshwater swamps.

In the last quarter of the seventeenth century, a group of Englishmen, some of them from Barbados, sailed into one such estuary to plant a colony. As Columbus had done almost two centuries before, the Englishmen took possession of the landscape in part by replacing Native American place-names with others of their own devising. Thus, the two

---

11. "An Old Letter, (About March 1671)," in Langdon Cheves, ed., *The Shaftesbury Papers and Other Records Relating to Carolina and the First Settlement on the Ashley River Prior to the Year 1676, Collections of the South Carolina Historical Society,* 5 (Charleston, 1897), 308. For a description of the low-country environment prior to European settlement, as well an examination of the impact of colonization on the region's ecology, see Timothy Silver, *A New Face on the Countryside: Indians, Colonists, and Slaves in South Atlantic Forests, 1500–1800* (Cambridge, 1990).

12. Robert L. Meriwether, *The Expansion of South Carolina, 1729–1765* (Kingsport, Tenn., 1940), 4.

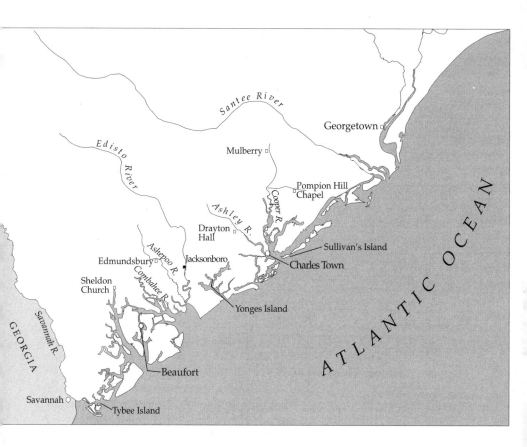

The South Carolina low country (places named in the text identified)

major rivers that formed this particular harbor were named Ashley and Cooper after the colony's principal proprietor. Similarly, the settlers named the colony itself, Carolina, and the town they founded, Charles Town, in honor of their king.

While the settlers may have hoped that these names would serve to remind them of the world they had left behind, they did not intend to re-create old England entirely. Within months, if not weeks, of the colony's establishment, its small population included Africans, and among its first institutions was chattel slavery.[13]

13. The best account of the early settlement of South Carolina remains Wood, *Black Majority*, 13–34.

In the three centuries that followed that fateful landfall, the low country has come to define a human as much as a natural landscape. In contrast to the apparent torpor of the region's natural environment, albeit an impression belied by the periodic hurricanes and earthquakes that have devastated the coast, the human history of the low country has been characterized by violent extremes. Since the early eighteenth century, the peoples of the South Carolina low country have been the advocates, and occasionally the instigators, of numerous political, economic, and social revolutions. Three times South Carolina's political leaders sought to overthrow their distant rulers: twice they were successful; once disastrously not. Likewise, elaborately constructed social systems, once thought divinely ordained, have fallen into disregard or ruin, to be replaced by systems that seemed equally natural once completed.

Alongside these violent changes, a series of equally violent continuities have shaped the low country's human history. Ideologies of race, of property, and of gender created stark dichotomies and dialectics that have proved remarkably resilient and persistent even as the political, economic, and social systems that originally created and supported them have risen, flourished for a time, and disappeared.

The years that passed between 1740 and 1790 saw the parallel "golden age" of two such systems, the collapse of one of these, and the maturation of a third. These decades saw the boom years of the low-country rice culture, whose roots lay the early eighteenth century, and which would continue, with steadily diminishing returns, until the early twentieth century. The third quarter of the eighteenth century also saw the final culmination of the colonial regime that was born a child of revolution in 1719 and died amid the chaos of a second revolution six decades later. Finally, this same era saw the codification and establishment of laws and practices that would largely define the low-country slave society from the mid-eighteenth-century until its own final downfall in 1865.

While it is set within a particular historic context, however, this book has a complex relationship to the passage of time. In order to reconstruct the day-to-day structures of power from a host of fragmentary and imperfect records, the central portion of this book, chapters two through five, treats the entire period from 1740 to 1775 as one historical "moment." The focus in these chapters is upon the internal dynamics, power relations, and languages within one particular facet of the social order, whether law, church, market, or plantation. To this end, evidence is called forth as needed with little regard to chronology. Examples drawn from before 1740 or after 1775 are even cited on occasion. That some chapters draw a preponderance of their evidence from the decade of the

1740s, and others from the 1760s, and so on, says far more about the idiosyncrasies of documentary survival than about the relative influence of any given institution at any given moment.

However necessary methodologically, this synchronic view of the past is obviously false. While it could be argued that many facets of the colonial slave society remained relatively constant through the years from 1740 to 1775, there was also a lot that changed. To give a simple example, it is almost certain that most of the people living in the low country in 1740 were dead by 1775, and the majority of South Carolina's inhabitants at the start of the Revolution had not even been born thirty-five years earlier. Thus, even if the stage and set remained in place, the roster of players was new. Moreover, the South Carolina low country was hardly at rest. In these years the region experienced tremendous growth in terms of its population and wealth.

Consequently, in order to provide a sense of movement and to place the low country in historical context, the first chapter of this book examines the larger forces and processes that were at work in the low country from 1740 to 1775. In this period, the low country developed in ways that were seemingly at odds. On the one hand, the region was undergoing a process of *creolization*, or adaptation to the local environment. In the middle of the eighteenth century, a majority of the low country's inhabitants, white and black, were for the first time native born. At the same time, however, the colony was also in the midst of a process of *Anglicization*, as the new-found wealth and stability of the region inspired low-country elites to reshape their society and themselves to resemble more closely the ruling establishment of eighteenth-century Britain. Given their contradictory nature, neither of these endeavors could be fully achieved.

Chapters 2 through 5 examine four different pillars of the social order in the colonial slave society. Chapter 2 examines the law and the slave court, chapter 3 the operation of the established church. Chapter 4 looks at the interactions that took place in the marketplace and through market relations. Chapter 5 studies the political economy of the plantations and the metaphors of patriarchy. In each of these arenas, masters' efforts to cultivate power and impose their rule was met by the slaves' own determination to secure a measure of autonomy within slavery or to deny their servitude entirely. Ultimately, a degree of order was obtained, but the culture of power rested uneasily upon a continuous dialectical process of contention and concession, coercion and appropriation.

Thus, slaves who were brought before the justices in the slave court or to the gallows contended with their masters about the message that such spectacles conveyed to white and black audiences. Slaves who accepted baptism into the Anglican church could turn their religious practice into a mode of protest against their masters. In the marketplace, black women were able to employ the "law of the market" as a weapon against their socially prescribed subordination. Even on the steps of the "great house," masters and slaves struggled over the metaphors through which their interactions were expressed and the meanings attributed to their relationships.

Chapters 2 through 5 are organized topically; each examines a different aspect of the social order in isolation. But most slaves, on most days of their lives, did not encounter these different institutions separately or even literally, but rather in their minds, perceptions, and expectations. The slave court, church, market, and great house could and did appear concurrently in the slaves' mental landscape. Therefore, to perceive the colonial slave society as it was, the roads that connected the various facets of the social order must also be imagined. For example, in one hypothetical journey, a slave might leave her home plantation, walk past an Anglican chapel, view a body hanging upon the gibbet outside of Charles Town, and eventually arrive at the public marketplace. In practice, the culture of power was designed to be both perpetual and inescapable.

The final chapter of the book views colonial slave society during the chaos of the American Revolution. The actions of slaves and masters in the turbulent years between 1775 and 1782 are explained in the light of the culture of power within which they had operated during the preceding decades. In this chapter the focus is not on large, impersonal historical forces, nor on the social institutions and rituals that lent an air of stability and permanence to people's lives, but instead on extraordinary and contingent events, the "hurricanes" that broke into the tyranny of the routine and enabled everyone to perceive ordinary social structures and social relations in new, and perhaps revolutionary, ways.

The low country's colonial regime, the world of kings and slaves, came to an end with the final British evacuation of Charles Town in December 1782. Eight months later, the South Carolina legislature passed an act of incorporation and colonial Charles Town became the republican city of Charleston. This fortuitous change of name is used to distinguish between the stories of the past that are told in Charleston in the late twentieth century and the evidence of Charles Town in the mid-eighteenth century that can be found in the archives.

Perhaps nowhere in America does the past seem as tangibly present as it does in the place that describes itself as "America's most historic city."[14] Charleston is indeed a remarkably beautiful and historic place. But, like many histories, the stories that Charleston tells visitors about its past are based as much upon forgetting as upon remembering.[15] While much in Charleston has been preserved, a great deal has also been lost. To get beyond "Historic Charleston" and to begin to approach the Charles Town of history, one must not only restore the silent and passive buildings of the old city but also recapture the voices and actions of the people who once lived in them. In part, this book is an attempt to achieve such a "restoration."[16]

14. Quoted in Walter J. Fraser, Jr., *Charleston! Charleston! The History of a Southern City* (Columbia, 1989), 373–74.
15. Of course, the South Carolina low country is not the only place in America to suffer from such a collective public amnesia. As Toni Morrison has written: "There is not a place you or I can go, to think about or not think about, to summon the presence of, or recollect the absence of slaves; nothing that reminds us of the ones who made the journey and those who did not make it. There is no suitable memorial, or plaque, or wreath, or wall, or park or skyscraper lobby. There is no 200 foot tower. There's no small bench by the road. There is not even a tree scored, an initial that I can visit or you can visit in Charleston, or Savannah, or New York, or Providence, or better still, on the banks of the Mississippi." Toni Morrison, "A Bench by the Road," *World Journal of the Unitarian Universalist Association* (January 1989), 4.
16. For a discussion of history and memory in modern Charleston, see Theodore Rosengarten, "History Alley, Memory Lane," in Mary Jane Jacob, ed., *Places with a Past: New Site Specific Art at Charleston's Spoleto Festival* (New York, 1991); and also V. S. Naipaul, *A Turn in the South* (New York, 1989), 77–117.

Charles Town at the end of the colonial era. The large structure dominating the city's Cooper River waterfront is the Exchange House, completed in 1772. On either side of the Exchange are some of the merchants' homes, stores and warehouses that formed a solid row for a half mile along the "Bay." Behind the waterfront, the city's skyline is pierced by the steeples of Charles Town's two Anglican churches. To the left is St. Michael's, from whose belfry city residents could watch "Ships at a distance sailing towards the port." To the right is St. Philip's, described as "the most elegant Religious Edifice in British America." In the foreground are several of the small vessels that plied the low-country waterways between the plantations and the city. This is a detail from a painting of the city waterfront made in 1773 by Thomas Leitch, an English artist. Leitch advertised in the Charles Town newspaper that he planned to return to England and produce an engraving based on the painting. Source: Museum of Early Southern Decorative Arts, Winston-Salem, North Carolina.

[1]

Between Rebellion and Revolution: Charles Town and the Low Country, 1740–1775

In the last half of the twentieth century, tourism has become an important part of the economy in Charleston and along the adjacent coast. Judging from travel literature and promotional brochures, many of those who visit the area are drawn by a romantic image of its past. A recent *Charleston Area Visitor's Guide*, for example, promises that "if history appeals to you, you'll be surrounded by it here."[1] "Historic Charleston," a term which embraces the various tours, house museums, and plantations as well as the shops, hotels, and guest houses that cater to the tourist trade, presents the past to visitors mostly in the form of stories. Perhaps the city's best-known storytellers are the drivers of the horse-drawn carriages that clip-clop through the streets of the old town each day. The carriage drivers, often costumed in "Gone with the Wind" style as "rebel" soldiers or southern "belles," have an established repertoire of tales and anecdotes tied to specific locations along their route. Sitting on a bench in the old town, a visitor hears the same old stories told again and again from a slow procession of carriages.

The intersection of Broad and Meeting Streets in the center of the old city is one such "storied" place. According to the horse-and-carriage drivers, this crossroads is known as the "four corners of the law" because

1. Charleston Trident Convention and Visitor's Bureau, *Charleston Area Visitor's Guide* (Charleston, S.C., 1994), 13.

the buildings on each of its corners embody the various "laws" that govern the city. On the southeast corner, or so the story goes, stands St. Michael's Church, representing "God's Law." On the west side of Meeting Street, a Federal Post Office and the Charleston County Courthouse signify federal and state authority. And on the northeast corner, in a building that originally housed the Bank of the United States, Charleston's City Hall now enshrines civic law.

However, like much of the low country's past, the history of the four corners is more interesting and more complicated than the story that Historic Charleston chooses to tell. For one thing, the tale of the four corners is almost certainly older than all but one of the buildings that now stand at the crossroads. Tourists have been coming to this spot for a very long time. In 1774, for example, an English visitor to Charles Town and to Broad and Meeting Streets noted that "at one of the four corners . . . stands the new English church [St. Michael's], and at another is the State House . . . [while] Opposite to it [on another corner] stands the Town Watch House." The anonymous tourist described the church and Statehouse as "handsome [and] substantial," and thought the Watch House a "plain good building." But he did not think much of the structure on "the fourth corner," which, he wrote, "does not answer the other three, for it is only a low dirty looking brick market house."[2]

The four corners complex was developed in the third quarter of the eighteenth century in a deliberate effort to provide Charles Town, and the entire colony, with a symbolic and "formal center."[3] On one corner, the colony's new Statehouse (completed in 1760) housed the South Carolina Commons House of Assembly, as the lower house of the legislature styled itself in imitation of the British House of Commons, as well as the Governor's Council and the colony court. Across the junction, the towering steeple of St. Michael's (modeled on the church of St. Martin-in-the-Fields, London) represented the authority of the established church. With the completion of St. Michael's in 1762, the intersection of Broad and Meeting became the seat of both church and state. Therefore, in the late-colonial era, the four corners were the source of South Carolina's laws in a very literal sense.

While the "handsome and substantial" church and Statehouse may have demonstrated colonial South Carolina's subordination to the rule

2. "Charleston at the End of the Colonial Era, 1774," in H. Roy Merrens, ed., *The Colonial South Carolina Scene: Contemporary Views, 1697–1774* (Columbia, S.C., 1977), 282.
3. George C. Rogers, *Charleston in the Age of the Pinckneys* (Norman, Okla., 1969), 58; see also Kenneth Severens, *Charleston: Antebellum Architecture and Civic Destiny* (Knoxville, Tenn., 1988), 8–15.

of God and King, other, less regal lords and laws were also seated at the junction. On the southeast corner, opposite the church and the State-house, the Town Watch House (completed in 1769) signified, as its name suggests, the constant surveillance that was required to police the col-ony's slave population. The Watch House was the headquarters of the night watch, whose task it was to enforce the ordinance against slaves being out on the streets after dark. Any slave truants whom the patrol apprehended on its nightly rounds were to be confined at the Watch House until they were claimed by their owners the next day. The junction also contained a public pillory where slaves convicted of petty crimes were brought to suffer the whippings, brandings, or ear-croppings to which they had been sentenced. Such sights and sounds were vivid re-minders of the collective and coercive power of the slave society or, more succinctly, of "Masters' Law."

The fourth corner of the crossroads, where the Bank of the United States (and City Hall) would later stand, contained the eldest and least distinguished resident of the junction in the late-colonial era: the 1739 public marketplace. Here, within the confines of the marketplace and beneath the shelter of the "low and dirty ... market house," money was both master and king, and the "Law of the Market" reigned su-preme.

Thus, as originally designed, and most likely as first described to vis-itors, the "laws" enthroned on the four corners of Broad and Meeting were not those of God, Nation, State, and City, but rather of God, King, Masters, and Market. This far more interesting and dramatic conjunction of laws may explain both why the story was invented in the first place and why it has survived even while (with the exception of St. Michael's) the original rulers of the crossroads have disappeared and have been written out of the tale.

Nor, of course, are "new lords and new laws" the only change the four corners have seen in the past two-and-a-quarter centuries. Unlike the tidy scene of today, where the carriage horses even wear canvas "diapers" to prevent unseemly sights and smells, sanitation in Charles Town left much to be desired. In 1757, for example, a contributor to the *South Carolina Gazette* wrote that he was disgusted "to see in our streets ... numbers of dead dogs and other animals, bloated and ready to burst with corruption ... [while] every bye corner and vacant lot becomes a receptacle for all manner of filth." Perhaps with a prophetic eye out for tourists, the correspondent worried "that the sight and smell of such things" might be "very offensive to strangers."[4]

4. *South Carolina Gazette*, 10 March 1757.

As this account suggests, the streets of Charles Town were once a lively scene of noise and stink, of confusion and chaos. In the mid-eighteenth-century, the four corners framed a contested space where masters and slaves, as well as horses and carriages, jostled for the right of way. Charles Town's slaves walked through the junction in a manner that suggests that they felt that they had as much right to be there as anyone. In 1777, a visiting Frenchman thought that the city's slaves had "a peculiar kind of pride and bearing . . . it at least gives the impression that they regard a man who is not their master simply as a man."[5]

If possession were ever indeed nine-tenths of the law, slaves may well have had a case for claiming the streets as their own. Slaves always formed the larger part of the people who walked or rode down the city's streets, who mingled and traded in the market, who were punished upon the pillory, and who stood in the aisles or gallery, or merely on the porch, of the church each Sunday. Charles Town's grand juries complained constantly of "the great insolence of the Negroes . . . gaming in the street and caballing in great numbers."[6] Likewise, visitors to the city wrote of the "blacks . . . playing paw-paw, huzzle cap, pitch penny, and quarrelling round the doors of the Churches in service-time."[7]

The buildings on each of the four corners may have symbolically sought to impose a measure of order over the crossroads, but the laws of Church, King, Masters, and Market seldom acted in perfect concert. Occasionally, or in moments of crisis, they could collude on the goal of self-preservation, but more often, and in more ordinary times, the "four laws," like the people at their feet, lived in daily contest and collision.

In truth, the social order of the mid-eighteenth-century low country was always based on more than buildings and the "laws" they represented. The institutions, ideologies, and relations embodied in the structures standing at Broad and Meeting were only the stages upon which living people, black and white, masters and slaves, royal officials and colonial subjects, acted to contest and negotiate their daily lives. The "laws" that governed the late-colonial low country were constructed out of tens of thousands of individual actions and decisions much more than from bricks, mortar, and whitewash.

5. On the Threshold of Liberty: Journal of a Frenchman's Tour of the American Colonies in 1777, ed. and trans. Edward D. Seeber (Bloomington, Ind., 1959), 14–15, quoted in Philip D. Morgan, "Black Life in Eighteenth-Century Charleston," *Perspectives in American History*, new series, 1 (1984), 187.
6. Presentments of the Grand Jury [Charles Town], 17 October 1744, JGC, microfilm, LC, 527–29.
7. Mark DeWolfe Howe, ed., "Journal of Josiah Quincy, Junior, 1773," Massachusetts Historical Society *Proceedings* 49 (1916), 455.

Of course, in the mid-eighteenth-century as much as today, people did not live entirely in the moment. Among the most powerful determinants of human choices and conduct are the experience of what is past and the expectation of what is to come. Before one can comprehend the words and deeds of past actors, one must first perceive the larger events, structures, and forces that both constrained and enabled their actions. Placing people in the context of their own history allows us to glimpse the nightmares of their memories and also their dreams for a future that is itself now long past. Accordingly, this chapter focuses upon the dramatic events and large developments that shaped and transformed lowcountry society in the years between the end of the Stono Rebellion and the outbreak of the American Revolution thirty-five years later.

Cultivating the Land of Egypt

In the small hours of Sunday, September 9, 1739, a group of perhaps twenty black men gathered on the banks of the Stono River twenty miles west of Charles Town. Earlier in the week, word had reached the colony that Britain and Spain were at war, and the men may well have discussed this news and the prospect of finding refuge (and freedom) in Spanish Florida some 150 miles to the south. While their precise motives and reasoning lie beyond historical inquiry, the result of their discussion is not. In the pre-dawn darkness, the men quietly resolved to strike out against the society that held them in bondage.[8]

In need of arms, the conspirators stole into a nearby store, confronted and killed the two resident storekeepers, and proceeded to ransack the place for firearms, ammunition, or other likely weapons. At this point, one can surmise that an excited mood of triumph and expectation may have swept over the little group. With the shedding of blood, they had

8. The details of the Stono Rebellion are drawn from the following contemporary accounts (listed in chronological order): Entry of 20 September 1739 in "A Ranger's Report of Travels with General Oglethorpe, 1739–1742," in Newton D. Mereness, ed., *Travels in the American Colonies* (New York, 1916), 222–23; "A Letter from South Carolina [dated 28 September 1739]," in *Boston Weekly News-Letter*, 8 November 1739; William Bull to the Board of Trade, 6 October 1739, in "Letters, Papers, &ca., from the Governors. March 1739–April 1740," originals BPRO, microfilm SCDAH, Co5/367, 114; Andrew Leslie, St. Paul parish, to the SPG, 7 January 1739 [1740], SPG Records, microfilm SCDAH, Reel 4, 19–20; James Oglethorpe, "An Account of the Negroe Insurrection in South Carolina" (1740), in Allan D. Candler and Lucien L. Knight, eds., *Colonial Records of the State of Georgia*, 26 vols. (Atlanta, 1904–16), vol. 22, pt. 2, 232–36; "Report of the Committee Appointed to Enquire into the Causes of the Disappointment of Success in the Late Expedition Against St. Augustine," *JCHA*, 1 July 1741, 83.

crossed the Rubicon that separated words from deeds, conspiracy from rebellion. There was, they knew, no going back. Perhaps it is in this spirit that one should interpret the rebels' last act before leaving the store. Returning to the corpses of the storekeepers, the rebels "Cut off their Heads and Set them on the Stairs" as a dread message of both their intentions and their resolve for those who would discover the scene the following morning.[9]

Now armed and determined, the group set off down the road toward Florida. Their actions, however, suggest that striking a blow against the slave society rather than seeking refuge with the Spanish was their primary objective. They made no effort to move quickly or clandestinely. On the contrary, the rebels deliberately attacked most of the plantations they passed, setting fire to houses and barns, killing any whites they could apprehend, and calling upon other slaves to join them. By their conduct, both at the store and on their march, the rebels declared themselves to be soldiers at war with the society that had enslaved them.

Through the rising daylight, the rebels continued southward, "calling out Liberty," and seeking further recruits from the plantations that they burned and plundered.[10] Some slaves resisted the rebels and were later rewarded by a grateful assembly, but other blacks chose to join the rebellion.[11] By mid-morning, with their numbers swelled to fifty or more, the rebel band began to take on the character of a little army. White observers later described the rebels as marching down the road "with Colours displayed, and two Drums beating."[12] Along the way, the rebels also displayed an ability to dispense mercy as well as retribution. For example, they were reported to have spared the life of a tavern keeper because "he was a good man and kind to his Slaves."[13]

That morning, by the rankest coincidence, William Bull, the lieutenant governor of the colony, was riding with four companions north along the high road toward Charles Town. At ten o'clock, the lieutenant governor and his party suddenly came face-to-face with the rebellion. At first, the five horsemen were unsure of what to make of the sight of

9. "A Ranger's Report," 222.
10. Ibid.
11. *JCHA*, 24 and 29 November 1739, 50–51, 63–64.
12. Ibid. Of West Africa (Benin) in this period, Olaudah Equiano noted "that when our people march to the field [of battle], a red flag or banner is born before them"; Olaudah Equiano, *The Interesting Narrative of the Life of Olaudah Equiano, or Gustavus Vassa, the African*, in Henry Louis Gates, Jr., ed., *The Classic Slave Narratives* (New York, 1987), 18. Conceivably, the flag of the Stono rebels may have been fashioned from a bolt of cloth taken from the store they ransacked at the start of the rebellion.
13. Oglethorpe, "An Account of the Negroe Insurrection," 234.

several score of determined black men striding down the road toward them. At the last moment, however, Bull and his companions "discerned the approaching danger," turned their horses about, "and with much difficulty escaped."[14] As the party rode off to sound the alarm, the rebels continued their march, their progress marked by the smoke rising from burning houses and barns.[15]

At mid-afternoon, having marched and plundered for ten hours and ten miles, and having "increased every minute by new Negroes coming to them" until they numbered one hundred or more, the rebel band turned into a field near the Edisto River ferry and "set to dancing, Singing and beating Drums."[16] Later, white contemporaries would deride the rebels' decision to halt, positing that they had become "drunk with the Rum they had taken in the Houses" and may have thought themselves "victorious over the whole Province."[17] But others, perhaps recalling their own very real vulnerability and fear, conjectured more plausibly that the rebels paused in their march so as "to draw more Negroes to them" and to allow stragglers to catch up. Most recently, it has been argued that what whites thought to be mindless "dancing" may in fact have been an African ritual that prepared the rebels for battle.[18]

At four o'clock, a hastily raised company of mounted militia arrived at the field where the rebels had halted. When the militia advanced to the attack, some of the rebels fled, but others "behaved boldly" and the two little armies clashed in a brief but desperate combat.[19] Later, the members of the South Carolina Commons described the battle: "The number was in a manner equal on both sides and an engagement ensued such as may be supposed in such a case wherein one fought for liberty and life, the other for their country and everything that was dear to them."[20]

The battle's outcome may perhaps be attributed to differences in firepower (the militia's first volley was said to have killed or wounded fourteen) or to culture (open-field, pitched battles were not in keeping with

14. William Bull to the Board of Trade, 6 October 1739; Oglethorpe, "An Account of the Negroe Insurrection," 234.
15. Oglethorpe, "An Account of the Negroe Insurrection," 234.
16. Ibid.
17. Ibid.
18. John Thornton, "African Dimensions of the Stono Rebellion," *American Historical Review* 96 (1991), 1112. For an analysis of the part African constructions of masculinity may have played in the uprising, see Edward A. Pearson, " 'A Countryside Full of Flames': A Reconsideration of the Stono Rebellion and Slave Rebelliousness in the Early Eighteenth-Century South Carolina Lowcountry," *Slavery & Abolition* 17 (August 1996), 22–50.
19. Oglethorpe, "An Account of the Negroe Insurrection," 235.
20. JCHA, 1 July 1741, 83.

the looser tactics favored in African warfare).[21] Whatever the cause, those rebels not yet wounded or taken abandoned the uneven contest and broke for the woods. Left in possession of the field, the victorious militiamen were in no mood for mercy; captured rebels and those who lay wounded upon the ground were briefly questioned and then "shot on the Spot."[22] As many as forty blacks may have been killed at this site, which was long remembered as "the battlefield."[23]

But, in the smoke and confusion, a good number of the rebels had managed to escape. Some of the fugitives returned to their home plantations hoping that they had not been missed. Most of these repentant rebels were seized and executed, but at least a few were able to convince their masters and the authorities that they had been coerced into joining the uprising and were spared. Several dozen rebels regrouped after the battle and sought to continue to St. Augustine. They had traveled thirty miles nearer to their goal before they were overtaken and annihilated a week later. Other participants in the uprising, unable to go forward and unwilling to go back, sought to take up a permanent residence in the woods and swamps of the area. One such fugitive was able to remain at large for more than three years.[24]

With the rebellion crushed, masters placated their anxieties by taking a savage retribution against the blacks involved. In a bloody counterpoint to the uprising's start (which may itself have been a counterpoint to the proceedings at public slave executions), the militiamen "Cutt off ... [the] heads" of the rebels they had killed and "set them up at every Mile Post they came to" as a gruesome example to the slaves of the parish.[25] In the days and weeks that followed, masters continued to vent their rage and fear on the slaves of the vicinity. Blacks convicted of taking part in the uprising were put to death in diverse ways: "some shot, some hang'd, and some Gibbeted alive."[26]

Gradually, as the ashes from the burnt plantations cooled, so, ultimately, did the masters' appetite for vengeance. But while public executions and the sight of heads on roadside posts reasserted the slave society's coercive power and gave low-country slaves pause to think and reason to grieve, they did little to restore low-country masters' optimism. As 1739 gave way to 1740, the dominant mood among masters was one of dismay for the colony's future. When the South Carolina

21. Thornton, "African Dimensions of the Stono Rebellion," 1112–13.
22. Oglethorpe, "An Account of the Negroe Insurrection," 235.
23. Henry A. M. Smith, "Willtown or New London," SCHM 10 (January 1909), 28.
24. South Carolina Gazette, 27 December 1742.
25. "A Ranger's Report," 223.
26. "A Letter from South Carolina."

Commons convened in December, the members declared that the combined effects of a fiscal crisis, the outbreak of war with Spain, and particularly "the unhappy Effects of an Insurrection of our Slaves within our Selves (an intestine Enemy the most dreadful of Enemies) which we have just Grounds to imagine will be repeated" had determined "many of our Inhabitants . . . to remove themselves and their Effects, out of this Province; insomuch, that upon the whole the Country seems to be at Stake."[27]

A year and a half later, when a measure of calm had been restored, the members of the Commons reflected further upon the psychological impact of the rebellion. The predominant sentiment the members recalled was of a loss of innocence. As the legislators described it, the planters of the low country awoke that September morning to discover that their dreams of progress and prosperity had gone terribly awry:

> On this Occasion every Breast was filled with Concern. Evil brought Home to us within our very Doors awakened the Attention of the most Unthinking. . . . every one that had a Life to lose were in the most sensible Manner shocked at such Danger daily hanging over their Heads. With Regret we bewailed our peculiar Case, that we could not enjoy the Benefits of Peace like the rest of Mankind and that our own Industry should be the Means of taking from us all the Sweets of Life and of rendering us liable to the Loss of our Lives and Fortunes.[28]

It would be easy to join the members of the Commons and depict the Stono Rebellion as a crucial turning point in the colony's history. It is both human nature and the nature of memory to explain great changes as being the result of great events. Moreover, such a depiction would not be entirely false. The Stono Rebellion did indeed have several important consequences. For example, there was clearly a causal link between the uprising and the passage of a new slave code the next year. Although interest in redrafting the slave code had been expressed prior to the rebellion, Stono provided the impetus finally to get the job done. But it is equally important to realize that Stono was not responsible for everything that came in its wake. The public drama and spectacle of the rebellion casts a shadow over other, more mundane and gradual, forces that were profoundly shaping the colony in the years between 1740 and 1775.

Nor was Stono the only problem that South Carolina faced. The out-

27. *JCHA*, 11 December 1739, 97–98.
28. *JCHA*, 1 July 1741, 84.

break of the rebellion marked the start of what proved to be a difficult decade for the colony. The next year was perhaps the worst of all. In the spring of 1740, a joint Georgia–South Carolina force was raised to invade Florida and destroy the "Town and Castle of St. Augustine," which was widely blamed for instigating the insurrection. The expedition had proceeded to within two miles of its objective when it was attacked at night by a party composed largely of former Carolina slaves who had been given refuge and arms by the Spanish. This time, in a turn-about from the battle of the previous fall, it was the whites who abandoned the field, leaving behind fifty dead and twenty captured. After this setback, the invasion collapsed, demoralized by defeat and torn by internal recriminations.[29]

Then, in the summer of 1740, a large slave conspiracy was uncovered "in the very Heart of the Settlements." Peter, a slave "belonging to Major Cordes," brought information that a plot was being hatched among the slaves in St. John Berkeley parish, a few miles north of Charles Town. On the basis of Peter's testimony, at least sixty-seven slaves were brought to trial and as many as two dozen may have been put to death.[30]

A few months later, on November 18, Charles Town was beset by another kind of "melancholly & fatal Calamity." In a massive fire that "Came so suddenly upon us" that many residents feared that it may have been deliberately set, "the best part of . . . Town . . . [was] laid in Ashes."[31] Before the flames could be extinguished they had destroyed "about 300 Dwelling Houses, besides a great number of Store Houses &

29. See "Report of the Committee Appointed to Enquire into the Causes of the Disappointment of Success in the Late Expedition Against St. Augustine," *JCHA*, 1 July 1741, 78–247; and Jane Landers, "Gracia Real de Santa Teresa de Mose: A Free Black Town in Spanish Florida," *American Historical Review* 95 (1990), 9–30.
30. As a reward, the assembly voted to give Peter "a Suit of Cloths, Shoes, Stockings and £20 in Cash," *JCHA*, 23 July 1740, 364; 13 August 1740, 377–78; 30 January 1741, 480, 482; 19 February 1741, 492. There is some disagreement in the Assembly record as to whether the conspiracy was hatched in the parish of St. John Berkeley or in nearby St. John Colleton (the confusion may stem from the fact that Sir John Colleton, a planter in St. John Berkeley, played a role in the trial), but St. John Berkeley seems the most likely location. The number of slaves who may have been executed is suggested by the Assembly's payment of 123 pounds to the attending constables. As constables were eligible to receive five pounds' compensation for every slave they executed, this sum would have accounted for twenty-four deaths, but because any recompense due for other expenses and punishments must be deducted from this amount, the actual number of slaves put to death was likely to have been somewhat fewer.
31. Robert Pringle to Andrew Pringle, 22 November 1740, in Walter B. Edgar, ed., *The Letterbook of Robert Pringle*, 2 vols. (Columbia, S.C., 1972), 1, 271–73; for suspicions of slave arson, see Peter H. Wood, *Black Majority: Negroes in Colonial South Carolina from 1670 to the Stono Rebellion* (New York, 1974), 295.

some of the Wharfs & . . . an Immence Quantity of all sorts of Merchandize."[32]

The years that followed brought further misfortunes. In 1742, a Spanish army, including the free black battalion, momentarily threatened the colony with invasion and the prospect of slave insurrection before it was checked and turned back at the battle of Bloody Marsh in Georgia.[33] In 1744, the conflict expanded when the king's declaration of war against France was publicly proclaimed in Charles Town.[34] Although the colony was not again directly involved in the fighting, the dangers posed by Spanish and French warships and privateers devastated the low country's export-driven economy. By 1746, rice prices had fallen to less than half of their prewar level.[35] Consequently, when news of the war's end finally reached Charles Town in 1749, the colony stood on "the Brink of Ruin."[36]

But, despite the gloom, the colony's condition was not as dire as it may have seemed. In the midst of the destruction and dislocation caused by rebellion, fire, and war, the decade of the 1740s was in many ways a creative and formative period. When the rubble of the fire was cleared, for example, Charles Town was rebuilt on a larger and grander scale than before. Similarly, with the rice trade disrupted by war, low-country planters turned their minds and their slaves' labors toward the development of alternate export crops. Indigo, a plant used to make textile dye, was the most successful of these experiments. By the 1750s, indigo had come to complement rice as the region's second export staple.[37]

In this same period, the low country's black inhabitants were engaged in a creative enterprise of their own. While their masters were cultivating a new crop, blacks were building a new culture. In 1740, the low-country slave population was overwhelmingly African. More than half of the low country's blacks were less than ten years removed from Africa, and a much larger proportion had been born in Africa.[38] In the five years be-

32. Robert Pringle to James Henderson, 17 December 1740, in Edgar, ed., *Letterbook of Robert Pringle*, 1, 277.

33. Robert M. Weir, *Colonial South Carolina: A History* (Millwood, N.Y., 1983), 117–19.

34. JGC, 19 July 1744, microfilm, LC, 420.

35. Peter A. Coclanis, *The Shadow of a Dream: Economic Life and Death in the South Carolina Low Country, 1670–1920* (Oxford, 1989), 106 (table 3–29).

36. Governor James Glen to Robert Dinwiddie, 13 March 1754, quoted in Russell R. Menard, "Slavery, Economic Growth, and Revolutionary Ideology in the South Carolina Lowcountry," in Ronald Hoffman et al., eds., *The Economy of Early America, The Revolutionary Period, 1763–1790* (Charlottesville, 1988), 252.

37. See Joyce E. Chaplin, *An Anxious Pursuit: Agricultural Innovation and Modernity in the Lower South, 1730–1815* (Chapel Hill, 1993), 187–208.

38. Wood, *Black Majority*, 302.

tween 1735 and 1740 alone, over twelve thousand Africans had been imported into the colony by way of the Atlantic slave trade and put into the burgeoning rice fields.[39]

The outbreak of the Stono Rebellion awakened low-country masters to the dangers inherent in a society in which slaves outnumbered their masters by more than two to one. In April 1740, in an effort to address this demographic imbalance, the South Carolina Assembly placed a prohibitive duty on any further slave imports. A portion of the money raised by the duty was to be used to defray the costs of settlement for "poor Protestants" who, it was hoped, might be encouraged to immigrate to the colony and thereby increase whites' numbers and security.[40] The imposition of the tariff, combined with the wartime drop in trade, reduced slave imports in the decade of the 1740s to a tiny fraction of their prewar level. Between 1741 and 1752, when the duty was repealed, less than sixteen hundred Africans were brought into the colony.[41]

The decade-long moratorium on slave imports coincided with a profound change in the low-country black population. Despite the fact that far fewer Africans were imported than in the previous decade, the number of slaves in the region did not fall. The slave population in 1750 was in fact slightly larger than that of ten years before.[42] Therefore, by the end of the 1740s at least, the colony's black population was capable of reproducing itself. This demographic trend continued until a watershed was reached early in the next decade. For the first time since large-scale rice cultivation had begun over thirty years before, births routinely outnumbered deaths in low-country slave quarters, and the black population began to increase naturally.[43]

It is possible that the achievement of a positive rate of natural increase among low-country blacks had little to do with the tariff. It may simply have been the result of gradual demographic processes: as more women were born in the colony, blacks would have greater opportunities to form families and have children.[44] Or perhaps it signified better living and

---

39. Daniel C. Littlefield, *Rice and Slaves: Ethnicity and the Slave Trade in Colonial South Carolina* (Baton Rouge, 1981), 116.

40. *JCHA*, 1739–41, 35, 52–56, 123–127, 306; see also Robert L. Meriwether, *The Expansion of South Carolina, 1729–1765* (Kingsport, Tenn., 1940), 27–30.

41. Littlefield, *Rice and Slaves*, 116.

42. Philip D. Morgan estimates the South Carolina slave population in 1740 as 39,000 and in 1750 as 40,000: Morgan, "The Development of Slave Culture in Eighteenth-Century Plantation America" (Ph.D. diss., University of London, 1977), 284 (table 4–1).

43. Philip D. Morgan, "Black Society in the Lowcountry, 1760–1810," in Ira Berlin and Ronald Hoffman, eds., *Slavery and Freedom in the Age of the American Revolution* (Charlottesville, 1983), 85.

44. Because planters primarily sought to buy male workers (and because Africans preferred

working conditions on the plantations: as the low country came to the end of the "heroic" age of plantation building, working conditions for slaves may have improved. The task of tending established rice fields was far less wasting than the herculean labors of creating rice fields out of virgin swamp.

But it is more than likely that the inability to replenish their labor force with further imports induced planters to be less profligate with the lives of their slaves. Similarly, memories of Stono may well have caused masters to pause before pressing their slaves to work ever harder in the pursuit of greater profits. (Given the wartime disruptions of trade, such profits may not have been available in any case.) To this end, the new slave code passed in the spring of 1740 threatened to impose fines on masters who failed to provide their slaves with sufficient food and clothing or made them work on Sundays.[45] After 1740, masters indicated a desire, collectively if not individually, to trade a slight reduction in productivity for a measure of increased security.

Whatever its causes, a naturally increasing black population soon had another consequence. By the end of the 1750s, despite the removal of the tariff and the resumption of large-scale slave imports, people born in the colony, or "creoles," formed a majority of South Carolina's slave population. Although the proportion of native-born blacks fluctuated according to the volume of the slave trade (falling to barely 50 percent on the eve of the revolution, for example), the emergence of this creole majority within the colony's larger black majority was a persistent and important fact.[46]

In some ways, the demographic experience of low-country whites in these decades was similar to that of blacks. Evidence suggests that the low-country white population also began to reproduce itself only during the 1740s.[47] Likewise, it was probably not until these years that a majority of low-country whites had been born in the colony. While the long delay before the colony's black population became predominantly creole can

---

to sell men) the common sex ratio in the slave trade was two men for every woman. The sex ratio among a native born or "natural" population is very close to parity, i.e., 1 to 1. Analysis of the sex ratio among low-country slaves reveals that in the period 1735–39, the proportion was 1.78 men to 1 woman, demonstrating the effects of large numbers of imports. Over the next thirty-five years, however, as the population began to increase naturally, the sex ratio fell; by 1775 it was down to 1.23 to 1. See Littlefield, *Rice and Slaves*, 58–59, and Morgan, "The Development of Slave Culture," 289 (table 4–2).

45. *Statutes*, 7, 404, 411.
46. Morgan, "Black Society in the Lowcountry, 1760–1810," 89 (table 4), 92 (table 7).
47. See George D. Terry, "Dying in Paradise: Malaria, Mortality, and the Perceptual Environment in Colonial South Carolina," *Journal of Southern History* 50 (1984), 541–49; and Coclanis, *Shadow of a Dream*, 161–74.

be explained as a result of both the sexual imbalance of the slave trade and the rigorous labors of rice cultivation, what can account for the like phenomenon among low-country whites? The answer lay in the low-country environment.

For most of the first seventy-five years of settlement, the South Carolina low country was a deadly place for newcomers. The marshes, swamps, and rice fields of the region were home to mosquitoes that infected humans with malaria and yellow fever. (Eighteenth-century observers noted the link between "fevers" and wetlands, but placed the blame upon the effects of breathing "air so poisoned by marshy swamps.")[48] These illnesses struck newly arrived Europeans and Africans alike. But while many Africans carried (and passed to their children) a genetic "sickle-cell" trait that offered them a partial immunity, afflicted Europeans could only chew on mouthfuls of "China bark" (extracted from the South American cinchona tree) to alleviate their symptoms and hope to survive. Gradually, however, as the population became creole and therefore more resistant to local diseases, the high rate of mortality in the low country declined. Those creoles who did not succumb to these diseases in childhood acquired an immunity that they in turn could pass on to their children. The low country was never a very healthy place, especially for newcomers, but after 1750 its creole inhabitants, both black and white, could at least sustain their numbers.[49]

Yet even while the low country's white and black creoles were undergoing a similar process of adaptation, the population figures for whites and blacks in the region were diverging ever more widely over time. In 1740, the total population of the low country (excluding Native Americans) was approximately sixty thousand, of whom forty thousand (or two-thirds) were black. Thirty years later, the low country's population had risen to about ninety thousand, an increase of 50 percent. But this growth was not equally shared. In fact, the white population did not grow at all in these three decades, remaining at around twenty thousand, while the black population rose to seventy thousand. In 1740 the ratio of blacks to whites in the low country was two to one; by 1770, the ratio had climbed to three-and-a-half to one. In 1780, when the black population had reached to almost eighty thousand, the region contained nearly four blacks for every white person.[50]

48. Alexander Hewatt, *An Historical Account of the Rise and Progress of the Colonies of South Carolina and Georgia*, 2 vols. (London, 1779), 1, 110.
49. This paragraph is based closely on Peter Wood's pioneering work on the epidemiology of the colonial low country; see Wood, *Black Majority*, 63–91.
50. These figures are extrapolated from those given in Coclanis, *Shadow of a Dream*, 64–68

The vast difference between the stationary white population and the steadily growing black population in these years can be explained in two words: immigration and choice. Whites, who were free to decide whether or not to come to the low country, largely chose to avoid the region. Before 1740, the promise of wealth drew European settlers despite the region's unhealthy reputation and record. After 1750, however, despite the Assembly's efforts to lure "poor Protestants" to the colony, white immigration to the low country slowed to a trickle. With plantations already established and the best lands already claimed, rice was no longer a poor man's crop. Would-be rice planters were told that it would require at least two thousand pounds to purchase a viable estate.[51] Anyone with that kind of money could well afford to stay home or to go some place where the returns might be smaller but where they would stand a better chance of living to enjoy them. Thus, while local whites were able to reproduce themselves, they could neither increase their own numbers nor attract many newcomers to the region.

Unless they were educated or already well-off, the few whites who did sail into Charles Town from Europe after 1750 generally did not linger in the low country but proceeded to the western part of the colony where land was cheaper and the prospects for their health and wealth more promising. After the mid-1750s, this slow trans-Atlantic migration into the Carolina "backcountry" was met by a flood of migrants traveling southward through the great valley of Virginia. As a result, the backcountry, which had been almost completely devoid of European settlers in 1740, contained by 1770 as many as thirty thousand whites.[52]

Here at last, unexpected and uninvited, were the "poor Protestants" that low-country masters had long sought in the hope of enhancing their own security from slave revolt. The frontier settlers were not hostile to slavery; on their pioneer farms they held perhaps as many as six thousand slaves in 1770.[53] But the backcountry settlements were separated from the low country by a fifty-mile-wide belt of sandy pine barrens, and the combined factors of distance, politics, and culture kept the whites of two regions apart until after the Revolution.[54]

In the same years, Africans, involuntary migrants who had no choice

---

(tables 3–1 to 3–5); and also Morgan, "Black Society in the Lowcountry, 1760–1810," 85–89 (tables 1–4).

51. *Gentlemen's Magazine* (London), May 1755, 25, 201–3.
52. Coclanis, *Shadow of a Dream*, 68 (table 3–4).
53. Ibid.
54. See Rachel N. Klein, *Unification of a Slave State: The Rise of the Planter Class in the South Carolina Backcountry, 1760–1810* (Chapel Hill, 1990).

whether or where they would go, poured into the booming rice and indigo fields of the low country. In the twenty-four years between 1751 and 1775, over fifty-six thousand people were brought into the colony from Africa.[55] Some of these Africans were sold to backcountry settlers, and a good number probably died within a few years of their arrival, but the remainder account for much of the rise in the low-country black population in these decades.

The low-country population on the eve of the Revolution might be counted in various ways. In terms of race and freedom, the twenty thousand free whites were vastly outnumbered by the perhaps eighty thousand black slaves. In terms of birthplace, the region's approximately sixty thousand creoles outnumbered the forty thousand immigrants, almost all of whom were Africans. Low-country whites were all "free" and overwhelmingly native born; while the eighty thousand low-country blacks were virtually all enslaved, and were almost equally divided between creoles and Africans. Meanwhile, to the west, the backcountry contained as many as forty thousand whites and ten thousand blacks. Most of these frontier settlers, black and white, were newcomers, either from the colonies to the north or from the other side of the Atlantic.

Obviously, low-country rice planters' eagerness to acquire additional slaves is a strong indicator of the profits they were both realizing and anticipating in this era. In fact, the low-country economy in the years between 1750 and 1775 grew at a much faster rate than its population. Following the end of the European war in 1749, with the resumption of the rice, indigo, and slave trades, the colony embarked upon a quarter-century of unprecedented economic expansion and prosperity. Between 1750 and 1770, the volume of the colony's rice exports more than doubled. Moreover, because the price of merchantable rice rose in the same period from five to eight shillings per hundredweight, the value of the rice crop more than trebled. Indigo, the low country's second crop, also enjoyed steadily rising productivity and prices through these decades.[56] By 1775, the colony's annual exports were estimated to be worth over six hundred thousand pounds sterling, almost a four-fold increase from its worth in 1748.[57]

By almost any measure, the late-colonial low country was among the fastest growing economies in all of the Atlantic world. The region's amazing potential to produce wealth was touted throughout the British

55. Littlefield, *Rice and Slaves*, 116.
56. Statistics on South Carolina's late-colonial economy are taken from Coclanis, *Shadow of a Dream*, 48–110.
57. "Dr. George Milligen-Johnston's 'Additions' to his Pamphlet," in Chapman J. Milling, ed., *Colonial South Carolina: Two Contemporary Descriptions* (Columbia, 1951), 109.

empire. In 1755, the *Gentlemen's Magazine* of London published an article that promised annual returns of 25 percent on an outlay of two thousand pounds sterling invested in "a plantation in South Carolina, within 40 miles of Charles Town." (Along with land, livestock, and tools, the initial expense included the purchase of thirty-two slaves.)[58] Twenty years later, the English author of *American Husbandry*, a survey of colonial farming, calculated that an investment of the same amount in low-country rice cultivation would, after a decade, have increased six-fold. "No agriculture in England will pay any thing like this," the anonymous author concluded.[59] That same year, a local resident described the colony as "the most thriving Country perhaps on this Globe."[60]

In the quarter-century between 1750 and 1775, the South Carolina low country seemed to many of its white inhabitants, and to most of its visitors, an early modern version of the British-American dream. Because the low country's free population had remained small, the region's new-found wealth did not have to be shared with many newcomers. Ironically, the rapidly increasing black population itself constituted an important part of the rising riches. An analysis of probate inventories filed in Charles Town in 1774 revealed that human property comprised 57 percent of the total value of the decedents' estates. The same study placed the average worth of these inventories at 2,337 pounds sterling. Charles Town's comparative wealth is suggested by the fact that this figure far surpassed the averages that were obtained for Annapolis (660 pounds), Philadelphia (396 pounds), and Boston (312 pounds).[61]

Stories were told in the late-colonial low country of people who not only had climbed from rags to riches but along the way had changed their status from servant to master and from plebeian to patrician. In 1765, Robert Wells, a Charles Town printer, wrote that "almost to a Man" the leaders of the colony had "risen from humble and moderate Fortunes to great affluence, from walking upon foot to the command of Conven-

58. *Gentlemen's Magazine* (London), May 1755, 25, 201–3.
59. Harry J. Carman, ed., *American Husbandry* (London, 1775; rpt. New York, 1939), 301.
60. "Dr. George Milligen-Johnston's 'Additions' to His Pamphlet," 109.
61. Alice Hanson Jones, *Wealth of a Nation to Be: The American Colonies on the Eve of the Revolution* (New York, 1980), 377–79 (tables B.1–B.3). Actually, while these figures do suggest the comparative wealth of the late-colonial low country, the difference may be exaggerated. Among the Charles Town decedents included in Jones's sample was Peter Manigault, the speaker of the Commons and one of the richest men in the colony. Manigault's estate was assessed at over 32,000 pounds, which was more than twice as large as that of his nearest rival, William White, a Boston merchant. If Manigault were removed from the sample, the low-country average would fall somewhat. However, it should be noted that, besides Manigault, the Charles Town district claimed nine of the ten wealthiest decedents in Jones's study. See Jones, *Wealth of a Nation to Be*, 170–71.

iences which render their Legs and feet almost useless."[62] In 1773, a low-country tourist visited the estate of Joseph Allston, a Georgetown rice planter who, the visitor reported, "a very few years ago begun the world with only five negroes—[and] has now five plantations with an hundred slaves on each." Allston proudly bragged to his guest that "his neat income was but five or six thousand pounds sterling per year."[63] To Wells and other observers, it may indeed have seemed as if "the planters here all got rich."[64]

While understandable, this impression was of course an exaggeration. The rising economic tide did lift all of the colony's boats, but at least a few of the colony's whites were left overboard. In 1765, for example, 130 Charles Town residents were poor enough to qualify for public assistance.[65] In terms of wealth, all low-country whites were not equal. In 1751, Governor James Glen sorted the colony's white population according to their living standards. Glen divided the colony into five groups. The top fifth, he thought, comprised those "people who have plenty of the good things of life," while the people in the second fifth "have some of the conveniencys of life." The third and fourth quintiles, Glen's description continued, "have the necessarys of life," while the bottom fifth could afford only "a bare subsistence."[66]

A more recent analysis of wealth distribution in eighteenth-century South Carolina reveals that Glen's rough estimate may have been reasonably accurate, although the governor slightly underestimated both extremes, the very well off and those who had to make do with "a bare subsistence." If an estate at death worth one hundred pounds or less is considered an indication of poverty, 23 percent of all Charles Town whites who died between 1766 and 1775 were impoverished. Conversely, if an estate of greater than one thousand pounds is considered an indication of wealth, 26 percent of Charles Town's white decedents in these same years died possessed of "plenty of the good things of life." When these groups are studied over time, the effect of the low country's decades of prosperity becomes apparent. Between 1736 and 1775, the proportion of decedents who were poor fell from 29 to 23 percent, while those who were rich rose from 12 to 26 percent.[67] Moreover, if an estate of five hundred pounds is considered the minimum necessary for one to

62. *South Carolina and American General Gazette*, 12 August 1765.
63. DeWolfe Howe, ed., "Journal of Josiah Quincy, Junior, 1773," 453.
64. *South Carolina and American General Gazette*, 12 August 1765.
65. Weir, *Colonial South Carolina*, 214, 222–23.
66. James Glen to the Board of Trade, March 1751, in Merrens, ed., *The Colonial South Carolina Scene*, 184.
67. Extrapolated from Richard Waterhouse, *A New World Gentry: The Making of a Merchant and Planter Class in South Carolina, 1670–1770* (New York, 1989), 64 (table 5).

aspire to "gentility," fully 40 percent of low-country whites (the same proportion that Glen thought could afford at least "the conveniencys of life") met this standard, a proportion twice as high as in the American colonies as a whole.[68]

By the end of the colonial period, white residents and visitors alike agreed that the South Carolina low country was a place in which wealth, while not equally shared, was nonetheless remarkably widespread. In 1770, an observer estimated that "the men and women who have a right to the class of gentry . . . are more numerous here than in any other colony in North America."[69] Another writer asserted that South Carolina contained "more persons possessed of between five and ten thousand pounds sterling that are to be found any where among the same number of people."[70] With such a large number of well-to-do residents, it was apparently easy to ignore not only less fortunate whites but also the colony's black majority. "We are a country of Gentry," a local contributor to the *Gazette* boasted in 1773; "we have no such thing as Common People among us."[71]

Clearly, by the start of the 1770s, low-country whites had reason to be pleased with their situation. Thirty years after the Stono Rebellion, Robert Pringle, a Charles Town jurist, expressed the popular sentiment when he proudly described South Carolina as "the most opulent and flourishing colony on the British continent of North America." Pringle regaled the assembled grand jurors with a short history of South Carolina that could not have been more different from that told by the assembly in 1741. "Some of your progenitures," Pringle began,

> arrived in this country when it was a dreary wilderness inhabited only by wild beasts, and great numbers of savages. . . . [Despite] the great hazard they ran of losing their lives, and the many hardships and disadvantages they labored under . . . they bravely maintained their ground . . . [until] by their great industry . . . [they] improved and cultivated the colony to so great maturity, that it became the land of plenty, as well as of liberty, and fruitful like the land of Egypt.[72]

68. Jackson Turner Main, *The Social Structure of Revolutionary America* (Princeton, N.J., 1965), 276–77, 113 (note); Waterhouse, *A New World Gentry*, 64 (table 5).
69. George Milligen-Johnston, "A Short Description of South Carolina" (London, 1770), reprinted in Milling, ed., *Colonial South Carolina*, 134.
70. Hewatt, *Historical Account* 2, 180.
71. *South Carolina Gazette*, 1 March 1773.
72. Quoted in Weir, *Colonial South Carolina*, 262. In the spring of 1764, Moses Lopez returned to Charles Town after an absence of over twenty years. To his amazement, he found the city "twice as big as when I was here in the year 1742. It has increased with sumptuous brick houses in very great number. One cannot go somewhere where one does not see new

As Pringle's boast indicates, the colony's leadership had overcome its brief crisis of confidence. From 1740 to 1775, between the Stono Rebellion and the outbreak of the Revolution, masters' designs and slaves' labors had cultivated and "improved" the low-country landscape. In the interval, South Carolina society had also "matured." But the liberty and plenty of which Pringle boasted was enjoyed by only a small minority of the low country's inhabitants. The African and creole blacks whose labor created this prosperity could not share Judge Pringle's smug assessment. For the region's black majority, however, Pringle's comparison of the low country to Egypt may have been unintentionally apropos. The blacks of the low country were like the ancient Israelites in bondage to Pharaoh. Just as the bricks they made formed the fabric of the colony's lavish new buildings, so their bodies and their labor were the source of the colony's wealth.

"Black and White all mix'd Together"

Travelers' accounts of the South Carolina low country in the late-colonial period are a study in contrasts. Visitors were captivated by the region's growth and prosperity and were attracted by its promise of easy riches. Travelers remarked approvingly upon the manners and sophistication of the low-country elite and on the refinement that was evident in Charles Town and in individual planters' homes. But the tourists were also confronted with sights that were far less familiar or comforting. Some complained about the low country's tropical climate, while many regarded low-country wildlife, such as alligators and rattlesnakes, with a mixture of fascination and fear. Above all, however, it was the institution of slavery, and the pervasive presence of Africans and their creole descendants, that told visitors that they were not in England (old or new) anymore. In the years between 1740 and 1775, travelers to the low country found the alluring alongside the horrifying and the familiar adjacent to the exotic.[73]

---

buildings and large and small houses started, half-finished, and almost finished. To me who comes from poor, humble, Rhode Island, it seems . . . a new world." Moses Lopez to Aaron Lopez, 3 May 1764, in Thomas J. Tobias, ed., "A View of Charleston in 1764," *SCHM* 67 (1966), 67–68.

73. Joyce Chaplin has cautioned that the eighteenth-century travel narrative genre was focused on issues other than verisimilitude and therefore should be used with care by historians. The discussion that follows focuses on what travelers *perceived* rather than taking their words for fact; see Chaplin, *An Anxious Pursuit*, 66–91.

Most tourists began their visit at Charles Town, the center of low-country society. It might fairly be said that, as in ancient Rome, all roads and rivers led to the capital city. One scholar has aptly described South Carolina under the royal government as a "city-state," so great was Charles Town's domination of the colony's political, economic, and cultural life.[74] The city was the seat of the colony's government and its courts and the center of its trade. One indicator of Charles Town's sway over the colony is the fact that in 1775, twenty-eight of the Commons House's forty-eight members came from Charles Town or from ten parishes lying within a day's ride of the city. By contrast, the backcountry's forty thousand white inhabitants were given only two seats.[75]

As the metropolis of the low country, the city benefited disproportionately from the region's prosperity in the third quarter of the eighteenth century. Between 1740 and 1775, the population of Charles Town increased from four to over twelve thousand inhabitants. By the end of the colonial period, Charles Town was the fourth-largest urban place in all of British America, behind only Philadelphia, New York, and Boston.[76] Moreover, the more than six thousand blacks who resided in Charles Town in 1775 formed a community larger than the combined black populations of its three continental rivals.[77]

Charles Town's continued growth, amid the larger low-country white population's numerical stagnation, indicates a gradual movement of whites from the countryside to the city. Increased prosperity allowed many planters to forsake their plantations for the social pleasures and cooling breezes of Charles Town and to live as absentee planters. Consequently, as Charles Town grew, the proportion of low-country whites who resided in the city rose from about one in ten in 1740 to nearly one in three by 1775. Meanwhile in the low country outside of Charles Town, the ratio of blacks to whites rose from about two to one to more than five to one; some low-country parishes had far higher ratios.

But Charles Town's growth was more than demographic. Although

---

74. Jack P. Greene, *The Quest for Power: The Lower Houses of Assembly in the Southern Royal Colonies, 1689–1776* (Chapel Hill, 1963), 35.
75. Jerome J. Nadelhaft, *The Disorders of War: The Revolution in South Carolina* (Orono, Maine, 1981), 12–13.
76. John J. McCusker and Russell R. Menard, *The Economy of British America, 1607–1789* (Chapel Hill, 1985), 184–85. In his "Additions" to his 1763 pamphlet, George Milligen-Johnston estimated the city's population in 1775 at 14,000; in Milling, ed., *Colonial South Carolina*, 109.
77. Morgan, "Black Life in Eighteenth-Century Charleston," 188.

the city's fortifications were dismantled in 1720, Charles Town had hardly outgrown its original eighty-acre site twenty years later. Beginning in the 1740s, however, creeks and marshes were filled in and streets laid out or extended, as the city expanded to the north, south, and west. In the 1750s the four corners were developed, and the town gate, which had been located at Broad and Meeting in the days when Meeting Street marked the western edge of the city, was relocated three-fourths of a mile to the north on King Street just beyond the appropriately named Boundary Street.

By 1760, Charles Town's most important activities were organized along a "T" pattern that was a classic part of eighteenth-century town planning.[78] Bay Street, along the Cooper River, formed the top of the "T." The solid row of merchants' houses, stores, and warehouses that lined "the Bay" for half a mile were the economic heart of the city and colony. Broad Street, which met Bay at a right angle midway along the waterfront, was the stem of the "T," and its base lay three blocks to the west at the four corners, where the colony's political and religious establishment was headquartered.

Charles Town may have been the metropolis of the low country, but London remained the great metropolis of the empire, as every white South Carolinian well knew. The colony's position on the periphery of an older, larger, richer, more powerful, and more sophisticated culture was an important factor shaping the social development of Charles Town and all of South Carolina society in the mid-eighteenth century. This relationship of colonial dependency powerfully influenced the perceptions, expectations, aspirations, and ambitions of Carolinians. Colonists judged themselves and their achievements according to English standards.[79] As early as 1740, Eliza Pinckney described her mode of life in South Carolina, somewhat implausibly, as "very much in the English taste."[80]

Like other *nouveaux riches*, the planters of the mid-eighteenth-century low country were eager to spend their new-found wealth to acquire the trappings of power and prestige. In the Anglo-American world, dressing

78. See Richard Bushman, *The Refinement of America: Persons, Houses, Cities* (New York, 1992), 150.
79. See Jack P. Greene, "Search for Identity: An Interpretation of the Meaning of Selected Patterns of Social Response in Eighteenth-Century America," *Journal of Social History* 3 (1970), 189–224; and Richard L. Bushman, "American High-Style and Vernacular Cultures," in Jack P. Greene and J. R. Pole, eds., *Colonial British America: Essays in the New History of the Early Modern Era* (Baltimore, 1984), 367–73.
80. Eliza Lucas to Mrs. Bodicott, 2 May 1740, in Harriet Horry Ravenel, *Eliza Pinckney* (New York, 1896), 5.

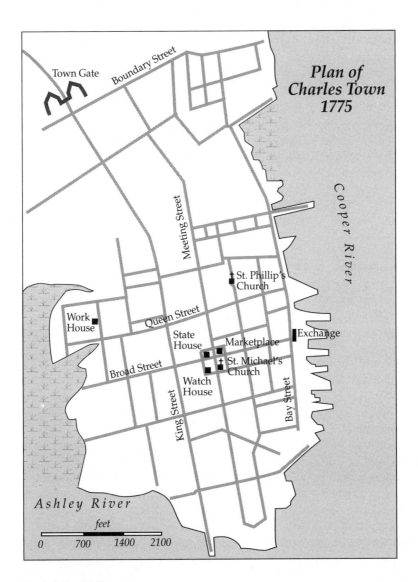

Plan of Charles Town, 1775

for success meant aping the lifestyle of the English gentry. In their homes, portraits, dress, and manners, members of the colonial South Carolina elite sought as much as possible to fashion themselves into English gentlemen and women.[81] David Ramsay, a Charles Town physician,

81. See Waterhouse, *A New World Gentry*, 106–7.

thought his fellow Carolinians "fond of British manners even to excess."[82]

Thirty years ago, cultural historians adopted the term "Anglicization" to describe the phenomenon by which American colonial elites in the eighteenth century sought to reform and reshape themselves and their societies in imitation of an English metropolitan model.[83] South Carolina's leaders were typical in this regard, although their wealth may have allowed them to carry imitation to greater lengths than most. Observing the audience at a concert in Charles Town in 1773, for example, Bostonian Josiah Quincy thought that "the gentlemen . . . dressed with richness and elegance uncommon with us, many with swords on."[84]

South Carolina's elite sought to copy British manners in other ways as well. When Quincy visited a session of the Commons House of Assembly, he noted that "the *first* thing done at the meeting of the house is to bring the mace (a very superb and elegant one which cost ninety guineas), and lay it on the table before the speaker. This I am told is the way in the Commmons of G[reat] B[ritain]." Quincy also noticed that "the members of the house all sit with their hats on" and was informed that this was done because "the members of . . . the Commons of England, always sat with their hats on."[85]

England, at least an ideal, imagined England, loomed large in wealthy Carolinians' hearts and dreams. In 1765, a British aristocrat, Lord Adam Gordon, arrived in Charles Town and was lavishly feted by the nabobs of the low country. Gordon found the South Carolina elite "the most hospitable and affable [people] . . . of any I have yet seen in America." "Almost all of them," he discovered, "first or last, have made a trip to the Mother-Country . . . [and] I am of opinion that the most opulent planters would prefer a home life," that is, to live in Britain.[86] Nine years later, an English visitor discovered that colonists need not actually have crossed the Atlantic to form such affective (if also fictive) attachments. This tourist noted that "most people that are born in Carolina can't help discovering in common conversation a great partiality towards England,

---

82. Ramsay, as quoted by William Henry Drayton in *The Letters of Freeman, Etc.: Essays On the Nonimportation Movement in South Carolina*, ed. Robert M. Weir (Columbia, S.C., 1977), xxiii.

83. John M. Murrin, "Anglicizing an American Colony: The Transformation of Provincial Massachusetts" (Ph.D. diss., Yale University, 1966); Greene, "Search for Identity," and John M. Murrin, "The Legal Transformation: The Bench and Bar of Eighteenth-Century Massachusetts," both in Stanley N. Katz and John Murrin, eds., *Colonial America: Essays in Politics and Social Development* (3rd ed., New York, 1983), 540–72.

84. DeWolfe Howe, ed., "Journal of Josiah Quincy, Junior, 1773," 442.

85. Ibid., 451–452, 447.

86. "Journal of an Officer who Travelled in America and the West Indies in 1764 and 1765," in Mereness, ed., *Travels in the American Colonies*, 397.

calling it their home tho' they have never been there and seem to wish much to have it in their power to be able to go and live comfortably in it.''[87]

Such Anglophilic impulses and tastes were not confined to the low-country elite. Other groups in the society also sought to appropriate English fashions and customs in an effort to enhance their status. In the year of Quincy's visit, an anonymous contributor to the *South Carolina Gazette* decried the "foolish vanity" that led everyone "to imitate ... [their] superiors." As a consequence, the correspondent continued, "the sons of our lowest mechanics are sent to the colleges of Philadelphia, England, or Scotland, and there acquire with their learning, the laudable ambition of becoming gentlefolks, ... [while] every planter of distinction is impatient for an elegant carriage, horses, equipage, &ca. and treads hard on the heels of Quality in dress & expences.''[88]

Of course, people's ability to refashion themselves into "gentlefolks" was closely tied to their disposable income. In this regard Governor Glen noted that it was "in proportion as they thrive" that the inhabitants of the colony "delight to have good things from England.''[89] But it did not require riches to take part in the "empire of goods" and to attempt to assert both one's Englishness and one's "Quality" through the purchase of consumables.[90] Almost every issue of the *South Carolina Gazette* printed between 1740 and 1775 carried lists of items "just imported ... from London." Those who could not afford to buy "silver hilted Swords" or "setts of Queen's Ware" might still be tempted by the "fashionable ribbons" and "linen handkerchiefs" the advertisements offered.[91]

Even slaves were not entirely excluded from the pull of Anglicization and the desire to imitate their "superiors." Most of what slaves knew of the fashions of the metropolis they gained second- or third-hand from watching their masters. However, at least a few low-country slaves learned from personal experience. For example, an advertisement described one runaway who "knows how to shave well, cook, &c, ... speaks good English, ... [and] has been in England.''[92]

---

87. "Charleston at the End of the Colonial Era, 1774," in Merrens, ed., *The Colonial South Carolina Scene*, 285.
88. *South Carolina Gazette*, 1 March 1773.
89. James Glen to the Board of Trade, March 1751, in Merrens, ed., *The Colonial South Carolina Scene*, 180.
90. See T. H. Breen, "An Empire of Goods: The Anglicization of Colonial America, 1690–1776," *Journal of British Studies* 25 (October 1986), 467–99; and Breen, " 'Baubles of Britain': The American and Consumer Revolutions of the Eighteenth Century," *Past and Present* 119 (1988), 73–104.
91. *South Carolina Gazette*, 6 November 1740, 19 March 1763, 24 May 1773.
92. *South Carolina Gazette*, 21 July 1766.

Other advertisements for runaways illustrate the degree to which some slaves succeeded in dressing like the very model of an early modern English gentleman or woman. For example, when Abraham left his master in 1771, he was thought to be wearing "a Coat, Waistcoat, and long trousers of blue Plains, good Stockings, Shoes, Silver buckles, and an old Beaver Hat."[93] The following year, a contributor to the *Gazette* complained that "there is scarce a new mode [of dress] which *favourite* black and mulatto *women slaves* are not immediately *enabled* to adapt."[94] But the ads also show that slaves could use English goods in un-English ways, for instance by wearing ribbons and handkerchiefs on their heads instead of on their clothes or around their necks.[95]

Low-country masters did not regard slaves' desire to imitate their dress as a form of flattery. Instead, the sight of slaves wearing the garments of gentility was interpreted as an inversion of the social order. The Negro Act of 1740 asserted that "many of the slaves in this Province wear clothes much above the condition of slaves" and directed that henceforth slaves' apparel be made from a specified list of coarse fabrics.[96] In practice, however, such sumptuary laws proved difficult to enforce, and the complaints continued. In 1773, for instance, one master described his own slave's clothes as "really too good for any of his Colour."[97]

Blacks' display of British goods and clothes may have walked a fine line between sincere imitation and subversive mockery. Like their masters, many slaves were inclined to judge a man by the cut of his coat. One low-country white wrote that "not many [slaves] will condescend to pay the compliment of taking off their hatt to a white man, who by his appearance, seems below affluence."[98] But slaves could also see beneath the fancy clothes and recognize their masters' pretensions for what they were. In 1772, for instance, the *Gazette* described "a Country Dance, Rout, or Cabal of Negroes" that had taken place one Saturday night a few miles north of Charles Town. The party "consisted of about 60 people 5–6ths from Town, everyone of whom carried some-

93. *South Carolina Gazette*, 11 April 1771, in Lathan A. Windley, comp., *Runaway Slave Advertisements, A Documentary History from the 1730s to 1790*, 4 vols. (Westport, Conn., 1983), 3 [South Carolina], 294.
94. *South Carolina Gazette*, 24 September 1772.
95. For examples, see *South Carolina Gazette*, 12 June and 27 August 1753, 9 April 1754, and 17 July 1755, in Windley, *Runaway Slave Advertisements*, 3, 121–22, 126, 135. For a provocative discussion of black clothing "style" as revealed in runaway advertisements, see Shane White, *Somewhat More Independent: The End of Slavery in New York City, 1770–1810* (Athens, 1991), 194–200.
96. *Statutes*, 7, 412.
97. *South Carolina Gazette*, 10 May 1773.
98. *South Carolina Gazette*, 17 September 1772.

thing . . . [such] as: bottled liquors of all sorts, Rum, Tongues, Hams, Beef, Geese, Turkies and Fowls . . . with many luxuries of the table [such] as sweetmeats, pickles, &c." The newspaper reported that the evening's "entertainment was opened, by the men copying (or taking off) the manners of their masters and the women those of their mistresses, and relating some highly curious anecdotes to the inexpressible diversion of that company."[99]

The mutual observation and close interaction between low-country slaves and masters that this accounts suggests had its origin in the first years of the colony. In 1974, historian Peter Wood chronicled the profound influence that Africans had on the early development of South Carolina.[100] Wood linked the considerable autonomy that Africans enjoyed in the colony's formative years to South Carolina's condition as a "frontier."[101] Whether tending isolated herds of cattle, working alone in the forest to turn pine tar into turpentine, voyaging independently into the backcountry to trade with Native Americans, or fighting beside their masters in the colonial militia, enslaved Africans were crucial and creative contributors in the establishment of low-country society.[102] While not discounting the harsh realities of slavery in this era, Wood portrayed a master-slave relationship of "forced intimacy and tenuous equality" that was shaped by the Africans' superior ability to adapt and survive in the low-country environment and the Europeans' need for able assistants in developing and defending the infant colony.[103]

However, as South Carolina evolved from a frontier to a plantation society in the first quarter of the eighteenth century, Africans' opportunities for initiative and autonomy were reduced. The large-scale cultivation of rice, which Africans most probably introduced into the colony, gradually transformed the low country into a land of plantations and large slave holdings.[104] After 1720, thousands of newly imported Africans were sent directly to labor in the swamps, clearing land for the cultivation of rice. These unwilling immigrants were as ingenious as their predecessors, and within the plantation slave quarters they built a distinctive culture and developed a language, Gullah, from a syncretic mixture of

99. *South Carolina Gazette*, 17 September 1772. For a fascinating study of how slaves could appropriate masters' culture while simultaneously subverting it, see James Sidbury, *Ploughshares into Swords: Race, Rebellion, and Identity in Gabriel's Virginia, 1730–1810* (Cambridge, 1997), 55–94.
100. Wood, *Black Majority*.
101. Ibid., 195–96.
102. Ibid., 28–34, 95–130.
103. Ibid., 196.
104. On the origins of rice culture in Carolina, see Wood, *Black Majority*, 35–62; and more particularly, Littlefield, *Rice and Slaves*, 74–114.

English and African influences.[105] Yet these later arrivals had little ability to shape the larger structures of their lives. By the 1730s rice and slavery were increasingly becoming the inescapable realities for the vast majority of low-country Africans.

The slow process by which the labor of low-country blacks inexorably forged the shackles of their own and their children's servitude is encapsulated in an anecdote passed down by the descendants of a white settler. A member of the Horry family recalled that at the end of the seventeenth century Elias Horry, his forebear and a Huguenot refugee, "worked many days with a Negro man at a Whip saw" clearing land on the Santee.[106] Three generations later, when this story was retold as an early version of the American dream, Horry's descendants constituted one of the richest families in South Carolina. For the great-grandchildren (if any) of the unnamed "Negro man" beside whom the elder Horry labored, the circumstances of their lives changed far less dramatically; they still "worked many days" at back-breaking toil. Amid their masters' wealth, they were chained in poverty and, of course, they remained unfree.

When Elias Horry, Jr., the son of the immigrant, died in 1783 at the age of seventy-six, he owned 104 slaves.[107] But stories such as those told around the Horry family dinner table were not the exclusive property of the very wealthy. If mastering the new world meant mastering people, most low-country whites could tell a similar tale. One indicator of how pervasive the impact of slaves and slavery was on white society by the third quarter of the eighteenth century is provided by an examination of slave ownership.

Possession of a slave had several meanings. Obviously, because slaves were valuable property, slave ownership was regarded as an important measure and marker of economic status among whites. As one visitor to the low country remarked, "if a man has not as many slaves as they, he is esteemed by them their inferior."[108] But possession of slaves had a social and political meaning as well as an economic one. Ownership of a slave automatically made one into a master and, in a slave society, into a member of the ruling "class."

By this criterion, the great majority of low-country whites were rulers.

---

105. Wood, *Black Majority*, 167–91.
106. Alexander S. Salley, Jr., ed., "Journal of General Peter Horry," *SCHM* 38 (1937), 51–52, quoted in Wood, *Black Majority*, 97.
107. Walter B. Edgar and N. Louise Bailey, eds., *Biographical Directory of the South Carolina House of Representatives*, vol. 2 (The Commons House of Assembly, 1692–1775) (Columbia, 1977), 330–31.
108. H. Roy Merrens, ed., "A View of Coastal Carolina in 1778: The Journal of Ebenezer Hazard," *SCHM* 73 (1972), 190.

An examination of slaveholding in Charles Town in the decade between 1766 and 1775 shows that only 23 percent of decedents' estates did not include at least one slave. As this is exactly the same proportion who died possessed of less than one hundred pounds' worth of goods, it suggests that one-fifth of Charles Town's white population, or around 1,400 individuals, were a slave-less working poor. Of the remainder, 41 percent had 1–10 slaves, 14 percent had 11–20 slaves, and 22 percent (the top fifth) died owning 21 or more slaves.[109]

While these figures suggest how very common the master-slave relation was in Charles Town, in the countryside it was virtually inescapable. A study of probate inventories filed between 1769 and 1779 in St. John Berkeley parish, just north of Charles Town on the Cooper River, revealed that 95 percent of whites died possessed of at least one slave. Sixty percent of decedents owned ten or more slaves. If the ownership of twenty slaves is used to define a "planter" (as is commonly done by scholars of the nineteenth-century South), more than two in five parish residents qualified as planters by the time of their death. Perhaps even more remarkably, fully one-fourth of all the estates inventoried in St. John Berkeley in these years included more than fifty slaves (compared to 8 percent in Charles Town).[110]

If the figures for St. John Berkeley can be taken as typical of the entire rural low country in this period, perhaps 90 percent of the entire low-country white population was directly involved in the slave-master relation, either as masters themselves or as members of families whose household heads were masters. Even the 10 percent of white householders who did not own slaves could hardly escape the institution's influence or avoid playing a role in its perpetuation. While poor whites were often suspected of having too much familiarity with slaves, they also filled the ranks of the town watch and the parish slave patrol and found employment as overseers on the large estates.[111]

Examining slaveholding from the perspective of the slaves reveals another picture. In this era, the free black population of the low country was minuscule, numbering at the very most 1 percent of the black population (or about 700 individuals).[112] For 99 percent of low-country

109. Waterhouse, *A New World Gentry*, 66–67 (table 8).

110. George D. Terry, " 'Champaign Country': A Social History of an Eighteenth-Century Lowcountry Parish in South Carolina, St. Johns Berkeley County" (Ph.D., diss., University of South Carolina, 1981), 249; Waterhouse, *A New World Gentry*, 66–67 (table 8).

111. For an example of poor whites' ambiguous relations with slaves, see Philip D. Morgan and George D. Terry, "Slavery in Microcosm: A Conspiracy Scare in Colonial South Carolina," *Southern Studies* 21 (Summer 1982), 121–45.

112. See Robert Olwell, "Becoming Free: Manumission and the Genesis of a Free Black Community in South Carolina, 1740–1790," *Slavery & Abolition* 17 (April 1996), 1–19.

blacks, the master-slave relation was an everyday, lifelong reality. However, while the typical low-country master possessed fewer than twenty slaves, the typical slave was owned by the master of a large plantation of twenty or more slaves. In the decade between 1760 and 1769, 75 percent of all low-country slaves lived on such estates. Fully 40 percent of all low-country slaves in these years lived on plantations with black populations of more than fifty persons. As many slaves lived in quarters of over a hundred individuals as lived in groups of less than ten.[113]

Over the course of the eighteenth century, masters and slaves on these plantations forged a working relationship that balanced the masters' willingness and ability to use power and violence to compel obedience with the slaves' ability and desire to shape their own mode of life. The central pivot of this "moral economy" was the task system of labor. Under the provisions of the task system, the rice fields were divided into sections of approximately one-quarter-acre each, and every adult slave was assigned one section to cultivate each day. The amount of labor to complete a "task" was such that by working steadily from sunup a slave could finish in about eight hours, or by mid-afternoon. After their task was complete, slaves could do what they pleased: spend the rest of the day cultivating their own garden plots, assist other family members in finishing their tasks, or merely enjoy a respite from labor.

The origins of the task system are unclear. It may have grown out of the productive processes of rice cultivation. Rice fields were naturally subdivided by sluices and dikes into small sections, and rice culture was ill-suited to gang labor. Just as likely, it may have been a result of the demographic and epidemiological realities of the colonial low country. Given their own relatively small numbers, masters may have been hesitant to drive their slaves harder or more closely. Likewise, given the threat of disease and the memory of the Stono Rebellion, masters may have welcomed the distance that the task system gave them both from their slaves and from the deadly fevers of the rice swamps.

By the middle decades of the eighteenth century, the task system had evolved from a form of labor into a way of life. For both masters and slaves, a "task" could mean a variety of different things according to context. It might denote an area of ground (a quarter-acre), or it might signify a particular job (splitting one hundred fence rails, for example), or it could be used to define a measure of distance (one task equaled approximately 105 feet).[114]

---

113. Morgan, "The Development of Slave Culture in Eighteenth-Century Plantation America," 2 (table 1–1).
114. See Philip D. Morgan, "Work and Culture: The Task System and the World of Low-

The emergence of the task system, a "culture" of work that was shared by low-country whites and blacks, illustrates how masters and slaves had learned to understand and respond to one another's demands by the mid-eighteenth century. Central to this process of education and negotiation was the emergence of a creole majority among both the white and the black population during this period. After 1750 or so, the vast majority of masters and a small majority of slaves were no longer "strangers," transplanted Europeans and Africans, regarding one another as aliens and contending with one another in an alien environment. Instead, most masters and most slaves, while still having distinct cultures and identities, were also fellow Carolinians, familiar with one another and with the low-country landscape.

Creole slaves had an importance that transcended their numbers. They occupied a crucial middle ground between their masters and newly arrived, African-born slaves. While they were the first generation to regard Gullah as their native tongue, black creoles were far more familiar with the English language and with English ways than their parents had been. Colony-born slaves were also more accustomed, from lifelong experience, to the practices, possibilities, and hazards of the slave society. Armed with this knowledge, creole slaves could function as cultural brokers between their masters and newly arrived Africans.

Certainly, masters regarded "country born" slaves as less alien, and therefore less threatening, than enslaved Africans. In a 1751 report on the colony, Governor James Glen distinguished those slaves who "are natives of Carolina, who have no . . . longing after any other country, that have been among white people, and . . . can all speak our language" from "new Negroes from Affrica."[115] While Glen's hopeful assertions that creole slaves had "no notion of liberty," were "pleased with their masters, contented with their condition, [and] reconciled to servitude" might safely be doubted, it is conceivable that people born into slavery may well have had different "notion[s] of liberty" and consequently may have resisted their masters in different ways than those who had memories of Africa and of freedom.

According to the governor, creole slaves were "seasoned to the country." By this, Glen apparently meant only that the country born had an acquired immunity to the low-country diseases that often proved deadly

---

country Blacks, 1700–1880," *William and Mary Quarterly*, 3rd series, 39 (October 1982), 563–99; and Morgan, "Task and Gang Systems: The Organization of Labor on New World Plantations," in Stephen Innes, ed., *Work and Labor in Early America* (Chapel Hill, 1988), 189–220.
115. James Glen to the Board of Trade, March 1750, in Merrens, ed., *The Colonial South Carolina Scene*, 182–83.

to new arrivals, African as well as European. But if his meaning is expanded to imply an acquired knowledge of the slave society, the remark is no less apt. Creole slaves, familiar with their masters' strengths and weaknesses, may have been more inclined to engage in "everyday forms of . . . resistance," working both with and *within* the slave system, seeking to expand upon or defend small freedoms, petty property "rights," and family ties, than to hazard everything in a desperate effort to escape or overthrow the only world they had ever known.[116]

Most travelers to the mid-eighteenth-century low country regarded slaves and slavery as the central, even dominant, reality of the region. Visitors were moved to remark upon the sheer numbers of slaves they encountered in the streets of Charles Town and along the roads of the rural low country. One indication of the impression that the sight of so many slaves had on the minds of visitors is the fact that their estimates of the proportion of blacks to whites in the colony were invariably grossly inflated. During a visit to the low country in September 1741, Henry Melchior Muhlenberg reported that "the heathen slaves are so numerous here that it is estimated that there are fifteen for every white man."[117] At that time, the true ratio was closer to two to one. In 1773, when there were about four blacks to every white, Josiah Quincy wrote: "I took great pains (finding much contrariety of opinion) to find out the true proportion. The best information I could obtain fixes it at about seven to one, my own observation leads me to think it much greater."[118] During his visit five years later, Quincy's fellow Yankee, Ebenezer Hazard, found the low country's black majority quite intimidating. While in South Carolina, Hazard copied into his journal rumors of slave uprisings in the Caribbean as well as the reflection that a "man can enjoy but little happiness who is under continual apprehensions from his slaves." When Hazard tried to gauge the racial balance, he placed it at "50 [blacks] for one white person," or more than twelve times the actual ratio.[119]

But the impact of slavery and slaves on the day-to-day life of the low country transcended mere demographic facts. In South Carolina during the third quarter of the eighteenth century, the presence and influence of slavery and slaves penetrated everywhere and everything. Josiah Quincy observed that the "general topics of conversation" at the elegant

---

116. For explication of the concept of "everyday resistance," see James C. Scott, *Weapons of the Weak: Everyday Forms of Peasant Resistance* (New Haven, 1985).

117. *The Journals of Henry Melchoir Muhlenberg*, trans. Theodore G. Tappert and John W. Doberstein, 3 vols. (Philadelphia, 1942), 1, 58; I thank Karin Wulf for this reference.

118. DeWolfe Howe, ed., "The Journal of Josiah Quincy, Junior, 1773," 456.

119. Merrens, ed., "The Journal of Ebenezer Hazard," 181.

dinners that he attended were of "negroes, and the price of rice and indigo."[120]

The stark contrast between the "hospitality, . . . good breeding, and politeness" they met with from their white hosts and the "great barbarity" of slavery struck many visitors.[121] Josiah Quincy described each course of the lavish dinners he attended in painstaking detail. At one dinner, he was captivated by "a very fine bird familiarly playing over the room, under our chairs, and the table, picking up crumbs, etc., and perching on the window, sideboard, and chairs: vastly pretty!" But Quincy also wrote of being rowed across the Hobcaw River to yet another dinner "by six negroes, four of whom had *nothing on* but their kind of breeches, scarce sufficient for covering."[122]

Travelers on low-country highways could, like William Bartram in 1773, be "agreeably" contemplating the "magnificence and grandeur" of "ancient sublime forests, frequently intersected with extensive avenues, vistas, and green lawns, opening to . . . far distant Rice plantations," only to round a bend and come face to face with the harsh reality of slavery.[123] Ebenezer Hazard had a roadside encounter with "a Negro man . . . who had runaway from his master":

> I came up just at the instant that another Negro was tying him with a hair rope; his young master was sitting by, on horseback, with a gun in his hand. The poor Negroe's looks arising from terrible apprehensions of future punishment were such as I think must have affected a savage; [but] his young master appeared unmoved.[124]

Slavery entered into Carolina whites' attitudes and behaviors as well as their conversations. Quincy felt sure that "the number and subjection of their slaves" explained the "life, sentiments, and manners of the leading people." For example, the Bostonian thought that the lack of "any warm or animated" opinions in the "political conversations" of the South Carolina elite was explained by the fact that "their fiercer passions . . .

---

120. DeWolfe Howe, ed., "The Journal of Josiah Quincy, Junior, 1773," 456.
121. Ibid., 462.
122. Ibid., 455, 452; the emphasis in the second quotation is in the original.
123. William Bartram, *Travels Through North & South Carolina, Georgia, East & West Florida* (Philadelphia, 1791; rpt. New York, 1996), 255. On another occasion, while riding alone north of Georgetown, Bartram came toward a "party of Negroes . . . armed with clubs, axes, and hoes." For a moment, Bartram feared they might be runaways and brigands. Upon their meeting, however, "their chief informed me who they belonged to, and said they were going to man a new quarter at the West end of the bay." Ibid., 373.
124. Merrens, ed., "The Journal of Ebenezer Hazard," 181.

[were all] employed upon their slaves."[125] In Hazard's eyes, the link between slavery and the mentality of "the country gentlemen" was even more direct. "Accustomed to tyrannize from their infancy," he wrote, "they carry with them a disposition to treat all mankind in the same manner they have been used to treat their Negroes."[126]

Low-country whites knew blacks as property (to be bought and sold, or merely accumulated) and as workers (to be commanded to labor or punished for disobedience), but they also knew them as persons. Blacks and whites lived in such close proximity in the colonial low-country that they could not but have watched, conversed, and learned from each other. Black women did the cooking in most wealthy white kitchens, and African culinary traditions soon found their way onto white tables and into white appetites. Lord Gordon noticed that, despite their proclaimed fondness for England, his Charles Town hosts preferred rice to bread at their meals.[127]

Likewise, while many colony-born slaves may have learned to speak or at least understand English, their masters also took linguistic lessons from their slaves. Both Hazard and Quincy noticed that low-country whites not only commonly spoke *of* blacks but also spoke *like* them. The two Yankees agreed on what they heard, but ascribed it to different causes. Quincy thought the causative factors were age and sex, reporting that white children "contract a negroish kind of accent, pronunciation, and dialect . . . even many of the grown people, and especially the women, are vastly affected with the same disorder."[128] Hazard preferred to place the blame on class, writing that "the common country people talk very much like negroes, and indeed many of the better sort use a little of that dialect."[129]

Masters and slaves also had sexual relations. "The enjoyment of a negro or mulatto woman is spoken of as quite a common thing," Quincy wrote; "no reluctance, delicacy, or shame is made about the matter." On two occasions, Quincy was taken aback as dinner guests playfully traced the close resemblance between the master of the table and a mulatto slave servant standing nearby. "The fathers," whom Quincy described as "men of worth, politeness and humanity," "neither . . . blushed or

125. Ibid., 455, 454.
261. Ibid., 190.
127. "Journal of an Officer who Travelled in America and the West Indies in 1764 and 1765," in Mereness, ed., *Travels in the American Colonies*, 400.
128. DeWolfe Howe, ed., "The Journal of Josiah Quincy, Junior, 1771," 456–57.
129. Merrens, ed., "The Journal of Ebenezer Hazard," 181. George Rogers has wittily described the speech of present-day Charlestonians as "high Gullah"; Rogers, *Charleston in the Age of the Pinckneys*, 79.

seem[ed] disconcerted."[130] On rare occasions, the children of such unions were acknowledged and freed. When John Williams manumitted two of his slaves in 1754, for example, he claimed to act from the "natural love and affection" that he felt toward "my own proper children & issue of my body."[131] Far more commonly, as Quincy noted, a master who fathered children on his slaves made "not one effort to redeem his blood" and left "his progeny in bondage and misery."[132]

By the end of the colonial period, low-country whites and blacks had come to know each other almost too well. Since the early years of the eighteenth century, the two groups had watched and struggled with one another until each of them dominated the other's vision of the past, present, and future. Thus, while one might write of black Carolinians or white Carolinians as if they each were distinct cultures, in reality the shadow of the other would always remain. In the words of an eighteenth-century tourist, the late-colonial low country was a world where "Black and White all mix'd together."[133]

On Saturday, September 8, 1739, a notice in the *South Carolina Gazette* offered for sale a plantation "on the Ashley-River, within 3 miles of Charles Town." The advertisement listed the usual details: acreage, buildings, livestock, "all kinds of plantation tools" and, of course, "negroes." The notice also included a description of the estate's "extensive and pleasant" gardens, which, the seller promised, "resemble old England the most of any in the province."[134] While this comparison might be dismissed as the usual real estate hyperbole, its prominence in the ad is nonetheless illustrative. Many colonial South Carolina masters apparently might have wished to imagine themselves in an England they had never known. In formal gardens (after the slave gardeners had returned to their quarters), planters could momentarily wash their hands of the barbarity of slavery, forget the dangers of the black majority, and escape the exotic character of the low country. Meanwhile, on the very night

130. DeWolfe Howe, ed., "Journal of Josiah Quincy, Junior, 1773," 463.
131. Miscellaneous Records, SCDAH, 6 June 1754, KK148.
132. DeWolfe Howe, ed., "The Journal of Josiah Quincy, Junior, 1773," 463. Given the enormous discrepancies of power that existed between masters and slaves, it seems pointless to ask if such sexual relationships were coerced. Even if physical violence were not used in the act itself (as it often was), brutal inequalities of every sort (economic, social, and political) shaped every encounter between masters and slaves, including sexual ones. In this vein, it is interesting to note that while "the enjoyment of a negro . . . woman" by a white man was condoned, sexual relations between a black man and a white woman were likely to end in the death of the former and the utter degradation of the latter.
133. "A Naval Officer's View of the Metropolis, 1769," in Merrens, ed., *The Colonial South Carolina Scene*, 230–31.
134. *South Carolina Gazette*, 8 September 1739.

that this advertisement appeared, a group of slaves were secretly gathering on the banks of the Stono.

A Colonial Slave Society

The sight of mulattoes strolling on the streets of Charles Town or serving in gentry dining rooms, like the presence of rice on white dinner tables and of African dialect in white speech, indicates the degree to which low-country planters, despite their Anglicized homes, clothes, portraits, and manners, had become something quite different from Englishmen and women abroad. Shaped by the colony's attraction for the metropolis and by the necessity of maintaining control over their slaves, the low-country society that emerged in the mid-eighteenth century was a hybrid mixture of English inheritance or imitation, African influence, and American experience.

There was irony as well as tragedy in the fact that the more low-country masters exploited their slaves' labor and sold their slaves' bodies in an effort to imitate English homes, fashions, and manners, the more they became the model of a *colonial* planter class. As Quincy noted, slavery, "generally thought and called by people . . . [a] blessing," was in reality the low-country's "peculiar curse."[135] The low-country elite may have dressed like the English gentry, but their fancy clothes bore the figurative spots of the rice fields' mud and of their slaves' blood.

More than fifty years ago, Frank Tannenbaum described the impact of slavery upon the "total culture" of what he termed "slave societies." In such societies, Tannenbaum wrote, slavery

> changed the form of the state, the nature of property, the system of law, the organization of labor, the role of the church as well as its character, the notions of justice, ethics, ideas of right and wrong. Slavery influenced the architecture, the clothing, the cooking, the politics, the literature, the morals of the entire group—white and black, men and women, old and young.

"Nothing escaped" the influence of slaves and slavery, Tannenbaum concluded; "nothing, and no one."[136]

135. DeWolfe Howe, ed., "The Journal of Josiah Quincy, Junior, 1773," 456.
136. Frank Tannenbaum, *Slave and Citizen: The Negro in the Americas* (New York, 1946), 117.

With a large majority of its inhabitants enslaved and most whites included in the master class, the mid-eighteenth-century low country was a slave society to the core. But in this same period, low-country society was also greatly influenced by its strong economic, cultural, and political ties to England. There were always institutions and individuals within the colony that served imperial and metropolitan authorities and interests. All colonial legislation was subject to metropolitan review and dismissal, every judicial decision was open to a royal pardon, and every Anglican missionary received materials, instructions, and recompense from the Society for the Propagation of the Gospel in London.

In a colonial slave society, social dynamics and relationships were constructed within a triangle formed by masters, slaves, and the metropolitan culture and polity. The resulting interactions could become exceedingly complex.[137] In most instances, the interests of masters and imperial ministers, of local and imperial rulers, coincided; both saw slaves as inferior, un-English and subordinate. In other cases, however, as with Anglican missionaries' desire to convert slaves to Christianity, metropolitan representatives might seek to cultivate an independent relationship with the black majority. In still other situations, slaves might look to the distant king for deliverance or to the local Anglican missionary for redress from their masters. Slaves might also take advantage of disputes between their local and imperial rulers and seek to gain freedom for themselves.

The conflict between metropolitan and local imperatives was not just a clash of rival structures, individuals, and authorities. A tension also existed in the minds, ambitions, and perceptions of all white Carolinians (and many black Carolinians as well). Colonists were torn between their desire to fashion themselves and their society in English ways and the need to construct and control that most un-English institution of slavery. In the eighteenth-century colonial world, the English establishment (the civil, political, and religious elite of the empire) was synonymous with civility, prestige, and power. South Carolina whites sought to Anglicize themselves and their colony as a mode of asserting control over (and, in some measure, escaping) the new world environment. At the same time,

---

137. For example, Stuart B. Schwartz writes of the slave society of colonial Brazil: "I have . . . become painfully aware that the role of the state in a colonial polity presents a peculiar set of problems because the apparatus of the state does not necessarily represent the interests of the dominant group *within the colony* but instead may be reflective of metropolitan situations and conflicts. At the same time, it is also possible that certain groups in the colony may be allowed control over social and economic resources and in fact be dominant, as long as their well being benefits those in the metropolis." Stuart B. Schwartz, *Sugar Plantations in the Formation of Brazilian Society, Bahia, 1550–1835* (Cambridge, 1985), 260.

South Carolina masters hoped to invoke the rituals and symbolic prestige of the English establishment to enhance their own authority within the colony and over their slaves.

Some slaves also sought to acquire attributes of Englishness in an effort to improve their own social status. To a degree, masters welcomed this: a measure of closeness between slaves and masters, and slaves' assimilation of the culture of those who dominated them, were important aspects of masters' control. But the virtues of Anglicization, like those of class, rested to a considerable degree upon exclusion. If Africans could become Englishmen, the concept lost all meaning and allure. Thus while masters allowed a few slaves to partake in the rites of Englishness, they also strove to deny that the slaves thereby became English or equal.

South Carolina masters may have chased after the elusive promise of Englishness from a desire to deny the extent to which they and their world had become something quite different from England. But they also sought to replicate the metropolitan establishment because they wanted to borrow the cultural legitimacy, authority, and power of the old world in order to govern the new. Like the English elite on whom they modeled themselves, the "gentry" of the mid-eighteenth-century low country saw themselves as a ruling class at the top of a rigidly hierarchical society. As Richard Waterhouse notes, "in seeking to impose their idealized version of English. . . . society in their own colony, the South Carolina elite . . . [sought] to maintain and extend [their] control over the black population."[138]

In a letter written to the *Gazette* in 1763, an anonymous writer, "Philopolis," compared Charles Town to other "large trading places [in which] artificers, labourers, and servants compose the bulk of the population." "The labourers, when compared with those of a higher rank," the letter continued, "are as the necessaries of life, when compared to the conveniencies and ornamental part of it." South Carolina was in keeping with this maxim, Philopolis reflected, but with a difference, for "the slaves, with a few exceptions, are the only labourers here." The "happiness of . . . [the] nation," the amateur philosopher went on, required that this laboring majority be "usefully and constantly employed," and this social goal was "the object of the police, the care of the legislature, and the duty of the magistrates and all other peace officers." In casting about for "Good laws" with which to control its "lower orders," Philopolis thought that South Carolina had

138. Waterhouse, *A New World Gentry*, 107–8.

a ready example. For "no people," he confidently asserted, could "boast of better [laws] than Britons."[139] In constructing the laws that sat enthroned upon the four corners, the masters of the colonial slave society may have been mimics, but the purpose of their mimicry was far from playful.

139. *South Carolina Gazette*, 19 March 1763.

The great house and slave street of Mulberry Plantation at the end of the eighteenth century. Mulberry was established in 1709 when Colonel Thomas Broughton obtained a grant for 4,400 acres of land on the Cooper River twenty-five miles north of Charles Town. By 1720, the great house, outbuildings, and rice fields of Mulberry were substantially complete. Thus, this Thomas Coram painting depicts a scene that may have changed little in the preceding seventy-five years. Coram's image of slaves returning to their homes after completing their tasks recalls the remark by an Anglican missionary that "the best planters' houses resemble Mannour houses surrounded with wooden cottages like poor villagers, the houses of their slaves." Although the Mulberry slave houses were destroyed early in the twentieth century, the original great house survives, as do many of the surrounding rice banks. Source. Carolina Art Association, Charleston, South Carolina. Gift of Friends of the Carolina Art Association.

[2]

Practical Justice: Slavery and the Criminal Law

U.S. highway 17 is known to low-country residents as the "old way."[1] South of Charleston, the highway follows the path of the colonial "high road . . . to Port Royal."[2] But the modern road gives little evidence of its long history. Only the passing place names evoke the past. The crossroads towns of Rantowles, Ravenel, and Yonges Island offer reminders of the families that brought these names to the low country in the colonial period. A sign pointing the way to the Stono bridge recalls the slave rebellion that began near there in the fall of 1739. (In fact, the rebels may have originally been part of a gang of slaves "working . . . upon the high roads.")[3] From the Stono bridge the rebels headed south along the path of what is now U.S. 17 until the uprising met its end in a field ten miles farther down the road, just east of Jacksonboro.

Farther south, on the far side of the Ashepoo River bridge, a solitary

---

1. A Savannah attorney quoted by Melissa Fay Greene in *Praying for Sheetrock: A Work of Non-Fiction* (New York, 1991), 9.
2. *Statutes*, 9, 96.
3. In 1770, Lieutenant Governor William Bull blamed the rebellion on the fact that "too great a number [of slaves] had been very indiscreetly assembled together for several nights to do a large work on the public road with a slack inspection"; William Bull to the Board of Trade, 30 November 1770, *DAR*, 2, 266–80. One of the first acts of the Assembly when it convened in the wake of the rebellion was one to "regulate the manner of working slaves upon the high roads, so that too great a number be not suffered to work together at the same place." *JCHA*, 14 December 1739, 119.

historic marker stands at the site of a forgotten but far more typical moment in the colonial slave society. The plaque marks the location of "Edmundsbury," a town laid out in 1740, and relates the story of the Anglican chapel that once stood on the spot. Phoenix-like, the chapel rose from its ashes three times before it was destroyed once and for all by marauding Yankees in 1865.[4] Today, no trace of the chapel or anything else survives to testify that a town once stood here. Without the lonely marker to pique their curiosity, passers-by would have no cause to stop or even slow down.

But Edmundsbury was always something of a mirage. The desire to establish towns was part of a common colonial desire to "improve" provincial society in familiar metropolitan ways.[5] Edmundsbury's founders hoped that the site they had chosen on the Ashepoo would grow into a "proper" country town. The plan they devised delineated ten streets laid out at right angles, including "Bridge Street," "Church Street," and "George's Street." The planners surveyed eighty-six building lots and set aside others for a school and a church.[6] However, like many other such schemes in the eighteenth-century South, Edmundsbury never lived up to the hopes of its promoters.[7] Only two of the lots, located at the foot of the bridge, were ever sold. The purchaser, William Buchanan, likely opened a branch of his Beaufort mercantile establishment, and the resi-

4. The marker reads:

Edmundsbury
A brick Chapel of Ease for St. Bartholomew's Parish was built here in 1785 in a town laid out in 1740 and named for Landgrave Edmund Bellinger. The vestry reported the chapel unfit for use in 1786, and in 1819 it fell in ruins. A new chapel was built in 1819, burnt in 1852, rebuilt in 1854, and was wrecked by Union troops in 1865. Erected by the Colleton County Historical Society—1961

The marker neglects to mention the first chapel on the site which was finished in 1760 and may well have been destroyed during the Revolution. Judith M. Brimelow, ed., *South Carolina Historical Marker Guide* (Columbia, 1992), 48.
5. See Jack P. Greene, *Imperatives, Behaviors, and Identities: Essays in Early American Cultural History* (Charlottesville, 1992), 190–94.
6. Details of Edmundsbury's history and a copy of the original (1742) town plan can be found in Henry A. M. Smith, *Cities and Towns of Early South Carolina* (Spartanburg, S.C., 1988), 2, 154–59.
7. For example, at the same time that Edmundsbury was being planned, William Byrd II was designing a similar town (which he evocatively named "Eden") on his land in the Virginia piedmont. Like the design for Edmundsbury, Byrd's plan for Eden included lots carefully set aside for churches. As with Edmundsbury, Byrd's "Edenic" dreams were unfulfilled. A recent study argues that Byrd's planned Eden was motivated by his desperate desire to assert control over nature and to develop colonial society in English ways; see Kenneth Lockridge, *The Diary and Life of William Byrd II of Virginia, 1674–1744* (New York, 1987), 137–41. A description and reprint of Byrd's plan for Eden can be found in Mechal Sobel, *The World They Made Together: Black and White Values in Eighteenth-Century Virginia* (Princeton, 1987), 88–89.

dent storekeeper and his family were probably the town's only inhabitants.[8]

If Edmundsbury never became what an Englishman would call a town, it may still have fulfilled many of the same economic and cultural functions for the residents of the vicinity.[9] The store and bridge became a meeting place for the local community. In 1745, the South Carolina Assembly described Edmundsbury as "very conveniently situated for a Chapel" and ordered one to be built.[10] But the completion of the chapel fifteen years later marked the end of Edmundsbury's rise and the beginning of a long period of stagnation. For over a century the store and chapel (in its various reincarnations) kept company beside the Ashepoo until Sherman's troops destroyed them both and erased Edmundsbury from the map.

On July 5, 1749, Edmundsbury was the site of drama that is not mentioned on the historic marker. John, a slave belonging to Walter Holman, had been charged with the murder of Duff, a slave belonging to Robert Wright, a prominent local planter and former assemblyman. At the head of their trial record, the justices who presided in John's case noted that the court was convened "at Edmundsbury." The accused was "called in" to hear the sentence pronounced, indicating that the affair was conducted indoors, presumably at the store (at that time still the only building at the site).[11]

The mere fact of the trial was itself unremarkable. Criminal proceedings against slaves were a regular part of the low-country social order. What happened after the case had concluded was far more unusual. When John's trial was over, the presiding justices sent a full record of their proceedings to Governor James Glen in Charles Town. When the governor brought the matter before his council eight days later, the attending clerk duly transcribed the justices' letter and the accompanying trial record into the council journal. As a result, the perfectly ordinary slave trial held "at Edmundsbury" in July 1749 is today unique. It is the only extant and complete record of a slave trial held in colonial South Carolina.

8. The lots were purchased in November 1744 by "William Buchanan of St. Helena Parish Merchant"; Smith, *Cities and Towns of Early South Carolina*, 154–59.
9. On 12 February 1778, Ebenezer Hazard, on a journey from Charles Town to Savannah, passed through the area and noted that "there are several houses at Ashepoo, which form something like a village"; see H. Roy Merrens, ed., "A View of Coastal Carolina in 1778: The Journal of Ebenezer Hazard," *SCHM* 73 (1972), 187. For a discussion of how country stores could act as "urban places" in the colonial South, see Joseph A. Ernst and H. Roy Merrens, " 'Camden's turrets pierce the skies!': The Urban Process in the Southern Colonies in the Eighteenth Century," *William and Mary Quarterly*, 3rd ser., 30 (October 1973), 549–74.
10. Quoted in Smith, *Cities and Towns of Early South Carolina*, 156.
11. JGC, 13 July 1749, microfilm, LC, 531–37. Unless otherwise noted, all references to this event are taken from this source.

In the course of John's trial, the two presiding magistrates and three freeholder jurists heard from four slave witnesses as well as the defendant. Most likely, the entire process was concluded within an hour. After the evidence had been presented, the justices and freeholders deliberated. When they had finished, a motion was made for the constable to bring the prisoner before the court. Solemnly, one of the justices told John that he had been found guilty of murder and was sentenced to be taken on "Fryday the 14th Instant between the Hours of ten and twelve at noon" to "some part of the High road between Ashepoo & Combee" and "hanged by the Neck till he should be dead."

The law that the justices invoked when condemning John to death was similar, in certain respects, to the place where the trial occurred. Like Edmundsbury, the South Carolina slave code was a carefully planned cultural edifice. As with the town, the law was both "imagined" and constructed to reflect and replicate a metropolitan ideal.[12] English jurisprudence presented colonial jurists with a powerfully influential code of judicial ethics and procedures. Given the absence of any alternative legal tradition and the imitative impulse of a colonial society, it was perhaps inevitable that South Carolina's legislators would borrow heavily from the English model when they created a system of criminal law for "the better ordering and governing" of their slaves. In part, the rituals of the law were an assertion of the colonists' membership in a common English world. The office of Justice of the Peace, for example, had existed in England since the fourteenth century, and magistrates' courts, a modification of which sat in judgment of John at Edmundsbury, dated back to the early seventeenth century.[13]

Yet, just as English visitors would not have considered Edmundsbury, despite its aspirations, to be a town on the metropolitan model, they would have been equally unlikely to mistake the proceedings at John's trial for what they had seen in English courtrooms. While magistrates' courts existed in the metropolis, they decided only small matters and imposed only fines.[14] In contrast, South Carolina justices exercised vast powers over accused slaves and had full authority to sentence convicts to "such manner of death . . . as they . . . shall direct."[15] After witnessing

---

12. See T. H. Breen, *Imagining the Past: East Hampton Histories* (New York, 1990), for a provocative discussion of how cultures can "imagine" themselves in relation to history, culture, and Providence.
13. Norma Landau, *The Justices of the Peace, 1679–1760* (Berkeley, 1984), 6–7.
14. Ibid., chap. 7.
15. William Simpson, *The Practical Justice of the Peace and Parish-Officer of His Majesty's Province of South Carolina* (Charles Town, 1761), 165.

a man tried and condemned in a South Carolina slave court, one English observer was moved to remark: "Surely there is no murder so cruel and dangerous as that committed under the appearance of law and justice."[16]

That colonial constructs did not conform to metropolitan norms did not mean that the example of the metropolis did not wield a significant influence. The justices in John's case, for example, might more accurately have reported that the trial had been conducted "at Buchanan's store." That they instead chose to locate themselves "at Edmundsbury" indicates their desire to measure up to English standards. In the trial record at least, Edmundsbury was a "real" town.[17]

The transcripts of magistrates' courts were ordinarily not public documents. In most cases, the justices who created them were also their sole audience. Consequently, the magistrates who imagined Edmundsbury into being did so not to deceive an uninformed outsider but for their own sake. They knew that in England trials were not conducted in storehouses but in towns, and they were determined to do likewise, even if in their case town and store were one and the same.

A similar process of imitation, imagination, and simplification can be seen at work within the low-country legal system. The statutes and procedures of the colonial South Carolina slave code could never fully replicate English law. Low-country society differed profoundly from that of the metropolis and consequently required different laws. The colonial institution of slavery, in particular, engendered conflicts and incongruencies between the ideals and practices of English justice and its provincial counterpart. Yet, while inimitable in fact, the example of English criminal justice was nonetheless a very real presence in the mental worlds of South Carolina jurists. Just as Edmundsbury, although not a town in reality, could serve as one in the life and imagination of its community, so the colonial slave society's criminal law, although quite different from its English progenitor, might still fill an equivalent place and act in a similar manner to uphold the provincial social order.[18]

16. George Milligen-Johnston to the Board of Trade, 15 September 1775, *DAR*, 11, 110–11.
17. A similar "fiction" was perpetrated in a 1757 map of the colony, on which "Edmundsbury" was printed in the same typeface as Beaufort, Georgetown, and other actual urban places, although at that time it still consisted of only one building. Smith, *Cities and Towns of Early South Carolina*, 2, 157.
18. My thinking in this chapter has been influenced by the writings of Douglas Hay, Peter Linebaugh, E. P. Thompson and other members of the "Warwick Social History Group." Their collective investigations into the social basis of the criminal law in eighteenth-century England resulted in two works: Hay et al., *Albion's Fatal Tree: Crime and Society in Eighteenth-Century England* (New York, 1975); and E. P. Thompson, *Whigs and Hunters: The Origin of the Black Act* (New York, 1975).

Black Acts

On May 10, 1740, at a ceremony held in the council chamber in Charles Town, Lieutenant Governor William Bull affixed his seal to the bottom of a piece of parchment, and South Carolina's new slave code became law.[19] The "Bill for the better ordering and governing of Negroes and other Slaves in this Province," or, as it was (and is) more commonly known, the "Negro Act," proved to be both enduring and influential. It provided the model for the slave law drawn up by the Georgia Assembly in 1755, five years after that colony had decided to permit slavery within its borders.[20] In South Carolina, the Negro Act was reaffirmed and "made perpetual" immediately after the Revolution. It continued, substantially unaltered, to be the basis for slave control in the state until emancipation finally rendered it obsolete in 1865.[21]

The Negro Act provided a statutory framework for the slave society.[22] It surrounded the lives of South Carolina's slaves with a deep ditch and tall hedge of legislation. The Negro Act constructed the legal condition of the slave in two ways. On one hand, the act stripped slaves of many of the individual protections customarily granted by the common law. To a large degree, it defined slavery as an absence of rights and slaves as legal non-persons. Slaves, for example, were denied the right to testify under oath. This bar rendered slave testimony inadmissible in the General Court where whites were prosecuted, and meant that whites' sworn testimony would be given preference to slaves' unsworn testimony in the magistrates' courts where slaves were tried. The Negro Act also reduced slaves' protection from deadly assault; the murder of a slave by a white was considered a misdemeanor, punishable with only a fine. At the same time, slaves were denied any right to defend themselves; slaves could "presume to strike" a white person to protect their master's life but not their own.[23]

Slaves, like all inhabitants of colonial South Carolina, were subject to the criminal laws of the colony, which were closely based on those of England. In 1712, the assembly passed an omnibus act that adopted the existing English criminal statutes wholesale.[24] But, as the Negro Act ex-

---

19. *JCHA*, 10 May 1740, 343–44.
20. Alan Watson, *Slave Law in the Americas* (Athens, 1989), 68–69.
21. Michael S. Hindus, "Black Justice under White Law: Criminal Prosecutions of Blacks in Antebellum South Carolina," *Journal of American History* 63 (December 1976), 576.
22. The full text of the Negro Act is printed in *Statutes*, 7, 397–417.
23. The fine for the murder of a slave was "seven hundred pounds, current money" (about one hundred pounds sterling); the fine was half this amount if the slave was killed as a result of "a sudden heat of passion" or "undue correction." *Statutes*, 7, 410–11, 405.
24. See Hindus, "Black Justice under White Law," 594 note; and Terry W. Lipscomb's pref-

plained, the "peculiar . . . situation and condition of this Province" also required the creation of another class of crimes that "could not fall within the provision of the laws of England" and that would apply to slaves alone.[25] Slaves, for example, could be executed if convicted of plotting insurrection (or merely conspiring to run away), of committing arson (even if it were only to burn a "stack of rice" or a barrel of tar), or of concocting poisons (or merely "teach[ing] another slave in the knowledge of any poisonous root, plant, [or] herb").[26]

The Negro Act sought to constrict slaves' lives with a host of minor regulations and prohibitions tied to their condition. By law, slaves were barred from traveling off their master's plantation without written permission. They were not to keep any firearms, boats, or livestock. Slaves were forbidden to trade goods in the market on their own account or to work on their own for hire. They were not to dress in a manner "above the condition of slaves," and their clothes were to be made only from a specific list of coarse fabrics. Any slaves found in violation of any of these provisions would be subject to whipping and to the forfeiture of the prohibited goods or money they had earned.[27] Finally, the Negro Act established a separate procedure for the trial of blacks charged with crimes. Any justice of the peace of the county where the crime had occurred was empowered to call together another local justice and any three freeholders of the vicinity to convene a slave court "to hear and determine the matter brought before them in the most summary and expeditious manner."[28] The justices and freeholders were authorized to impose any sentence they saw fit, up to and including death. If the slave was charged with an offense that did not carry the death penalty, a single justice and two freeholders could preside at the trial. No appeal from the verdict of a slave court was allowed.[29]

Because the execution of a slave entailed not only the punishment of a criminal but also the destruction of property, the authors of the Negro Act worried that financial motives might lead some masters to "conceal the crimes of their slaves to the prejudice of the public."[30] The law therefore allowed owners of executed slaves to receive two hundred pounds current money (the equivalent of about thirty pounds sterling)

ace to the *JCHA* volume covering the period from November 21, 1752, to September 6, 1754 (Columbia, 1983), xxvii note.
25. *Statutes*, 7, 402.
26. Simpson, *Practical Justice of the Peace*, 167–68, 186.
27. Ibid., 163, 173–76.
28. *Statutes*, 7, 400.
29. Simpson, *Practical Justice of the Peace*, 164–65.
30. *Statutes*, 7, 403.

in compensation from the colonial treasury, minus whatever amount the presiding justices felt should be paid to those injured by the crimes of the condemned. If, however, the slave was convicted of the murder of a white person or of rebellion, the owner was not to receive any recompense. Apparently, masters whose slaves committed such particularly heinous crimes were thought to bear some of the blame and therefore did not deserve compensation.[31]

In earlier slave codes, the need for such "peculiar" legislation, and for the institution of slavery itself, had been explained defensively and apologetically. The preambles to these codes frankly admitted that the foundations of slavery and the slave code were based not upon "the laws, customs, and usages of England" but rather on a mixture of economic necessity and self-preservation.[32] The slave code in force in the fall of 1739 (at the time of the Stono Rebellion), for example, began by noting that

> as the plantations and estates of this Province cannot be well and suffi-
> ciently managed and rendered useful, without the labour and service of
> negroes and other slaves, and as the said negroes are generally of a bar-
> barous and savage nature, and unfit to be governed by the laws, customs,
> and usages of England, . . . it is found to be absolutely necessary that such
> laws, rules and orders should be made and enacted for the good regulating
> and ordering of them, as may restrain the disorders, rapines, and inhu-
> manities to which they are naturally prone and inclined, and may also
> tend to the safety and security of the white people of this Province and
> their estates.[33]

This preamble conceded the dangerous and degenerate state of colonial society. By its own description, colonial South Carolina was an unstable world populated by savages, threatened by violence, and beyond the pale of English law.

Although the Stono Rebellion seemed to offer ample proof of slaves'

---

31. *Statutes*, 7, 403. In 1746, for example, the Commons House rejected a petition for compensation for two slaves executed for "Rebellion in tying their Overseer up, and Murder in Whipping him to death"; *JCHA*, 15 February 1746, 99. Fearing that the denial of recompense for slaves convicted of murder and rebellion gave masters an incentive to conceal the most serious crimes of all, the legislators removed this provision in 1751. At the same time, the compensation offered was increased to forty pounds sterling, *Statutes*, 7, 424.

32. The texts of all the colonial South Carolina slave codes can be found in *Statutes*, 7, 352–97.

33. *Statutes*, 7, 352. The wording of this preamble is closely based upon the Barbadian slave code of 1688; Richard Dunn, *Sugar and Slaves: The Rise of the Planter Class in the English West Indies, 1624–1713* (Chapel Hill, 1972), 242.

inclination for the "disorders" that the existing slave code had anticipated, the Negro Act of 1740, written in the aftermath of the revolt, was not the product of panic and paranoia. In the eight months that passed between the quashing of the uprising and the passage of the new law, South Carolina's legislators deliberated carefully about the place of slavery in their society and their society's place within the Anglo-American world. As a result, the preamble to the Negro Act used language strikingly unlike that of any previous South Carolina slave code:

> WHEREAS, in his Majesty's plantations in America, slavery has been introduced and allowed, and the people commonly called negroes, Indians, mulattoes and mustizoes, have been deemed absolute slaves, and the subjects of property in the hands of particular persons, the extent of whose power ought to be settled and limited by positive laws, so that the slave may be kept in due subjection and obedience, and the owners and other persons having the care and government of slaves may be restrained from exercising too great rigour and cruelty over them, and that the public peace and order of this Province may be preserved.[34]

The framers of the Negro Act made no apologies. Neither slavery nor the slave code was explained as an unfortunate necessity required to prevent the "rapines" to which "barbarous" Africans were "naturally prone." Rather, the Negro Act was described as a part of a system of "positive laws" designed to keep slaves "in due subjection and obedience." Nor was slavery excused as an unpleasant by-product of the colonial condition caused by social, economic, or climatic imperatives. That "the people commonly called negroes . . . [were] absolute slaves, and the subjects of property in the hands of particular persons" was described as a simple fact.

In the same year the Negro Act was drafted, an influential Charles Town jurist provided an indication of the spirit that guided the slave code's creators. In 1739, former chief justice Nicholas Trott advised his fellow South Carolinians that "in most cases, the laws of England, are the very best pattern & example we can follow in America," for, he continued, quoting the famed English judge Sir Matthew Hale, " 'they are not the product of the wisdom of one man, or society of men, in any one age, but of the wisdom, council, experience and observation of many ages.' "[35]

---

34. *Statutes*, 7, 397.
35. Nicholas Trott, "Observations on the Present State of the Courts of Judicature in his Majesty's Province of South Carolina," undated manuscript (date attrib. 1739), microfilm, SCDAH. Trott was a graduate of the Inner Temple who arrived in Charles Town to serve

In South Carolina the desire to pattern the criminal code of the colony after "the laws of England" was strengthened by the fact that a significant proportion of the colony's lawyers had a personal acquaintance with the English legal system. Men who had been students at the Inns of Court dominated the South Carolina bar in the colonial era and were also prominent in the colonial assembly.[36] Those who had attended at the Inns held the experience in high regard. For example, despite the fact that he never practiced law in South Carolina, Peter Manigault, Speaker of the Assembly from 1765 to 1772, always appended to his signature the words: "Barrister of the Inner Temple."[37]

South Carolina's lawyers eagerly sought information about their English counterparts. While Manigault was a student in London, for instance, he received a letter from a prominent Charles Town attorney saying that "I should esteem it a particular favour to be obliged with an account of what you think observable" when "any Considerable Causes are argued at any of the Courts" in the metropolis.[38] Similarly, when a new chief justice arrived in Charles Town in 1753 he was quickly sized up by the local legal fraternity and esteemed "to have been in England a good circuit lawyer, for he is very ready & clear in observing upon evidence and giving a cause to a jury."[39]

Where previous slave codes had emphasized their deviation from the "laws, customs, and usages of England," the Negro Act sought to locate itself and slavery within the established practices of the metropolis. In describing their society in the first sentence of the Negro Act as one of "his Majesty's plantations in America," South Carolina's legislators placed themselves squarely under the English crown and asserted that, while the requirements of their society may have engendered a legal system in some ways different from that which prevailed in England,

---

as the colony's Attorney-General in 1699. He became Chief Justice in 1703 and held that post until South Carolina became a royal colony in 1719. He won considerable fame in England after publishing transcripts of the trials of several pirates held in Charles Town in 1718. In 1721, he was awarded an honorary doctorate of civil law from Oxford University. After resigning his justiceship, Trott continued to practice law in Charles Town and trained several men who also became prominent lawyers in the colony. In 1736, Trott published the first compendium of South Carolina Statutes. See L. Lynn Hogue, "Nicholas Trott: Man of Law and Letters," *SCHM* 76 (January 1975), 25–34.

36. Paul Hoyt Canaday, Jr., "Gentlemen of the Bar: Lawyers in Colonial South Carolina" (Ph.D. diss., University of Tennessee, 1979), 211–15.

37. Walter B. Edgar and N. Louise Bailey, eds., *Biographical Directory of the South Carolina House of Representatives*, vol. 2, *The Commons House of Assembly, 1692–1775* (Columbia, 1977), 431.

38. Andrew Rutledge to Peter Manigault, 16 December 1750, Peter Manigault Papers, SCL-USC.

39. Andrew Rutledge to Peter Manigault, [no date] 1753, Peter Manigault Papers, SCL-USC.

they were partakers of a shared tradition. The first words of the Negro Act implied that since the king had permitted slaves to be "introduced and allowed" in "his . . . plantations," he had tacitly consented to the existence of both slavery and slave codes.

The desire to Anglicize the slave code, to minimize the difference created by slavery, and to situate the Negro Act in an imperial context was in keeping with simultaneous efforts in many colonies to bring colonial jurisprudence more in line with the standards of the metropolis.[40] In the case of the Negro Act, this process of convergence was made simpler by the trend underway in England itself toward more punitive legislation and a greater resort to the death penalty.[41] The Negro Act of 1740 does not seem uniquely harsh when compared to the laws in force in mid-eighteenth-century England. At the same time that a black man could be lawfully executed in South Carolina for crimes as petty as burning "a stack of rice" or a barrel of tar, an Englishman faced death if convicted of such crimes as poaching rabbits, stealing fish, cutting down trees, or burning a haystack.[42] If the draconian provisions of the Negro Act were rooted in the rice fields of South Carolina, its seed came from the criminal law of early modern England, which included a grim "Black Act" of its own.[43]

While the members of the South Carolina Assembly strove to fit the Negro Act within the parameters of metropolitan authority and custom, the process of revising the slave code nonetheless forced them to acknowledge the ways in which the society they had built differed from metropolitan norms. Governor James Glen's dispute with the South Carolina Commons in 1751 on the issue of the proper qualifications for jurors offers an example of how English legal traditions were modified to suit colonial requirements. Glen contrasted the English practice of juries composed only of property holders with the mode in South Carolina, "where all [white] persons . . . tho' perhaps they have neither estates in lands or

40. See John M. Murrin, "The Legal Transformation: The Bench and Bar of Eighteenth-Century Massachusetts," in Stanley N. Katz and John M. Murrin, eds., *Colonial America: Essays in Politics and Social Development*, 3rd ed. (New York, 1983), 540–72; and also Peter Charles Hoffer, *Law and People in Colonial America* (Baltimore, 1992), 62–67.
41. Between 1688 and 1820 the number of capital offenses on the English statute book grew from about fifty to over two hundred; Douglas Hay, "Property, Authority, and the Criminal Law," in Hay et al., *Albion's Fatal Tree*, 18.
42. Thompson, *Whigs and Hunters*, 271. Thompson gives two examples of death sentences being imposed for the burning of haystacks, one in 1788, the other in 1802; ibid., 246–47, 256.
43. The "Black Act," enacted by Parliament in 1723, was designed to suppress poachers and trespassers in private game parks. It imposed death sentences for offenses as petty as poaching hares or deer, breaking down the head of a fish pond, maiming cattle, or cutting down trees. See Thompson, *Whigs and Hunters*, 21–24.

goods, may be . . . returned as jurymen."[44] Like other eighteenth-century Britons, Glen saw the main object of the law to be the defense of property.[45] Seating a propertyless man in the jury box was therefore like setting a fox to guard the chickens. "Nothing," the governor asserted, "can be . . . more contrary to the constitution, more opposite to the laws, custom and practice of Great Britain." The governor repeated the maxim that "it is the Birth-right of British subjects to be tryed by their Peers and Equals, by their Country." But, he declared, "Persons having no estates either in lands or goods are not that Country, They are in the eye of the law, Strangers, a sort of Sojourners among us."[46]

In colonial South Carolina, however, race rather than property was the crucial wall dividing "the Country" which was to rule from the "Strangers" who were to be governed. The assemblymen may have resented Glen's observations on their provincial deviance, but they did not adopt his proposed reform. They saw no reason to examine a man's purse to discern his allegiance when they could more readily look at the color of his skin.

As its popular name implied, the Negro Act centered around the concept and construction of a racial hierarchy in which whites ruled blacks. A nineteenth-century judge explained that the South Carolina slave code "contemplate[s] throughout the subordination of the servile class to every free white person."[47] The Negro Act, for instance, gave every "white person" a police power over any slave encountered off their master's plantation. Any white could demand that any slave met on the road produce a "ticket," a pass from his or her owner giving permission for the slave to be off the plantation. If the slave could not do so or if it was thought that any slave, "though such slave . . . have a letter or ticket," was not about "on lawful business," the inquisitor could, then and there, administer "a moderate whipping." Slaves who refused "to submit to . . . examination" could likewise be seized and whipped. If slaves so accosted dared to offer physical resistance, they could be summarily killed.[48]

44. James Glen to the Commons House of Assembly, JGC, 23 April 1751, microfilm, LC, 38–39. After 1720, an English juryman was required to be possessed of a minimum of either a ten pound per annum freehold or a twenty pound per annum leasehold; J. M. Beattie, *Crime and the Courts in England, 1660–1800* (Princeton, 1986), 378–79. The hegemonic purposes of the property qualification for English juries are discussed in Hay, "Property, Authority, and the Criminal Law," 38–39.
45. According to John Locke, for example, "government has no other end but the preservation of property." Locke, *The Second Treatise of Government* (London, 1690), paragraph 94.
46. James Glen to the Commons House of Assembly, JCHA, 4 May 1751, 398.
47. Judge D. L. Wardlaw (1847), cited in Hindus, "Black Justice under White Law," 579.
48. *Statutes*, 7, 176, 163.

If white skin meant freedom, dominion, and power, black skin signified slavery, submission, and powerlessness. Free people of color were so rare that the chances that a non-white was also a slave were overwhelming. Indeed, the act directed that it "shall always be presumed that every negro . . . is a slave" until proven otherwise.[49] Several times in the text, as in the phrase "negroes and other slaves" which appears in the act's official title, race and caste were conflated as if they were synonymous terms. On the few occasions that the act troubled to acknowledge the existence of "free negroes" it contradicted itself, twice combining their treatment with that of slaves and twice making a distinction.[50]

Free blacks were combined with whites as "free persons" without reference to race only once, when the act prohibited the renting of houses or rooms to slaves. The majority of blacks transcended their caste on only two instances, when the statute referred to the "rebellious negroes" killed at Stono and when it spoke of "negroes . . . put to death" for crimes.[51] In using race instead of caste to describe such persons, lawmakers seemed grudgingly to acknowledge that, while those who violently resisted their servitude had to be destroyed, they could no longer be aptly described as "slaves." In their last moments on the gallows or battlefield at least, the condemned or rebellious were freed from the semantic chains of slavery.

A judicial system founded on the principle of racial caste suited the domestic requirements of South Carolina masters, but the colony was part of a larger legal and economic system based upon the primacy of property. Consequently, while one side of the colonial law code was adapted to maintain masters' control over their slaves, another side of the legal system had to enforce the laws of contract and credit that enabled the low country to take its part in the metropolitan trading network.

The contradictions and compromises that ensued when the principles

49. *Statutes*, 7, 398.
50. Besides the exception made for "negroes, mulattoes, and mustizoes, who are now free" in the first paragraph of the Act (which otherwise defines all members of these groups as *ipso facto* slaves), the category of "free negroe" appears three times in the slave code. In paragraph XIV, the law first directs that slave testimony (without oath) was admissible in the trial of "free negroes," but then immediately afterward decrees that free negroes accused of crimes should be tried in the same manner as slaves, which seemingly rendered the preceding point moot. In paragraph XVI, free negroes are also to suffer death if convicted of any of the "peculiar" crimes (i.e. arson, poison, conspiracy, etc.) directed against slaves. Slave and free blacks are not conflated in paragraph XXIX, which subjects "free negroes" convicted of harboring runaways to fines while slaves convicted of the same offense are to be whipped. *Statutes*, 7, 397, 402 and 407.
51. *Statutes*, 7, 403, 416.

of race and property collided were characteristic both of early modern merchant capitalism and of new world slavery.[52] The law supported racial hierarchy at the expense of property when, for instance, it refused to permit slaves to testify against whites even though this practice allowed criminal whites to defraud and rob plantations with relative ease. Conversely, the law enforced the primacy of property when it allowed slaves to be seized for debt, although this violated the masters' claim that market forces could not intrude in their patriarchal relations with their slaves.[53]

When the interests of race and property coincided the law could bear down with uncommon force. For example, three of the six white men executed in the colony between 1769 and 1776 were convicted of the crime of "inveigling or stealing negroes." This offense was also the only one (murder included) for which condemned whites were more likely to suffer death than to receive a pardon.[54] In 1754 a special legislative act removed Negro stealing from the benefit of clergy and therefore the possibility of judicial clemency.[55] The crime of Negro stealing was considered uniquely "pernicious" and "wicked" because it trespassed the boundaries of both property and race. In practice, slaves were rarely stolen against their will. Negro stealing usually required an active collusion between the black "property" and the white "thief" against the interests of the slave's master and the larger slave society.

In 1773, Josiah Quincy, a Boston attorney, visited Charles Town and dined at the home of Miles Brewton. The company included Charles Cotesworth Pinckney, a prominent assemblyman and wealthy attorney who, Quincy was quickly informed, had been "educated at the Temple."[56] In "the grandest hall I ever beheld" and over glasses of "the richest wine I ever tasted," Quincy's hosts entertained him with descriptions of South Carolina's slave code. He was told, for example, "that neither negroes or mulattoes could have a Jury," and that "for killing a

52. For a discussion of this point, see Elizabeth Fox-Genovese and Eugene D. Genovese, *Fruits of Merchant Capital: Slavery and Bourgeois Property in the Rise and Expansion of Capitalism* (Oxford, 1983).
53. The practical contradictions of a law based on white supremacy enmeshed in a larger legal network based on private property are discussed at length in Eugene D. Genovese, *Roll, Jordan, Roll: The World the Slaves Made* (New York, 1974), 25–49. For another view, see Charles S. Sydnor, "The Southerner and the Laws," *Journal of Southern History* 6 (February 1940), 3–23.
54. Of five men convicted of "negro stealing" in these years, three were actually executed, while only one of four convicted murderers actually perished; Journal of the Court of General Sessions (Charles Town), 1769–1776, SCDAH.
55. *JCHA*, 26 April 1754, 446.
56. Mark DeWolfe Howe, ed., "Journal of Josiah Quincy, Junior, 1773," in Massachusetts Historical Society *Proceedings* 49 (Boston, 1916), 444–46. All subsequent information about this incident comes from this source.

negro, ever so wantonly, as without any provocation, there could be nothing but a *fine*." The Carolinians graciously provided their guest with "a late instance of this." What astonished Quincy most of all, however, was the discovery that "by the provincial laws of the place . . . to *steal* a negro was death, but to *kill him* only fineable."[57] "Curious laws and policy!" the Bostonian exclaimed. "Very true," his Charles Town hosts replied, "but this is the case."[58]

In devising the Negro Act, South Carolina's masters, legislators, and lawyers (like C. C. Pinckney, low-country leaders usually wore all three hats) sought to graft slavery onto the existing English criminal statutes. In the dark soil and peculiar climate of the low country, those limbs of "Albion's Fatal Tree" that were unequal and brutal flourished, while other branches that stressed due process and equality before the law withered. Just as the ancient live oaks of Carolina could, from a distance, be mistaken for the familiar oaks of England, so the colonial slave society's criminal law resembled in its broad structures the criminal law of the metropolis. Up close, the differences became evident. Draped with Spanish moss as if in mourning, the huge live oaks that lined the approaches to many low-country estates perhaps aptly symbolized colonial South Carolina's own "fatal tree" of justice.

Practical Justice

Between the slave code and the slave stood the justices of the peace who transformed the letter of the law into practice. The ordinary operation of the law in the eighteenth-century Anglo-American world deliberately gave magistrates a great deal of discretion in rendering their verdicts. Like the bewigged judges who presided at an English

---

57. They may have been discussing the assize session of the preceding October when, on the same day that Dempsey Griffin was sentenced to death for negro stealing, John Milner pled guilty to killing a slave, was fined the equivalent of 50 pounds and was released. Journal of the Court of General Sessions (Charles Town), 1769–1776, 30 October 1772, SCDAH, 207.

58. Some Carolinians were more troubled by this deviation and sought to explain it. In a letter to the board of trade written in 1770, Governor William Bull (whose father had signed the Negro Act thirty years earlier) noted: "The royal humanity has often recommended to governors that a white who murders a Negro should be punished with death. It is so in all of the English colonies *north of Maryland*, where the number of Negroes is small. But in *Maryland, Virginia, and all southern colonies and islands*, it has been thought dangerous to the public safety to put them on a footing of equality in that respect with their masters, as it might tempt slaves to make resistance, and deter masters and managers from inflicting punishment with an exemplary severity tho' ever so necessary." "Governor William Bull's Representation of the Colony, 1770," in H. Roy Merrens, ed., *The Colonial South Carolina Scene: Some Contemporary Views, 1697–1774* (Columbia, 1977), 260.

assize, colonial South Carolina's justices of the peace, as they sat in judgment of slaves, were able to decide, through their interpretation of loosely constructed rules of evidence and proof, when to be harsh and when to be firm, and whether to make any particular criminal slave an example of the slave society's "justice" or of its "mercy."[59]

According to Chief Justice William Simpson, justices of the peace were chosen by the royal governor from among "the most sufficient persons dwelling in . . . [each] county."[60] A more recent assessment of the commission of the peace in the mid-eighteenth century supports this assertion and shows that the colonial justices were, without exception, also slaveholders.[61] South Carolina's justices were not only drawn from the same social rank as the members of the assembly, but the same men often held both offices. Of the 199 justices holding commissions in 1756, for example, 27 were also assemblymen, while a further 71 had either formerly been or later would be assemblymen.[62] Thus future, former, or current legislators comprised half of the colony's 200 justices; likewise, justices occupied half of the 47 seats in the 1756 assembly.

Upon receiving their commission, all justices of the peace participated in a ritual of oathtaking which articulated the idea that the colonial magistrate was "serving . . . King & Country" and also emphasized the close ties between the Anglican church and the state.[63] The would-be justice pledged allegiance to the King, denounced as "impious and heretical" the doctrine that subjects might justly depose or murder "princes excommunicated by the pope," took the "Oath of Abjuration" against the Jacobite pretender, affirmed the Hanoverian succession, and finally, swore to the "Declaration Against Popery."[64]

The authority of an individual justice of the peace was more punitive and preventative than judicial. A solitary justice could impose a host of small fines for such minor offenses as neglecting to attend militia muster or using false weights and scales. To prevent trouble, a justice could swear prospective offenders to keep the peace in the parish. When faced

59. Hay, "Property, Authority, and the Criminal Law," 17–63; for a similar process of mitigation at work in eighteenth-century North Carolina, see Donna J. Spindel, *Crime and Society in North Carolina, 1663–1776* (Baton Rouge, 1989), 116–25.
60. Simpson, *Practical Justice of the Peace*, 1.
61. Of the 199 justices commissioned in 1756, the largest slaveholder was Edward Fenwicke, who held 470 slaves. The justice with the fewest slaves was Douglas Campbell, who owned only seven. See David Morton Knepper, "The Political Structure of Colonial South Carolina, 1743–1776" (Ph.D. diss., University of Virginia, 1971), 139–42.
62. Ibid., 141–42.
63. William Henry Drayton to Peter Manigault, 21 December 1754, Peter Manigault Papers, SCL-USC.
64. Simpson, *Practical Justice of the Peace*, 3–5.

with more serious offenses, a lone justice could only issue warrants, levy bail, and remand accused criminals to trial. The role of a justice acting alone accurately fit within his duties as a "Parish Officer."[65]

When two or more justices acted together, however, they assumed a judicial authority. Magistrates' courts, or "petty sessions" as they were also known, had evolved in England as a way of clearing the court docket of minor offenses. By the eighteenth century magistrates' courts determined cases of petty theft or other "small and mean causes" for which the penalties did not exceed fines, a few hours in the stocks, or a dose of corporal punishment. Petty sessions dispensed a rough-and-ready justice without recourse to lawyers or juries.[66]

In South Carolina, justices exercised a similar authority and acted in a similar manner as "Parish Officers." Magistrates' courts existed but appear to have been less active than was the case in the metropolis. Soon after the founding of the colony, however, South Carolina justices were given a new field upon which to exercise their judicial ambitions. The magistrates' court, slightly modified, became the slave court, and assumed a sole jurisdiction (including powers of life and death) over criminal slaves.[67]

The practice of trying slaves before justices rather than before the colony court in Charles Town had several attractions. First, the ad hoc character of the justices' court meant that trials could be convened in the immediate neighborhood in which the crime occurred, reducing the disruption of plantation routine. Also, the creation of a special court for slave crime placed the government of slaves under law without the awkward racial leveling that might have occurred had slaves been allowed to take the stand to challenge white testimony in the colony court. The justice dispensed in the slave court was both distinctly separate and unmistakably unequal.

Moreover, the expeditious manner in which justice could be dis-

---

65. Landau, *Justices of the Peace*, 173–208.

66. Ibid., 209–39; see also Beattie, *Crime and the Courts in England*, 269–70. Peter Hoffer describes a very similar informal justices' court, termed a "called court," which existed in colonial Virginia; Peter Charles Hoffer and William B. Scott, eds., *Criminal Proceedings in Colonial Virginia, Fines, Examinations of Criminals, Trials of Slaves, etc., from March 1710 [1711] to [1754] [Richmond County, Virginia]* (Athens, 1984), xxxv–xliv.

67. The practice of trying slaves before courts comprised of justices and freeholders was first developed in Barbados in 1661 and later adopted in the slave codes of Jamaica, the Carolinas, Georgia, Pennsylvania, and Delaware. In Virginia and Maryland slaves were tried before courts comprised of justices alone. See Hoffer and Scott, eds., *Criminal Proceedings in Colonial Virginia*, xlv–xlvi; and also Thomas D. Morris, *Southern Slavery and the Law, 1619–1860* (Chapel Hill, 1996), 210–20, although Morris is mistaken in asserting that the selected freeholders were required to be slaveowners—in South Carolina at least, they were not.

pensed by the slave court allowed punishment to follow hard upon the heels of the crime. In 1733, for example, the newspaper reported the case of a slave who robbed a white boy on Saturday and who was "taken on Sunday, on Monday brought to Town, tried and condemned; and the next Day, about Noon, . . . was hanged."[68] Although justice was uncommonly swift in this instance, in most cases the original crime and the final punishment were separated by only a few weeks.[69] While such haste doubtless came at the expense of the accused's ability to make an able defense, it satisfied masters' appetite for revenge and allowed "the example of justice" to blot out the memory of the crime in the vicinity.[70]

The belief that the judicial process should not be separated from the locality in which both accuser and accused were well known was a basic principle in this system of law. The court in which slave crimes were tried was therefore deliberately structured as a form of neighborhood justice.[71] Consequently, the slave court was also very much a masters' court. Not only were justices all themselves masters, but prosecutors were free to choose which of the numerous justices in the parish would hear their case. Although justices were forbidden to judge their own causes and to give counsel to either party, they were not barred from presiding over cases in which the principals were close friends or relations. In the close-knit and intermarried planter communities of the rural low country, such "incestuous" proceedings may well have been the rule rather than the exception.

Most cases that appeared before the slave court involved crimes that transgressed plantation boundaries.[72] The law was a convenient arena to arbitrate disputes between masters concerning the trespasses of their slave property. Although justices were charged to "inquire . . . [into] all manner of felonies . . . and offenses whatsoever committed by negroes," in most cases they waited passively for a charge to be brought to the

68. *South Carolina Gazette*, 27 January 1733, quoted in Peter H. Wood, *Black Majority: Negroes in Colonial South Carolina from 1670 to the Stono Rebellion* (New York, 1974), 213.
69. In John's case at Edmundsbury, for example, the crime occurred on 25 June and John was sentenced to hang on 14 July 1749.
70. *South Carolina Gazette*, 16 October 1736.
71. Discussing justice in the nineteenth-century South, Bertram Wyatt-Brown notes that because "law is a cultural artifact, the more personal, oral, and small scale the community in which it is administered, the more certain it is that the law will reflect the neighborhood will." Bertram Wyatt-Brown, *Southern Honor: Ethics and Behavior in the Old South* (Oxford, 1982), 364.
72. This was true of John's case at Edmundsbury, in which the slave of one master was charged with the death of the slave of another. Michael Hindus argues that the law acted as an arbiter of inter-plantation crime in nineteenth-century South Carolina; Hindus, "Black Justice under White Law," 582–83.

court by someone willing to undertake the costs and trouble of prosecution.[73] Justices seldom intruded into private plantation affairs.

Even when slave trespasses occurred, the white parties involved on each side often settled the matter privately "out of court." One low-country account book, for example, noted a payment of five pounds to "the Dutch Servant for smart and hush money on being wounded by Negro Billy."[74] Similarly, in 1771, when two of James Grant's Florida slaves "were detected in a robbery" and the stolen goods were found in their homes, Grant's overseer wrote that he agreed "to make it up" with the victim of the theft. After he paid damages of nine pounds sterling, the charges were dismissed.[75] The extent of such arrangements can only be surmised, but as the compensation for an executed slave was barely half the cost of a prime field hand, the owner of the accused had a strong incentive to buy off the prosecution.

The places in which slave courts were held also indicates their impromptu and local character. Magistrates' courts were often convened in taverns.[76] In England, where this practice was common, some tavern owners even maintained a special "justice's room."[77] Although few Carolina taverns could have afforded such a facility, their well-known and central location, relatively large rooms, and ample refreshments for the court and the assembled spectators made them popular sites for conducting judicial business.[78] Other slave trials were, as in John's case, con-

73. Simpson, *Practical Justice of the Peace*, 2. Similarly, in eighteenth-century England the cost of bringing charges, summoning witnesses, etc., was to be borne by the plaintiff, even in criminal cases; see Beattie, *Crime and the Courts in England*, 35. Evidence that this was also the case in South Carolina slave courts can be found in JCHA, 11 February 1756, microfilm, LC, 90.

74. Quoted in Philip D. Morgan, "The Development of Slave Culture in Eighteenth-Century Plantation America" (Ph.D. diss., University of London, 1977), 171.

75. David Yeats to James Grant, 31 August 1771, Ballindalloch Castle Muniments, Ballindalloch, Scotland, O771–250.

76. For example, Charles Woodmason complained to a gathering of backcountry magistrates of their practice of "holding . . . courts in taverns"; Richard Hooker, ed., *The Carolina Backcountry on the Eve of the Revolution: The Journal and Other Writings of Charles Woodmason, Anglican Itinerant* (Chapel Hill, 1953), 128. In this disapprobation, as in so many of his other reactions to backcountry culture, Woodmason was probably out of step with his parishioners.

77. Landau, *Justices of the Peace*, 231.

78. Two accounts survive of tavern owners who sought recompense from the assembly for "provisions supplied at the tryal" of slaves. In one instance, from 1754, the bill was over 23 pounds currency; in the other, from 1767, it was 30 pounds. These relatively large sums of money may indicate both the duration and degree of public interest in what were both celebrated cases. The first involved slaves suspected of fatally poisoning their master, a militia colonel; the second required "sundry meetings . . . on the examination and trial of slaves suspected of a conspiracy." JCHA, 13 March 1754 and 27 January 1767. In more ordinary cases, justices probably paid for their refreshment out of their own pocket. For example, Henry Ravenel noted in his daybook on 12 May 1764 one pound fifteen shillings

ducted in country stores. Some Carolina justices, more in keeping with the ideal of the gentleman magistrate, convened slave courts in their own homes.[79] The home of Richard Richardson, who held multiple offices as a justice, militia officer and assemblyman, was said to have "the appearance of the assizes" to the inhabitants of his Peedee River neighborhood.[80] In fair weather, justices might choose to convene a slave court out of doors. The record of a slave trial in October 1783, for example, notes that the proceeding was held "at the French Quarter Musterfield in St. Thomas Parish."[81]

The convening of a slave court was an important local event. One former justice wrote that the inhabitants of the neighborhood treated the meeting of a magistrates' court as "a Sort of *Fair*."[82] The drama of watching a slave being tried for his life probably drew the idle and curious (perhaps including slaves) whenever a slave court was convened in their vicinity. Justices probably welcomed the opportunity to exhibit their authority before an audience and, like one South Carolina circuit court judge, may have hoped in their own small way that "the solemnities attendant upon a court, . . . [would] drive the people into respect."[83] Given the ready presence of drink and the constant murmuring and mixing of the crowd, however, the atmosphere that prevailed may have been less sober and attentive than the justices would have liked.[84]

Later critics of the slave court decried the ability of the attending audience to influence the decisions of the justices. In the nineteenth century, when some South Carolina judges were attempting to establish a more

---

"paid Mary Jane for two Dinners on the tryal of slaves"; Daybook of Henry Ravenel [1744–1785], SCHS.

79. However, the prevailing atmosphere may still have been rather like a tavern. For example, Woodmason also complained of justices who took the opportunity presented by the court day crowd to engage in the "retailing of Liquors in their own Houses (most of them without License)"; Hooker, ed., *Carolina Backcountry*, 128.

80. Joseph Johnson, *Traditions and Reminiscences Chiefly of the American Revolution in the South* (Charleston, 1851), 158–59. For the black population of the area, for whom Richardson's powers really did extend to life and death, the resemblance to the assize was more than symbolic.

81. The case, "The State against a Negro Man named Charloe & a Negroe Woman Named Bess," was held on 3 October 1783, and a copy of the sentence was included in a petition from their owner to the Assembly seeking recompense (both slaves were executed for poisoning). General Assembly Papers, Petitions 1785-05-03, SCDAH.

82. Hooker, ed., *Carolina Backcountry*, 127.

83. *South Carolina Gazette*, 15 June 1765.

84. Charles Woodmason ridiculed the bustle at a typical country magistrate's court: "Here have I seen, the Bible, the Cards—the Brutes and the Laws, on one Stool—The Magistrate sitting in his Chair, and administering Oaths—rabbling over the Form, so as none to understand his Speech—many in the Crowd, at the instant Cursing and Swearing—While others intoxicated with Liquor, were calling for 'tother [half] Pint." Hooker, ed., *Carolina Backcountry*, 127.

professional judiciary, Judge John Belton O'Neal attacked "the tribunal for the trial of slaves" as "the worst system which could be devised . . . The passions and prejudices of the neighborhood, arising from a recent offence, enter into the trial and often lead to the condemnation of the innocent."[85] To the slave court's supporters, however, it was only right that "the prejudices of the neighborhood" play an important role in the judicial process. In the eighteenth-century understanding of the law a good jurist was supposed to take local opinion into account when rendering his verdict.

A 1791 record of a slave trial in Georgia suggests how public opinion could shape the verdict of the slave court. Billy had been convicted of burglary and sentenced to death. As this was Billy's first offense, his owner, Thomas Stone, petitioned the governor complaining that the sentence was uncommonly harsh. In reply, the justices who presided at Billy's trial described the accused as "a notorious thief . . . [who was] perverse in all his conduct." They defended their verdict not by citing the facts of the case but by arguing that "it is the general voice of the people that he should be executed." The justices claimed that the governor's grant of a stay of execution to allow an inquiry into the verdict had "very much incurred the displeasure of nineteen twentieths of the vicinity."[86]

Public participation in the operation of the slave court was more than informal. The inclusion of three freeholders on the panel alongside the two justices put the will of the neighborhood in the judges' chambers as well as in the spectators' gallery and the jury box. All verdicts and sentences the slave court produced had to be agreed upon between the justices of the peace, representing the law, and the freeholders representing local opinion. Before any decision could be pronounced at least one of the justices and one of the freeholders had to support it.

Such a subjective system of justice could not, of course, be "blind," in the sense of being detached from personalities. Nor was it supposed to be. For eighteenth-century Anglo-Americans the personal nature of the law was one of its greatest virtues. As one of the system's defenders explained, a system of justice based upon local feelings and personal ties "knew how to discriminate between a friend and an enemy" and had "room for favour and for kindness."[87] In a similar vein, one of South

---

85. John Belton O'Neal, *The Negro Law in South Carolina* (Columbia, 1848), 35.
86. Betty Wood, " 'Until He Shall be Dead, Dead, Dead': The Judicial Treatment of Slaves in Eighteenth-Century Georgia," *Georgia Historical Quarterly* 71 (Fall 1987), 393.
87. Edward Christian, *Charges Delivered to Grand Juries in the Isle of Ely* (1819), 278–79, cited in Hay, "Authority, Property, and the Criminal Law," 58. A sermon delivered by a South Carolina parson on Good Friday 1770 provides a fascinating insight into the logic that

Carolina's royal governors celebrated "the happy temperament of justice and mercy in our Negro Acts."[88]

To assist justices in making these subjective deliberations, the slave code allowed them an extraordinary latitude in determining their verdicts and freedom in mitigating their sentences.[89] In 1743, for example, Sambo, a Charles Town slave, stood before a magistrates' court charged with burglary. "For want of sufficient evidence and out of great tenderness to his life," the justices at his trial "acquitted . . . Sambo of the burglary . . . and found him guilty of felony only." After being whipped as punishment and branded on the cheek to indicate that he had claimed his pardon, Sambo was released.[90] At the same time that it made room for such acts of mercy, however, the law also insisted that when a group of slaves was capitally convicted, at least one must "be executed for example."[91]

The slave society demonstrated its ultimate expression of authority— the power to destroy its "enemies"—far more often upon a black body than upon a white. Likewise, the law's most solemn ritual—the passing of the death sentence—was pronounced with far greater frequency by magistrates presiding at the trial of slaves in their local parishes than by the judges who attended the General Court in Charles Town. In all, between the passage of the Negro Act and the outbreak of the Revolution, the assembly compensated the masters of 191 slaves who were executed by law.[92] Because the "ordering" of slaves was always the slave society's most important concern, the slave court, despite (or because of) its local status, was always the colony's most important and deadly judicial arena.

Because the assembly allowed owners of executed slaves to claim compensation from the public treasury, the number of slaves who were executed each year appeared in the colony's annual budget. In most years the clerk merely noted the redemption of certificates presented by slaveholders and signed by magistrates "for a Negroe executed" with no

---

underlay this "old" system of justice. In "The Severity and Goodness of God," Paul Turquand, minister at St. Matthew parish, chose to focus his sympathy not on Christ the innocent martyr but on God the stern judge. Reverend Paul Turquand Sermon Books, 1766–72, St. Matthew Parish, SCHS, 1/582/1–3

88. "Governor William Bull's Representation of the Colony, 1770," 260.

89. *Statutes*, 7, 402–3, 425.

90. JGC, 8 October 1743, microfilm, LC, 354–55.

91. *Statutes*, 7, 403.

92. The total number of slaves executed must be higher, for this figure would not include either slaves executed for murder or rebellion prior to 1751 (when the law was amended) or any slave master who neglected to apply for recompense (although given the large sums at stake, this latter figure must be very small).

detail as to the offense that made a given slave's death a budgetary matter.[93] In the decade from 1750 to 1759, however, the clerk was uncommonly curious and noted the condemned slave's crime in nearly four-fifths of the cases.[94] The resulting sample of 38 executions represents only one-fifth of the slaves executed at law between 1741 and 1775, but an analysis of these cases suggests which offenses were punished most severely.[95]

While the death sentence was attached to a wide variety of crimes by statute, in practice capital punishment was reserved for a narrow category of offenses. The offenses dealt with most harshly involved crimes of violence. Nearly four-fifths of all the slaves who were executed in the 1750s fell into this category.[96] Convictions for murder accounted for over

93. See for example the budget of 1764, which was recorded by the clerk on 11 January 1765, JCHA, microfilm, LC, 11–15.

94. Crimes were listed with executions in 38 of 49 instances in this decade.

95. Crimes for Which Slaves Were Executed, 1750–59

	No.	Pct.
Violent Crimes	30	79%
Against whites	24	63%
Murder	8	21%
Poisoning	14	37%
Assault	2	5%
Against slaves	6	16%
Murder	5	13%
Poisoning	1	3%
Property crimes	7	18%
Arson	2	5%
Burglary	1	3%
Misc. "felonies" (probably theft)	4	10%
Conspiracy to revolt	1	3%
Total	38	100%

Source: Annual budgets as recorded in the *JCHA* and JCHA, 1751–1760. The Commons Journals have been published from 1736 through 1757; for the years after 1757 they are available on microfilm at SCDAH and LC. Not included in this table are the eleven executed slaves whose deaths were compensated for but whose crimes were not specified, and any slaves executed for murder or rebellion in 1750.

96. This pattern corresponds very closely with that found among slaves executed in colonial North Carolina, as well as nineteenth-century South Carolina and Virginia. Alan Watson notes that in colonial North Carolina the death penalty was "reserved . . . for the crimes of arson, poisoning, murder, and rape"; Alan D. Watson, "North Carolina Slave Courts, 1715–1785," *North Carolina Historical Review* 60 (January 1983), 33. In South Carolina from 1800 to 1854, 58 percent of slaves were executed for violent crimes and 21 percent for property offenses. The high proportion of executions for "insurrection" (21 percent) occurred as a result of the Denmark Vesey conspiracy of 1822; if this unusual event is removed, the percentages are much closer to those found in the eighteenth century. Hindus, "Black Justice under White Law," table XI, 59. A study of slaves executed in Virginia between 1785 and 1865 found that 69 percent were convicted of crimes "against persons" and only 13 percent

a third of the condemned. Poisoning, the most common single offense that brought slaves to the gallows, was responsible for two-fifths of judicially imposed deaths. Not surprisingly, violence against whites was far more harshly punished than that directed against fellow slaves; executions for the former outnumbered the latter nearly four to one. By contrast, less than one in five of the condemned were convicted of property crimes. Moreover, most of those executed for trespasses against property were multiple or repeat offenders.[97]

In eighteenth-century England the pattern of punishment was almost exactly the opposite. Convictions for property offenses accounted for over four-fifths of those who were hanged from "Albion's Fatal Tree."[98] The primary interest of English judges, prosecutors, and juries was the protection of property. Accordingly, the English bench bore down most heavily against criminals whose actions were "a stab at commerce."[99] Englishmen or women convicted of crimes of violence, on the other hand, were often treated with remarkable forbearance. Interestingly, this metropolitan pattern also emerged in colonial South Carolina in the trials of criminal whites. Most of the white men convicted of murder in Charles Town between 1769 and 1776 were pardoned. Among the six whites actually hanged, five were convicted of property crimes and only one of murder.[100]

Three months after John's trial at Edmundsbury, a contributor to the *South Carolina Gazette* offered as "an excellent Charge to Justices" a list of "rules, which the great judge [Sir Matthew] Hale prescribed to himself in the Execution of his Office." The first rule was "that in the administration of justice, I am intrusted for God, the King and Country." The majority of the remaining eighteen rules concerned the importance of impartiality, objectivity, and careful deliberation. The justices were reminded that in rendering judgment "it be a measuring Cast to incline to

---

of crimes "against property"; Philip J. Schwarz, *Twice Condemned: Slaves and the Criminal Laws of Virginia, 1705–1865* (Baton Rouge, 1988), 15.

97. This at least is my interpretation of the clerk's notation of the plural and vague term "felonies" beside the names of four of the condemned.

98. Beattie, *Crime and the Courts*, 433.

99. John Holliday, *Life of Lord Mansfield* (London, 1797), 149, quoted in Hay, "Property, Authority, and the Criminal Law," 19.

100. Of the six white people executed in South Carolina between 1769 and 1776, three were convicted of Negro stealing, and one each was convicted of horse stealing, forgery, and murder. Three other convicted murderers were pardoned compared to two men convicted of Negro stealing; Journal of the Court of General Sessions (Charles Town), 1769–1776, SCDAH. Michael Hindus makes the same point in a comparison of the criminal or slave codes of nineteenth-century Massachusetts and South Carolina in his book, *Prison and Plantation: Crime, Justice, and Authority in Massachusetts and South Carolina, 1767–1878* (Chapel Hill, 1980), 250–55.

Mercy," but were called on to consider that "in Business capital, though my nature prompts me to Pity, yet to consider, that there is also a Pity due to the Country."[101]

South Carolina's justices filled many roles. It was their responsibility as parish officers to regulate the markets held in their parishes and to "try all weights and measures, beams and scales" to discover if they were "false."[102] The slave court was a balance of another kind. In the slave court justices and freeholders also were called upon to "try" what was brought before them and to decide upon its truth. But the "business" of the slave court, as the correspondent quoted above reminded his readers, was not merely to weigh the facts of the case but to measure the seriousness of the crime against the character of the defendant. In the "scales of justice" as tried in the slave court, the heaviest weight was given not to evidence of guilt or innocence but rather to considerations of deference and "pity." When the balance tilted against them, convicted slaves went to the gallows or the whipping post to pay "the Country" its "due."[103]

"To Speak the Real Truth"

Each year, alongside the compensation given to the owners of executed slaves, the assembly listed payments made to constables for their effort and expense in putting the decisions of the slave court into effect. The constables were entitled to claim twenty shillings for every slave they whipped or branded and five pounds for every slave they executed. Constables could, if they chose, "press one or more slaves" in the vicinity to impose the sentence, and administer twenty lashes to any who refused. But, with a macabre generosity, the Negro Act also directed that any slave who was forced to play the part of hangman was to be rewarded with five shillings by the attending constable.[104]

The annual payments made "for executing a Negro," "for whipping and branding a negro man," "for maintaining and keeping in custody three criminal negroes," or for "apprehending and punishing Negroes and for carrying a Hue and Cry" give evidence of the routine adminis-

---

101. *South Carolina Gazette*, 9 October 1749.
102. Simpson, *Practical Justice of the Peace*, 134–35.
103. On Good Friday 1770, an Anglican minister explicitly compared the scales of justice to the scales of the market, justifying Christ's death for mankind's sin by saying: "one man may answer for another's crime as well as another's debt"; Reverend Paul Turquand Sermon Books, 1766–1772, St. Matthew Parish, SCHS, 11/582/1–3.
104. Simpson, *Practical Justice of the Peace*, 170–71.

tration of justice.[105] Like the twenty-five pounds' compensation paid to "John Axson, Blacksmith, for making gibets for a negro fellow sentenced for poisoning" in 1758, such banal transactions formed the sinews of the criminal law.[106] Like slavery itself, the justice of the slave society was a "business" in which money was passed over the bodies of slaves.

Unfortunately, apart from these terse notations in the colonial budget, little evidence survives of the routine proceedings or verdicts produced at the vast majority of slave trials that did not result in executions. The dearth of documentation for the everyday practice of slave courts is largely a by-product of their local and ad hoc nature, and is matched by a similar lack of surviving evidence on the practice of English petty sessions, which were also "not required to explain themselves to any higher authority."[107] Although Chief Justice Simpson thought it "highly necessary" that a public record of slave trials be kept and proposed "the office of the clerk of the Crown and Peace" as "a proper place for lodging such records," his recommendation went unheeded, and the preservation of slave trial records was left to the discretion (or indiscretion) of the justices who presided at them.[108]

What little record exists of trial procedure concerns disputed or notorious cases that warranted mention in the journals of the council or assembly or publication in the newspaper. Although it is impossible to reconstruct a detailed picture of the day-to-day operation and sentences of the colonial slave court from such unrepresentative evidence, these bits and pieces can be used to suggest the rituals of the slave court in ordinary as well as extraordinary cases.

When justices were called upon to defend their rulings in these unusual and contentious cases, they often appealed to the standards and procedures that prevailed in more typical trials, thus describing judicial norms that usually remained unquestioned and unspoken. Moreover, if the slave court was an unequal "contest" between the slave defendant and masters posed as justices, those cases that for some reason defied the silence of routine might represent instances when slaves managed to throw a wrench into the machinery of the law, even if they did not always succeed in saving their lives.

In the colonial slave society the shackles of the law were forged in the statute book but hammered out in the courtroom through the dialogue between the justices and the accused. The eighteenth-century "trial" was

105. *JCHA*, 8 April 1743, 376; 22 May 1761, 89, 93; *JCHA*, 17 March 1774, microfilm, LC, 129–37.
106. *JCHA*, 21 April 1758, microfilm, SCDAH, 163.
107. Landau, *Justices of the Peace*, 209–10.
108. Simpson, *Practical Justice of the Peace*, 189.

meant to be quite literally that: an ordeal in which the accused was put to the test.[109] In the slave court slaves were not merely objects—so many bodies to be whipped, hanged, or pardoned—but were vital, if unwilling, participants in the drama of the law. In the slave court justice was a process and not a product.

To begin to perceive the part that slaves themselves played in the theater of the court and in the production of justice, we return to the episode that began this chapter. A detailed examination of John's trial held at Edmundsbury in July 1749 illuminates in microcosm both the possibilities and the pitfalls that awaited the accused brought before the slave court. John's case also provides a model *in toto* to set against the mass of slave trials for which only fragmentary evidence survives.[110]

As Judge Simpson's manual later directed, John's case began with a round of oathtaking.[111] The two justices in attendance, Henry Hyrne and James Skirving, first swore each other in and then administered the same oath to the three freeholder jurors (Peter Girardeau, David Godin, and William Webb).[112] When the trial was ready to proceed the justices called upon the constable to bring the prisoner into the room. John was told "that he stood accused of the wilful Murder of one Duff, a Negro," and asked to plead "if he were guilty or not." According to the transcript, John answered carefully that "he was not guilty of killing him wilfully."

The court proceeded to hear the witnesses, four slaves belonging to Robert Wright, the owner of Duff, whom John was accused of murdering. One after another, Wright's slaves stood before the justices and freeholders and related what they knew pertaining to the case. Simon began by testifying that on Sunday morning, June 25, "about first Cockcrow," he was in his house in Wright's slave quarters when "he heard the prisoner knock at the deceased's Door and call to him." The noise continued "some time," Simon thought. Finally, Simon heard Duff come out of his house and "tell the Prisoner he was a Fool and that he did not want to see him," to which John replied that "he was no Fool, but that he [Duff] was a Scoundrell and had used him ill." Simon then heard Duff run after John, calling out his name and asking where he was. The witness claimed

109. Beattie, *Crime and the Courts in England*, 271–72.
110. JGC, 13 July 1749, microfilm, LC, 532–35. Unless otherwise noted, all references to the proceedings at John's trial are taken from this source.
111. Simpson, *Practical Justice of the Peace*, 166–67.
112. Indicative of interrelationships that were possible on a slave court is the fact that one of the freeholders in John's case, David Godin, was brother-in-law to James Skirving, one of the justices, and at his death in 1754 left his estate (including 132 slaves) to the widow of William Webb, his neighbor and another of the freeholders impaneled at Edmundsbury in 1749. Edgar and Bailey, eds., *Biographical Directory of the South Carolina House of Representatives*, 2, 284–85, 619–20.

that he did not hear any answer but reported that suddenly he "heard Duff hollow and cry out twice he was Murthered." Simon, who explained that he was "a Cripple . . . and not able to go out," then woke his sister Hannah and "bid her run over to the Brickyard for that he heard Duff cry out Murder there and he believed John had killed him."

The eyes of the court now turned to Hannah, who told the justices and freeholders that the evening before, "coming pretty late out of the Field from her Work she had laid down upon her Bed with all her Cloaths on, and fell asleep." She slept until Simon woke her to tell her what he had heard and to ask her to go out and "see what was the matter." Hannah testified that she "accordingly run over" to the brickyard, where she met John. "Upon her asking him where Duff was," Hannah recalled to the court, "[John] said he could not tell, [but said] that Duff had beat him very much and knocked him down three times." When the slave woman asked John if he had killed Duff, he answered, "how should he kill Duff that was as strong as a Horse[?]" Seeing "a large Butchers Knife" in John's hand, Hannah replied that "she supposed he had stabbed him with that Knife." John gave no answer to this bold riposte. Hannah then began to search about the area while John stood and watched. "At length," she reported, "going into a little Foot Path," John "cried out to her 'not thear.'" But this only "made her the more Earnest to proceed." A few steps farther down the same track she came upon Duff's body and cried out, "here is Duff!" Upon which, Hannah's testimony concluded, "the Prisoner immediately fled."

The remaining two witnesses offered strangely conflicting testimony. First, Ned reported "that he used frequently to go to Mr. Stocks Plantation where the Prisoner lived." He recalled that several weeks before Duff's death, "Duff had twice bid him to tell John that he wanted to speak with him which he had done and John accordingly went . . . but on what account he could not tell." He added that "he knew nothing of any Quarrel between them in the meantime." Pompey, on the other hand, testified that on the Friday before his death, Duff, who evidently had exercised some authority, had told Wright's slaves that he "had forbid . . . [John] coming there anymore and that if any of the Negroes saw him they must call him." Pompey reported that Duff declared that "he hated to see . . . [John] and would drive him off the Plantation."

With the prosecution case completed, John was now called upon to speak in his own defense. It is unclear whether John had heard the preceding testimony and so knew of the evidence brought against him. In any case, John's testimony shows evidence of a preplanned strategy. Earlier, while admitting that he had killed Duff, John had been careful to add "not . . . wilfully." Now John apparently hoped to persuade the court to find him innocent of murder and guilty of the lesser and pardonable crime of manslaughter. To do this John had to convince the justices and freeholders that Duff's death had been the unintended result of a "hasty quarrel."[113] Pompey's testimony, by implying that John may have come to Duff's house on the night of June 25 anticipating a violent and hostile reception, had undermined this defense.

Perhaps in an effort to counter this evidence, John chose to begin his testimony by admitting to the court that he and Duff had been conspiring to escape from the colony to Spanish Florida. John reported that Duff had told him "that he was barbarously used and wanted to get off the Country," and that "they had some discourse together about it." Conspiring to run away was itself a capital crime, and admitting his complicity in such a dangerous endeavor may have seemed to John ample proof of the friendship and trust that had existed between Duff and himself. John may have hoped that this confession would negate Pompey's assertion that there had been preexisting malice between himself and the deceased.

On the night "the accident happened," John continued, he had been to see Duff at his house when "some angry words Passed between them." John testified that he then "went away . . . towards the Brickyard (being his way home) . . . [when] to his surprise he found Duff before him." According to John, after declaring that " 'he would now give him what he wanted,' . . . [Duff] immediately fell on him with his Stick and struck him several blows." John reported that "he fended them off . . . as well as he could [until] Duff . . . threw him down three times and . . . struck him over the head." At this, John testified that he became "blinded with Passion . . . drew his knife and struck at . . . [Duff]," stabbing him fatally in the chest. John asserted that he had acted "with no design to kill but [sought] only to wound him," and "that there had . . . been no previous Quarrel between them." He concluded his defense by showing the court "a pretty large Cut in his Head" and bruises upon his right arm that he said were inflicted by Duff during his attack.

The prisoner and the witnesses were taken from the room, and the justices and freeholders consulted together to consider their verdict. Two of the freeholders were sufficiently swayed by John's testimony to argue

---

113. The eighteenth-century distinction between manslaughter and murder centered upon the question of the defendant's intent. Murder was defined as the result of a preexisting malice (i.e., done in "cold blood"). Manslaughter, by contrast, was described as "the unlawful killing of another, without malice either express or implied." A person found guilty of manslaughter was too culpable to be acquitted on the basis of pure self-defense. Killings that were judged to be manslaughter were often the result of a sudden "heat of passion" (or "hot blood"). See Beattie, *Crime and the Courts*, 79–96.

that he should be declared not guilty of murder. At this point, John's admission that he and Duff had planned to escape from the colony intruded into the proceedings. The two justices, better acquainted with the responsibilities of the law as it dealt with slaves, pointed out that John had committed a crime merely by visiting Duff in the night without the knowledge and permission of his master. "The occasion of his going there," the justices added, referring to John's admission that he and Duff had been conspiring to run away, was "in all Probability a much greater [crime]."

According to the law, slaves could be found guilty of conspiracy only if they were found with arms, food, and other materials "whereby such their intentions shall be manifested."[114] Slaves could not be executed on the basis of their words (often idle talk) alone. Although John had hinted that such materials might indeed have existed (according to John, Duff had promised that "he would take good care to supply all things necessary"), John could not be convicted of conspiracy with no other evidence than his own confession. The justices seemed to admit as much when they remarked that only "in all Probability" had John committed the "greater" crime of conspiracy.

The defendant's admission of his intent to escape from slavery was nonetheless important because it cast a shadow over his character in the eyes of the court. As the case turned upon the purely subjective matter of John's intentions when he came to Wright's plantation, gaining the sympathy of the court was crucial to his prospects. In this case, as in all cases, the court's deliberations entailed two decisions: before they could reach a decision concerning the nature of the offense, the justices and freeholders had to come to a verdict upon the nature of the offender. John's admission that he had conspired with Duff to run away inadvertently revealed to the court his own disaffection with the established authority of the slave society. In the first part of their deliberations, therefore, the court found John's "character" to be highly suspect.

If John had been brought up before the law on this matter alone, that is, if he had been overheard while talking of running away, the justices might have released him after a warning and a whipping, given the lack of corroborative evidence and John's apparently submissive demeanor before the court. Disaffection, by itself, was not a capital offense. John's mistake was to have placed the sincerity of his submission into question at the very moment when it was needed to save his life.

Whatever the evidence, permitting a slave accused of murder to escape the gallows by pronouncing a sentence of manslaughter was regarded as

114. Simpson, *Practical Justice of the Peace*, 168.

an act of mercy on the part of the court. It implied a willingness to "negotiate" with the accused and to accept the defendant's version of events and description of his or her intentions. In return for this act of mercy, the court expected some kind of reciprocity from the accused. To qualify for the mitigating provisions of the law, slaves were expected to make a sincere demonstration of their submission to and respect for the law and, by implication, to the social order that it represented. By admitting that he had been conspiring to escape, John had admitted that he had rejected the slave society's authority. His outward deference to the justices was thus reduced in value. In the justices' view, John had nothing worthwhile to offer them in return for their allowing him the "favor and kindness" that a mitigation of his crime from murder to manslaughter implied.

Having decided upon the proper sentence, the justices were easily able to construct a verdict to support it. The justices deftly argued that by entering into Wright's plantation illegally and with criminal intent, John "thereby became answerable for all the Consequences and . . . that he was guilty of the Crime wherewith he was charged." In explaining their reasoning the justices frankly admitted that John's "criminal intent" (i.e. his disaffection) made him "answerable for all the Consequences" (that is, unfit to be allowed any mercy).[115]

Had John been spared, he would have returned to the slave quarters, both his life and the brand on his thumb testifying to the law's "kindness" to its friends. Instead, a few days later, John's corpse, suspended from a tree beside the high road, bore silent witness to the law's treatment of its enemies.[116]

---

115. The court was divided in its opinion, with two freeholders (Godin and Webb) favoring acquittal and the two justices and Peter Girardeau voting to find the prisoner guilty. Unanimity was not required to convict according to the law, but the majority opinion had to include the vote of at least one justice to be valid. Thus an accused slave had to gain the support of at least one of the presiding justices in order to be declared innocent. Ibid., 166.
116. Evidence that John was duly executed is provided by the Journal of the Commons, which records "an order drawn by two Justices and one Free holder" for compensation to be paid to Holman and Wright respectively for John's execution and Duff's murder; JCHA, 24 April 1750, 31. The justices did not seek the governor's advice about their verdict; rather, they were concerned about the prisoner's claim that he was a free man and a Spanish citizen. Appended to the trial transcript was this account of John's life:

He says he was born of free parents at the Havanah and was chiefly bred to the Sea, that he sailed from thence to Acapulco where he went on board a ship bound to old Spain, but happening to fall in with Admiral Anson was taken and carried to England there he continued near three years, and at length got again to the Havanah, from whence sailing to Augustine in a vessel bound thither with Provisions he was again taken by a Privateer from Frederica [Georgia] and carried in there where not withstanding the Master of the Spanish Vessel made oath that he was a free Man, he was sometime after sold for a Slave into this Province and in that Station of Life has continued under different Masters something more than a year.

All accused slaves brought before the court had first to answer the question that the justices had posed to John when they asked him "if he were guilty or not." This introductory query was far more than a mere point of procedure. The proceedings at the slave court, like the criminal courts of early modern Europe, focused intently upon securing a confession from the accused.[117] With no recourse to fingerprints or other forensic evidence, it was often difficult to prove a charge in the face of the prisoner's stout denials or stubborn silence. Consequently, a prisoner's refusal to admit guilt might cause the entire case to fall apart. In one instance, a slave charged with burglary was given "by divers adjournments on his tryal, almost three weeks" to confess. Confronted with the prisoner's "obstinate" refusal to cooperate, the justices were finally forced to declare that "for want of sufficient evidence" the charges were dismissed.[118]

But the accused's confession did more than satisfy the justices' need to uncover the "facts" of the case. The confession also served as a demonstration of the accused's deference and submission. Simply put, slaves who freely admitted their guilt threw themselves upon the mercy of the court and placed their lives in the hands of the justices. A confession instantly changed the dynamic of the trial from a contest between the accused and the law to a more familiar and far less confrontational negotiation between slaves and masters over degrees of deference, submission, and punishment. An accused slave might, as John did, attempt to confess to a lesser charge. To protest one's complete innocence, however, not only rendered inoperative the deference-

---

Given these "particular circumstances," the justices inquired whether the governor might wish to extend a pardon to the prisoner. Unfortunately for John, however, at this time white South Carolinians were considerably worried about Spanish interference with their slaves. The Stono Rebellion of ten years earlier had been widely blamed on "infiltrators" from St. Augustine. Thus news that John spoke Spanish and had lived in the Spanish colonies probably made him all the more "suspect." After reviewing the transcript, the governor and council found nothing "that could recommend the Criminal to Mercy"; JGC, 13 July 1749, microfilm, LC, 532–35.

117. Similar practice (and reasoning) was followed at magistrate's courts in colonial Connecticut. As John T. Farrell notes: "Every attempt was made [by the justices] to clinch matters at this point. If possible, a confession was secured, the first question often being such as to put the accused immediately to plead Guilty or Not Guilty. The character of the whole proceeding was that of an inquisition." Farrell, ed., *The Superior Court Diary of William Samuel Johnson, 1772–1773* (Washington, D.C., 1942), xliii.

118. Actually this case, like John's, illustrates the malleability of the law in the hands of the justices. Although they decided that without a confession they could not convict the accused of the capital crime of burglary, they did, on the same evidence, convict him of "felony only," and sentenced him to suffer "three concurrent public whippings." JGC, 7 October 1743, microfilm, LC, 347–48.

punishment balance that lay at the heart of the slave court's system of justice but appeared to defy the law's right to have brought the charge in the first place. In some sense, a stout refusal to confess was itself a suspect and hostile act.

A 1756 case in which two slaves were tried for complicity in a robbery provides an example of the slave court's peculiar logic in this regard. The magistrates explained their verdict by saying that "what induced us on the tryal of the said negroe[s] to condemn Mr. Tucker's Negro, and to mitigate the punishment of Mr. Drayton's, was because we believed that the latter very fairly related and confessed the fact as far as he knew it . . . but that the former prevaricated on his tryal."[119] Tucker's slave's lack of cooperation "induced the Justices and Freeholders to think him a hardened sinner and unfit for mercy."[120]

The central place that the confession occupied in the trial often led justices to take great pains to coerce or cajole prisoners into self-incrimination. Many trial proceedings seem to have been reduced to little more than a struggle between the justices and the accused over this issue. Slave suspects were repeatedly "pressed . . . under the most awful and solemn considerations to speak the real truth" and admit their guilt.[121] To obtain the information they required and the submission they demanded, justices utilized a variety of "promises" and "threatenings."[122]

In a world in which death was omnipresent and the idea of divine judgment was regarded with great seriousness, religion could be a powerful instrument in the hands of an inquisitor. One Anglican minister approvingly described how justices could employ the fear of God to terrify witnesses. The Bible oath was no mere formality. When told "in the most solemn manner" that those who "swear falsely . . . hazard the loss of their souls," the minister wrote, "I have known . . . persons [to] tremble and falter and chuse to give up the point, rather than run such a terrible risque."[123] A defendant's testimony was not sworn to avoid the dilemma of choosing between self-incrimination and self-damnation.[124]

---

119. JGC, 22 April 1756, microfilm, LC, 214–15.
120. JGC, 22 April 1756, microfilm, LC, 213–14. Later, after Tucker's slave "had become very penitous and . . . had discovered the whole fact to the best of his knowledge," the justices recommended him "as an object of mercy" to the governor, who commuted the sentence of death to one of transportation; JGC, 22 April 1756, microfilm, LC, 213–15.
121. JGC, 7 February 1749, microfilm, LC, 163–64.
122. Governor James Glen wrote in 1748 that "God Almighty, in his moral Government of the World is pleased to make use of both love and fear, of promises and also of threatenings." James Glen to the Board of Trade, 10 October 1748, BPRO transcripts, microfilm, MEL-JHU, 23, 236–38.
123. Hooker, ed., Carolina Backcountry, 126–27.
124. Beattie, Crime and the Courts, 348.

By law, slaves were not allowed to present sworn testimony, in aid of either the defense or the prosecution, and there is no evidence that justices either allowed or compelled accused slaves to do so. But they could seek to remind prisoners in a less formal way that testimony calculated to save their mortal lives might put their immortal souls at risk. A slave woman pressed "to speak the whole truth" and confess was also "put . . . in mind, that there is a God who knows all things, and a Heaven to reward the good and a Hell to punish all Lyars and wicked Persons."[125] Similarly, a slave being tried before a North Carolina slave court was told that anyone who testified falsely would be sternly dealt with by God "the Revenger."[126]

On the other hand, at least one slave turned the tables and sought to invoke the aid of the eternal in his case to add weight to his testimony. He began his confession by declaring: "It is true that I am not a white Man, but I have a Soul as well as others, and I believe there is a Heaven and a Devil."[127]

Most often, however, the "awful considerations" that justices employed to badger witnesses to confession threatened earthly rather than spiritual torment. However uncertain slaves in the dock might have been about divine retribution, they knew only too well that the power that justices wielded was genuine. One justice, for example, bluntly told a slave to "tell the truth for if he did not he would be hanged."[128] Similarly, the magistrates who presided at another trial admitted that they had threatened an accused slave. However, they explained, they had "but talked of it in *terrorum*, to see if by imprinting the fear and danger of death upon him we might bring so obstinate and obdurate a slave . . . to repent and make an ample confession."[129]

When several slaves were accused of the same crime, each individual's choice of whether or not to confess directly impinged upon the lives of his or her fellow suspects. In such cases, justices commonly offered one of the accused a pardon in exchange for testimony against the others. In 1742, for example, when a group of slaves were charged with conspiring to run away, one of the suspects, "Mr. Rantowles's Peter . . . was allowed to be evidence for the King, with a promise of pardon, if he would make a full discovery." In this case, the purported leader of the suspects was

---

125. JGC, 7 February 1749, microfilm, LC, 162.
126. Watson, "North Carolina Slave Courts," 27.
127. JGC, 2 February 1749, microfilm, LC, 99.
128. JGC, 30 January 1749, microfilm, LC, 82.
129. This petition is unusual in that the owner was not seeking a pardon but rather demanding that his slave be executed; JGC, 7 October 1743, microfilm, LC, 347–48.

hanged and another "accomplice" was sentenced to be "severely whipped and pickled, on three several days round the square of Charles Town."[130]

Such cases forced accused slaves to choose between their own lives and those of their loved ones. In August 1749, for example, the wife of Thomas Miles, a planter on the Stono River, "was taken so suddenly and violently ill that she immediately suspected herself to be poisoned." Mrs. Miles survived, and suspicion immediately focused on Kat, one of Miles's slaves, who had "dropt some hints" about poison in conversation with another slave. But, despite being examined "in the strictest manner," Kat resolutely maintained his innocence. The examiners, frustrated in their efforts to wring a confession from Kat, turned to Venus, "a Negro Girl . . . about 15 years of age . . . whom . . . Kat has lately taken to wife." At last, "by great persuasions and repeated promises of safety," Venus was "prevailed upon to make an ample confession." She testified that "at the Instigation of . . . Kat [she] had mixed poison with the water of which her mistress drank, which poison had been furnished by a slave . . . named Frank." On the basis of Venus's evidence, both her husband and Frank were sentenced to death while she was pardoned by the governor.[131]

In the summer of 1754, the entire colony was caught up in the newspaper reports of a notorious crime, and the subsequent investigation, confession, and final punishment. The story began on July 25, when the *Gazette* reported that "the body of Mr. Charles Purry . . . was found in the River, with Bags of Shot tied to each of his wrists and feet, a Stab in his breast and one of his eyes thrusted out of his head." Purry was last seen the previous evening "sitting in his piazza alone." After a fruitless search in the night, the morning light revealed "his hat and wig, with the track of some bare feet" on the riverbank near where his body was soon discovered. "Two or three of . . . [Purry's slaves]," the paper concluded, "have been taken up on suspicion."[132]

After weeks of fruitless inquiry, the paper disclosed that "three of the late Mr. Charles Purry's negroes [were] concerned in the murder of their Master, a wench and two fellows (her brothers)."[133] The case was broken, the paper reported, when the woman had agreed to testify against her brothers in return for her life. The final episode in the tragedy was reported in the *Gazette's* August 29 issue:

130. *South Carolina Gazette,* 10 January 1742.
131. JGC, 7 November 1749, microfilm, LC, 677.
132. *South Carolina Gazette,* 25 July 1754.
133. *South Carolina Gazette,* 15 and 22 August 1754.

The Negro who was gibbeted at Beaufort for the Murder of Mr. Charles Purry, did not die before last Thursday, and 'till within an hour before he expired constantly declared his innocence; but at last he confessed that he himself had perpetrated that murder, and at the same time disclosed a scene equally shocking in which he and eight other Negroes were to have been concerned, i.e., the murder of two other gentlemen at Beaufort on the night after Mr. Purry's death (which only the discovery of his body had prevented) after which they were to have taken a schooner in the harbour . . . and in [it m]ade the best of their way to St. Augustine.[134]

With this array of anxieties and fears, "threats" and "promises" playing upon their minds, the mental and emotional state of slaves brought before the slave court can well be imagined. Slave suspects, if they were to save themselves, had to speak persuasively and in public before a panel of white judges in a language with which many of them were barely familiar. In these circumstances, it is perhaps understandable that while under close questioning one slave was said to have had "some confusion and disorder in her countenance" and another was described as "scared and could not speak."[135] Nor is it surprising that when placed in the dock of the slave court some slaves could make only a feeble effort at defending themselves. One North Carolina slave, for example, freely confessed to burning his master's barn but, when asked if he could give any reason why he should not be executed, remained fatally silent.[136] Familiarity with the dominant language and with the ways of the master class was obviously an asset in the slave court. In this vein, a slave arrested on suspicion of conspiracy was overheard to say that "he knew how to go before Gentlemen for he had waited on his Master . . . & was used to it, but Kent was a fool and did not know how to talk before white people."[137]

Not only were accused slaves in a situation fraught with deadly consequences if they misspoke, but it was not always clear what sort of testimony would lead them to safety. Confession could lead directly to condemnation. On the other hand, an "obstinate" refusal to cooperate might be regarded as an affront and a challenge to the authority of the court, a crime against deference that might be considered more serious than the original charge. Thus a slave who pled guilty and begged the

134. *South Carolina Gazette*, 29 August 1754.
135. JGC, 7 and 1 February 1749, microfilm, LC, 162 and 99.
136. Watson, "North Carolina Slave Courts," 28. Similarly, a Virginia slave charged with burglary in 1749 conducted his defense ineptly and was sentenced to death; Hoffer and Scott, eds., *Criminal Proceedings in Colonial Virginia*, 240–241 and xlix.
137. JGC, 1 February 1748, microfilm, LC, 98.

justices for mercy might be given a lesser punishment than another who defiantly proclaimed his or her innocence. The slave court dealt slaves a very weak hand; if they were to survive they had to play their few cards with great care.

For the accused it might well be a matter of life and death to be able to distinguish when the situation called for denial and "prevarication" and when a full confession and admission of guilt was the only safe course. In rare instances slaves could manipulate the justices' need for information to extricate themselves from the snares of the law. Sambo, a slave belonging to John Stone, belied the reputation for slow-wittedness often ascribed to his name when he was twice charged with burglary before slave courts. In the first instance, in October 1743, he steadfastly refused to confess despite being threatened with death, and ultimately the charges were dropped for lack of evidence.[138] Two years later, despite having "violent presumptions against him," the justices again admitted that there was "no sufficient proof" to convict Sambo. Again, despite "being urged very closely to a confession," Sambo held out. Only after he had secured a promise from the justices presiding at the trial that his life would be spared did he at last admit his guilt.[139]

If Sambo's experience provides a glimpse of how a slave could turn the justices' need for a confession into a powerful bargaining chip, John's unhappy example is a reminder that the justices' receptivity to such information was tempered by their subjective deliberations on the attitude and character of the slave defendant. In many trials the opinion the justices reached of the accused's character and attitude were more important in shaping their final verdict and sentence than were the facts of the crime itself. While the transgression of a properly deferential slave might be accepted as a negotiable matter that could be balanced by a dose of corporal punishment, a slave whose submission was thought to be wanting could expect little mercy.[140]

The accused's previous reputation in the community and demeanor at the trial were therefore crucial to the outcome of the case. As with John, this information could tell against the prisoner, but for an obedient slave it might be a lifesaver. In 1751, for example, Tom was "convicted of

138. JGC, 7 October 1743, microfilm, LC, 347–48.
139. JGC, 27 April 1745, microfilm, LC, 188. As agreed with the justices at his trial, Sambo's sentence of death was commuted to one of transportation.
140. On this point, Bertram Wyatt-Brown writes: "if slaves merely pretended to offer respect, the essence of honor would be dissolved; only the appearance, shabby and suspect, would remain. Hence it was important that blacks show obedience with apparently heartfelt sincerity. Grudging submission to physical force would not suffice. In part, slave codes were designed to that end. They heavily penalized the slave for infractions to deference." Wyatt-Brown, *Southern Honor*, 363.

breaking open and robbing a store" and sentenced to death. In petition-
ing the governor for a pardon, his owner, Helen Cobley, freely acknowledged Tom's guilt but asked Glen to consider "the youth and folly of
the . . . fellow" and the fact that he "has hitherto been reckoned a faithful
slave." Her petition was supported by the justices and freeholders who
had sentenced Tom and who wrote that "some favorable circumstances
attending . . . the said Negro fellow, on his tryal, . . . [led them] to recommend him to your excellency for mercy." After considering the matter, the governor granted Tom "his Majesty's most gracious pardon."[141]

The greater the crime with which a slave was charged, the more abject
and reliable the submission of the slave had to be to balance the scales
of justice. Some crimes, especially those involving violence against whites
or crimes against white authority, could never be redeemed and would
inevitably end in execution. Repeat offenders who had previously been
granted mercy and whose promises of good behavior and fidelity had
proved false were also shut out of the bargaining process. Their deferential and submissive behavior could not be trusted and was of little
worth. They, too, usually went to the whipping post or gallows.

Occasionally, slaves who appeared before the court would take no part
in these negotiations, despite the consequences. One slave charged with
plotting to run away to St. Augustine "behaved at his tryal with a good
deal of Insolence and said he would not live with his Master if he was
sure to be hanged."[142] Similarly, a low-country planter reported "that he
knew [of] several negroes who had refused to implore a forgiveness
when under sentence of death, though a pardon was assured [them] on
this easy term."[143] When faced with such defiance, justices usually had
no difficulty in finding the prisoners guilty.

The importance that the justices accorded to the accused's reputation
and behavior gave great weight to the testimony of any "character witnesses" who might appear to speak on behalf of the prisoner. As in
England, the "quality" of these supporting witnesses counted far more
than their quantity. A few good words from the suspect's master would
make all the difference. Suspects, white or black, knew that their life
might depend upon the willingness of the powerful and influential to
come to their aid at the trial. The desperate tone of a letter written "in
prison" by a white man seeking a wealthy patron's help in defending
himself against a charge of theft perhaps gives some of the flavor of these
entreaties. After meekly acknowledging that "what your Hon[o]r says is

141. JGC, 8 February 1751, microfilm, LC, 30–31.
142. JGC, 19 February 1750, microfilm, LC.
143. DeWolfe Howe, ed., "Journal of Josiah Quincy, Junior, 1773," 457.

very true, had I stayed at home and minded my own business I never should have been in this misfortune," the accused begged that "your Hon[o]r will see me mercifly," and concluded abjectly, "your poor and unfortunate wretch till death."[144]

A 1762 newspaper exchange illustrates the central role that a master could play in the trial of his slaves. The dispute began when Thomas Wright published an open letter in the *South Carolina Gazette* addressed to John Remington, a Charles Town magistrate. Wright complained that "my slave [Caesar] was punished agreeable to your award of justice; he was whipped 'round the town, when no offence criminal was really committed" and "tho' his crime could only be grounded on suspicion."[145]

Remington defended his conduct in the paper's next issue. "Your negro Caesar," the magistrate replied, "was ... charg'd by Mr. Thomas Smith, Jnr., of Charles Town ... with having ... feloniously entered the dwelling house of the said Mr. Smith, and hid or secreted himself in the garret with intention to commit some felony; he was try'd and convicted agreeable to the Negro Act, and sentenced to be whipp'd at [the] four corners of the town." Remington wrote that before Caesar's trial he had sent a message to Wright asking "if any person there would appear on his [the accused's] behalf ... but was told ... [Wright] would have nothing to do with him." He asserted that "had the freeholders been acquainted" with Caesar's "distinguishing qualifications" from his master's own testimony, he was "pretty confident" the outcome of the trial would have been different. The offended magistrate implied that if Wright did not like the verdict, he had only himself to blame for not appearing in court to point the justices in the proper direction.[146]

Masters could seek to place their thumb upon the scales of justice by altering their description of a slave's character according to their desire to increase or decrease the punishment accorded. Thomas Broughton, a justice in St. John Berkeley parish, complained in 1749 that "Mr. Akin's Character of [his slave] Robin at the Time that Joe [another of Akin's slaves] was condemned was very black but that Mr. Akin had given the same fellow Robin a different character now ... to wit that he is a good clever fellow."[147] Although in this instance Akin may have gone too far in proclaiming the virtues of a notorious offender, courts probably tended to accept such a change of heart on the part of masters.

Certainly, the presence and support of a master or mistress at the trial

144. Richard Cromwell to Charles Pinckney, 27 May 1747, Charles Cotesworth Pinckney Papers, LC.
145. *South Carolina Gazette*, 30 October 1762.
146. *South Carolina Gazette*, 6 November 1762.
147. JGC, 6 February 1749, microfilm, LC, 146.

could greatly strengthen an accused slave's defense. Eliza Pinckney described an incident in 1742 in which her slave "Mullatto Quash" was charged with plotting to escape to St. Augustine. "I was at his tryal," she wrote, "when he proved himself quite innocent."[148] Similarly, when Peter Manigault attended the trial of Polydor, a slave in his charge who was accused of robbery, Manigault's description of the principal witness for the prosecution (and Polydor's wife) as "a Lying Jude" probably indicates which side he was on. Not surprisingly, Polydor was also acquitted.[149]

The influence that masters exercised at the slave court by their testimony or mere appearance beside the accused served to reinforce their role as the benevolent patriarchs of their plantations. An extreme example of the way masters could use the law to suit their own ends is provided by a Virginia master who, after discovering one of his slaves in the act of robbery in 1770, "prosecuted him and got him pardoned with a halter round his neck."[150] Slaves who hoped to survive the slave court had to throw themselves not only upon the mercy of the court but first, and more importantly, upon the mercy of their master. On the day of their trial, slaves who, like Caesar, had disobeyed or rejected their master's rule might find that their master wanted "nothing to do with them." In this way, the criminal justice system of the slave society both recognized and fortified masters' personal authority. As Douglas Hay argues was the case for eighteenth-century England, the law "was part of the tissue of paternalism."[151]

For those slaves whose crime was thought too serious to be redeemed or who were judged "unfit for mercy," there was a final, solemn, act in the drama of the law. Even more than slave trials, slave executions were carefully planned public spectacles. When they took place in Charles Town they attracted large crowds and were reported in the newspaper. The ideal execution provided an exhibition to onlookers of the power and righteousness of the law. In their last speech the condemned were expected to confess to the crime, accept the justice of the verdict, and pray for their salvation.[152]

The hanging of a slave in April 1739 followed this formula perfectly:

148. Journal entry of 7 January 1742, Elise Pinckney, ed., *The Letterbook of Eliza Lucas Pinckney, 1739–1762* (Chapel Hill, 1972), 57–58. "The ring leader [of the slaves] is to be hanged and one [other] Whyped," Pinckney concluded.
149. Peter Manigault to Daniel Blake, 10 March 1771, Peter Manigault Letterbook, SCHS.
150. Jack P. Greene, ed., *Diary of Landon Carter of Sabine Hall, 1752–1778* (Charlottesville, 1965), 1: 397.
151. Hay, "Property, Authority, and the Criminal Law," 47.
152. The ritual (and intended moral) of public execution was very much the same in

On Saturday last the said Caesar was executed at the usual Place. . . . Before he was turned off he made a very sensible Speech to those of his own Colour, exhorting them to be just, honest, and virtuous, and to take warning by his unhappy Example; after which he begged the Prayers of all Christian People, himself repeating the Lord's Prayer and several others in a fervent and devout Manner.[153]

Not surprisingly, the fear of impending death often dominated the thoughts and words of the condemned. Some slaves may have directed their last words not to the surrounding crowd but to the divine judge before whom they soon expected to appear. This apparently was the case with one slave who had been captured and sentenced to death after hiding out for more than six years. "When he came to the Gallows," the paper reported, "he kneel'd at the foot of the Ladder and prayed very devoutly; after he had ascended the Ladder, he likewise prayed again for a short time, when he turn'd himself gently off the Ladder, with a fervent petition to the Almighty, to have mercy upon his poor Soul." In a conclusion that starkly contrasted the hope of divine mercy with the cruelty of earthly justice, the story reported that "after he was dead, his Head was sever'd from his Body, and fixed upon the Gallows."[154]

But not all slave executions proceeded as smoothly or, in the eyes of the law, provided as satisfying a spectacle of piety and punishment as these cases. In 1751, Henry Fielding, an English magistrate (and novelist), criticized the proceedings at Tyburn, London's place of execution. According to Fielding, the political "art" of the execution ceremony was "to raise an object of terror, and at the same time, as much as possible, to strip it of all pity and admiration." In practice, Fielding declared, the lesson that the crowd took from a public hanging was far from clear. "To unite the ideas of death and shame is not so easy as may be imagined," he wrote.

I will appeal to any man who hath seen an execution, or a procession to an execution; let him tell me, when he hath beheld a poor wretch, bound in a cart, just on the verge of eternity, all pale and trembling with his approaching fate, whether the idea of shame ever hath intruded on his

eighteenth-century England. See Peter Linebaugh, "The Ordinary of Newgate and His Account," in J. S. Cockburn, ed., *Crime in England, 1550–1800* (Princeton, 1977), 246–69.
153. *South Carolina Gazette*, 12 April 1739.
154. *South Carolina Gazette*, 6 April 1734.

mind? much less will the bold daring rogue, who glories in his present condition, inspire the beholder with any such sensation.[155]

Slaves brought to the gallows had little to gain by adhering to the part they were assigned in the ritual of execution. Descriptions of slave executions provide a glimpse of a final struggle between slaves and the law. With their final words and deeds, some condemned slaves contended with the authorities and their masters not to save their lives but to control the meaning and message of their deaths.

A few slaves used their dying speech to clear their conscience and save others from their fate. "At her Death" in 1749, for example, Hannah declared "that she could not be easie" because "she had told so many lyes upon so many People"; in particular, she declared that her husband Will "was innocent in having any hand or part in poisoning his Master."[156]

In some cases, the messages slaves delivered from the gallows were ambiguous. The condemned might go silently to their death, leaving onlookers only to guess at their final thoughts and emotions. Of two men hanged in 1771, for example, the paper could only say that "they behaved as became persons in their unhappy situation."[157] In 1769, two slaves, a man and a woman, were convicted of poisoning their master and his child and were sentenced to be burned at the stake on Charles Town green. At the place of execution, each chose a different path. The woman, the newspaper reported, "made a free confession, acknowledged the justice of her punishment, and died penitent, but the fellow did neither."[158]

Occasionally, however, the condemned actively sought to invert the moral of the drama and, with their last words, to assert a continued defiance. When a slave named Boatswain "was burnt to death" in 1741 after being convicted of arson, for example, the *Gazette* was forced to report that "he would make no confession at the stake but died like an impudent hardened wretch." In his final speech as the faggots were lit, Boatswain defiantly proclaimed that "he looked upon every white man he should meet as his declared enemy."[159]

155. Henry Fielding, *An Enquiry into the Causes of the Late Increase of Robbers* (London, 1751), section 11.
156. Hannah's gallows confession moved her master (who had survived the putative poisoning) to petition for Will to be pardoned. Whether Will was spared or not is unknown; JGC, 7 November 1749, microfilm, LC, 674–75.
157. *South Carolina Gazette*, 7 March 1771.
158. *South Carolina Gazette*, 1 August 1769.
159. *South Carolina Gazette*, 15 August 1741. The phrase "at the stake" was written in the

Masters continued to hope that the "example of justice . . . will deter other Negroes from committing such insolencies and crimes in the future."[160] But the lessons slave witnesses took from these spectacles were not always those that their masters had intended. The sympathies of slave onlookers were often on the side of the condemned. On several occasions, guards were hired to attend executions, apparently out of fear that the crowd might attempt to aid the prisoner or to prevent the sentence of death from being carried out.[161] Likewise, a slave who witnessed a hanging in 1748 reportedly described it as "the spilling of Innocent Blood" and was heard to predict darkly that "that day twelve months that he was hanged his Blood would boil from under the Gallows."[162]

The Rule of Law and the Law of Rule

To speak of "the criminal law" is to encapsulate in one phrase an entire complex of statutes and institutions, ideals and motivations, verdicts and punishments. Without recourse to such a convenient label it would be impossible to see the law in its larger context, but in using such a term there is always a danger that "the criminal law" may take on a life of its own and acquire an independent consciousness and purpose. In reality, of course, no system of law can exist apart from the ongoing process of its creation and legitimization. To speak of the "criminal law," therefore, is to describe the consequences of myriad individual actions, not a single prescient actor.

The criminal law of the colonial slave society was constructed each day by the decisions and choices of the living men and women, white and black, who cooperated with or contested against one another in the legislature, at the slave court, or upon the gallows. Catherine the Great, who knew something about arbitrary power, expressed the essence of this sort of personal and subjective system of justice when she reputedly remarked that law was written not on paper but on "human skin."[163]

In creating the Negro Act the members of the South Carolina Assembly were forced to reconcile the conflict between their perception of them-

---

paper's margin by an anonymous reader of the newspaper who apparently had attended the execution.

160. *South Carolina Gazette*, 27 November 1736.

161. See for example JCHA, 27 January 1767, microfilm, SCDAH, 263–65; and JCHA, 20 January 1768, microfilm, SCDAH, 500–6.

162. JGC, 7 February 1749, microfilm, LC, 160.

163. The actual quotation is "je travaille sur la peau humaine"; Louis Philippe, Comte de Segur, *Memoires, ou souvenirs et anecdotes*, 5th ed., 2 vols. (Paris, 1844), 2, 127.

selves as Englishmen and the necessity to "order and govern" the colonial institution of slavery. The slaveholders of the colonial low country valued the law and its rituals in part because their existence and exercise helped masters assert their claim to belong to a civil society. Colonial South Carolina's masters would no more have governed their slaves without recourse to the law than they would have served dinner without wine.

But the criminal law of slavery was far more than empty rhetoric or sham ritual. The law acted to further the slaveholders' imperative of "ordering and governing" the slave society. The Negro Act defined the legal condition of the slave and created a host of slave "crimes." The law was above all an assertion of masters' (and whites') power over slaves (and blacks). The men who created the Negro Act may have been guided by the same mimetic desires as the men who, in the year the act was signed, created and imagined Edmundsbury, but, as the bodies upon the gibbet could attest, the law was no mirage. Once framed, however awkwardly and imperfectly, the criminal law assumed a tangible and terrible reality.

For the masters who sat in judgment in the slave court, as well as for the masters who stood behind their slaves as they testified, the day-to-day operation of the law served to reinforce and reenact social hierarchies. The most important of these, of course, was the dominance of whites over blacks and masters over slaves. But the verdicts of the slave court also weighed the influence of local planters against the will of the parish and against each other. The bodies of accused slaves served as surrogates for white struggles over status. When John lost his case and his life at Edmundsbury, for example, the verdict was also a triumph for Robert Wright, the former assemblyman and Duff's owner, over Walter Holman, the master of John.[164]

The slaves brought before the slave court could not have been surprised when they were not treated equally or fairly. All courts reflect the world in which they are embedded. The slave court was no exception. It was a rare prisoner who defied the court and thereby ensured his or her own destruction. For most of the accused, the primary concern was self-preservation. They did what was necessary to gain this end. Witnesses who testified before the slave court had their own agendas. The slaves who testified in John's case at Edmundsbury may have sought to gain a measure of revenge for the murder of a member of their plantation

164. Not only did the verdict deprive Holman of a valuable piece of property, but the sentence directed that the forty pounds' compensation for John's execution be divided between Holman and Wright.

community by an outsider. Other witnesses may have sought to reconcile their need to placate onlooking masters with their desire to assist the accused. At the gallows, as some slaves faced death and others watched, slaves on occasion loudly shouted or clandestinely whispered the truth: the criminal law of slavery was made from their flesh and blood.

[3]

Communion and Community: Slavery and the Established Church

Anyone wishing to visit the colonial parish chapels that lie northwest of Charleston would do well to start the tour at the office of the Berkeley County tax assessor. A tour of the chapels does not entail a long journey, but it does require some initiative and determination. The chapels are all within thirty miles of the city, but neither they nor most of rural Berkeley County are shown on commercially available maps of the Charleston area. Perhaps it is assumed that people who travel the back roads of a region recently described as "one of the poorest parts of one of the poorest states" already know where they are going.[1] It does seem that the only glimpse of Berkeley County desired by the millions of annual visitors to Charleston or the Carolina beaches is that gained through their car windows as they speed through the western edge of the county on the interstate.

The assessor's office will provide, upon request, a blueprint map of the county tax districts.[2] Beneath the boldly delineated tax boundaries, a plan of the local roads can dimly be seen. Other words, barely legible in the faded blueprint, mark the location of the colonial chapels and the site of long-vanished rice plantations. Thus equipped with a late-twentieth-century tax collector's map, one can confidently venture into

---

1. Peter A. Coclanis, *The Shadow of a Dream: Economic Life and Death in the South Carolina Low Country, 1670–1920* (Oxford, 1989), 155 and note.
2. Berkeley County Assessor's Office, Moncks Corner, South Carolina.

the Berkeley County countryside and spend the afternoon in the eighteenth century.[3]

Today the chapels seem humble in size and simple in plan, but when they were built they must have made a more substantial impression. Brick construction was a statement of sophistication in the mid-eighteenth century and, while the chapels are by no means large, they would have been equal in size to the homes of all but the wealthiest planters in the parish.

Primarily, however, the chapels' builders sought to evoke order rather than awe and to inspire decorum rather than devotion. As the only public buildings located within the boundaries of a rural parish, the chapels served as the local representatives not only of the Anglican church but also of the British state. Anglican parishes served as the basis for representation in the colonial assembly. The responsibility to conduct elections was vested in the churchwardens of each parish. Notice of an impending election was posted on the chapel door, polling was conducted by secret ballot in the chapel aisle, and the results were announced from the chapel porch. As S. Charles Bolton notes, "the connection between church and state was obvious to all . . . [who] took part in the secular political process."[4] The conflation of sacred and secular power is vividly illustrated to visitors to the chapel at St. James Goose Creek, where an elaborate royal coat-of-arms still decorates the chancel above the altar.

The "venetian" windows, careful symmetry, and other decorative elements of the chapels reflect, in a provincial form, the architectural taste of Georgian Britain and indicate the builders' desire to locate themselves and their colony within the mainstream of the larger metropolitan culture.[5] The chapels are silent witnesses of an era when the Cooper River was a well-traveled highway in a trans-Atlantic trading network. In the mid-eighteenth century the region bordering the river was popularly termed the "Champaign Country" for the enormous profits that the local planters extracted from the labor of slaves in the rice and indigo fields.

3. Five colonial parish chapels survive within the boundaries of modern Berkeley County: St. James Goose Creek Church (St. James Goose Creek parish), St. Thomas and St. Denis Church and Pompion Hill Chapel (both St. Thomas and St. Denis parish), Strawberry Chapel (St. John Berkeley parish), and St. Stephen's Church (St. Stephen parish). In addition to these buildings, the brick walls and arches of Biggin Church (St. John Berkeley parish), burned by the British in 1781, remain as a picturesque ruin three miles northeast of Moncks Corner.

4. S. Charles Bolton, *Southern Anglicanism: The Church of England in Colonial South Carolina* (Westport, Conn., 1982), 148–49.

5. Descriptions and photographs of several of the colonial chapels can be found in Mills Lane, *Architecture of the Old South, South Carolina* (Savannah, 1984), 16–63.

Two-hundred-and-fifty years ago, St. John Berkeley was one of the richest parishes in one of Britain's wealthiest colonies.[6]

Today, the chapels are like aging dowagers, oddly out of place amid the climate, flora, and isolation of the rural low country. But this impression is not entirely due to the passage of time. Long before they became the relics of a bygone era, the chapels were colonial outposts in an alien landscape. Even when they were first constructed, the chapels' uneasy relationship to their surroundings must have been evident. In the eighteenth century the small, white, Anglo-Carolinian population of the region was overshadowed by a much greater black, Afro-Carolinian and African, presence. In 1747, for instance, the resident Anglican minister reported that the parish of St. John Berkeley contained only 530 "White People" but over 3000 "Blacks."[7]

Standing in the churchyard of Pompion Hill chapel, one can easily imagine this black majority walking or riding down the road to Charles Town, drifting past in their canoes and boats on the Cooper River that flows nearby, working and living in the rice fields and slave quarters of the adjacent Middleburg plantation, or meeting secretly at night in the nearby woods—all the while talking, singing, and worshiping in ways that both ignored and refuted the chapel's attempt to define the colonial social order in Anglican terms.[8]

The paradox of an "English" church located in a subtropical American environment and surrounded by African slaves encapsulates the complexities and contradictions inherent in colonial low-country society. It also serves as a starting point for inquiry, for it poses a number of interesting questions. Put simply, how did these disparate pieces fit to-

6. See Coclanis, *Shadow of a Dream*; George D. Terry, " 'Champaign Country': A Social History of an Eighteenth Century Lowcountry Parish in South Carolina, St. Johns Berkeley County" (Ph.D. diss., University of South Carolina, 1981); and John J. McCusker and Russell R. Menard, *The Economy of British America, 1607–1789* (Chapel Hill, 1985), 169–88.

7. Daniel Dwight to the SPG, 29 September 1747, SPG Records, microfilm, SCL-USC, Reel 5, No. 180.

8. A surviving ledger for the Cooper River ferry at Strawberry Chapel suggests the amount of black traffic on the roads. The vast majority of those using the ferry were black, often traveling in groups and almost always unaccompanied by a white. Passing slaves either paid the ferryman from their own pockets or charged their toll to their master's "tab"; see Strawberry Ferry Ledger, Lancelot Smith, 1777–79, microfilm, SCHS, Box 49. Testimony gathered in a slave conspiracy investigation in 1749 revealed the common practice of slaves traveling on the Cooper River to trade and visit at plantations located along its banks; see Philip D. Morgan and George D. Terry, "Slavery in Microcosm: A Conspiracy Scare in Colonial South Carolina," *Southern Studies* 21 (Summer 1982), 121–45. The slave quarter of Middleburg plantation (which was established in 1699) was located approximately a quarter-mile from the Pompion Hill chapel. In 1772, fifty-nine slaves lived at Middleburg; see Leland Ferguson, *Uncommon Ground: Archaeology and Early African America, 1650–1800* (Washington, 1992), xxiii–xxxi.

Pompion Hill Chapel (photograph by author)

gether to create the social order? Or, more elaborately, what were the interactions between the established church (metropolitan and Anglican), local authorities (low-country slaveholders), and the slave population (Africans and their Afro-Carolinian descendants)?

Most studies of the relationship between Anglicanism and slavery have about them an air of doom and futility. Previous examinations of the Anglican clergy's efforts to baptize colonial South Carolina's slaves have disagreed on the ministers' zeal and purpose, but have concurred in depicting the church's campaign as a dismal failure.[9] Certainly, plenty

9. For examples, see Frank J. Klingberg, *An Appraisal of the Negro in Colonial South Carolina: A Study in Americanization* (Washington, 1941); Peter H. Wood, *Black Majority: Negroes in*

of evidence demonstrates the difficulties that Anglican parsons faced. In December 1738, for example, the minister to the parish of St. George Dorchester complained to his superiors of the "gross neglect, not to say . . . unchristian aversion of too many [slaveholders] to instruct their Negroes in the Christian principles and bring them to Baptism."[10]

Such interpretations are built, however, upon a misconception of how the Anglican church actually functioned and a false assumption that a mass conversion of the entire slave community was what the church-state establishment desired. Rather than study what did not take place (i.e., mass conversion), perhaps attention should be directed at the sort of slave-church interaction that did, in fact, occur. For instance, in the same letter quoted above, the minister continued: "At Easter 1738, 27 White Persons and 13 Negroes [took communion], and within the year . . . [I] had baptized 11 White Children and 6 Negroes, 5 of whom were adults." Three years later, the same minister estimated that his parish contained 468 whites and 3,347 slaves, of whom 430 and 100 respectively were baptized.[11] That the parish contained one hundred slave converts (almost one-fifth of the church membership, if only 3 percent of the slave population) and that slaves constituted one-third of all communicants and baptisms suggest that, while the church may have been of small importance in the lives of most slaves, slaves played a significant part in the life of the church.

In theory, the Anglican church was a metropolitan institution constructed in a colonial setting by a colonial ruling class. But in practice, low-country realities, such as the distance from central authority and the existence of slavery, influenced the resulting religious establishment. Low-country elites confronted a dilemma that was typical of all colonial societies. They were torn between their desire to imitate the form of metropolitan institutions and the requirement to adapt to local innovations, such as slavery. The contrast between the chapels' Anglican style and their "exotic" locale is symptomatic of the perpetual tension between the metropolitan ideal and provincial reality that defines the colonial condition.[12]

This chapter examines the role played by the established church in

Colonial South Carolina from 1670 to the Stono Rebellion (New York, 1974), 133–42; Bolton, *Southern Anglicanism*, 102–20; and Margaret Washington Creel, *A Peculiar People: Slave Religion and Community Culture among the Gullahs* (New York, 1988), 67–80.

10. Stephen Roe, St. George Dorchester, to the SPG, December 1738, SPG records, microfilm, SCL-USC, Reel 3, 246.

11. Stephen Roe, St. George Dorchester, to the SPG, 22 December 1741, SPG records, microfilm, SCL-USC, Reel 4, 138.

12. See Jack P. Greene, *Imperatives, Behaviors, & Identities: Essays in Early American Cultural History* (Charlottesville, 1992), chaps. 1, 4, 6.

upholding the low-country social order. Its focus is on the central facet of that task: maintaining control and authority over slaves. The church lent support to this cause both through the exclusion of the majority of slaves and through the inclusion of a select few. In the center of what was from the first a slave society, the Anglican church in colonial South Carolina was woven into the fabric of the ongoing contention between masters and slaves. The church was consequently profoundly shaped by slavery even when it did not convert or include the majority of slaves. The rituals of the established church offered one way for the slave society publicly to divide itself into distinct communities of rulers and ruled. To examine how and why a small minority of slaves became Anglicans and the differing ways slaves, masters, and Anglican ministers interpreted that experience is to examine how domination could be exercised and resisted via cultural processes.[13]

The Church Established

From the start, the Anglican church in colonial South Carolina was closely tied both to the secular establishment in the colony and to the metropolitan culture. The creation of the church was due to a combination of provincial and metropolitan initiatives. In 1706, the colonial assembly legally established the Anglican church, drew the boundaries of ten parishes, and provided funds for the building of parish churches, chapels of ease, and parsonages.[14] In the same year, the London-based Society for the Propagation of the Gospel in Foreign Parts

13. My thinking in this chapter (as well as my title) has been shaped by David Warren Sabean's portrayal of the relationship among state authority, the laity, and the church in early modern Germany. In a key passage Sabean notes: "communion made Württemburg subjects members of what one might call a sacral community. It was one of the institutions which defined people as belonging to a lord under the Lord. Since the community was understood as being constituted within ritual, the problem for analysis is how that relationship—community/ritual—was understood in different ways and subject to different practices on the part of authorities and community members." Sabean, *Power in the Blood: Popular Culture and Village Discourse in Early Modern Germany* (Cambridge, 1984), 40. By focusing on the relationship between masters, slaves, and the colony's religious establishment, that is, the Anglican church, I do not mean to suggest or imply that there were no other religious denominations or movements at work in the low country in this period. Recent works examining these low-country "dissenters" include Carl Erskine, *Our Southern Zion: A History of Calvinism in the South Carolina Low-Country, 1690–1990* (Tuscaloosa, 1996); and Christine Leigh Heyrman, *Southern Cross: The Beginnings of the Bible Belt* (New York, 1997). For studies of the impact of eighteenth-century evangelicalism on some low-country whites and blacks, see Creel, *A Peculiar People*, 81–109; and Alan Gallay, *The Formation of a Planter Elite: Jonathan Bryan and the Southern Colonial Frontier* (Athens, 1989), 30–54.
14. Bolton, *Southern Anglicanism*, 28. By 1765 the number of parishes had increased to twenty, largely through the subdivision of the original parishes.

(or SPG) elected to sponsor ten Anglican missionaries to the colony. In its instructions, the SPG particularly charged its missionaries to attend to the conversion of the native Indians and of slaves, as well as to minister to the resident English population.[15] For the next fifty years, the SPG supplied nearly two-thirds of South Carolina's Anglican clergy.[16] The missionaries were expected to write London regularly reporting the state of their missions. In return they received an annual stipend of fifty pounds sterling, along with material support in the form of Bibles and printed tracts.[17]

The great majority of the Anglican clergy who served in South Carolina during this period arrived in the colony fresh from Britain with no prior experience of the low-country society.[18] At the start, therefore, each missionary drew his understanding of a minister's rightful place in his parish from the British example. This perception may have influenced the ministers' initial attitudes toward the black population of their parishes. One newly arrived missionary, for example, remarked to his superiors in London that "the best planters houses resemble Mannour houses surrounded with wooden cottages like [those of] poor villagers, the houses of their slaves."[19]

Slaveholder parishioners were generally pleased to have educated men fresh from Britain for their ministers, for in most regards they wanted

15. "Instructions for the Clergy Employed by the Society for the Propagation of the Gospel in Foreign Parts," reprinted in Frederick Dalcho, *An Historical Account of the Protestant Episcopal Church in South Carolina* (Charleston, 1820), 46.
16. The actual figure is 51 of 77, from Bolton, *Southern Anglicanism*, 166–71. After the retirement of commissary Alexander Garden in 1754, the SPG largely ceased operation in the colony and sent only one additional missionary between 1755 and 1775.
17. In addition to the stipend provided by the SPG, the South Carolina Assembly paid each missionary a further 75 pounds sterling from the provincial treasury each year. Nonmissionary parsons were given a salary of 105 pounds annually. Ministers could also expect to supplement their salary with "benefits" (i.e., fees) obtained for conducting weddings, baptisms, and burials. In the Charles Town parishes of St. Philip and St. Michael the annual "benefits" could easily equal the parson's salary. See Bolton, *Southern Anglicanism*, 98–99.
18. In the period 1706–1756 (roughly those of SPG activity), 74 percent of the Anglican clergy whose country of origin is known came from the British Isles (44 percent from England); another 14 percent were French Huguenots; native born colonists tied with Swiss Protestants at 6 percent each. Interestingly, in the two decades after the SPG ceased to send missionaries to the colony (i.e., 1755–1775), South Carolina's reliance upon Britain for Anglican clergy became even more pronounced. In this period fully 89 percent of the ministers were British born (73 percent English) while Switzerland and Germany accounted for another 5 percent each. Not a single minister whose place of birth is known was native to the colony in this latter period. Ibid., 166–74.
19. Richard Ludlam, St. James Goose Creek, to the SPG, 12 December 1727, quoted in John Donald Duncan, "Servitude and Slavery in Colonial South Carolina" (Ph.D. diss., University of Virginia, 1971), 249. For other ministers the likeness was less compelling. For instance, Levi Durand of Christ Church parish wrote the SPG on 23 April 1747 "that he should endeavour to content himself with that Province God had allotted him in one of the dark corners of the world"; SPG Records, microfilm, SCL-USC, Reel 5, 152.

the church to adhere as closely as possible to the metropolitan standard. In 1753, one Charles Town resident was so pleased with the appearance of the city's Anglican church, St. Philip's, that he sent an engraving of it to be published in the *Gentlemen's Magazine* of London. Twelve years later, another inhabitant boasted, "this Church is allow'd to be the most elegant Religious Edifice in British America."[20]

In colonial South Carolina, as in England, the representatives of the Anglican church saw it as their duty to ally themselves closely with secular authority.[21] In its architecture, liturgy, and ceremony, the established church upheld and celebrated the rightful authority of the government and its local representatives. According to Rhys Isaac, through its practices and doctrines the Anglican church "clearly asserted the hierarchical nature of things, confirming definitions of authority within the rural community itself."[22]

As a study of Anglicanism in eighteenth-century England notes, the seating plan of a parish church provided all in attendance with "a kind of map of village society."[23] It was customary for the wealthiest and most prominent families in each parish to claim the largest and most central pews. In a 1740 seating plan for the parish church of St. John Colleton, two box pews were even located within the chancel. On Sunday, whenever the minister and congregation looked to the altar, they also gazed upon the families of Isaac Waight and Captain Stanyarne.[24] In this hierarchical order, those slaves in attendance occupied the lowliest places: in the gallery at the rear, on benches in the aisles, or merely standing outside at the windows.[25]

20. R. M. Kennedy, "Extracts from the *Gentlemen's Magazine* [Pertaining to South Carolina], 1731–1792," typescript, SCL-USC, 64; Richard J. Hooker, ed., *The Carolina Backcountry on the Eve of the Revolution: The Journal and Other Writings of Charles Woodmason, Anglican Itinerant* (Chapel Hill, 1953), 70.
21. For South Carolina, see Bolton, *Southern Anglicanism*, 140–52; for Virginia, see Rhys Isaac, *The Transformation of Virginia, 1740–1790* (Chapel Hill, 1982), 58–65. For England, see Alan Smith, *The Established Church and Popular Religion, 1750–1850* (Bristol, England, 1971), 8–12; and also Arthur Warne, *Church and Society in Eighteenth-Century Devon* (Newton Abbot, Devon, 1969), 56–57.
22. Isaac, *Transformation of Virginia*, 64.
23. Anthony Armstrong, *The Church of England, the Methodists and Society, 1700–1850* (Totawa, N.J., 1973), 13.
24. St. John Colleton Parish, Church Book, 1738–1874, seating plan [circa 1740], St. John Colleton Vestry Book, SCL-USC, 8. Isaac Waite held 62 slaves at his death in 1745; in 1740 he was on the St. John Colleton vestry and earlier he had served in the colonial Assembly. In 1740, John Stanyarne was churchwarden for St. John Colleton; he served in the Assembly in 1746 and at his death in 1772 he owned 286 slaves. See Walter B. Edgar and N. Louise Bailey, eds., *Biographical Directory of the South Carolina House of Representatives*, vol. 2, *The Commons House of Assembly, 1692–1775* (Columbia, 1977), 654–55 and 691–92.
25. In 1723, a new church was erected in St. Andrew parish in the shape of a cross that included a gallery at the west end "[which was] appropriated to people of colour"; St.

As representatives of the established church, parish clergy deliberately sought to secure and maintain a close relationship with the local elite. The Anglican church and the British state were perceived as mutually supporting institutions. In this vein, the English poet William Cowper wrote of the "Squire, who, like the King, may be styled the Head of the Church in his own parish."[26] Colonial South Carolina's Anglican clergy endorsed this view. In 1768, for example, James Harrison, minister at St. James Goose Creek, who had earlier complained that "the most opulent . . . [planters] in my parish . . . reside in Charles Town," wrote of his delight that Henry Middleton, a wealthy slaveholder and prominent assemblyman, had decided to take up residence in his parish, "since his acknowledged integrity and abilities joined to his extensive influence may be productive of substantial benefits."[27]

Their desire to uphold and celebrate social hierarchy and secular authority led ministers to preach a doctrine of civil obedience to their assembled congregations. In 1738, the parson of Prince Frederick Parish wrote to the SPG that where there was no resident minister "people are very ignorant of their Duty to God, their Neighbours, and their Prince and those in authority under him."[28] Similarly, in 1744 the Anglican clergy of South Carolina published a joint address to Governor James Glen in which they assured him that "we shall not fail in our dutiful affection to Your Person, and submission and Obedience to your Government; nor neglect our best Endeavours to influence those of our several Charges to the same Behaviour."[29]

If on these occasions the rites and trappings of the church were employed to uphold the state, in other instances parsons could also invoke the power and majesty of the state to uphold the authority of the church. In particular, the ceremonies and drama of the law provided ministers

Andrew Parish Records, Church History 1706–1816, original at SCHS, microfilm, MEL-JHU. In 1773 the vestry of St. Michael parish (Charles Town) ordered "that the Sexton . . . remove the Benches the property of Negroes, now plac'd in . . . [the aisle leading from the north to the south door] either into the gallerys, or under the Bellfry" so that poor white people could sit there; Minutes of St. Michael's Church, Charles Town, 27 April 1773, typescript, SCL-USC, 93. On 14 July 1710, Francis LeJau, minister at St. James Goose Creek, wrote to the SPG that slaves attend "near and about the windows of our church, which cannot contain them when the parishioners are met"; quoted in Duncan, "Servitude and Slavery in Colonial South Carolina," 300.

26. Quoted in Smith, Established Church, 81.

27. James Harrison to the SPG, 6 August 1766, and 14 October 1768, quoted in David Morton Knepper, "The Political Structure of Colonial South Carolina, 1743–1776" (Ph.D. diss., University of Virginia, 1971), 19–20, 26. The "benefits" Harrison was anticipating may have been as much personal and financial as public and social.

28. John Fordyce, Prince Frederick, to the SPG, 1 February 1738, SPG records, microfilm, SCL-USC, Reel 3, 240.

29. South Carolina Gazette, 16 April 1744.

with a useful source for analogies in their sermons. For example, parishioners in one congregation were solemnly warned that "they shall [one day] appear before the impartial tribunal of the grat Judge of the World, & . . . as it shall upon that tryal appear that they have demeaned themselves in this world, they shall be sentenced to an eternal . . . Happiness or Misery."[30] On another occasion, the same minister compared the plight of sinners on the day of "judgement" to "a criminal . . . at the bar, when the sentence of condemnation is awarded against him."[31]

The surviving sermon book of one parson reveals that exhortations to support the secular establishment could be a steady refrain from the pulpit. On a September Sunday in 1767, for example, Reverend Paul Turquand called upon his listeners at St. Matthew Parish to "submit . . . to every ordinance of man for the Lord's sake." Turquand even repeated the Pauline doctrine that made it a religious duty for "servants to be obedient to their own masters." In another sermon Turquand defended and sanctified inequality, pointing out that "ranks & orders" exist even among "the holy Angels" so that "some [are] more excellent & honourable than others, & yet . . . they are all perfectly and completely happy."[32]

From the other side of the pulpit, members of the local elite could use the social gathering occasioned by church service as an opportunity to affirm their own exalted place amid the "ranks & orders" in their local community. For example, a tradition in Prince William Parish recalled the practice of Colonel Stephen Bull who, after church, "usually invited as his guests [to his home], . . . the more respectable part of the congregation who attended divine service; while his overseer, by his direction, and at his expense, liberally entertained the rest."[33]

Church service itself was as much a social event as a time for sober religious reflection. When George Whitefield first preached in Charles Town in January 1740, he found "the auditory large, but very polite." "I question," he wrote, "whether the court-end of London could exceed them in affected finery [and] gaiety of dress."[34] Thirty years later, a visitor from Boston described a service he attended at St. Philip (Charles Town) in similar terms:

30. Rev. Paul Turquand Sermon Books, 1766–1772, St. Matthew Parish, SCHS, 11/582/3.
31. Ibid., SCHS, 11/582/2. The appropriation of judicial metaphors by eighteenth-century Anglican clergy is noted in Douglas Hay, "Property, Authority and the Criminal Law," in Hay et al., *Albion's Fatal Tree: Crime and Society in Eighteenth-Century England* (New York, 1975), 29–30.
32. Rev. Paul Turquand Sermon Books, 1766–1772, St. Matthew Parish, SCHS, 11/582/1–3.
33. Dalcho, *An Historical Account of the Protestant Episcopal Church in South Carolina*, 383.
34. William V. Davis, ed., *George Whitefield's Journals, 1737–1741* (Gainesville, Fla., 1969), 382.

A young scarcely-bearded boy read prayers, with the most gay, indifferent and gallant air imaginable; very few men and no women stand in singing-time. A very elegant piece of modern declamatory composition was decently delivered by another clergyman, by way of a sermon from these words in Job "Acquaint now thyself with God, that good will come of it." Having heard a young church-parson very coxcomically advance a few days before, that no sermon ought to exceed twenty-five minutes, I had the curiosity to see by my watch whether our clerical instructor was of the same sentiment, and found that he shortened the space above seven and one-half minutes.

"It was very common in prayer as well as sermon time," the observer concluded, "to see gentlemen conversing together."[35]

Most ministers were assimilated into the ranks of the slaveholders soon after their arrival because most parsonages and glebe lands included slaves to serve them.[36] Charles Boschi wrote in October 1745 that "as soon [as] I arrived in the Parish several Parishioners persuaded me to buy Negroes. [After protesting] . . . I consented . . . not knowing full well the ways and management of country affair[s]. Therefore I bought a Negroe man with his wife and daughter."[37]

If they enjoyed the benefits of slave labor along with other low-country whites, Anglican clergymen also shared the risks. Josiah Smith, a plantation agent, wrote of one minister who was "so beat by one of the Parsonage Negroes . . . as to lose his life thereby."[38] The assembly journal records that Thomas Millechamp, parson at St. James Goose Creek, was paid four hundred pounds compensation in 1746 for two of his slaves executed "pursuant to the directions of the [Negro] Act."[39]

The South Carolina elite accepted and promoted strong ties with the local representatives of the Anglican church because they were able, through their control of parish vestries, to keep the clergy and the church under their control.[40] According to law, once a minister was appointed

35. Mark DeWolfe Howe, ed., "Journal of Josiah Quincy, Junior, 1773," Massachusetts Historical Society *Proceedings* 49 (Boston, 1916), 444.
36. At a meeting of the vestry of St. John Berkeley parish on 14 November 1765, for example, the arrival of a new minister was cause for the vestry to resolve "that a subscription be put about for the purchasing of Parish Negroes—also one other subscription put about for the purchase of a Horse"; Records of St. John Berkeley Parish, 1753–1819, Extracts from the Minutes, SCL-USC.
37. Charles Boschi to the SPG, 30 October 1745, in Florence Gambrill Geiger, ed., "St. Bartholomew's Parish as Seen by Its Rectors, 1713–1761," *SCHM* 50 (1949), 185.
38. Josiah Smith to John Jacob Zubly, 22 August 1780, Josiah Smith, Jr., Letterbook, SHC-UNC.
39. *JCHA*, 15 March 1746, 141; the crime of which they were convicted was not specified.
40. See Bolton, *Southern Anglicanism*, 140–53.

to the rectorship of his parish he could not be removed except by the Bishop of London or his commissary. A rector became chairman, with life tenure, of the vestry of his parish. South Carolina vestrymen, however, evaded this limitation on their authority by deliberately leaving rectorships vacant. They preferred to hire clergy on a year-to-year basis, thus depriving them of even a vote at vestry meetings.

Although ministers constantly complained of this practice, they could do little to counteract it. In 1734 Andrew Leslie, parson to St. Paul Parish, demanded that the vestry of his parish put his elevation to the rectorship to a vote. To his chagrin, however, he found that

> a considerable Majority voted against & rejected him; giving for their Reasons, not any Objections against either his Life or Doctrine, but [rather] that they thought Electing a Minister, was putting it ... in his Power to ... Lord it over them; [and] that it was more reasonable a whole Parish shou'd govern one man, than one man shou'd govern ... a whole Parish.[41]

In 1742, "Dr. Skirvin," a vestryman in St. Bartholomew Parish, put the same idea more crudely, telling the resident minister that "if a clergyman was Elected [rector] instead of coming to officiate at church perhaps he would stay at home drinking his Bottle with his negroe woman."[42]

With its suspicion of racial as well as sexual and professional misdeeds, this remark may hint at a reason vestries had for keeping a close rein on their parsons. If missionaries gained independence from vestry control, they could not be trusted to adhere to the planters' opinion on how the church should confront the slave population. The SPG in particular was known to advocate a wider campaign of slave conversion than most masters thought prudent. A story that is probably apocryphal but may well illustrate popular attitudes on this subject tells of a "clergyman settled ... at Georgetown" who "warmly recommended ... from the pulpit, ... a greater degree of compassion toward ... slaves than had hitherto been customary." After the service, the tale continues, a member of the congregation took the parson aside and explained, "we pay you a genteel salary to read to us the prayers of the liturgy and to explain to us such parts of the Gospel as the rule of the church directs, but we do

---

41. Alexander Garden to the Bishop of London, 18 April 1734, in George W. Williams, ed., "Letters to the Bishop of London from the Commissaries in South Carolina," *SCHM* 78 (1977), 219.
42. "Dr. Skirvin" was probably James Skirving, a prominent planter who resided in the parish; he served as one of the presiding magistrates at the 1749 slave trial of John discussed at length in chapter 2. Charles Boschi to the SPG, 7 April 1746, in Geiger, ed., "St. Bartholomew's Parish as Seen by Its Rectors," 192.

not want you to teach us what we are to do with our blacks." "The clergyman," the story concludes, "found it prudent to withhold any further admonition."[43] Certainly, the power parish vestries wielded over the clergy effectively doomed any project that offended local sensibilities. As one parson put it, "if a few of the leading men [in the parish] are so disposed, 'tis enough to prevent the doing of anything."[44]

Colonial South Carolina's established church was what the planters themselves chose to make it, and the rituals of the church reflected and sanctified the social order as the slaveholders perceived it. While the colony's slaveholding elite greatly desired the trappings of legitimacy that the Anglican establishment offered them, they were careful to keep the church and its ministers subordinate to their will. They borrowed from the cultural authority of the church without acknowledging any obligation to the metropolitan church establishment. In this way, planters could bask beneath religious doctrines of civil obedience without having to cope with the meddling of a bishop or recognize any clerical superior. In practice, if not in theory, South Carolina's Anglicans, as one parson disgustedly described them in 1765, "[were as] independent in matters of religion as ... [they were] republican in those of government."[45]

"The Society of Christians"

David Hall has suggested that historians who seek to understand the link between religion and culture should "reflect upon the ritual process," for "ritual represents and acts out a myth of collective identity."[46] In this way, the participants in the rites of the Anglican church in colonial South Carolina could be said to have formed a self-defined ritual community. By partaking in church ceremonies and visibly conforming to the doctrines of the established church, parishioners demonstrated their acceptance of the existing social order and in turn secured public recognition of their rightful place within the social hierarchy.

43. "Description of Charlestown," in J. Hector St. John deCrevecoeur, *Letters from an American Farmer and Sketches of Eighteenth-Century America*, ed. Albert E. Stone (New York, 1981), 172–73.
44. William Orr to the SPG, 29 September 1743, quoted in Knepper, "The Political Structure of Colonial South Carolina," 25.
45. Charles Martyn to the SPG, 20 October 1765, SPG records, microfilm, SCDAH, Reel 7, 230.
46. David D. Hall, "Religion and Society: Problems and Reconsiderations," in Jack P. Greene and J. R. Pole, eds., *Colonial British America: Essays in the New History of the Early Modern Era* (Baltimore, 1984), 336.

Through the rituals of the established church one could define oneself as a Christian and an Englishman and gain a sense of belonging to the local Anglican community.[47]

Doubtless, slaves knew of the existence of the chapels and something of their role in colonial society. They must have fit the chapels into their mental landscape. A belief in spirits may have led them to give the churchyards a wide berth during their nocturnal travels.[48] On occasion, slaves no doubt watched as their masters, dressed in their finest clothes, processed on horseback or in carriages to attend a church service or a burial. Indeed, some slaves always went along on such outings, if only to stand in the churchyard holding their masters' guns and horses during the ceremony.[49] For most slaves, however, the ceremonies of the established church were rituals of exclusion that served as reminders of their inferior and outsider status.

But members of the slave community were not all on the outside looking in. Slaves were inside the church too. Membership in the ritual community of the established church was never wholly restricted to white Carolinians. Slaves were present and often played a substantial part in church ceremonies. In 1759, for example, James Harrison, minister at St. James Goose Creek, reported to the Society that "his Congregation generally consists of about one hundred and fifty Whites, and from fifty to sixty Negroes . . . and his Communicants consist of thirty-one white, and twenty-six Negro Persons."[50]

Although Anglican missionaries continued to "hope [that] God in his due time will afford a probable means for converting many of the poor

---

47. Of eighteenth-century England, historian J. C. D. Clark has argued that "religion provided for Anglicans a nationwide definition of unity, and, for non-Anglicans, the definition of their inferior status." Clark, *English Society, 1688–1832: Ideology, Social Structure and Political Practice During the Ancien Regime* (Cambridge, 1985), 90.

48. See, for example, Albert Raboteau, *Slave Religion: The Invisible Institution in the Antebellum South* (Oxford, 1978), 85. White Carolinians shared these beliefs in the power of the dead; for example, a visitor to the region in 1783 was told by his host that if he relocated the family crypt (which the visitor thought too near the house) "his people would consider themselves unfortunate" (i.e., cursed). Francisco de Miranda, *The New Democracy in America: Travels of Francisco de Miranda in the United States, 1783–84*, trans. Judson P. Wood (Norman, Okla., 1963), 29.

49. Although masters were charged to bring arms to church so that they might quickly respond to a Sunday insurrection, the grand jury complained in 1756 of "the neglect of carrying arms to church and other places of worship, and against the bad custom of delivering their arms to Negroes or other slaves to keep while they are at divine worship"; *South Carolina Gazette*, 17 March 1756.

50. The SPG was so pleased with Harrison's report that it was printed in the Society's annual, *An Abstract of the Proceedings of the S.P.G.* (London, 1760). The abstract's summary of Harrison's letter of 12 May 1759 is quoted in Klingberg, *An Appraisal of the Negro*, 96.

unhappy infidels [i.e., slaves] here," they also recognized that such work depended upon the good will of local planters.[51] Consequently, ministers were careful to obtain the master's permission before offering religious instruction to any slave.[52] In 1749, for instance, Robert Stone, parson at St. James Goose Creek, hesitated to baptize one slave because "his Master sent word that he desired to speak with me first."[53] The minister of St. Paul wrote in 1744 that he had delayed the baptism of several slaves until "proper sponsors can be provided for them."[54] The clergy's need to wait upon the slaveholders' approval and consent placed the final decision as to whether any particular slave would be offered baptism in the hands of the slave's master.

While only a crude estimate of the proportion of the total slave population that was baptized into the established church in the colonial period is possible, the figure was certainly small. Four parish surveys exist and can serve as rough guides.[55] The highest estimate of the four surveys is James Harrison's computation in 1766 that 12 percent of the slaves in the parish of St. James Goose Creek were Christians. The lowest estimate is that of Charles Martyn, who reckoned in 1762 that only 1 percent of the slaves in the entire colony were baptized. The percentage must have varied widely from parish to parish according to the zeal of the local

51. Richard Ludlam, St. James Goose Creek, to the SPG, 3 July 1724, SPG records, microfilm, LC, Mss.B, vol. 4, Reel 59, 181.

52. Earlier in the century, a minister wrote that "several sensible and sober slaves have asked me also to be baptized and married according to the form of our Holy Church. I could not comply with their desire without the consent of their Masters, but I have exhorted them to perseverance and patience"; Francis LeJau, St. James Goose Creek, to the SPG, 22 March 1709, quoted in Klingberg, *An Appraisal of the Negro*, 12.

53. Robert Stone, St. James Goose Creek, to the SPG, 6 March 1749, SPG records, microfilm, SCDAH, Reel 6, 182.

54. William Orr, St. Paul, to the SPG, 30 March 1744, SPG Records, microfilm, SCL-USC, Reel 4, 288.

55. All the figures given in the text are rounded to the nearest whole percent. The four surveys are listed here in chronological order. "Notitia Parochialis, or, an Account of ye spiritual state of St. Thomas parish in South Carolina [1721]" estimated "between 900 and 1000 Negroes" in the parish and "about Ten or 12 Baptized Negroes," or approximately 1.2 percent; SPG records, microfilm, LC. Stephen Roe, St. George Dorchester, 1741, estimated that among "3347 slaves in the parish" 100 are baptized, or approximately 3 percent; Stephen Roe, St. George Dorchester, to the SPG, 22 December 1741, SPG records, microfilm, SCL-USC, Reel 4, 138. In 1762, Charles Martyn figured that "the number of Negroes [in the colony] consists of forty-six thousand out of which I imagine that there are five hundred who are Christians," or approximately 1.1 percent; Charles Martyn, St. Andrew, to the Bishop of London, 11 April 1762, Bishop of London's Papers, originals at Lambeth Palace Library, London, microfilm, SCL-USC, vol. 9, 153. Lastly, James Harrison wrote in 1766: "there are about 1300 Negroes in this parish [St. James Goose Creek] of whom 150 or more are Christians," or approximately 11.5 percent; James Harrison, St. James Goose Creek, to the SPG, 8 August 1766, SPG records, microfilm, SCDAH, Reel 5.

minister and the prevailing custom of the region. While a reliable figure remains elusive, an estimate of about 3 to 5 percent for the proportion of slaves baptized into the Anglican church seems reasonable.[56]

Because Anglican parish registers were considered public records and were used for secular as well as religious purposes, ministers were reluctant to clutter their pages with what were, from the white society's point of view, useless notices of slave baptisms. Some ministers maintained a separate account of slave baptisms for their own records, but none of these "private registers" has survived. Confronted with the resulting documentary silence concerning slave baptism, one might share the sentiments of the newly arrived parson who lamented to the SPG "that there is no easy way of knowing . . . [which slaves] were baptized in Church."[57]

Certainly, common sense and the necessity of "sponsorship" suggest that baptism was offered most often to those slaves with whom masters were most familiar. For example, Richard Ludlam, parson at St. James Goose Creek, noted in 1724 that because of "the diffidence of the [slave] owners . . . it [is] at present almost impractical to convert any but here & there a favourite house slave."[58]

If local parish registers were largely silent on slave baptisms, a whisper of these baptisms can be heard in the reports, or *Notitia Parochialis*, which missionaries sent to London. In response to a directive from the SPG, the *Notitia* were supposed to include records of the number of slaves baptized in the parish during the preceding year. Although the *Notitia* were to be made annually, most ministers were far more sporadic in fulfilling their duty, seldom compiling more than two or three in a decade. Yet, despite these gaps and their other obvious limitations, the surviving *Notitia* allow an imperfect portrait of the typical slave convert to be drawn.

A sample of forty *Notitia* completed between 1736 and 1768 includes the record of 158 slave baptisms (along with the baptisms of 1096

---

56. The average of the four accounts cited above is 4 percent, and the median is 3 percent. If one takes the *Notitia Parochialis* (see below) as a guide, one might conclude that since 12.6 percent (158 of 1254) of those given baptism were slaves, slaves probably comprised a similar proportion of Anglican congregations. If the low-country white population numbered approximately 20,000 (see Coclanis, *Shadow of a Dream*, 68) throughout this period, the proportional number of slave Anglicans would then be about 2,500, or approximately 5 percent of the slave population of 50,000 in 1750. This figure, however, would not account for those slave attendees who were not formally baptized or, of course, for those low-country whites who were not Anglican.

57. William Cotes, St. George Dorchester, to the SPG, 17 April 1751, quoted in Klingberg, *An Appraisal of the Negro*, 88.

58. Richard Ludlam, St. James Goose Creek, to the SPG, 3 July 1724, SPG records, microfilm, LC, Mss. B, vol. 4, Reel 59, 181.

whites).[59] An examination of these baptized slaves reveals several significant characteristics of slave converts as a group. First, a fifth of slave Anglicans (and over a third of those slaves baptized as infants) were described as mulattoes, a proportion more than five (and eight) times greater than that found in the slave population at large.[60] Apparently, many of the slaves who attended church with their masters represented the fruits of miscegenation. Such, at least, seems to have been the case with the "one Adult *Negroe* Woman, and six of her Children *Mulattoes*" (emphasis in original) baptized by John Fordyce in Prince Frederick Parish in 1737.[61]

Moreover, most white and black church members encountered the sacrament of baptism in very different ways. While 97 percent of whites were baptized in infancy, 53 percent of the slaves who experienced baptism did so as adults.[62] This difference is significant; according to the practices of the church, before adult converts could be baptized they had to demonstrate their knowledge of church doctrine and testify to their faith before the entire congregation. Unlike infant baptism, which was a private, family affair, adult baptism was a public ceremony of communal acceptance.

The Anglican church did not adhere to the Catholic custom of universal baptism. Instead, past infancy, would-be converts to the Church of England had to undergo a program of religious instruction in accordance with the Anglican doctrine of "preparation." In 1743 William Orr, parson at St. Paul Parish, noted that "he was instructing and preparing a very sensible sober Negroe woman for Baptism"; three years later he reported that he was "preparing some Adult Negroes for the holy Sacrament of Baptism."[63]

Given the importance of scripture in Protestantism and the Church of England's reliance upon the Book of Common Prayer for its liturgy, a

59. The forty *Notitia* were gathered from microfilm copies of the SPG records held at various repositories, including SCL-USC, SCDAH, and LC.
60. The actual figures are 32 mulattoes in 158 total baptisms and 26 mulattoes among 74 slave children baptized. In a profile of the South Carolina slave population based upon an analysis of runaway slave advertisements from 1732 to 1782, Philip D. Morgan has estimated that mulattoes made up 3.7 percent of the general slave population; Morgan, "Colonial South Carolina Runaways: Their Significance for Slave Culture," *Slavery and Abolition* 6 (December 1985), 60.
61. John Fordyce, Prince Frederick, to the SPG, 25 July 1737, SPG records, microfilm, SCL-USC, Reel 3, 192. The fact that Fordyce underscored the words "Negroe" and "Mulattoes" in his letter may indicate an indirect criticism of evident miscegenation.
62. There were only 27 adults among 1096 total white baptisms, while 84 of 158 slaves baptized were adults.
63. William Orr, St. Paul, to the SPG, 18 November 1743, SPG Records, microfilm, SCL-USC, Reel 4, 228.

large part of this instruction entailed teaching slaves to read and recite from religious texts.[64] Alexander Garden, rector at St. Philip's Church in Charles Town and the Bishop of London's commissary in South Carolina, thought that slaves should be "instructed in the Principles of the Christian Religion as contained in the Church Catechism, to read the Bible, and to make use of the Book of Common Prayer."[65] Likewise, the SPG expected that slave converts would be taught to exercise "their own Reason; by carefully reading and considering the *Bible*," and directed missionaries to "excite in them an earnest Desire to read the *Bible* as soon as they can."[66]

Ministers differed in how far they adopted the SPG's proposed curriculum. For some, instruction involved little more than rote memorization and repetition. William Guy, minister at St. Andrew, noted that he had taught three slaves "to say the creed, the Lord's Prayer, & the ten Commandments" along with other lessons "in the Church Catechism."[67] Similarly, a Georgia minister wrote that such slaves as were "not capable of learning to read, I instruct in as plain a manner as I can in such principles of our holy religion as suits best with their condition and capacity."[68] Some slaves, however, did learn to read as part of their religious instruction and preparation for baptism. In 1741, Lewis Jones informed the SPG that two slaves under his care in St. Helena parish "can read well in the New Testament and two more learn to spell."[69]

In 1740 Alexander Garden asked the SPG for funds to purchase "3, 4, or 5, more or less, . . . Home born male slaves not under the age of 12, nor exceeding that of 16 years, and who shall appear to be of Sober and Docile dispositions." Garden proposed that after being "instructed in the Principles of the Christian Religion" and taught to read "the said slaves [would] be employed as schoolmasters . . . under the immediate care and supervision" of ministers to teach other slaves what they had learned. Garden hoped that if "every owner of 80 or 100 slaves" would send one

---

64. On the central place of the Book of Common Prayer in eighteenth-century Anglican ceremony, see Isaac, *Transformation of Virginia*, 63–64.

65. Alexander Garden to the SPG, 6 May 1740, SPG records, microfilm, SCL-USC, Reel 4, 33–35.

66. "Directions to the Catechists for Instructing Indians, Negroes, &c.," reprinted in Dalcho, *An Historical Account of the Protestant Episcopal Church*, 47–50.

67. William Guy, St. Andrew, to the SPG, 30 September 1742, SPG records, microfilm, SCDAH, Reel 7.

68. Joseph Ottolenghe, Georgia, to the SPG, 9 September 1751, SPG Records, microfilm, SCDAH, Reel 6, 149.

69. Lewis Jones, St. Helena, to the SPG, 25 September 1741, SPG records, microfilm, SCL-USC, Reel 4, 102.

slave to be so instructed, and if such slaves, upon their return to their native plantations, would

> read the Bible . . . and other proper tracts of Instruction [to the other blacks] at evenings and other spare hours, especially Sundays . . . [in] the space of 20 years, the knowledge of the Gospel among those other slaves . . . excepting those newly imported, would not be much inferior to that of the lowest sort of white people, Servants and Day Labourers (especially in the Country) either in England or elsewhere.

The SPG concurred, and in 1742 Garden purchased two young slaves, Andrew and Harry, to be trained as "schoolmasters." "In the space of eight months" Garden taught Harry, who was fourteen years old, "to read the New Testament exceeding well."[70] The "Negroe School" was opened on September 12, 1743, and for the next twenty-five years the rectors of St. Philip periodically reported to London on the school's progress. Garden projected that the school would "annually send out 30 or 40 young negroes capable of reading the Scripture and instructed in the chief principles of Christianity." By 1750, Garden reported that Andrew, having proved to be of "weak understanding," had been sold and the proceeds applied to the purchase of books, leaving Harry to tend the school alone. Ten years later, the school was said to be "in a flourishing state." In 1768, however, the vestry of St. Philip "ordered that Harry, the Negroe that keeps School at the parsonage . . . be put into the Mad house, there to be kept till Orders from the Vestry to take him out." The orders never came and the school was never reopened.[71]

After the successful completion of "preparation," the next step in the process of conversion, baptism, was a ceremony of acceptance and adoption into the church community. The rite of adult baptism in the Anglican Church had two distinct parts. The first constituted something of a public trial, in which candidates had to demonstrate to the satisfaction of the minister and the congregation their comprehension of and conformity to

70. Alexander Garden to the SPG, 17 December 1742, SPG records, microfilm, SCL-USC, Reel 4, 168.
71. Records of the "Negroe School" are taken from the following sources: Alexander Garden to the SPG, 6 May and 4 October 1740; 20 May 1741; 9 April and 24 September 1742; 10 October 1743; 18 October 1744; 19 September 1746; 22 August 1747; and 9 September 1750, SPG records, microfilm, SCL-USC, Reel 4, 33–35, 37, 89, 143–44, 168, 182, 250, Reel 5, 104, 119, 266; Alexander Garden to the SPG, 11 February 1751; and also, Robert Smith to the SPG, 25 July 1759; 18 November 1760; and 29 April 1761, SPG records, microfilm, SCDAH, Reel 6, 183, and Reel 7; St. Philip's vestry book, from Bolton, *Southern Anglicanism*, 118. For a detailed account of the "Negroe School," see also Klingberg, *An Appraisal of the Negro*, 101–22.

accepted religious doctrine. Having passed this test, a candidate then underwent the more familiar baptism ceremony, the minister's blessing and the symbolic immersion at the baptismal font after which, according to the SPG, they emerged as an accepted member of the "Society of Christians."[72]

Surviving accounts differ as to the nature of slave candidates' testimony. John Fordyce described the case of one woman in Prince Frederick Parish "who gave an account of her faith, and read several portions of Scripture, particularly the 10th Chapter of the Epis[tle of] P[aul] to the Romans."[73] William Guy of St. Andrew wrote of the baptism of five slaves who gave "a pretty good account of their faith . . . before the publick congregation in my church."[74] A decade later, in the same parish, Charles Martyn reported upon the baptism of a "very sensible" black man who, under examination, provided "a rational account of the principles of the Christian religion."[75]

In some cases the public declaration of faith slave candidates underwent before they were baptized was apparently more of a trial than a testament. William Orr, minister at St. Paul, recorded a baptism performed in his church in 1744 at which the candidate (a slave woman) "behaved well, and answered to the satisfaction of every one present."[76] In practice, such must have always been the case, at least implicitly, for any slave candidate would have had to respond successfully to any doubts that on-looking church members had as to the nature of their testimony, sincerity, or good character. The requirement to conform to the expectations and attitudes of Anglican slaveholders in order to gain acceptance into the church community may have had a powerful and transforming effect on those slaves who underwent adult baptism. Through the "ritual process" of adult baptism the candidates "emptied

---

72. Dalcho, *An Historical Account of the Protestant Episcopal Church*, 49.

73. John Fordyce, Prince Frederick, to the SPG, 1 February 1738, SPG records, microfilm, SCL-USC, Reel 3, 240. While there are a multitude of possible interpretations of this particular passage and of the public ritual in which the slave candidate recited it, I would suggest that the first thirteen verses speak to the conversion of slaves ("they, being ignorant of God's righteousness, and going about to establish their own righteousness, have not submitted themselves unto the righteousness of God"). The eleventh verse perhaps addresses the slave convert's potential alienation from the rest of the slave community ("whosoever believeth on him shall not be ashamed"). The remaining eight verses describe the importance of the ministry ("how shall they believe in him of whom they have not heard? and how shall they hear without a preacher?").

74. William Guy, St. Andrew, to the SPG, 30 September 1742, SPG records, microfilm, SCDAH, Reel 7.

75. Charles Martyn, St. Andrew, to the SPG, 28 December 1752, SPG records, microfilm, SCDAH, Reel 6.

76. William Orr, St. Paul, to the SPG, 30 March 1744, quoted in Klingberg, *An Appraisal of the Negro*, 81.

themselves" via personal testimony, "reshaped themselves" via their response to real or implied questions, and eventually were "reborn" as Christians and church members.

Because the established church identified itself so closely with the secular elite in the slave society, the "worldly" dimensions of the baptismal rite were difficult to distinguish from its purely spiritual aspect. Many of the onlookers regarded the public baptism of slave converts as a ceremonial acceptance into the slaveholders' earthly community as well as their spiritual communion. In the rituals of the church the rhetoric of inclusion could at times be quite explicit. For example, at the conclusion of the baptism ceremony missionaries enjoined converts "heartily to love their Fellow-Christians."[77]

Anglican doctrine deliberately blurred the boundaries between church and state. Consequently, for most Anglican slaveholders the distinction between the church communion and the social community was vague at best. In their minds the church embodied not only Christianity but also the persistence of their metropolitan cultural identity in the colonial environment. To partake in the rituals of the church was to assert one's "Englishness" as well as one's piety. This conflation of communion and community affected individual planters' attitudes toward the baptism of slaves.[78]

Some slaveholders found the idea of fellowship with slaves abhorrent. One missionary, for example, reported that a "Lady" of his parish, certain of her own salvation, worriedly asked him if she would have to share heaven with her slaves, while a "young Gent" told him "that he is resolved never to come to the Holy Table while slaves are rec[eive]d there."[79] In the minds of these slaveholders, the inclusion of slaves in communion breached the boundary between English and African and undermined the exclusiveness that was the whole point of colonial Anglicanism.

At the opposite extreme, the conflation of communion and community meant that for a fortunate few conversion went hand-in-hand with freedom. Prince, a slave belonging to Alexander Inglis, was manumitted on the same day that he was "baptized and received into the holy communion."[80] Soon after Hester Dwight's slave, Plymouth, was "Baptized and received into Christ's flock" in 1749, he was freed, al-

77. Dalcho, *An Historical Account of the Protestant Episcopal Church*, 49.
78. See for example Orlando Patterson, *Slavery and Social Death, A Comparative Study* (Cambridge, Mass., 1982), 72–73.
79. Francis LeJau to the SPG, 18 September 1711 in Frank Klingberg, ed., *The Carolina Chronicle of Dr. Francis LeJau, 1706–1717*, (Berkeley, 1956), 102.
80. Miscellaneous Records, 14 July 1784, AAA67, SCDAH.

though he also paid Dwight a considerable sum of money for his freedom.[81]

The persistent belief either that Christians should not be slaves or, more conveniently, that slaves should not be Christian was a strong impediment to slave conversion. The SPG and its ministers attacked this notion, insisting that baptism wrought only a spiritual improvement in slaves' condition but did not compromise the "secular excommunication" and "social death" that was one of the foundations of the slave society.[82] In 1727, Edmund Gibson, Bishop of London (whose diocese included all of America), sent a "pastoral letter to the Masters ... [of] English Plantations" assuring slaveholders that "so far is Christianity from discharging Men from the Duties of the Station and Condition in which it found them, that it lays them under stronger Obligations to perform those Duties with the greatest Diligence and Fidelity, not only from the Fear of Men, but from a Sense of Duty to God."[83]

Ministers argued that baptized blacks would be new and improved slaves. "Those [Christian] slaves behave very well," one parson wrote in this vein, "and do better for their masters profit than formerly, for they are taught to serve out of Christian love and duty."[84] Moreover, parsons asserted, the privileges of church membership offered the slave society another avenue of control. If baptized slaves failed to do their "duty," ministers had a ready response. Francis LeJau, of St. James Goose Creek, reported that he made baptized slaves "promise they'll spend no more the Lord's day in idleness" and warned them that "if they do I'll cut them off from the Communion."[85]

Whether or not they were persuaded by such reasoning, most slaveholders apparently were able to reconcile Anglican baptism with continued servitude. The majority of planters and vestrymen, however, continued to resist and prevent the SPG's program of mass conversion.

81. Plymouth (rechristened "Charles Cordes") paid Dwight 750 pounds currency (or approximately 107 pounds sterling), which raises the question as to whether the prime motivation in Dwight's action was communion or commerce. Both factors may well have been operative; becoming a Christian allowed Plymouth successfully to petition Dwight for his freedom, which he obtained only after reimbursing her for his economic worth. Miscellaneous Records, 19 September 1749, HH101, SCDAH.
82. Patterson, *Slavery and Social Death*, 5.
83. Edmund Gibson, "Pastoral letter to the Masters and Mistresses of Families in the English Plantations abroad: Exhorting them to encourage and promote the Instruction of their Negroes in the Christian Faith" (London, 1727), reprinted in Dalcho, *An Historical Account of the Protestant Episcopal Church*, 104–12.
84. Francis LeJau, St. James Goose Creek, to the SPG, 13 June 1710, quoted in Klingberg, *An Appraisal of the Negro*, 18.
85. Francis LeJau, St. James Goose Creek, to the SPG, 20 October 1709, quoted in ibid., 13.

Anglican slaveholders demonstrated their belief in the Society of Christians neither by freeing their converted slaves nor by imposing a total ban on slave conversion but instead by permitting only a few, carefully selected slaves to be baptized.

If conversion had existed as an avenue of status and self-esteem for slaves independent of their masters, it would have worked against the authority of the slaveholders. For example, a slave field hand who took part in the ceremonies of the church might come to feel himself the equal or superior of his unconverted driver. Instead, slaveholders insisted that baptism only take place with their consent and, by limiting baptisms to a select few, sought to use the conversion of slaves to support and enhance their authority.

Church membership was only one of several avenues through which the slave society sought to differentiate and order the slave population. Other "defining characteristics" of status included mulatto over black, creole over African, skilled over unskilled, and those able to understand and converse in the language of the dominant culture over those who could not. These attributes, which whites perceived as positive or negative, tended to coincide in the slave population. A hypothetical portrait of the slave most likely to be a church member would depict a mulatto, creole, skilled slave able to speak English well. Conversely, those slaves who were least likely to be baptized would be black, African born, unskilled, and unable to understand English.[86]

It was when the ministers sought to extend the communion of the church beyond this select few to the slave population at large that slaveholders manifested an "unchristian aversion" to widespread proselytization. Slaveholders sought to employ the established church to support the social order of the slave society by elaborating upon and enhancing the hierarchy that they strove to impose upon the slave population.

In arguing for the positive benefits of conversion, even Anglican parsons at times adapted themselves to the slaveholders' beliefs and conflated religious communion with social community. Ministers entertained hopes that baptized slaves would identify themselves with their "Fellow-Christians" in moments of crisis. One minister thought that

---

86. Stuart Schwartz has written of the slave society of colonial Brazil: "A system that combined social definitions and rankings based on estate, function, corporate identity, religion, culture, and color might have proved so confusing and liable to inherent contradiction as to become no system at all. But such was not the case, the tendency was always for the various criteria of rank to become congruent in a single individual. Thus a . . . [native] African was most likely to be a pagan, black, unacculturated, unskilled, a field hand, and certainly a slave." Stuart B. Schwartz, *Sugar Plantations in the Formation of Brazilian Society: Bahia, 1550–1835* (Cambridge, 1985), 250–51.

through Christianity slaves, "from being suspected enemies to their masters, may be made their real friends and safeguards against the barbarous surprises of the savage Indians."[87] One missionary reported that "the most sensible of our slaves, whom I have admitted to [the] Holy Sacrament have solemnly protested to me that if ever they hear of any ill design of the slaves, I shall know it from them that it may be prevented, and I can't but depend upon the truth of those words, knowing them to be exemplary and honest."[88]

The position of slave converts within the Anglican church was ambiguous. They were both part of the slaveholders' community and were excluded from it. They were invited within the family of the church, yet were rebuffed if they presumed familiarity. Baptized slaves stood with one foot within the door of the church and one outside with the rest of the slave community. This awkward stance served the interests of the slave society, for converts could not report the "ill design[s] of the slaves" if baptism allowed them to cease to be slaves themselves. What masters had not considered, however, was the fact that, because the converts lived in both worlds, they had not only divided identities but also divided loyalties.

The Kingdom of Heaven

The facet of the Anglican-slave relationship that is most difficult to recover is that of slaves' own experience. The few accounts that provide a slaves'-eye view of Anglicanism were published under the auspices of the evangelical churches and were shaped by their authors' later conversion from Anglican to evangelical forms of Christianity. For example, David George, a Baptist preacher in Sierra Leone in 1793, recalled that, while a slave in Virginia thirty years before, he had often walked "eight or nine miles" to attend services at "the English Church." But despite this apparent mark of devotion, George remembered himself at that time as "with out knowledge" because he "did not fear hell."[89]

Olaudah Equiano, who later became a Methodist, described his own state of mind immediately preceding his conversion to Anglicanism in 1759 at the age of fourteen:

---

87. Richard Ludlam, St. James Goose Creek, to the SPG, 3 July 1724, SPG records, microfilm, LC, Mss. B, vol. 4, Reel 59, 181.

88. Francis LeJau, St. James Goose Creek, to the SPG, 22 January 1714, quoted in Klingberg, *An Appraisal of the Negro*, 25.

89. "An Account of the Life of Mr. David George, from Sierra Leone in Africa; Given by Himself," in John Rippon, ed., *Baptist Annual Register* (London, 1793), 1, 473–84.

I could now speak English tolerably well, and perfectly understood everything that was said. I not only felt myself quite easy with these new countrymen, but relished their society and manners, I no longer looked upon them as spirits, but as men superior to us; and therefore I had the stronger desire to resemble them, to imbibe their spirit, and imitate their manners.[90]

While acknowledging their evangelical bias against the formal and emotionless Anglican liturgy, both of these descriptions suggest that what slaves may have sought and found in Anglicanism was less a spiritual than a cultural communion. Equiano closely equated his desire to become Christian with a desire to assimilate into the dominant culture. By becoming Anglican, slaves may have sought to gain membership in the slaveholders' cultural community and to secure a corresponding enhancement in their earthly condition.

Evidence of South Carolina slave converts' motives and aspirations are provided by instances in which slaves who were both baptized and manumitted changed their names. Six days after being freed, Abba Camfill was baptized into the Anglican church and exchanged her African first name for "Lucy."[91] Alexander Inglis's ex-slave Prince became "William" after baptism; Plymouth, who soon bought his freedom from Hester Dwight, was rechristened "Charles Cordes."[92] If the act of taking on a new name is symbolic of the rebirth that baptism ritually celebrates, it is significant that neither Abba, Plymouth, nor Prince chose to mark his or her conversion by assuming an overtly "Christian" name, such as that of a saint. Instead, the fellowship suggested by such names as "Lucy," "William," and "Charles Cordes" is of a secular and English communion. Cordes was, in fact, the surname of a prominent low-country family. In the year that Plymouth was reborn as Charles Cordes, two men surnamed Cordes were serving as assemblymen from St. John Colleton and St. John Berkeley and another was acting as Anglican churchwarden in the latter parish.[93]

As their masters had feared, many slave converts sought to interpret their ritual fellowship in the community of the ruling caste literally. Converted slaves may have seen themselves less as newborn Christians than

90. Olaudah Equiano, *The Interesting Narrative of the Life of Olaudah Equiano or Gustavus Vassa, the African, Written by Himself* (London, 1789), reprinted in Henry Louis Gates, ed., *Classic Slave Narratives* (New York, 1987), 51–52.
91. Miscellaneous Records, SCDAH, 30 June 1749, HH135. "Abba" (Thursday) was a common "day-name" for women in West Africa; see Wood, *Black Majority*, 183.
92. Miscellaneous Records, SCDAH, 14 July 1784, AAA67; and 19 September 1749, HH101.
93. Edgar and Bailey, eds., *Biographical Directory of the South Carolina House of Representatives*, 167–70.

as newborn Englishmen; more likely, slave converts would have had difficulty recognizing a distinction between the two. A Virginia parson, for example, wrote that in his opinion, "the greater part of [slave converts] . . . little mind the serious part, [and] only are in hopes that they will meet with so much the more respect, and that some time or other Christianity will help them to their freedom."[94]

In South Carolina, many slaves apparently felt that baptism gave them at least a claim to membership in the ruling caste and therefore removed, or at least loosened, the chains of their servitude. One slave who had been "baptized and instructed so that he was able to read and write well" refused to work and, armed with his Bible, wanted to "spend half the day in the shade with his devotions."[95] Other baptized slaves were reported to have refused to work on "the holy days" which, the resident minister reported, "greatly displeased the[ir] Masters."[96]

Slaveholders used such incidents to cast doubt upon the utility of baptizing any slaves at all. In 1752 Charles Martyn, parson at St. Andrew Parish, reported: "Masters seem[ed] rather averse to their [slaves] being admitted to the Christian faith; because after their admission . . . they become lazy and proud, entertaining too high an opinion of themselves and neglecting their daily labour."[97]

In an effort to placate the doubts of his slaveholder parishioners, one minister required would-be slave converts to make clear the break between religious communion and social community by including the following oath in the ceremony for adult slave baptism:

You declare in the Presence of God and before this Congregation that you do not ask for the holy baptism out of any design to free yourself from the Duty and Obedience you owe to your Master while you live, but meerly for the good of Your Soul and to partake of the Graces and Blessings promised to the Members of the Church of Jesus Christ.[98]

While Anglican parsons talked of the "Society of Christians," they made it plain that this was not a society of equals. After all, "ranks & orders" existed even in heaven among the angels. The place of Christian

94. Raboteau, Slave Religion, 123.
95. Theodore G. Tappert and John W. Doberstein, eds., The Journals of Henry Melchior Muhlenberg, 2 vols. (Philadelphia, 1942, 1958), 2, 637–38, quoted in Betty Wood, Slavery in Colonial Georgia, 1730–1775 (Athens, 1984), 163.
96. Francis LeJau, St. James Goose Creek, to the SPG, 9 February 1710, SPG records, microfilm, SCL-USC, Reel 3, 66–67.
97. Charles Martyn, St. Andrew, to the SPG, 25 June 1752, SPG records, microfilm, SCDAH, Reel 6, 320.
98. Bolton, Southern Anglicanism, 109.

slaves in the earthly religious hierarchy was equally plain. Moreover, in the rituals of the church slave converts were called upon to demonstrate their subordination to the religious and secular authorities. Anglican slaves were continually reminded of and ceremoniously accepted their low status. Slave church members sat in the gallery or in the aisles (they may even have stood while others sat), they were the first to enter, the last to leave, and the last to receive communion.

Slave converts who presumed to assert a social as well as a religious communion quickly discovered their mistake. But if their adoption into the Anglican church did not make slaves into honorary Englishmen, it did have the consequence of changing their perspective on the slave society and their own place within it. Baptized slaves were to some extent in a cultural "no man's land"; if they could not go forward into the community of the ruling class, it was equally impossible for them to return to where they had been.

The process of slave conversion had another consequence beyond that of teaching slaves to read and acquire a familiarity with the scriptures. The acquisition of literacy distinguished converts from the vast majority of unconverted and non-literate slaves. As was the case with Jesuit missionaries to the Indians, Anglican ministers were well aware of the "power of print."[99] The SPG authorized its missionaries "to give prayer books or other small tracts according to . . . [their] own discretion amongst such Negroes as are baptized and come constantly to church."[100] Equiano recalled that at the same time that he was baptized, the presiding minister gave him "a book . . . written by the Bishop of Sodor and Man."[101] Such small tokens marked the baptized slaves' separateness by providing them with tangible relics of their new religion to carry into the slave quarters.

For non-literate slaves, printed matter seemed imbued with spiritual

99. See James Axtell, "The Power of Print in the Eastern Woodlands," in Axtell, *After Columbus: Essays in the Ethnohistory of Colonial North America* (Oxford, 1988), 86–99.
100. "Minutes of the Meeting of the Society," 9 February 1710, SPG records, microfilm, SCL-USC, Reel 3, 66–67. Similarly, in 1745, Alexander Garden wrote the Society that "the poor Negroes [at the Charles Town "Negroe School"] are thankful for the books [you] sent them"; Alexander Garden to the SPG, 23 April 1745, SPG records, microfilm, SCL-USC, Reel 5, 38.
101. Equiano, *The Life of Olaudah Equiano*, 52. The book which Equiano received was probably the same one to which William Guy, minister of St. Andrew, referred in a 30 September 1742 letter to the SPG: "I have . . . dispersed a dozen of the Bishop of Sodor & Man's Essays towards an Instruction of the Indians among my Parishioners, and hope by the Blessing of God they will be of Great Service towards the Conversion of the Negroes (there being no Indians in my Parish)"; SPG records, microfilm, SCDAH, Reel 7. The tract was actually entitled *The Knowledge and Practice of Christianity Made Easy; or An Essay Towards an Instruction for the Indians* (London, 1741); Klingberg, *An Appraisal of the Negro*, 65–66 and note.

and temporal power. A slave woman's effort to save her husband, who was awaiting trial for arson, by stealing "away with [her master's copy of] the Negro Law" reveals an interesting conflation of the law as a tangible text and the law as abstract authority.[102] Similarly, most eighteenth-century slave narratives made reference to the "talking book." Equiano's version is typical:

> I had often seen my master . . . employed in reading; and I had a great curiosity to talk to the books, as I thought . . . [he] did; and so to learn how all things had a beginning. For that purpose I have often taken up a book, and talked to it, and then put my ears to it, when alone, in hopes it would answer me; and I have been very much concerned when I found that it remained silent.[103]

The religious nature of most printed matter and the fact that the church was the slaves' primary route to literacy may have enhanced the idea among slaves that print itself was somehow sacred.

But if literacy was a source of power and personal liberation for slave converts, it also alienated them from the majority of slaves. As Jean Comaroff notes, in a non-literate society the ability to read "transforms the consciousness of those who acquire it, setting it off, in unprecedented ways, from the world views of their . . . fellows."[104] By teaching would-be Anglican slaves to read, the conversion process may have weakened the converts' ties to the rest of the slave community, in which knowledge and religion were based upon an oral tradition. Perhaps the fate of Harry, the baptized slave teacher banished to the Charles Town "Mad house" in 1768, was a result of pressures accumulated during the quarter-century during which he lived a solitary life in the inhospitable terrain between the cultural lines.

That non-Christian slaves sometimes ridiculed baptized slaves' efforts to demonstrate publicly their new religion and literacy indicates the divisive effect conversions might have within the slave community. For example, Francis LeJau, minister to St. James Goose Creek, observed: "Our Baptized Negroes . . . have behaved themselves very well upon all

102. JGC, 6 February 1749, microfilm, SCDAH, 144.
103. Equiano, *The Life of Olaudah Equiano*, 43–44. For an interesting discussion of this point, see Henry Louis Gates's introduction to Charles T. Davis and Henry Louis Gates, Jr., eds., *The Slave's Narrative* (Oxford, 1985), xi–xxxiv.
104. Jean Comaroff, *Body of Power, Spirit of Resistance: The Culture and History of a South African People* (Chicago, 1985), 143; and Jack Goody and Ian Watt, "The Consequences of Literacy," in Goody, ed., *Literacy in Traditional Societies* (Cambridge, 1968), 27–68. See also Houston A. Baker, Jr., "Autobiographical Acts and the Voice of the Southern Slave," in Davis and Gates, eds., *The Slave's Narrative*, 242–61.

occasions, So as to disarm and silence envy itself. They pray'd and read some part of their Bibles in the field and in their quarters, in the hearing of those who could not read; and took no notice of some profane men who laught at their Devotions."[105] Similarly, another minister reported that one of the chief obstacles to preparing slaves for baptism was the fact that "all other slaves do laugh at them."[106] It is perhaps significant in this regard that one of the scriptural passages slaves were reported to recite at their baptism intoned that "whosoever believeth on him shall not be ashamed."[107]

Through their participation in church ceremonies and their outward conformity to Anglican doctrines of hierarchy, slave converts seemingly accepted their subordinate status and sanctified their servitude. In many ways, their struggle for respect earned them only rebuke from their masters and derision from many unconverted slaves. But Anglican slaves were not merely passive recipients of the dominant culture. Slave converts filtered the religious doctrines of the church through their own experience of the society and conditions in which they lived. It is possible to discern among Anglican slaves the shadows of a distinctive religious expression. The implications of black Anglicanism were not at all what the ministers of the established church had promised or what the slaveholders had hoped for.

Even conformity to Anglican doctrine and to the church's call for "Christian love and duty" could be used by slave converts as a source of power and as a critique of the social order. Slaves could hold their owners accountable to the standards of Christian behavior. For example, one minister reported the case of "a negro boy of 14 . . . [who,] being blamed by his mistress (as she was going to church) for some things he had done amiss, was heard to say, 'My mistress can curse and go to church.' "[108]

Slaves also could, through the ceremonies of the church, assert a spiritual equality with or even superiority to their masters. The Anglican communion rite conflated the secular and spiritual by evoking the patriarchal metaphor of genteel hospitality. In the house of God, an eighteenth-century commentator explained, "Christ is . . . the Master of the Feast, and . . . We are his Guests; 'tis his Table at which we are en-

105. Francis LeJau, St. James Goose Creek, to the SPG, 19 March 1716, SPG Records, microfilm, LC, Mss B., Vol. 4, Reel 59, No. 58.
106. Klingberg, *An Appraisal of the Negro*, 24 note.
107. William Guy, St. Andrew, to the SPG, 30 September 1742, SPG records, microfilm, SCDAH, Reel 7.
108. Francis Varnod, St. George Dorchester, to the SPG, 1 April 1724, quoted in Klingberg, *An Appraisal of the Negro*, 56.

tertained, his Provisions which we eat and drink; and we have the great Honor . . . of eating and drinking in his own Presence."[109] Wooden communion tables were almost indistinguishable from the tables found in gentry dining rooms and were similarly arrayed with linen table cloths. The silver cup and plate on which the sacrament was administered reinforced the idea of communion as a meal.[110] Ordinarily, slaves' only business in a gentry dining room would have been to wait upon the table; at the "Lord's supper," however, slaves broke bread with their masters.[111]

Like other forms of patriarchal benevolence, Christ's hospitality imposed reciprocal demands of loyalty and gratitude upon its recipients. The rituals of communion were fraught with great drama and solemnity in the eighteenth-century Anglican church. The sacrament was administered only four times in the year, at Easter, Whitsuntide (May), Michaelmas (September), and Christmas. Popular belief and Protestant doctrine agreed that to take communion lightly was to risk damnation. According to scripture, "he who eats and drinks in an unworthy manner eats and drinks judgement to himself."[112] An Anglican minister in Pennsylvania reported that "the dreadful Apprehensions which some People conceive about receiving [communion] unworthily, frighten many a religious well-meaning Person from the Lord's Table."[113] Similarly, colonial Virginians were said to consider communion "a dangerous thing to meddle with."[114]

To walk to the front of the church and kneel at "the holy table" was to testify to the rest of the onlooking congregation about the state of one's soul. Only those confident that they were in a state of "grace" were advised to take communion. A popular Anglican work counseled: "he that lives in the habitual practice of any known sin, without repentance, must not approach the holy table lest he be found to mock God, and

109. Thomas Bennet, *A Paraphrase with Annotations Upon the Book of Common Prayer*, 2nd. ed. (London, 1709), 303, quoted in Dell Upton, *Holy Things and Profane: Anglican Parish Churches in Colonial Virginia* (New York, 1986), 164.
110. A description of South Carolina's Anglican churches and chapels in 1765 noted that St. Philip's had "a very large Service of Plate" and described the plate at St. Michael's as "superb." Both were in Charles Town. Of the "Country Churches," it was only remarked that "All the Churches have a Service of Plate"; Hooker, ed., *The Carolina Backcountry*, 70–71, 75.
111. This paragraph draws upon the analysis found in Upton, *Holy Things and Profane*, 147–58, and 163–73.
112. I Corinthians 11:29.
113. Thomas Barton, Lancaster, Penn., to the SPG, 16 November 1764, quoted in Patricia U. Bonomi, *Under the Cope of Heaven: Religion, Society, and Politics in Colonial America* (Oxford, 1986), 89.
114. *The Life of Devereaux Jarrat* (Baltimore, 1806; rpt. New York, 1969), 102, quoted in Bonomi, *Under the Cope of Heaven*, 89.

contemn his authority."[115] Given this context, it is perhaps not surprising that most parishioners decided to remain in their pews when the sacrament was administered.

According to the missionaries' reports a significantly higher proportion of black Anglicans chose to take communion than was the case for the congregation at large.[116] Although slaves constituted only one-eighth of Anglican baptisms, they constituted a third of Anglican communicants.[117] In 1768, James Harrison reported the remarkable fact that in his parish the thirty-five slave communicants actually outnumbered whites who took the sacrament by a margin of two to one on most occasions.[118]

Slaves converts' greater participation in the sacrament may be indicative of their greater stake in the church and its rituals. In one sense, partaking in communion was an act of accommodation on the part of Anglican slaves. By accepting their place at the end of the communion line they symbolically accepted their place at the bottom of society. Similarly, because Anglicans were told not to come forward for communion if they had "any malice in . . . [their] hearts," black Anglicans' willingness to do so seemed publicly to demonstrate their "brotherly love" for the assembled congregation, white and black, master and slave.[119]

Yet, at the same time, slave communicants posed a silent challenge to the Anglican social order. When slaves knelt at the holy table while their

---

115. *The New Whole Duty of Man* (London, 1759), 143.
116. Ministers simultaneously gave the number of slave church members and that of slave communicants in two instances. In the first, Stephen Roe estimated he had 100 slave parishioners and 15 slave communicants (or 15 percent of the total); Stephen Roe, St. George Dorchester, to the SPG, 22 December 1741, SPG records, microfilm, SCL-USC, Reel 4, 138. In the other, James Harrison estimated that 30 (or 20 percent) of his 150 slave members were regular communicants; James Harrison, St. James Goose Creek, to the SPG, 8 August 1766, SPG records, microfilm, SCDAH, Reel 5. The aggregate average of these two estimates is 18 percent. In contrast, the average proportion of communicants among white church members (from four examples) was only 10 percent (with the largest single instance being 13 percent); John Fordyce, Prince Frederick, to the SPG, 25 July 1737, SPG records, microfilm, SCL-USC, Reel 3, 192; Stephen Roe, St. George Dorchester, to the SPG, 22 December 1741, ibid., Reel 4, 138; William Guy, St. Andrew, to the SPG, 26 March 1742, ibid., Reel 4, 144; Daniel Dwight, St. John Berkeley, to the SPG, 29 September 1747, ibid., Reel 5, 180. Patricia Bonomi and Peter R. Eisenstadt estimate the proportion of communicants among white members of the Anglican church in British North America at 26 percent, based on a survey of the Anglican *Notitia Parochialis* of 1724. However, in the one instance they provide in which slave and white communicants were both counted, slaves still took communion at a higher rate. See Bonomi and Eisenstadt, "Church Adherence in the Eighteenth-Century British Colonies," *William and Mary Quarterly*, 3rd ser. 39 (April 1982), 261 and appendix.
117. Slaves constituted 172 of 523 recorded communicants in a survey of 13 *Notitia Parochialis* written between 1738 and 1768.
118. Harrison noted that he had 35 "faithful" black communicants, 16 "constant" white communicants, and 16 whites who only took communion occasionally; quoted in Klingberg, *An Appraisal of the Negro*, 97–98.
119. *The Whole Duty of Man*, 85. For an exploration of the potential for coercion in the sacrament see Sabean, *Power in the Blood*, 38–60.

masters looked on, the back of the church momentarily became the front. By quietly asserting that they possessed a larger share of God's grace than those who occupied the largest pews, black Anglicans inverted the social pyramid and reminded the minister, their masters, and the rest of the congregation that in heaven, if not on earth, the last shall be first.

Some black Anglicans were not content to wait upon God's judgment but, strengthened by their faith, sought to enact their own vision of justice. In 1751, William Cotes, parson at St. George Dorchester, reported to the SPG that "a horrid practice of poisoning their masters, or those set over them . . . [had] lately prevailed among" the slaves of his parish.[120] The poisoners' most prominent victim was Colonel Joseph Blake, a member of the Governor's Council and owner of 283 slaves.[121] Among those sentenced to death for this notorious crime was a slave woman who was a baptized member of Cotes's church. In speaking with the woman while she awaited execution, Cotes was horrified to find that, far from instilling obedience and acceptance of her station, Christianity had helped provide her with the courage to act. He discovered that the woman, despite her crime, "still hoped to be saved because she believed in Christ." Cotes reported that he showed the woman her error and explained "the true import and meaning" of Christianity, until "she at last . . . made some kind of confession & desired to be remembered in our prayers."[122]

With Bibles and other religious tracts to take back to their quarters, slaves were free to ponder what they read and draw their own conclusions. Missionaries had encouraged converts to use religion as a source of strength against sin and the ridicule of the unconverted. The SPG told Anglican slaves that "by exercising their own Reason; by carefully reading and considering the *Bible*; [and] by praying earnestly to God . . . He will . . . afford them his assistance."[123] Ministers discovered, however,

120. William Cotes, St. George Dorchester, 2 December 1751, to the SPG, SPG records, microfilm, SCDAH, Reel 6, B19, 141; all of Cotes's references to this incident are taken from this letter.
121. Edgar and Bailey, eds., *Biographical Directory of the South Carolina House of Representatives*, 81–82. This was apparently not the first occasion on which Blake's slaves had sought to poison him. Seven years earlier, the newspaper reported that "an old Negro Man belonging to the hon. Joseph Blake, Esqr., was hanged in chains on a Gibbet near Dorchester" having attempted to poison his Master"; *South Carolina Gazette*, 30 July 1744.
122. In January 1752, the Assembly Journal recorded receipt of "an order of Magistrates & Freeholders for payment of the sum of eighty pounds to William Simmons (being for a Negro Woman executed for poisoning the honourable Joseph Blake, Esqr.)" The journal also recorded the execution of a slave man, Primus, for his part in the crime. *JCHA*, 9 and 23 January 1752, 36, 88–89.
123. "Directions to the Catechists for Instructing Indians, Negroes, &c.," in Dalcho, *An Historical Account of the Protestant Episcopal Church*, 49.

that the message many black Anglicans found in the writings of the church and the "assistance" they sought from God differed profoundly from the doctrine the parsons had propounded from their pulpits.

Far from sanctifying the status quo and celebrating the existence of "ranks & orders" in accord with mainstream Anglican doctrine, the God in whom black Anglicans found solace was profoundly disturbed by the state of the world and his church. Black Anglicans were not inspired by St. Paul's call for Christians to acknowledge earthly power and for servants to obey their masters; instead, their scriptural exegesis was focused on the Book of Revelations and the apocalypse. As Francis LeJau recorded:

> The best scholar of all the negroes in my parish and a very sober and honest liver, through his learning was like to create some confusion among all the negroes in this country. He had a book wherein he read some description of the several judgments that chastise men because of their sins in these latter days, that description made an impression upon his spirit, and he told his master abruptly there would be a dismal time and [the] moon would be turned into blood, and there would be a dearth of darkness and went away.[124]

LeJau reported that he confronted the slave "scholar" and "charged him not to put his own constructions upon his reading after that manner, and to be cautious not to speak so, which he promised to me." Nonetheless, he added, "some [other] negro overheard a part, and it was publically blazed abroad that an angel came and spake to the man. He had seen a hand that gave him a book; he had heard voices, seen fires, etc."

Given their very different perspectives, it is perhaps not surprising that slave converts saw their world in a light unlike that of their masters and ministers. What is significant, however, is the ability of black Anglicans radically to invert the Anglican message while remaining within Anglican (and Christian) religious discourse. Where the front of the church saw "duty," "love," and "obedience," at least some of the slaves attending in the gallery, aisles, or windows saw instead only "sin," "blood," and "darkness." Pondering black Anglicans' ability to find their own subversive truths in scripture, LeJau wondered if "it had been better if persons of a melancholy constitution . . . had never seen a book."[125]

In 1759, a black man used a mixture of religion and literacy to cast

124. Francis LeJau, St. James Goose Creek, to the SPG, 1 February 1709, quoted in Klingberg, *An Appraisal of the Negro*, 16.
125. Ibid., 17.

judgment upon the slaveholders themselves and to enlist God's help, not in the battle against sin, but against slavery. In February Richard Clarke, rector of St. Philip's Church in Charles Town, "preached some sermons in which he asserted that the world would soon be at an end" and predicted that "some great calamity would befall" South Carolina in September.[126] Soon, to the astonishment of his parishioners, Clarke began to act the part of an Old Testament prophet. According to Governor Henry Lyttleton, "he let his hair grow and ran about the streets of the city crying 'repent, repent, for the Kingdom of Heaven is at hand.' "[127] The strange affair appeared to have ended at the end of March when Clarke suddenly resigned his office and left the colony for England.

Three months later, however, the governor received word from the southern part of the colony that three black men (two free and one slave) had been charged with "promoting and encouraging an insurrection of the Negroes against the white people."[128] Traces of the strange doctrines propounded by Reverend Clarke were revealed when it was reported that Philip Johns, one of the free black men, had told slaves that "he had seen a vision, in which it was revealed to him, that in the month of September the White People should be all under ground, that the Sword should go through the land, & it should be no more White King's Governors or great men but the Negro's should live happily & have Laws of their own."[129]

In testimony gathered by the governor and council, several of Johns's slave listeners indicated that he had drawn inspiration and authority from a "written paper," which he passed among his non-literate audiences. The witnesses, for example, testified that:

[Johns] said to them that God Almighty had given much for them to do and he delivered to them a written paper and charged them to carry it to all the negroes and show it [to] them [and say] that Philip Johns told . . . [them] that the 1st day of June was fixed upon for killing the Buckraas [i.e., Whites] but afterwards told . . . [them] that it was agreed to wait till the corn was turned down . . . that the Justices before whom he had been had taken his paper from him but he did not care if the devil had it for

126. Governor Henry Lyttleton, Charles Town, to the Board of Trade, 1 September 1759, BPRO records, microfilm, SCDAH, CO5/376, D 438, 107–8.
127. Ibid.
128. JGC, June 20, 1759, original at SCDAH, microfilm LC, 105–6.
129. Governor Henry Lyttleton, to the Board of Trade, 1 September 1759, BPRO, microfilm, SCDAH, CO5/376, D438, 107–8. The Governor referred to the suspect as "Philip Jones"; the "Jones/Johns" confusion exists throughout the documentary record of this affair. The *South Carolina Gazette*, in its accounts of the incident, 18 August and 1 September 1759, uses "Johns"; I have followed this example.

he had another and would go to Charles Town with it and would do the work God Almighty had set him about [and] that in six weeks time all the Buckraas would be killed.[130]

Several factors suggest that Johns's "written paper" may have been a printed religious tract such as he might have purchased from booksellers in Charles Town. First, Johns cast his predictions in religious terms; he seems to have been influenced by Clarke in his prophecy of a September apocalypse. Second, he appeared to borrow authority from the "written paper" and use it almost as an talisman among the non-literate slaves. Finally, even after a magistrates court "had taken his paper from him," Johns was released with only a whipping. If the paper had contained overt plans of rebellion, Johns would surely have been executed—as he eventually was after his second arrest. But a millennial religious tract was sufficiently ambiguous and, in the eyes of the justices, legitimate for Johns to have escaped with a few stripes and a warning about the hazards of drawing faulty analogies.

The cases of Philip Johns and of Parson LeJau's "scholar" demonstrate that the cultural divide that separated black Anglicans from unconverted slaves and literate from oral culture could be breached. Slave converts may have sought to employ their literacy to gain status for themselves in the slave community. Although some unconverted slaves mocked the religious devotions or social aspirations of baptized slaves, most also privately acknowledged the supernatural "power of print." The use of "scraps" of print as religious talismans and belief in "literary magic" were common in the region of West Africa from which many of South Carolina's African slaves were drawn.[131]

In his plan for gradually converting the slaves of the low country, Commissary Alexander Garden had hoped that slaves educated at his school would "read the Bible . . . and other proper tracts . . . at evenings and other spare hours" to the remainder of the slave population. Garden had assumed however, that his pupils would be merely passive conduits of received Anglican doctrine, parsons' mouthpieces multiplied. But the

130. JGC, July 9, 1759, microfilm, LC, 110–11. An interesting parallel that illuminates this episode can be found in the chapter in *Power in the Blood* in which a German vintner, who was an avid reader of religious tracts, made prophecies of impending doom which have politically subversive undertones; Sabean, *Power in the Blood*, 61–93.
131. Jack Goody, "Restricted Literacy in Northern Ghana," in Goody and Watt, eds., *Literacy in Traditional Societies*, 199–246. In an analysis of the eighteenth-century South Carolina slave trade, Daniel Littlefield estimates that one-third of the slaves imported from Africa to the low country in the 1750s came from the "Windward Coast" region of West Africa, approximately the same area covered by Goody's study; see Daniel C. Littlefield, *Rice and Slaves: Ethnicity and the Slave Trade in Colonial South Carolina* (Baton Rouge, 1981), 125.

message which black Anglicans received from their Bibles and delivered to their listeners was shaped by their experience at the bottom of the Anglican social pyramid and was quite unlike that which the ministers had sent down from above. While the ritual aspects of Anglicanism may have acted to divide the slave community, the shared experience of slavery bound black Anglicans and unconverted Africans together. They found common ground in their hope for a better world to come.

Communion and Community

An examination of the relationship among the Anglican church, the masters, and the slaves reveals both the possibilities and the limitations of cultural hegemony in a colonial slave society. In the eighteenth century, the slave society of the South Carolina low country was sharply divided into two cultural communities: white, "English" masters and black, "African" slaves. But the boundaries between these two communities were not impermeable. The creation, through miscegenation, of an intermediate category between white and black, English and African, immediately foreclosed any thought of strictly dividing the society along absolute lines of culture, race, and freedom.

Such a stark divide would have worked against the interest of masters by placing the entire body of slaves into the alien camp. Instead, masters sought, through the selective adoption of slaves into the Anglican communion, to incorporate chosen segments of the slave population into their own ritual community and to blur the boundary between the dominant culture and the culture of the dominated.

Anglican missionaries, acting on behalf of the metropolitan power, wanted to create an expansive church that offered the entire population of the slaves an opportunity to partake in the Anglican communion. Masters disagreed. For them, a universal church would have been at best useless and at worst dangerous to the social order of the slave society, because it might have allowed the church to become an independent source of social self-esteem for slaves and would have made it difficult to prevent the intervention of the metropolitan church on behalf of its slave membership. Masters much preferred to limit church membership to a chosen few who, through their assimilation into the dominant culture, could serve as useful and reliable intermediaries between masters and the unassimilated majority of the slave population.[132]

132. Stuart Schwartz has depicted a similar process of differentiation through conversion at work in the slave society of colonial Brazil: "As pagans, Indians and Africans were

If most slave converts accepted and desired the enhancement in status and self-esteem church membership offered, they did not always then become the loyal supporters of the social order their masters had sought. Interpreting the church's teachings in their own way, some black Anglicans were able to reject the subordinate and submissive implications of Christian doctrine and sought to take their own, often subversive, message to the slave community outside the doors of the church.

---

outside the limits of the body politic. But as Christians, they had to be found a place. Religious orthodoxy and acceptance of European culture became measures by which they were judged. Distinctions between *gentios* (gentiles) and *indios aldeados* (village Indians) or between *bocal* (newly arrived) and *ladino* (acculturated) Africans were essentially cultural rankings to mark off those within and those outside or almost outside society. Once part of society, Indians or Africans could simply be placed in the existing hierarchy as new corporations, strata derived by color." Schwartz, *Sugar Plantations in the Formation of Brazilian Society*, 249–50.

[4]

Mastering Money:
Slavery and the Market

For three centuries, in slavery and in freedom, black women have been making and selling sea grass baskets in Charleston and the adjacent low country. Broad and shallow "fanner baskets," used to separate the rice grain from the chaff, were included among a deceased planter's effects as early as 1730.[1] In 1766, planter Henry Ravenel noted in his "Day Book" that he had paid one of his slaves, Lucrecia, two-and-a-half shillings "for a Baskt."[2] Eight years later, another master carefully recorded sums ranging from three to nine shillings that he "pade for baskets" made by his slaves.[3] In recent years, the sea grass baskets of the low country have been widely recognized and celebrated as an important expression of African-American folk art.[4]

For many low-country inhabitants, white and black, the baskets and their makers have become a familiar and welcome sign of home. Driving

1. Peter H. Wood, " 'It Was a Negro Taught Them': A New Look at Labor in Early South Carolina," *Journal of Asian and African Studies* 9 (1974), 172.
2. Entry of 14 March 1766, Day Book of Henry Ravenel [1744–1785], SCHS.
3. Dale Rosengarten, *Row upon Row: Sea Grass Baskets of the South Carolina Lowcountry* (Columbia, 1986), 14–15.
4. The most comprehensive treatment of sea grass baskets and their makers is Rosengarten, *Row upon Row*. Other writings on low-country basketry include: Gerald L. Davis, "Afro-American Coil Basketry in Charleston County, South Carolina," in Don Yoder, ed., *American Folklife* (Austin, Texas, 1976), 151–84; Skip Rozin, "The Handmade Baskets of Charleston," *New York Times*, 13 February 1983; John Michael Vlach, *By the Work of Their Hands: Studies in Afro-American Folklife* (Charlottesville, 1991), 20–23; and Wood, " 'It Was a Negro Taught Them,' " 159–79.

"past the shopping malls and subdivisions" outside of Charleston, Dale Rosengarten writes, "you might not know what state you were in, if it weren't for the palmetto trees and the basket stands."[5] The baskets are a marker of identity and cultural persistence as well as a source of income for the women who make them and for the low-country black community as a whole. In 1983, one of the basketmakers proudly declared: "These baskets are special things . . . something the slaves brought over from Africa. . . . As long as nobody takes our baskets away from Charleston, away from me and the black people here, then we'll never be obsolete. These baskets are part of us."[6] Perhaps significant in this regard is the fact that low-country slaves referred to their personal, African-derived names (as opposed to the Anglophone names given them by their masters) as their "basket names."[7]

Today, baskets are made and displayed each day at the nineteenth-century market house in Charleston, at the corner of Broad and Meeting in the center of the city's historic district, and at roadside stands set up along U.S. highway 17 at the north end of the Cooper River bridge. The basketmakers are local black women, generally middle aged or older. They work surrounded by completed baskets, which are laid out on the ground or hang from wooden frames. As passing tourists examine their wares, the women take bundles of dried sea grass and pine straw from a box at their feet and carefully shape them into the tight coils that will eventually form a new basket.

The women who tend the basket stalls are as adept at selling their baskets as they are in making them. "The basket sellers, like other marketeers," one scholar notes, "are professionals in the art of bargaining."[8] As all basket prices are negotiable, the bargaining process is something of a contest between the tourist-buyer and the basketmaker-seller. Because the basketmakers have a keen sense of the worth of their product, and because their pride as well as their income is at stake, they are seldom mastered in these negotiations.[9]

5. Rosengarten, *Row upon Row*, 5.
6. Quoted in Rozin, "The Handmade Baskets of Charleston," 10, 30. Likewise, a basket I purchased in 1991 carried a tag that described "Historic Sweet Grass Baskets" as "a craftsmanship handed down from generation to generation by slaves from West Africa" and added that "though the art is hundreds of years old, it has never changed and is found only in this part of the U.S.A."
7. Charles Joyner, *Down by the Riverside: A South Carolina Slave Community* (Chicago, 1984), 217–18.
8. Patricia Jones-Jackson, *When Roots Die: Endangered Traditions in the Sea Islands* (Athens, 1987), 21.
9. Of course, each "contest" between tourist and basketseller takes place within the public space of the market and has a social context. Patricia Jones-Jackson notes that "it is a bad reflection on one's selling skills to be pressured into parting with a basket at a price lower

The basketmakers prize the ability to shape the product of their labor and to set the terms under which it is sold, as much as the money that they earn. As one of them put it, "You can make your basket the way you want and you can make 'em the price you want."[10] The wide degree of self-control and self-esteem basketry provides is in sharp contrast to the low-paid work (often as maids or nannies in the homes of wealthy Charleston whites) that is otherwise available to the basket women and their peers. Basketmakers disparagingly term such employment "working for nothing."[11] The expression "working for nothing," applied to labor that is financially rewarded (albeit often at the minimum wage), may at first seem inappropriate. But, like their eighteenth-century ancestors, the basket women do not consider money to be the sole object of their labor. Menial labor as "domestics," for example, might be said to offer "nothing" because the small financial gains it promises are canceled out by the requisite loss of autonomy.

The basket women, like the rest of the low country's inhabitants, are enmeshed in the contradictions and ambiguities engendered by a market economy. As a *place*, the market offers autonomy and opportunity to the basketmakers and other traders. Likewise, in the contingent and contested terrain of market relations, which are negotiated day-to-day in the marketplace and elsewhere, people appear to enjoy a wide discretion as consumers of commodities and as sellers of their labor or its product. As a *process*, however, the market is controlled by large and impersonal forces that act to perpetuate economic and social inequalities and to limit and constrain the choices and opportunities that the marketplace seemingly promises. The attraction of basket making is in part derived from the lack of other employment opportunities for low-country black women. For the basket women and their community, therefore, the "freedom" of the market is tightly woven within narrow limits whose boundaries are dictated by structures far beyond any individual's control.[12]

The colonial slave society was also situated at the nexus of markets large and small. Colonial South Carolina was itself a product of larger Atlantic, and ultimately global, market forces. As Peter Coclanis has noted, "It was the expansion of the market economy in the West that

than that established by the community; such an act may bring censure from . . . [other] members of the [basketmaking] community." Ibid., 21–22.

10. Quoted in Rosengarten, *Row upon Row*, 37.

11. Kay Young Day, "My Family Is Me: Women's Kin Networks and Social Power in a Black Sea Island Community" (Ph.D. diss., Rutgers University, 1983), 21.

12. The distinction between the market as a *place* and the market as a *process* is detailed in Jean Christophe-Agnew, *Worlds Apart: The Market and the Theater in Anglo-American Thought, 1550–1750* (Cambridge, 1986), 17–56.

brought Europeans to South Carolina originally."[13] The same forces soon led Europeans colonists to bring Africans as slaves to the low country. Throughout the colonial era, and indeed throughout the history of slavery in South Carolina, the plantations of the low country were organized for the production of commodities that were exported for profit to the wider world.[14]

A keen desire for economic accumulation and a belief that property was "sacred" were part of the English inheritance and identity of colonial South Carolina's masters. According to eighteenth-century theorists, the practice of commerce embodied the highest level of human civilization, and respect for the "law of the market" was both the marker and the maker of a civil society.[15] When they compared Charles Town to other "large trading places," colonial South Carolinians asserted that their colony had also progressed to this ultimate stage.[16] The conflation of Anglicization, civility, and commerce in colonial South Carolina is, perhaps, best encapsulated in the last public building erected in Charles Town before the Revolution: the lavishly appointed Exchange house, which still stands at the east end of Broad Street.[17]

The market had two faces and two very different meanings to colonial South Carolina's slaves. On one hand, the market as a *process* controlled by larger economic forces forged the chains of their servitude. Slavery, as well as the ongoing African slave trade, could not have existed or long continued outside the Atlantic economy and the dictates of what has been termed "the modern World System."[18] Without these macroeconomic forces there would have been no new world slavery and perhaps no "new world." Likewise, the need to balance their accounts, both

13. Peter A. Coclanis, *Shadow of a Dream: Economic Life and Death in the South Carolina Low Country, 1670–1920* (Oxford, 1989), 31.
14. See Coclanis, *Shadow of a Dream*, 48–110; and also John J. McCusker and Russell R. Menard, *The Economy of British America, 1607–1789* (Chapel Hill, 1985), 169–88.
15. See J. G. A. Pocock, *Virtue, Commerce, and History: Essays on Political Thought and History Chiefly in the Eighteenth Century* (Cambridge, 1985), 114–19; and also Joyce Chaplin, *An Anxious Pursuit: Agricultural Innovation and Modernity in the Lower South, 1730–1815* (Chapel Hill, 1993), 23–33.
16. *South Carolina Gazette*, 19 March 1763. For an intriguing discussion of how South Carolinians reconciled slavery and modernism in this era, see Chaplin, *An Anxious Pursuit*, 53–65.
17. An English visitor to Charleston in 1774 described the newly completed "royal exchange and custom house" as "a very substantial handsome large building of brick, faced with stone round the arches of the windows, etc.," but noted regretfully that while the building "cuts a very good appearance all up and down . . . [Broad] street," its construction blocked what would otherwise have been "a fine prospect of the bay"; H. Roy Merrens, ed., *The Colonial South Carolina Scene: Contemporary Views, 1697–1774* (Columbia, 1977), 281–82.
18. Immanuel Wallerstein, *The Modern World-System II: Mercantilism and the Consolidation of the European World Economy, 1600–1750* (New York, 1980), chap. four.

with their neighbors and with their English creditors, often led masters to convert their human property into cash. The market posed a constant threat to every slave family and all slaves' hopes for their posterity. On the other hand, the market as a *place*, and day-to-day market relations, could offer slaves a degree of autonomy, self-control, and *de facto* freedom within the confines of their condition. The collision and collusion between these two sides of the market and the contradictory dictates of market relations played an important role in the social order of the slave society.

Agents of Property

As *chattel personal*, low-country slaves were only too aware of the shadow that market processes cast over every black family and household. All slaves constantly faced the threat of being brought to the public vendue house in Charles Town and auctioned to satisfy their masters' debts or heirs, or merely to further their masters' acquisitive endeavors. Slaves were regarded as property, first, last, and always. The Negro Act defined slaves as "subjects of property in the hands of particular persons." Therefore, before slaves could attempt to use the "law of the market" to their own advantage, they had to perform something of a sleight of hand. Transcending, or at least disguising, their legal condition as property, slaves had to become property owners, not only objects "in the hands" of others but agents in their own behalf. The first step in this process was the acquisition of property.

Most low-country slaves became possessors of property through a method as simple as it was irrepressible. On Sundays, or in the evenings after they had completed their daily labors in the plantation fields, slaves often did not put down their hoes but rather went to work for themselves cultivating small gardens beside their homes or on nearby "vacant" land.[19] Alternately, slaves could spend their evenings engaged in other activities, such as raising poultry or livestock or producing handicrafts. The products of their labors could be eaten to supplement the rations slaves drew from their masters, or they could become the basis for trade to obtain clothes and other manufactures. The desire to produce, to possess, and to trade was so common in new world slave societies as to suggest that it constitutes a universal expression of the human spirit.[20]

19. See Philip D. Morgan, "Work and Culture: The Task System and the World of Low-country Blacks, 1700–1880," *William and Mary Quarterly*, 3rd series, 39 (October 1982), 537–74.
20. Recent works that demonstrate the breadth and significance of slaves' role in the "do-

Evidence of low-country slaves' engagement in such activities dates from the earliest decades of the colony. In 1712, Anglican missionaries reported that slaves were commonly allowed time to "plant for themselves as much as will cloath and subsist themselves and their family." The parsons complained that when they pressed slave converts to cease their labors and to respect the Sabbath, the slaves "always have it to say" that it would be unjust to deny them the liberty to spend their Sunday afternoons working for themselves.[21]

Two years later, perhaps persuaded by the clergy's sabbatarian campaign, but perhaps merely seeking to render slaves legally more dependent upon their owners, the assembly declared it unlawful for slaves to "plant for themselves any corn, peas or rice."[22] However, this act, like many others, was a dead letter. Records indicate that slaves continued to cultivate provision grounds and garden plots with their masters' consent and cooperation. In 1751, for example, Johann Bolzius noted that "after they have done their required day's work" slaves were "given as much land as they can handle" on which to grow food for themselves.[23] A generation later, a visitor to the North Carolina low country watched as slaves who had completed their work in their master's fields diligently tended their own "little piece[s] of land." Comparing the state of slaves' gardens to the plantation fields, the visitor concluded that slaves were "much better [farmers] than their Master."[24]

In their private plots, slaves generally chose to plant a diversity of crops rather than to concentrate on one or two staples. In their gardens, Johann Bolzius observed, slaves "plant for themselves corn, potatoes, tobacco, peanuts, water and sugar melons, pumpkins, [and] bottle pumpkins (sweet ones and stinking ones which are used as milk and drink vessels and for other things)."[25] Other crops grown by the slaves "for themselves" included peas, rice, and peppers.[26] The variety of produce

mestic economy" of slave societies include: Ira Berlin and Philip D. Morgan, eds., *Cultivation and Culture: Labor and the Shaping of Slave Life in the Americas* (Charlottesville, 1993); Larry E. Hudson, Jr., ed., *Working toward Freedom: Slave Society and Domestic Economy in the American South* (Rochester, Ill., 1994); Betty Wood, *Women's Work, Men's Work: The Informal Slave Economies of Lowcountry Georgia* (Athens, 1995).

21. "The Instructions of the Clergy of South Carolina Given to Mr. Johnston [1712]," SPG, microfilm, LC, A8 429.

22. *Statutes*, 7, 11, 368.

23. Klaus Gloewald, Beverly Starika, and Paul S. Taylor, ed. and trans., "Johann Martin Bolzius Answers a Questionnaire on Carolina and Georgia," *William and Mary Quarterly*, 3rd series, 14 (April 1959), 259.

24. Evangeline Walker Andrews and Charles McLean Andrews, eds., *Journal of a Lady of Quality* [Janet Schaw] (New Haven, 1923), 176–77.

25. Gloewald, Starika, and Taylor, ed. and trans., "Bolzius Answers a Questionnaire," 259.

26. Morgan, "Work and Culture," 573–74.

that they were able to harvest from their gardens allowed slaves to keep their options open. They could use the product of their provision grounds for their own consumption or to trade. Slaves added variety both to their diet and to their merchantable wares and did not depend upon one crop as their sole source of either cash or calories.

Keeping domesticated animals afforded slaves another avenue for the accumulation of goods to consume or to trade. The law apparently conceded to slaves the right to keep poultry, but not larger livestock. Laws repeatedly prohibited slaves from keeping "any stock of hogs, cattle, or horses."[27] But slaves (and their masters) evaded these legal restrictions. In 1740, the Negro Act complained that in spite of previous laws, "owners of slaves have permitted them . . . to breed and raise horses, neat cattle and hogs."[28] The new slave code was no more successful in this regard than its predecessors. In 1772, for instance, the Charles Town grand jury complained yet again of "Negroes being allowed to keep Horses & carry Firearms contrary to Law."[29]

Masters probably permitted slaves to circumvent the laws against accumulating and holding property because it suited their own immediate goals to do so. As such activities were confined to the slaves' "free" time and to "waste" ground, they came at no cost to the master and may have promised a more contented labor force.[30] Masters also hoped that allowing their slaves to acquire property would strengthen their own hand in other negotiations. At the turn of the nineteenth century, one Carolina planter wrote that slaves would be reluctant to run away if they had "too much property to leave"; a generation earlier another planter described her slaves as very "attached to their homes and the little they have there."[31]

Masters defended their slaves' right to property when it was threatened by the law or its agents. In February 1749 Ammon, a slave belonging to Thomas Akin, gave testimony in a slave conspiracy investigation and was asked "where he got the rice which he had sold

---

27. According to a law of 1734, patrollers were to confiscate "all fowls and other provisions" found in the possession of "straggling negroes." But this statute was aimed more at stopping clandestine trading than at prohibiting poultry raising. Otherwise, the law makes no mention of slaves keeping poultry. *Statutes,* 3, 398, 489; and 7, 368, 382.

28. *Statutes,* 7, 409.

29. Presentments of the Grand Jury of Charles Town, 24 January 1772, Journal of the Court of General Session (Charles Town), 1769–1776, 170, SCDAH.

30. Sidney Mintz notes: "From the master's short term perspective, whatever kept the slaves contented and spirited, without reducing the real available labor supply or raising the cost of labor was good." Sidney Mintz, "Slavery and the Rise of Peasantries," *Historical Reflections* 1 (Summer 1979), 241.

31. William Read to Jacob Read, 12 March 1800, Read Family Papers, SCHS; Eliza Lucas Pinckney to Thomas Pinckney, 17 May 1779, Pinckney Family Papers, SCHS, 38–3–6.

to [his brother] Joe?" Ammon answered "that the rice was his own and that he had planted it himself in his own time and by his Masters allowance and leave." The journal recorded that Akin, who was apparently standing nearby, "acknowledged [this] . . . to be true." Although legally Ammon could neither grow rice for himself or sell it to his brother, the Council was satisfied and asked no further questions on the matter.[32] A few months earlier, Edmund Atkin had petitioned the governor and council complaining that a passing slave patrol had abused one of his slaves who was "then peaceably and quietly in . . . [his] plantation." After whipping the slave, the patrollers "also broke open a box, and took away several things belonging to the said Negro." Ignoring the fact that his slave could not legally possess property, much less be the victim of theft, Atkin wanted the patrollers charged with "breach of the patrol laws." Significantly, Atkin went on to justify this selective enforcement of the statutes in a way that might well speak for all planters in their reasoning about slave property holding. "Slaves," he argued, "have undoubtedly a right to their master's protection from abuse when they do not offend against the laws, and, . . . it much concerns the public welfare also, that they should not be dissatisfied in their state of slavery."[33]

The law acknowledged slaves' "right to their master's protection" in a legal fiction that founded slaves' enjoyment of property firmly upon the sufferance of their owners. Although slaves were barred from owning property *de jure*, they could still be allowed *de facto* possession of it. Hence the master of any slave whose goods were impounded could recover them by testifying that "the . . . [confiscated] goods were in the possession of the said slave . . . to be kept *bona fide*, for my use, . . . and not for the use or benefit of any slave whatsoever."[34] When both slaves and slaves' property belonged by law to the master, what any master chose to do with his or her goods was considered a private affair.

In law, masters' power over slaves' property was deemed to be absolute, but within plantation boundaries matters were conducted quite differently. In everyday practice, slaves' property right rested on slaves' own determination. Masters who wished to avoid trouble were careful to acknowledge their slaves' claims to property. When organizing a transfer of slaves from one of his plantations to another, for example, Henry Laurens advised his overseer that "it will be kind in you

32. JGC, 7 February 1749, microfilm, LC, 160.
33. JGC, 20 December 1748, microfilm, LC, 3–4.
34. *Statutes*, 7, 409.

& quiet their Minds much, if you will see all their Little Estates packed up. Take an Account of them & give the strongest assurances that each Man's property shall be safely deliver'd to them." Laurens's final word of advice indicates that slaves held their property in family groups. "Pitch upon Married Men," he wrote, when choosing who was to be transferred first, for "their Wives will give an eye to their respective goods."[35]

Laurens's remark suggests that the desire to "quiet ... [slaves'] minds" and to avoid trouble led most masters to recognize slaves' claims to property. By threatening disruption and conflict to any master or overseer who encroached upon it, slaves themselves took on the major burden of defending their property right. When masters failed to acknowledge slave property, slaves could be quick to make their feelings known. In 1781, for example, the newspaper printed an account of "a disturbance that happened ... amongst the negroes on Dr. Carson's estate on John's Island."[36] According to the *Gazette*, "the negroes ... that morning attacked the overseer ..., with hoes, axes, and poles." Even after one of them was killed and two were wounded, the enraged slaves pressed their attack, "one attempting to cut ... [the overseer's] throat with a rice hook, another to beat out his brains with his own musket while others were mauling him with his own powder horn and sticks." Amidst this "confusion and bustle" the overseer somehow broke free, "took to his heels," and escaped. Hearing of the trouble on Carson's plantation, which was adjacent to his own, the paper's correspondent rode over to investigate. "The negroes," he wrote, "appeared to be in a state of madness which conveyed an idea of an insurrection amongst them, and made me at a loss how to act."

In the end, the local militia was called to the scene. Upon their arrival the next morning, the militiamen "secured seven of the ringleaders," and the following day a magistrates' court hurriedly convened and tried the prisoners on the spot. After what the paper assured its readers was "a fair and candid examination," the magistrates sentenced one of the prisoners to be put to death, another to be "cropped and branded," and the rest to be "severely flogged." These draconian measures restored order, but the disruption and two deaths were described as a "heavy loss" to the plantation's owner. "The ostensible cause" of the "insurrection," the report concluded, "was because the overseer wanted to remove the corn of seven negroes who had the

35. Henry Laurens to Theodore Rossel, 8 April 1766, *PHL*, 5, 99–100.
36. *South Carolina and American General Gazette*, 20 January 1781. All the following references to this incident are taken from this source.

evening before gone off in a boat." Perhaps this sort of "disturbance" is what a nineteenth-century low-country slave was hinting at when he testified that any "master who would take property from his slaves would have a hard time."[37]

The repetitious complaints of grand juries and the reenactment of apparently futile laws suggest that masters were less troubled by the practice of slaves producing and claiming property than they were by the thought (or sight) of slaves using the fruits of their labor to gain independent access to the market. From the slaves' perspective, any surplus beyond what they or their families required for subsistence was of limited value if it could not be traded for other, less perishable, goods. Some small-scale trade was possible within the slave quarters. A slave could give fowls or peppers in exchange for corn, or trade a hog or a calf for a basket or a canoe. But the manufactured goods and "creature comforts" which slaves most lacked and most wanted could only be obtained through trade with the world outside the plantation.

Slaves who sought to participate in market exchange did not lack opportunities. White shopkeepers and laborers were ready to accept slaves' goods and asked few questions. As early as 1686, the assembly prohibited trade with servants or slaves.[38] In 1738, the assembly passed an act to prevent "Hawkers Pedlars and petty Chapmen" from trading with slaves; these men, the act claimed, traveled "from one plantation to another, both by land and water, exposing to sale rum, sugar, and other goods, wares, and merchandises, and take in payment, therefore, from negroes and other slaves, hogs, fowls, rice, corn and other produce, to the great prejudice of the planters their masters."[39] As with provision grounds, the passage of laws could not stem the flood, and the complaint of "evil disposed persons in the Country who make a Common Practice of selling Rum to Slaves" soon became familiar.[40]

Most bargains struck in this manner were undoubtedly small in scale. In 1749, for example, a white man accused of trying to persuade slaves to run away testified that he had given a slave a small hog in exchange "for a Deers skin and upon no other account whatsoever."[41] But the cumulative effects of such petty trading might still reach quite large proportions. In 1775, the Beaufort Grand Jury condemned "the abominable custom of several petty traders, who settle in every parish and carry on

37. Philip D. Morgan, "The Ownership of Property by Slaves in the Mid-Nineteenth-Century Low Country," *Journal of Southern History* 49 (August 1983), 411.
38. *Statutes*, 2, 22.
39. *Statutes*, 3, 487–90.
40. JGC, 30 October 1752, microfilm, LC, 462.
41. JGC, 30 January 1749, microfilm, LC, 85.

a clandestine trade with Negroes. . . . By which method [these illicit traders] generally have several hundred bushels of corn, and other provisions to sell, at a time when perhaps no planter in the parish has a bushel to spare."[42]

An idea of what slaves may have sought to obtain through such market transactions can be seen in the account "Muso, [a] Negroe Fellow," kept with a low-country storekeeper.[43] In February 1773, Muso entered Edward Telfair's store in Savannah and purchased (apparently on credit) one pound of "pigtail tobacco," two jackets, a one-shilling knife, and three "gallons West India Rum." On April 15, he returned to the store for another half-pound of tobacco. In May, he was back for three more gallons of rum, another knife, and four shillings' worth of nails. The next month, Telfair credited Muso with a further three gallons of rum, another half-pound of tobacco, and a "Cuttoe knife." By year's end, Muso had visited Telfair's store nine times and had been credited with purchasing over four-and-a-half pounds' worth of goods.[44]

The ability to purchase small items through trade could have a considerable impact on slaves' lives. The large quantities of pipe fragments discovered in two excavations of eighteenth-century low-country slave quarters, for example, led archaeologists to speculate that "pipe smoking . . . played a major role in [slaves'] leisure time activities."[45] But before they could enjoy a quiet smoke in the evening or treat friends to a pipe of tobacco, slaves had first to gain access to the market.

Slaves found other avenues to trade besides those offered by white "Chapmen." A constant and clandestine traffic was carried on between plantation slaves and their city counterparts. In 1744, for example, the grand jurors complained of "Negroes being allowed to go from town into the country, under the pretence of picking myrtle berries etc., and who at the same time carry rum and other goods to trade with Negroes

---

42. *South Carolina Gazette and Country Journal*, 13 June 1775.

43. Edward Telfair Papers, WPL-DU. Telfair kept a store in Savannah, Georgia. It is possible that "Muso" was a free black man and not a slave. Interestingly, however, the former slave Olaudah Equiano described a visit he made to Savannah in 1767 during which he "went to a friend's house to lodge, whose name was Mosa, a black man [and a slave]"; Olaudah Equiano, *The Interesting Narrative of the Life of Olaudah Equiano or Gustavus Vassa, the African, Written by Himself* (London, 1789) reprinted in Henry Louis Gates, Jr., ed., *The Classic Slave Narratives* (New York, 1987), 117. Perhaps Equiano's "Mosa" and Telfair's "Muso" were in fact the same person.

44. Ibid. The total was £4.13s.9d. In October Muso bought a "scarlet cloak," and in November "1 Quire post papers."

45. Thomas R. Wheaton et al., *Yaughan and Curiboo Plantations: Studies in Afro-American Archaeology* (Marietta, Ga., 1983), 265; and also Lesley M. Drucker and Ronald W. Anthony, *The Spiers Landing Site: Archaeological Investigations in Berkeley County, South Carolina* (Columbia, 1979), 122.

in the country."[46] Similarly, plantation slaves with access to Charles Town may have sought to act as retailers to their country fellows. In 1765, for example, Amos, one of Henry Laurens's slaves, was said to have "a great inclination to turn Rum Merchant." Laurens instructed his overseer "to search narrowly & if he has more than One bottle to seize it. I suspect he has or may send up some by my flat Boat to Mr. Mayrant's Landing."[47]

The slaves with the greatest opportunity to travel between Charles Town and the plantations were the crews of the boats that plied the colony's rivers. Many of these boats had no white crewmen at all and were regarded as notorious conduits for this illicit trade.[48] Laurens had particular difficulties in this regard, and warned his overseer "to give a watchful eye to the behaviour of Abraham [Laurens's boat captain] & his gang. I will have no traffick carried on by them & he is so very sly & artful that you will find all your skill necessary to counteract him. If he or any one of his people are detected in any trade or trick don't spare them."[49]

Masters sought to deny their slaves access to the market for several reasons. Many masters feared that their slaves would be "debauched" by market exchange, by which they meant that they would develop so strong an appetite for market goods that they would be led "to steal and robb their masters of their corn, poultry, and other provisions" in order to have goods to barter.[50] Masters may also have resented the role the market could play as a source of self-esteem and material improvement that did not require slaves to go cap in hand to the great house.

Masters' initial response to this challenge was to attempt to prohibit slaves' access to the market by making such trading (and indeed all slave property) illegal. In the assembly, the slave society's representatives proclaimed in their laws that the masters' authority was absolute and that slaves were to look to the great house for all things. While such proclamations may have assuaged masters' pride, they had little practical effect in stemming the tide of trade. In 1751, the assembly fi-

46. *South Carolina Gazette*, 5 November 1744.
47. Henry Laurens to Abraham Schad, 30 April 1765, *PHL*, 4, 616.
48. For examples of boats without white crewmen, see *South Carolina Gazette*, 3 April 1762 and 30 April 1771, and also JGC, 25 January 1744, microfilm, LC, 69. In 1785, the inhabitants of St. James Santee Parish petitioned the assembly "that patroons [i.e., boat captains] of schooners and other small craft are allowed (as they pass and repass up and down our rivers) to trade, traffick, barter, and sell to and with Negroes to the great prejudice of their owners"; South Carolina Assembly Petitions, 1785–100–01, SCDAH.
49. Henry Laurens to John Smith, 5 September 1765, *PHL*, 5, 2–3.
50. *South Carolina Gazette*, 5 November 1744.

nally acted to bring the law more in line with practice and conceded to slaves the right to grow and to trade "rice or Indian corn" provided it was done with their master's permission.[51] But, even after this limited recognition of slaves' property right, slaveholders did not always confine themselves to trading with their slaves in the legally permitted commodities.

Most masters resorted to a different method to prevent their slaves from going to the market; they decided that they would bring the market to their slaves. The account book kept by one rice planter recorded buying eighteen "fowls" from a slave man in 1728, as well as paying a "negro wench" eight pounds for hogs two years later.[52] In 1736, twenty-two slaves on the same plantation were paid more than fifty pounds for selling their master rice.[53] A "Day Book" kept by the planter Henry Ravenel from 1750 until 1772 contains myriad references to his purchases from his slaves. Along with rice and corn, foodstuffs Ravenel bought from his slaves include fowls, honey, catfish, hogs, and beef; he also purchased canoes, baskets, and "myrtle wax," which slaves had produced in the quarters.[54]

Nor did planters prevent their slaves from selling to others when such business could be conducted within the confines of the plantation. For example, while traveling from Charles Town to Savannah in 1742, Johann Bolzius recorded the following incident in his journal:

> At this plantation I would have liked to buy two quarts of corn from the German overseer for my horse; but he had no authority over it and directed me to the Negroes. One of them gave me some, but I had to give him a half crown of local paper currency for it, which amounts to almost five pence sterling. In addition, it was so dirty that the horse did not wish to eat it.[55]

Some masters even allowed their slaves to raise and sell horses. For instance, the agent for the absentee planter Thomas Boone wrote his employer in 1760, "I have been a second time at your Plantation & have paid your Negroes in full for their horses which I should have done before but could not get a Bill changed in the Parish."[56] Perhaps most

51. *Statutes*, 7, 423.
52. Ball Family Account Book, Elias Ball Papers, 11–515–5, SCHS.
53. Ibid.
54. Day Book of Henry Ravenel, Ravenel Family Papers, SCHS.
55. George Fenwick Jones, trans., "John Martin Boltzius' [Johann Bolzius] Trip to Charleston, October 1742," *SCHM* 82 (1981), 104.
56. Robert Raper to Thomas Boone, 19 November 1760, Robert Raper Letterbook, WSCRO.

remarkable of all, one slave was apparently able to trade three horses to his master in exchange for his freedom.[57]

Such successful and large-scale entrepreneurship was not typical of most slaves' trading. The vast majority of slave marketing was undoubtedly far more modest. Comparing the records of several plantation account books yield a rough estimate of the scale of slaves' bargaining. In the records of six plantations dating from 1767 to 1784, a total of 56 different slaves sold their masters 157 bushels of rice or corn. Of these transactions, more than half involved the sale of two bushels or less, one-third involved the sale of two to five bushels, and only six slaves sold their masters quantities larger than five bushels.[58] Most slaves probably traded small surpluses from crops that were raised primarily for the consumption of themselves and their families in exchange for small quantities of tobacco, clothing, or manufactured goods.

The ability to acquire and trade property may have worked to strengthen black families. After the Civil War, a low-country slave recalled of the provision grounds that "my wife and I raised this corn together," and another testified that he and his wife had "put their labor together" when not working for their master.[59] As Philip Morgan has pointed out, this practice meant that "slave kin groups and families in

57. The record is as follows:

> This is to certify that in the year 1781 or 82 I heard Mr. Lewis Dutarque say to his old fellow Will that as he had been a faithful servant to him and if he had a mind to purchase his freedom he should obtain the same by paying him three hundred pounds old currency and says he Will you have two horses which will nearly pay me I will allow you two hundred pounds old currency for a Roan gelding and fifty-five currency for your gray for which the fellow Will readily consented to the proposals and Mr. Dutarque took possession of the horses and the fellow Will was to pay the balance as soon as he could make it up. Mr. Dutarque also borrowed of the old fellow a black mare which he lost and he said she was worth six guineas [approximately 42 pounds currency] and would allow him that price for her April 25, 1788.
> Wm. Blake, Georgetown, April 29, 1788

Miscellaneous Records, VV 473, SCDAH.

58. The sources used for this calculation are as follows: "Mandorum [sic] of Farley's Negros Corn 1767," William Gibbons, Jr., Papers, WPL-DU; Account Book, River Side [plantation] (1773), Wragg Family Papers, SCHS; Memo Book (undated but circa 1780), Ball Family Papers, SCHS; "John Ball's Planting book for the Year 1780," Ball Family Papers, WPL-DU; Fairfield Plantation Book, 1773–1797 (record circa 1784), Pinckney Family Papers, SCHS. To go further out on a speculative limb, one might hazard a guess at what slaves might have earned through such petty trading. Between 1758 and 1760, the slaves belonging to the estate of James Hartley were paid 124 pounds for 290 bushels of corn, or roughly two pounds six shillings per bushel; Morgan, "Work and Culture," 28. Therefore, if a typical slave traded two bushels per year at this price, he or she would have earned slightly over four and a half pounds, or approximately what Muso spent at Telfair's store in 1773.

59. Morgan, "The Ownership of Property by Slaves in the Mid-Nineteenth-Century Low Country," 403.

the low country could function as significant *economic* units for at least part of the working day."[60]

Moreover, family property may have given slave men an opportunity to act as the economic heads of their households. Although husbands and wives worked together in the provision grounds, it seems to have been the man's responsibility to trade the family's produce in the market. Of the 92 purchases from his slaves which Henry Ravenel recorded in his daybook between 1750 and 1772, for example, 69 (or three-fourths) were from men and only 23 from women.[61] Likewise, of the 56 slaves recorded to have sold corn or rice to their masters between 1767 and 1784, 45 (or 80 percent) were men.

The relationship between a master and his slaves took on a different character when the two parties were engaged in negotiations according to the "law of the market." Henry Laurens, for instance, told his overseer to "purchase of your own Negroes all [the provisions] that you know Lawfully belongs to themselves at the lowest price they will sell it for."[62] This instruction suggests a process of bargaining in which the master or his representative, the overseer, momentarily faced the slaves as equals. Laurens implied that if the price offered were *too* low, slaves would refuse to sell.

Of course, master-slave bargaining could never be entirely separated from its social context and was therefore never genuinely equal. As in the case of Laurens and his slave boatmen, masters strenuously sought to prevent slaves having other outlets to market their goods. The practice of masters buying their slaves' provisions was less a "free market" than it was a forced purchase by right of "eminent domain." Slaves could either sell to their master for whatever price he offered, see their surplus wasted, or attempt to trade off the plantation and risk the consequences if caught. Such restricted conditions may have led slaves to sell their goods for a price that was less than its full market value.[63]

But masters who cheated their slaves outrageously risked engendering ill will in the quarters and squandering a chance to demonstrate their

60. Ibid. See also Larry E. Hudson, Jr., *To Have and to Hold: Slave Work and Family Life in Ante-bellum South Carolina* (Athens, 1997).
61. Day Book of Henry Ravenel, Ravenel Family Papers, SCHS. Of course, the fact that Ravenel wrote only the men's names in his record may suggest his own imposition of a patriarchal construct upon his slaves' families. Twice in his account, however, Ravenel recorded the names of slave couples, "Buss & Amey," and "Dublin & Dorothy," suggesting that in most cases only the husband came to the great house.
62. Henry Laurens to Frederick Wiggins, 30 November 1765, *PHL*, 5, 41.
63. In a study of such transactions in the South Carolina upcountry in the nineteenth century, John Campbell found that the price masters paid slaves for their cotton averaged 18 percent below the price it would have commanded in the open market; John Campbell, "As 'A Kind of Freeman?' Slaves' Market Related Activities in the South Carolina Up Country, 1800–1860," in Berlin and Morgan, eds., *Cultivation and Culture*, 259–64.

beneficence. By keeping trade within the boundaries of the plantation, slave owners could minimize the harmful effects of slaves' marketing on their own authority and make use of the opportunity it provided for symbolic gestures. In this context, a master might view the exchanges made on the steps of the great house less as a business transaction conducted between equals than as another of the rituals of patriarchy.

Masters would have gained little from purchasing their slaves' crops if the slaves simply took they cash they received from their master to purchase goods in the marketplace. Consequently, having entered into business with their slaves as a purchaser of their crops, many masters quickly took the further step of acting as vendors of manufactured goods to their slaves. In this way, masters could hope to recoup the money they had spent on buying their slaves' produce. In fact, by selling to his slaves on credit, a master need never pay them cash at all. Finally, by bringing both sides of the market within the plantation bounds, masters could deter their slaves from outside trading.

Henry Laurens gave perhaps the best surviving description of this practice in a letter to an overseer written in 1765:

> I enclose you an Account of sundry articles sent to be dispos'd among the Negroes for their Rice at the Prices mark'd to each article which I hope they will take without too much fuss & trouble that I may not be discouraged from being their Factor another Year.
>
> Their several names are set down & your quantity of each ones Rice on the Credit side at 7/6 per Bushel, which is its full value & opposite to that you must make them Debtor for such goods as they take.[64]

In another instance, Laurens wrote, "you must take Account of . . . the [ten gross, short] pipes . . . & also the Yellow Porringers & Muggs that are given to the Negroes that they may be paid for according to the Planter's custom."[65] In a third letter, he delivered "15 very gay Wastcoats which some of the Negro Men may want at 10 Bushels per Wastcoat unless you shall think them worth more or less."[66]

Laurens was not the only master to acknowledge this "planter's custom." In his day book, Henry Ravenel kept track of what his slaves bought from him as well as the reverse. Among the items he sold them were cloth, rice, and "Beefs."[67] The back of the Ball family "Memo Book," which includes a record of corn and rice purchased from the estate's

64. Henry Laurens to Abraham Schad, 30 April 1765, *PHL*, 4, 616.
65. Henry Laurens to John Smith, 29 January 1766, *PHL*, 5, 57.
66. Henry Laurens to Abraham Schad, 7 October 1765, *PHL*, 5, 20.
67. "Day Book of Henry Ravenel," Ravenel Family Papers, SCHS.

slaves, carries the brief note that Surry "owes for a Lock."[68] Another planter's papers include an itemized record of the "store for the plantation" that was kept in 1773. Items slaves purchased at the "store" included foodstuffs such as "Malasies" [molasses] and vinegar, and manufactured goods such as combs, tools, hats, knifes, and a "saddel well fitted with girth."[69]

The "planter's custom" seems to have been one in which masters both bought from and sold to their slaves and thereby sought to contain slaves' economic initiative within the small world of the plantation. One mid-eighteenth-century observer explained the practice this way:

> [In their provision grounds, slaves plant] rice, corn, potatoes, tobacco, &c. for their own use and profit. . . . In some plantations, they have also the liberty to raise hogs and poultry, which, with the former articles, they are to dispose of to none but their masters (this is done to prevent bad consequences) for which, in exchange, when they do not chuse money, their masters give Osnaburgs, negro cloth, caps, hats, handkerchiefs, pipes, and knives.[70]

By restricting slaves' access to the market to a context in which the master could still play the central and dominant role, masters reconciled their slaves' assertion of property right and market relations with their own claims of authority and need to maintain control.

Moreover, by limiting slave purchases to the plantation "store" or, as Laurens suggests, to the master or overseer acting as the slaves' "factor" or conduit to the marketplace, masters could restrict the slaves' choice of consumer goods. Liquor, for example, one of Muso's staple goods from Telfair's store, is notably absent from any of the slaves' plantation purchases. Masters chose to keep a firm control on the rum barrel, and

68. "Memo Book [circa 1780]," Ball Family Papers, SCHS. Lawrence McDonnell has argued that slaves' decision to spend some of their hard-earned income on locks (presumably for the purpose of deterring other slaves from theft) "symbolized how insidiously private property and market exchange fractured slave society"; Lawrence T. McDonnell, "Money Knows No Master: Market Relations and the American Slave Community," in Winifred B. Moore and Joseph F. Fripp, eds., *Developing Dixie: Modernization in a Traditional Society* (New York, 1988), 37. While slaves' property ownership was an obvious prerequisite to such theft, its net effect on the slave community was far more complex and not nearly as negative and divisive as he suggests. Slave property holding and the ability to accumulate may have strengthened the slave family, for example. Furthermore, slaves had to be able to set aside selfish interest and act collectively to defend their individual property right.
69. "The Expence of the store for the plantation," River Side and Middle Plantations, 1773, William Wragg Papers, SCHS.
70. ["Scotus Americanus"], *Information Concerning the Province of North Carolina*, in William K. Boyd, ed., "Some North Carolina Tracts of the Eighteenth-Century," *North Carolina Historical Review* 3 (1926), 616.

distributed its contents sparingly and without charge as a principal source of reward for good work or customary "treats" for holidays or other "occasions" in the slave quarters.[71] In this way, masters attempted to take some of the most valued commodities "off the shelf" and hold them outside the market where the master's will still reigned supreme.

While the development of slaves' property right and the ability of slaves to trade their surpluses in the market for other goods contradicted many of the basic tenets of the slave society, the contradiction happened to suit the short-term goals of both slaves and masters. In the immediate context, as Sidney Mintz points out, the ability to gain a degree of economic independence "reduced the hunger of the slaves, increased their autonomy *while still slaves*, allowed them to accumulate [wealth] . . . and otherwise benefitted the slaves economically and socially—but all *within slavery*." Yet in the long run, Mintz adds, the economic self-control slaves enjoyed "*may* have cooled rebellious ardour, [and] fostered acceptance of slave status and resignation."[72]

All this may well be true. Yet, as Dr. Carson's overseer discovered when he tried to confiscate slaves' corn in 1781, slaves' conception of their property right contained rebellious implications as well. Most importantly, the ability slaves gained through their provision grounds and market relations to provide something for themselves and their families allowed them to construct a part of their lives and self-esteem away from the shadow of the great house. By working "for themselves" in their gardens and elsewhere, low-country slaves were able to acquire, hold, and trade a small part of their labor product.

The Wages of Slavery

In the colonial slave society it was not only the product of the slaves' labor that masters bought and sold; slaves' labor could itself become a marketable commodity. Some masters, particularly in the metropolis of Charles Town, where a significant demand for labor existed throughout the eighteenth century, did not put their slaves to work at "home," but instead hired the labor of their slaves to another. A master

71. Plantation records are replete with examples of masters using rum both as an emblem of their patriarchal benevolence and in order to extract labor. For instance, Josiah Smith, a plantation agent, wrote his employer, George Austin, on 22 July 1774: "Although the grass was very bad in all your fields, none of your people had run from it, they being kept to their work by mere dint of encouragement of a beef & some rum, added to lenient treatment by the overseer"; Josiah Smith, Jr., Letterbook, SHC-UNC.
72. Mintz, "Slavery and the Rise of Peasantries," 240.

who wished to sell the labor of a slave might simply hire out the slave temporarily to another white person for an agreed upon sum. In November 1774, for example, one master advertised the services of "a Sober, remarkably honest, and handy House Wench . . . to be hired out by the Month."[73] "Thus," one visitor to the city in 1785 commented, "many idlers place their capital in negroes and, in the strict sense, are by them supported, living careless on the bitter sweat of the hired."[74]

To masters, such arrangements offered a way to maximize their economic return from the available labor of their slaves. The possible dividends from slave hire were substantial. One account estimated that "in the average . . . a hired negro is worth a yearly interest of 15–20 per centum."[75] The actual returns to masters from hiring out slaves can be gauged from two surviving accounts. Two slave women whom Charles Pinckney hired out in 1753 earned him an amount equivalent to only about six percent of their value.[76] But James Laurens, who departed Charles Town for London and left his brother Henry to manage his affairs and to hire out his nine slaves, received dividends exceeding 15 percent per year.[77] Henry Laurens informed his brother that his slaves,

73. *South Carolina Gazette*, 21 November 1774.
74. David Johann Schoepf, *Travels in the Confederation*, ed. and trans. Alfred J. Morrison, 2 vols. (New York, 1968), 2: 201.
75. Ibid.
76. According to Pinckney's account book, which runs from April through November 1753, his two slaves, Bettina and Abba, brought in wages of thirty-eight pounds. In the same period Pinckney spent nine-and-a-half pounds on expenses, including medical and dental care, buying each woman a pair of shoes, and advertising them both for hire in the newspaper. Thus, he had a net gain in eight months of twenty-eight-and-a-half pounds. Extrapolated over the year, the net gain would be approximately forty-two pounds and fifteen shillings (or the equivalent of six pounds two shillings sterling). As the average slave was valued at about fifty pounds sterling, this sum would equal a return of approximately 6 percent on the one-hundred pounds capital represented by Bettina and Abba. The account book notes that within this eight-month period, Bettina gave birth to a child who later died and Abba was sick for three months, so this may have been an unusually low rate of return. Charles Pinckney Account Book, 1753–1757, Pinckney Family Papers, LC.
77. In a letter, Henry Laurens detailed how his brother James's slaves were employed:

Auba (& Walley to attend her Child) hired to Mr. Thomson [the] Schoolmaster at £90 p[er]/an[num] from 12 June 1775
Betty allowed by Mrs. Thomson to stay with her Mother till she is brought to Bed and able to go to service
Satira—[hired out] the 28th June to the Reverend Mr. Tennant for easy service in the House @ £60 p[er]/an[num].
Ishmael . . . is to go to service the 3rd July with Rob[er]t Pringle, Esqr. @ £7 p[er]/mo[nth]
George—the 29th June hired to Mr. Sody at £7 p[er]/mo[nth]
Cato—to go to Mr. Phipoe the 3rd July @ £6 p[er]/mo[nth]
Chloe—to work at a stated Washerwoman's & to bring in her Wages weekly 30/ p[er]/Week & maintain [i.e. feed and clothe] Stepney [Laurens's slave gardener]

hired out to others in the city, "are earning more Money upon the whole than you would expect."[78]

Slaves who were hired out might continue to look to their owner for their food, shelter, clothing, and other subsistence needs; alternatively, the contracting (white) parties might agree that such necessities were to be provided by the "leasee" of the slave, who would then act as a sort of surrogate master. In either case, the master or surrogate continued to provide the slave's subsistence, and money was passed from the "leasee" to the master without touching the hand of the laboring slave. In these cases, as on the plantations, the master's economic gain from the slave's labor (or its product) was obscured, and master-slave relations took place at one degree of removal from the cash nexus.

In other hiring practices, the reduction of slaves' labor to cash was more obvious. While the work of skilled slaves such as glazers, bricklayers, or carpenters was in great demand, few persons required such skilled workers for as long as a month or even a week at a time. It was more practical and profitable to hire the labor of skilled slaves by the day or for the completion of a certain job. Rather than devote themselves to seeking casual work for their skilled slaves, many masters charged the slaves themselves with the task of finding employment and with returning a specified sum of money (called a "wage") to their master.

The labor of unskilled slaves could also be sold on a casual basis. Charles Town masters with no work for their slaves might simply send them into the street equipped with a wheel barrow or a spade charged to seek work as porters or casual laborers and with directions to return a set amount of money per day or week. In August 1753, for example, Charles Pinckney noted in his account book that he "paid 2 negroes for 14 days wages filling marsh mud before . . . [my] house."[79]

The unspoken corollary of such arrangements was that any money slaves earned in excess of their "wage" was theirs to keep. In other cases, slaves were expected to feed and clothe themselves from their earnings. Some slaves also found their own lodgings in the town and

---

Henry Laurens to James Laurens, 2 July 1775, *PHL*, 10, 203. Together these eight slaves (including Walley and Betty who were not earning wages, but excluding both Stepney, who was working as Laurens's gardener, and Auba's unnamed child) stood to earn Laurens an annual return of 468 pounds in colonial currency or 67 pounds sterling. If they were worth approximately 50 pounds sterling each, the annual return was 16.75 percent. Moreover, Laurens's three slaves who were not earning wages were to be supported at the expense of those slaves who were.

78. Henry Laurens to James Laurens, 28 March 1777, *PHL*, 11, 323.

79. Pinckney recorded that he paid the slaves about one shilling sterling per day for their labor. Charles Pinckney Account Book, 1753–57, Pinckney Family Papers, LC.

consequently might only turn up on their master's doorstep once a week or month to pay their "wages." In 1772, for example, a contributor to the *Gazette* complained "that *many rooms, kitchens,* &c. are hired to or for the use of *slaves* in *this town*; and by such slaves, let to others, in *subdivisions*."[80]

Masters who left their slaves to find work for themselves, as well as to feed, clothe, and shelter themselves in return for a weekly wage, did not live up to the slave society's idea of masters' proper duties and responsibilities. In such cases, masters appeared to sell their authority and control for a cash payment. To some observers, such slaves seemed to have escaped the ordinary bonds of slavery and, as Henry Laurens wrote to his brother, "in some measure Govern themselves."[81]

As evidence of the disquiet that the sight of slaves selling their own labor engendered, the colonial assembly passed a law prohibiting this practice as early as 1712.[82] Like prohibitions on slave property, this law was ineffective, as the grand jurors of Charles Town complained two decades later.[83] In 1740, the assembly tried again. Section 33 of the Negro Act stated that "several owners of slaves do suffer their slaves to go and work where they please, upon condition of paying to their owners certain sums of money agreed upon between the owner and the slave." This custom, the law averred, encouraged slaves to steal and allowed them to obtain money so "as to maintain themselves in drunkenness and evil courses."[84]

The Negro Act sought not only to prohibit masters from sending their slaves out to "work where they please" but also to discourage others from hiring them. After 1740, not only the owners of self-hire slaves but also the people who employed them would be subject to fines. In an effort to undercut slaves' ability to obtain "sums of money" from selling their own labor, the Negro Act decreed that whenever slaves were hired, it was the employer's responsibility to see that "the master . . . receive the whole of the earning of such slave or slaves."[85] Moreover, to prevent

---

80. *South Carolina Gazette*, 24 September 1772.
81. Henry Laurens to James Laurens, 6 January 1776, *PHL*, 11, 5.
82. *Statutes*, 7, 362.
83. *South Carolina Gazette*, 30 March 1734. This presentment was the first ever printed in the colony and therefore the first to make what would become a familiar complaint: "We present . . . that it is a common practice by several persons in Charlestown, to suffer their Negroes to work out by the week, and oblige them to bring in a certain hire which is not only contrary to the law now subsisting, but a great Inlet to Idleness, Drunkenness, and other Enormities. . . ." Reprinted in Maria L. Weber, ed., "Presentment of the Grand Jury, March 1733/34," *SCHM* 25 (October 1924), 193–94.
84. *Statutes*, 7, 408.
85. William Simpson, *The Practical Justice of the Peace and Parish Officer of His Majesty's Province of South Carolina* (Charles Town, 1761), 174–75.

slaves from living out, the Negro Act declared that "no slave or slaves shall be permitted to rent or hire any house, room, store or plantation, on his or her own account."[86]

However strongly the law condemned the practice of self-hire the demand for labor was too great for many employers to take care that the master of a hired slave would receive "the whole of the [slave's] earning." Likewise, despite the stern pronouncements of the law, masters knew that their slaves would seek work more earnestly and would return them a larger wage if they were given a stake in their own labor. As with slaves' garden plots and petty trading, the practice through which slaves sold (and profited from) their own labor contradicted basic principles of the slave society but suited the short-term interests of both slaves and masters.

However, unlike the garden-marketing complex, the implications of which masters could mask or dilute by restricting slave trading to the confines of the plantation, the practice of slaves' selling their own labor could not be so easily "domesticated." Such slaves glaringly exposed and put a monetary value upon masters' profit from "the bitter sweat" of all their slaves. Each time slaves placed their earnings in their masters' hand, they were reminded anew of the injustice of the system.

It is not surprising that slaves constantly sought to keep what they had earned for themselves. Less than six months after the passage of the Negro Act, for instance, Elizabeth Smith advertised in the *Gazette* that her slave "Lancaster, commonly known about town for a white washer and fisherman, has of late defrauded me of his wages." She warned "all persons not to employ the said Lancaster, without first agreeing with me, or his producing a proper ticket, unless they are willing to pay the fine prescribed by law."[87] Smith's warning, coupled with the new law, was evidently ineffective. Ten months later Smith wrote the *Gazette* once more: "Whereas I have formerly advertised all Persons not to employ my negro-man Lancaster in white washing or any kind of work whatever, but to little purpose; since he constantly earns money (which he loses either by gaming or among the little punch houses)."[88] Fifteen years later, another Charles Town slave owner complained of "my Negro fellow Cuffee (with a wooden leg) frequently hiring himself out without my knowledge, whereby I am defrauded of his wages."[89]

Slaves who hired themselves out became the practical masters of their

---

86. *Statutes*, 7, 412–13.
87. *South Carolina Gazette*, 25 December 1740. Smith warned that "all Negroes who shall carry the said Lancaster a fishing shall be rigorously prosecuted."
88. *South Carolina Gazette*, 17 October 1741.
89. *South Carolina Gazette*, 23 September 1756.

own labor. Even at its most innocuous, the bargaining between the slave and his potential employer took on an air of momentary equality. When Robert Pringle undertook to hire several slaves to work on his coasting vessel, for example, he wrote to the boat's white captain: "I have also hir'd & sent by Mr. Coneur's boat four stout Negro men to assist you on board & who are us'd to be upon the water & understand to work on ship-board, & desire you may let the said Negroes have Provisions & Drink while on board, as I have agreed with them."[90]

Henry Laurens's dealings with his brother's slaves demonstrate the degree of independence such slaves routinely exercised in terms of both their work and the money they gained thereby. They could choose to change work, as did Joe, who "disagreeing with Mr. Creighton [his employer], [now] works out and is to bring in his Wages."[91] They also made decisions as to whether or not they would work on a given day. On one occasion "Chloe . . . deducted 3 days [wages] . . . for Sickness which," Laurens wryly commented, "is all the Certificate she has produced of her invalidity."[92] In some cases slaves could decide not to work at all. In 1775 Laurens wrote his brother that "Ishmael & George kept themselves aloof & whenever I summoned them to account for their time, pretended they were in search for Master's & employment & Cato followed their example." "The former two," he added, "I suspected were working jobbs about Town [and keeping the money], the latter passing his day in Play."[93]

With such loose arrangements, the difference between a dutiful slave and an "audacious" one could be as little as the failure to turn up at the end of the month to pay in the required wages. In 1759, John Paul Grimke advertised that "I am informed that several persons in town employ my run-away negro fellow Sharper" and "forewarn[ed] all persons not to employ him again till he produces a ticket from me."[94] But was "run-away" even the proper term for Sharper? Presumably he had not run very far. By refusing to pay the "sums of money agreed upon" to their owners, such slaves sought to sever one of the principal ties that marked them as unfree.

Those whites who sought to employ slaves encountered another aspect of their "masterlessness." Free for once to contract the terms of their own labor, slaves were not afraid to drive a hard bargain. Grand juries re-

90. Robert Pringle to John Evans, 24 January 1743, in Walter B. Edgar, ed., *The Letterbook of Robert Pringle*, 2 vols. (Columbia, 1972), 2, 489–90.
91. Henry Laurens to James Laurens, 7 June 1777, *PHL*, 11, 346.
92. Henry Laurens to James Laurens, 20 August 1775, *PHL*, 10, 317.
93. Henry Laurens to James Laurens, 2 July 1775, *PHL*, 10, 201.
94. *South Carolina Gazette*, 3 November 1759.

peatedly protested against such a galling and resolute lack of deference from slaves. In 1746, the grand jury complained of "the slaves of Charles Town, who act as porters & who refuse to work for a reasonable hire, when they are frequently found Idle, & often insist on as much for an hour or two as pays their Masters for a whole day."[95] In 1750, the jurors again objected to the slave porters, particularly "that it is left in their power to chuse or refuse such work as are required and the exorbitant wages demanded by them."[96] Twenty years later, little had changed. In a familiar refrain, the city grand jury recommended that the "commissioners of the streets . . . punish such Negroes as refuse to work, unless it be such work as shall be agreeable to themselves and such pay as they may require."[97] In 1763, one correspondent to the *Gazette* complained that the slave chimney sweeps of the city had even organized a strike for better wages. "They have had the insolence," he wrote, "by a combination amongst themselves to raise the usual prices and refuse doing their work unless their exorbitant demands are complied with."[98]

In 1751, the city commissioners passed a regulation that recognized and to a degree legitimated the practice of slaves selling their own labor. The commissioners agreed to license and issue badges to a limited number of "male slaves to work out for hire, as Porters, Laborers, fisherman, or handicraftsmen."[99] At the same time they established set rates to be paid for porterage and other types of casual labor, thereby seeking to eliminate the threatening and "levelling" give-and-take that took place before a slave would consent to work.[100] Through these decrees, the commissioners attempted to set up the entire community as a sort of collective master over those slaves who hired themselves out.

But, as with laws restricting slaves' trading to their masters, attempts to regulate and restrict slave hire were unsuccessful. In 1755, the commissioners reminded city residents that slaves were not to be hired unless they were licensed and wore badges. The lack of cooperation from those in need of temporary slave labor was not the only problem. Slaves apparently continued to set their own prices for their labor in defiance of the law. The exasperated commissioners were driven to decree that "if any licensed slave refuse to work at the rates ascertained . . . anyone of the commissioners may order such slave to be whipped."[101]

95. JGC, 17 April 1746, microfilm, SCDAH.
96. JGC, 22 November 1750, microfilm, SCDAH.
97. *South Carolina Gazette*, 7 February 1771.
98. *South Carolina Gazette*, 5 November 1763.
99. *South Carolina Gazette*, 13 May 1751. The number of licenses was limited to two per white inhabitant.
100. *South Carolina Gazette*, 10 June 1751.
101. *South Carolina Gazette*, 1 May 1755.

Such independent slaves could not have existed if colonial South Carolina's masters had lived up to the ideal that placed all slaves under the authority of a single master and defined the slave's labor as a duty rather than a commodity. While slaves' provision grounds and petty property holding originated in slaves' spontaneous determination to claim the product of their labor without regard for or in spite of the actions or desires of their masters, the practice of slaves selling their labor for money required an active collusion with members of the master class. As long as the demand for labor remained greater than the supply, some masters would be willing to exchange their "duties" for monetary rewards. Likewise, other whites would always be equally willing to bargain with slaves for their labor.

The dictates of larger market processes allowed some slaves an opportunity to utilize market relations in their own interest and to carve out a degree of autonomy and self-control while still slaves. But, as with the provision grounds, the economic independence they achieved may have had the long-term side effect of furthering accommodation to the slave system and making rebellion less likely.

Two of James Laurens's slaves, Betty and Ishmael, provide an example of how blacks may have chosen to use the opportunity of selling their own labor to create an independent life for themselves within slavery. In July 1775, Henry Laurens wrote his brother that Betty was pregnant while her mother, Auba, still had an infant child.[102] Betty was therefore probably under thirty years old at that time. In the same letter Laurens wrote that Ishmael "struggled hard to follow" the trade of a porter. In 1777, Ishmael was abducted by a British privateer while "fishing without Charles Town Bar" on a Sunday.[103] A few months later Laurens reported that Betty had become "very troublesome," adding, "I believe while Ishmael was at home he maintained her & paid the principle part of her Wages."[104]

These oblique references appear to indicate that Ishmael and Betty were a couple, that Ishmael was the father of the child Betty was expecting in 1775, and that he had "struggled hard" as a porter partly to earn enough money to allow him to "maintain" his wife so that she could stay home with their child and not have to work out for wages. Consequently, among the things Ishmael chose to do with the money he earned by selling his own labor was to withdraw his wife from their master's labor force. This choice was not open to many slaves. Interest-

102. Henry Laurens to James Laurens, 2 July 1775, *PHL*, 10, 201–3.
103. Henry Laurens to James Laurens, 7 June 1777, *PHL*, 11, 346.
104. Henry Laurens to John L. Gervais, 5 September 1777, *PHL*, 11, 486.

ingly, however, after emancipation one of the things freedmen were most determined upon was that their wives would no longer work in the fields.[105]

The practice of selling their labor every day at the city waterfront may have also inculcated among urban slaves an understanding that their labor or even their time was something they owned of themselves which no one else, including their master, could claim without their consent and an agreed-upon compensation. For example, Laurens reported that he was forced to pay Ishmael ten shillings just to stay home one Sunday, "although I had no real service for him."[106]

Slaves who traded their labor for cash also recognized the opposite side of such transactions, that services, or at least compliance, could be had at a price. For instance, in 1772, the Charles Town Grand Jury complained of:

> the disorderly behaviour of the Town-Watch by which they defeat the good intended by watching and preserving the property of the people from harm; instead whereof they are become a very great nuisance by beating and abusing negroes sent on errands by their masters with tickets, and letting others escape who have none; by which irregularities the Negroes in general disregard them and if they can but raise the sum of ten shillings to pay for their release, are not afraid of being out all night.[107]

With money in their pockets and white men ready to look the other way in exchange for it, slaves had a key they could use to unlock some of their chains.

"Loose, Idle and Disorderly"

In late-colonial Charles Town there were three places where the "law of the market" was allowed a free rein. Beneath the arcade and within the richly decorated rooms of the Exchange, the colony's planters sold their rice and indigo crops and balanced their accounts with the larger Atlantic economy. A few blocks to the west, at the intersection of Broad and Meeting Streets in the center of Charles Town, stood the public market house. The bargains struck here satisfied the city's hunger for

---

105. Leon Litwack, *Been in the Storm So Long: The Aftermath of Slavery* (New York, 1979), 244–45, and also Jacqueline Jones, *Labor of Love, Labor of Sorrow: Black Women, Work, and the Family from Slavery to the Present* (New York, 1985), 44–78.
106. Henry Laurens to James Laurens, 7 June 1777, *PHL*, 11, 346.
107. *South Carolina Gazette*, 25 January 1772.

food and other vendibles and served the colonial slave society's "domestic" economy. Finally, at "public vendues" held on the wharves along the Cooper River, Africans who had survived the rigors of the "middle passage," as well as other property (including slaves) disputed among creditors and heirs, were sold to the highest bidder.

Travelers to Charles Town regarded these "markets" quite differently. Few visitors failed to notice and approve of the Exchange house. Josiah Quincy, for example, thought it made "a most noble appearance" to ships approaching the city.[108] More often than not, however, eighteenth-century observers entirely excluded both the vendue and the marketplace from their depictions of the city. Beyond advertisements placed in the city newspaper, there are no surviving descriptions of the proceedings at the public auctions. Not yet sensitized by the abolitionist movement to regard the slave auction as an object of horrid fascination, colonial travelers appear to have taken its existence for granted and regarded it as unworthy of remark. But the tourists' "blindness" toward the market house was more deliberate. In most accounts, the Anglican Church and Statehouse, which occupied the other corners of Broad and Meeting, were lavishly praised. But the same observers turned their backs (both literally and figuratively) upon the adjacent public market.[109]

Perhaps Charles Town's visitors elided the market house from their vision of the city because they were disturbed and troubled by what they saw there. The bustle and confusion of the marketplace could not easily be reconciled with the image of orderly and civilized progress that the other structures presented. Moreover, in stark contrast to the subordinate (or commodified) position in which slaves, blacks, and women were relegated in the liturgy and rituals in the Exchange house, the established church, and the legislature, female slaves played a central and active role in the Charles Town marketplace. Under the roof of the "low and dirty . . . markethouse," and behind the mask of market relations, slave

---

108. Mark DeWolfe Howe, ed., "Journal of Josiah Quincy, Junior, 1773," Massachusetts Historical Society *Proceedings* 49 (Boston, 1916), 441.

109. For example, William Dillwyn, who visited Charles Town in November 1772, admired the Statehouse, Guard House, St. Michael's, and the statue of William Pitt that stood in the center of the four corners, but he said nothing of the marketplace, although he must have walked right past it; A. S. Salley, ed., "Diary of William Dillwyn during a visit to Charles Town in 1772," *SCHM* 36 (1935), 6. In 1778, Ebenezer Hazard described the "exchange, state house, [and] St. Michael's Church" as "rough-cast," but made no mention of the market; H. Roy Merrens, ed., "A View of Coastal South Carolina in 1778: The Journal of Ebenezer Hazard," *SCHM* 73 (1972), 183. In 1780, during the royal occupation of the city, a Hessian officer's description of the "public buildings" of the city included the "beautiful statehouse, . . . the main guardhouse, the exchange, and the two churches, Saint Philip and Saint Michael" but again utterly ignored the marketplace; Johann Conrad Dohla, *A Hessian Diary of the American Revolution*, ed. and trans. Bruce E. Burgoyne (Norman, Okla., 1990), 125.

women as marketeers could assert and exercise a large measure of *de facto* liberty and self-control.

Charles Town's public marketplace, where slaves predominated numerically, practically controlled, and daily acted in ways that defied their proscribed subordination, encapsulated the dynamic that existed between the market as a place and the market as a process. The activities and relations that "governed" the marketplace stood in stark contrast to the social order that prevailed in the remainder of the colonial slave society. Periodically, individual masters or representatives of the state made forays into the marketplace to assert their power and to keep the "presumption" of the slave marketeers within acceptable parameters. On the whole, however, masters chose to avert their gaze, in part because they realized that the slave marketeers played a vital role in provisioning the city. The encounters which took place every day in the marketplace offer a glimpse of how the social order of the colonial slave society was constructed and perpetuated.

In the early modern world, markets often existed outside of ordinary law. The Charles Town marketplace was legally established in 1739, but other markets had long existed and would continue to exist in the city.[110] In a 1741 petition to the assembly, the commissioner of the new market complained that the "market Act appoints but one public Market place, and yet there were two in the . . . Town; the one established by Law, the other by Custom."[111] It is apparent that from the earliest days slaves sought a temporary refuge from their masters' power in the marketplace. Only two years after the market house was built, for example, it was noted that "Negroes went so much to Market."[112]

The South Carolina slave code of 1740 permitted slaves to attend the market to buy or sell on behalf of their masters, provided that they carried tickets "particularly enumerating" what was to be bought or sold.[113] From the beginning, however, slave marketeers sought to do more. Many worked out an arrangement with their masters by which they not only sold their master's produce but also used their earnings to purchase goods in their own right and resell them for their own personal profit. After paying their master an agreed-upon wage, these slave marketeers could retain for themselves whatever they had earned in excess of that amount.

In the short term, such arrangements suited masters, who could thereby continue to collect a steady income from their slaves and from

110. *JCHA*, 11 April 1739, 698.
111. *JCHA*, 21 May 1741, 23.
112. *JCHA*, 21 May 1741, 16.
113. Simpson, *The Practical Justice of the Peace*, 137.

the market even when they had no work for the slaves to do or produce of their own to sell. In the long run, however, as slaves came to play a larger and larger role in the marketplace and took on an increasingly important role in providing the city's white and black inhabitants with basic necessities, whites came to resent both the independence of the slave marketeers and their control over the city's food supply.

For this reason, even while individual masters allowed their own slaves to become "independent" marketeers, white society collectively censured the practice. Attempts to prohibit or at least limit the subversive aspects of slaves' trading can be traced back to the late seventeenth century. In 1686, for example, the assembly enacted a law prohibiting any person from buying goods from servants or slaves.[114] In 1734, the Charles Town Grand Jury complained "that Negroes are suffered to buy and sell, and be Hucksters of Corn, Pease, fowls, &c. whereby they watch night and day on the several wharves, and buy up many articles necessary for the support of the inhabitants and make them pay an exorbitant rate."[115] The establishment of the "official" marketplace in 1739 was aimed in part to "prevent the injurious and illegal Practice of ... Negro-huckstering."[116] A year later, when the assembly revised the slave code in response to the Stono Rebellion, it renewed the prohibition on independent slave trading.[117]

However, despite their stern words and prescribed penalties, these successive laws and regulations were ineffective in curtailing the slave marketeers. In 1744, for instance, the grand jury again objected that "many Negroes in Charles Town (in defiance of the 31st paragraph of the Negro Act) do openly buy and sell sundry sorts of wares."[118] The recurrent complaints of Charles Town grand juries indicate that the sight of slaves acting as independent traders in the market was a commonplace.

This ongoing discrepancy between statute and custom suggests that the constant repetition of prohibitions by the legislature may actually have placated white resentment and allowed masters to accept the intru-

---

114. *Statutes*, 2, 22.
115. *South Carolina Gazette*, 30 March 1734; Weber, contrib., "Presentment of the Grand Jury," *SCHM* 25 (October 1924), 193–94.
116. *JCHA*, 21 May 1741, 16.
117. The Negro Act of 1740 directs that "no slave who shall dwell ... or be usually employed in Charles Town, shall presume to buy, sell, deal, traffic, barter, exchange or use commerce for any goods, wares, provisions, grain, victuals, or commodities, of any sort or kind whatsoever ... On pain that all such goods, wares provisions, grain, victuals, or commodities, which by any slave shall be ... used in commerce, shall be seized and forfeited ... and moreover ... every slave who shall be convicted of such offence [is] to be publicly whipped on the bare back not exceeding twenty lashes." *Statutes*, 7, 407–8.
118. *JGC*, 17 October 1744, microfilm, LC, 527–529.

sion of the market into their everyday relations with their slaves. In this way, the law may have served as an ideological "citadel," a secure retreat, within which masters' absolute authority could be kept safe, while in practice and in the marketplace master-slave interactions were conducted on a very different and far more negotiated basis.

Two accounts, a generation apart, provide a fair picture of the nature and extent of slave participation in the marketplace in the mid-18th century. A 1747 petition to the assembly complained that "white people . . . are . . . entirely ruined and rendered miserable . . . by the great liberty and indulgence which is given to Negroes and other slaves in Charles Town to buy, sell, and vend . . . valuable commodities." The petitioners' description of the slave marketeers is worth quoting at length:

> [Their masters] give them all imaginable liberty, not only to buy and sell those commodities, but also, . . . to forestall the markets of Charles Town by buying up the Provisions, &c. which come to town for sale, at dear and exorbitant prices, and take what other indirect methods they please, provided they pay their masters their wages, which they seldom or never enquire how they came by the same, . . . [further] those Negroes and other slaves, being possessed of large sums of money, purchase quantities of flour, butter, apples, &ca., all [of] which they retail out to the inhabitants of Charles Town, by which means leading lazy lives, and free from the government of their masters.[119]

An equally vivid portrayal of the market scene, which was printed in the *Gazette* a generation later, documents the continuing slave presence in the market. In 1772 an anonymous observer wrote that

> almost every day . . . in and near the Lower Market, . . . poultry, fruit, eggs, &c. are brought thither from the country for sale. Near that market, constantly resort a great number of loose, idle and disorderly negro women, who are seated there from morn till night, and *buy* and *sell* on *their own accounts*, what they please, in order to pay their wages, and get so much more for themselves as they can; for their owners care little, how their slaves get the money, so they are paid.[120]

Furthermore, runaway slaves were often described in the colony's newspapers as being "well known in Charles Town" for their activities

119. "Petition of Sundry Inhabitants of Charles Town," *JCHA*, 5 February 1747, 154–55.
120. *South Carolina Gazette*, 24 September 1772.

in the market.[121] Bella, for example, was said to be "almost every day at Market selling diverse things."[122] Another advertisement described "the widow Brown's old Negro wench, named Lizette, who attends the lower market and frequently has things to dispose of there."[123]

Slave marketeers soon outnumbered and displaced white traders and made the Charles Town marketplace their own particular domain. By the mid-eighteenth century, in terms of race as well as tolerated illegalities, the public marketplace might be justly termed a "black market." Consequently, the public market was the only official institution in the colony where slaves predominated not only in numbers but in power.[124]

In regard to gender as well as race, day-to-day activity in the Charles Town marketplace defied ordinary rules. For, with the exception of butchers and fishermen, the vast majority of the slaves who came to trade were women. On one day in 1778, for example, an observer "counted in the market and different corners of this town, sixty-four Negro wenches selling cakes, nuts, and so forth."[125] Perhaps slave women dominated the market because other casual work as porters or day laborers was closed to them. More likely, by acting as market traders they were taking on a role traditionally allotted to women in West African, Caribbean, and most other preindustrial societies.[126]

The central position that black slave women occupied in the Charles Town marketplace had social as well as economic ramifications. In the early modern world, as E. P. Thompson notes, "the market . . . [was] a social as well as an economic nexus."[127] It was the place where the town met the country and where news and gossip were exchanged along with goods and money. Much of the produce sold by the slave marketeers "on their own accounts" had been grown by other slaves in their private

---

121. *South Carolina Gazette*, 6 December 1751.
122. *South Carolina Gazette*, 10 November 1746.
123. *South Carolina Gazette*, 31 May 1770.
124. In this regard, Betty Wood has noted that "by the late eighteenth century, the Low-country's urban markets were dominated by black vendors." Betty Wood, " 'White Society' and the 'Informal' Slave Economies of Lowcountry Georgia, c. 1763–1830," *Slavery and Abolition* 11 (December 1990), 317.
125. *South Carolina and American General Gazette*, 19 February 1778.
126. According to Philip Morgan, "by the late eighteenth century . . . black women had assumed an important role in the town's daily economic affairs, not unlike the place traditionally held by female entrepreneurs in the trading centres of West Africa"; Morgan, "The Development of Slave Culture in Eighteenth Century Plantation America" (Ph.D. diss., University of London, 1977), 138. Sidney Mintz notes the predominance of women in Jamaican markets after emancipation (1838), while also noting that because of a lack of evidence the sex of the Jamaican marketeers during slavery can not be known; Sidney Mintz, *Caribbean Transformations* (Baltimore, 1974), 216.
127. E. P. Thompson, "The Moral Economy of the English Crowd in the Eighteenth Century," *Past and Present* 50 (February 1971), 135.

gardens. In this way, slave marketeers became an important source of cash and manufactures to their country counterparts, and the marketplace became one of the central crossroads of the low-country black community. In trade, town and country slaves could cooperate to their mutual advantage.

Studies of present-day markets in Jamaica and Haiti have detailed the existence of "trading partnerships" between rural peasant producers and urban market traders.[128] Such economic ties and clientage may have existed among colonial South Carolina slaves. For instance, in 1772 an observer reported that black market

> women have such a connection with and influence on, the country negroes who come to market, that they generally find means to obtain whatever they may chuse, in preference to any white person; . . . I have seen the country negroes take great pains, after having been first spoke to by those women to *reserve* whatever they chose to sell to them only, either by keeping the particular articles in their canows [canoes], or by sending them away and pretending they were not *for sale*; and when they could not be easily retained by themselves, then I have seen the wenches so briskly hustle them about from one to another that in two minutes they could no longer be traced.[129]

Slaves' numerical predominance in the market may have given them an opportunity to defy white authority in ways that would have been impossible individually. Whites may have recognized that in the marketplace the ordinary powers of the slave society were to some extent suspended. In 1770, the commissioners noted that the fish market, where "the business . . . is principally carried on by negroes . . . [was] apt to be riotous and disorderly."[130]

The most common sentiment expressed in the collected grand jury pre-

128. In Haiti such "trading partnerships" are known as "pratik." Sidney Mintz provides a description of their operation: "A buying pratik who knows her selling pratik is coming will wait at the proper place and time, refusing to buy stock from others that she is sure her pratik is carrying. . . . to the extent that her stock is committed in such arrangements a selling pratik will refuse to sell to others until she has met her pratik buyer." Quoted in Stuart Plattner, "Equilibrating Market Relationships," in *Markets and Marketing: Monographs in Economic Anthropology*, ed. Stuart Plattner (Lanham, Md., 1985), 137.
129. *South Carolina Gazette*, 24 September 1772.
130. The commissioners decreed that stocks be erected near the fish market and empowered local magistrates to confine "riotous, disorderly or drunken Negroes . . . buying, selling, or being in and about the said market in the stocks . . . for a space not more [than] two hours." *South Carolina Gazette*, 15 November 1770. According to E. P. Thompson, "the market was the place where the people, because they were numerous, felt for a moment that they were strong"; Thompson, "The Moral Economy of the English Crowd," 135.

sentments and other white complaints about the slave marketeers was a frustration at the large degree of discretion that slaves exercised during transactions in the market and the consequent powerlessness of white inhabitants. As masters, Carolina whites felt that slaves should be subordinate in all circumstances, but as property holders and capitalists they also had to recognize the legitimacy of the market. Sellers had the right to seek the highest price for their goods. In the market, slaves could turn the contradictions of the system they labored under to their own advantage.

Within the marketplace, slaves could use the "law of the market" to complicate the patriarchal authority under which masters ordinarily sought to contain their relations with their slaves. Masters were very familiar with the "law of the market" and were bound to respect it. For slaves, the distance that market relations allowed them to create between themselves as unfree laborers and the commodities they produced could be a source of liberation. Behind the mask of a commodity and governed only by the "law of the market," slave marketeers could challenge their masters and assert a *de facto* equality every time they refused to sell except upon their own terms.

Furthermore, because slave marketeers did not trade their labor, but instead merely exchanged goods for money, the relationship between them and their white "customers" ended as soon as each bargain was transacted. Buyer and seller were momentarily equal, and no other connection existed or was thereby created. As a result, no restoration of the dominant social hierarchy took place after the subversive equality of the bargaining process was concluded. A white person who was faced with the choice of paying a black butcher thirty-two shillings "for a quarter of a hog" or going hungry might well have felt a sense of outrage and humiliation at having been placed in such a predicament.[131]

The grand jurors and others who objected to the black market protested most often against this so-called profiteering. That slaves should profit from masters was a galling contradiction of the social ideal. Black marketeers were accused of selling goods "at 100 or 150 per cent advance" from what they had paid for them.[132] In 1763, the city's market commissioners protested that "Negroes and other slaves . . . have of late actually raised the price of almost every necessity of life beyond anything heretofore known."[133]

Some of the hostility directed at the market women may have also reflected an unease about the growing dominance of the cash nexus over

131. *South Carolina Gazette*, 26 November 1772.
132. *South Carolina Gazette*, 24 September 1772.
133. *South Carolina Gazette*, 22 October 1763.

older, more personalized forms of economic relations. To buy their stock, market women were required to have a considerable amount of cash on hand each day. Envious white observers decried the fact that the slave marketeers were "possessed of large sums of money." In their daily business black marketeers had to be able to recognize, exchange, and discount a confusing variety of "good" and "bad" currency, notes, and coin. It seems likely that the black marketeers possessed a far greater knowledge of and facility with the "new economy" than did many whites. Whites feared that market women could "hustle" money in the same way that they did goods, cashing and exchanging notes "so briskly . . . that they could no longer be traced."[134] In 1770, for example, one correspondent to the newspaper suspected that "an old negro wench . . . who attends the lower market" would have had no difficulty in redeeming stolen exchange notes worth sixty-five pounds sterling.[135]

It is difficult to judge how much of the money that passed through slave marketeers' hands ended up in their pockets. At least some slaves who engaged in trade were able to save enough money to purchase themselves. In 1770, for example, Leander paid his master the equivalent of 130 pounds sterling in exchange for his freedom. The money, Leander's master reported, "was delivered to me . . . from time to time as Monies which he had by his great care diligence and industry in his business trade or occupation of a Butcher for several years past got together and earned."[136]

In the market, slaves appeared to have evaded the basic principles of the slave society. For many whites, this development may have aroused latent fears that slaves might begin to assert their independence in other areas of society as well. Consequently, many whites couched complaints about slave marketeers in terms that seemed to describe a far more direct insubordination and rebellion. For example, one complaint described slave marketeers as acting "in open violation and contempt" of the law and of "combining together in the most impudent and notorious manner."[137] In a similar vein, another observer, after depicting the little regard blacks paid to white supremacy in the market, remarked that *"they are your slaves"*—as if the matter were in doubt.[138]

In extreme cases, whites spoke of the market as if it had already turned their world upside down. They described their relationship to market slaves in terms that revealed both their unease at slaves' control of the

---

134. *South Carolina Gazette*, 24 September 1772.
135. *South Carolina Gazette*, 31 May 1770.
136. Miscellaneous Records, 11 October 1770, OO385, SCDAH.
137. *South Carolina Gazette*, 22 October 1763.
138. *South Carolina Gazette*, 24 September 1772.

market and their own feelings of dependency. The commissioners wrote of the "manifest oppression . . . of the inhabitants" by slave marketeers.[139] Another account was even more explicit: "it plainly appears that we are at the mercy even of the lowest and most abandoned scoundrels, who dispose not only of our fortunes but our lives, according to their insatiable thirst for gain—and this is permitted in contempt of government, which ought to exert itself."[140]

Of course, exchange is a cultural as much as an economic phenomenon. It cannot be separated from its social context or from the structures of power within which it is conducted. Even if the transaction itself takes place within a momentary "social vacuum" of *de facto* equality, each participant can remember what had come before and, more importantly, anticipate what will follow after the exchange is concluded. Therefore, a truly "free market" can exist only when both participants in exchange are in a relation to each other that is genuinely equal.[141]

Two social and cultural factors acted to deflect or contain the challenge that the market activities of slaves posed to masters' authority. First, the majority of market traders were women, which rendered their challenge to the social order less threatening. Even if, through their actions in the market, black marketeers defied the principle of white supremacy, as women they could still be subordinated within the larger patriarchal social order.

The words that were used to describe the slave marketeers are illuminating in this regard. In 1768, for instance, the grand jurymen complained of the "many idle negro wenches, selling dry goods, cakes, rice, etc. in the markets."[142] Four years later, the market women were similarly described as "loose, idle and disorderly."[143] Other complainants depicted the market women as "insolent," "Abusive," "notorious," and "impudent."[144] The female slave marketeers were said to be both "free from the government" and contemptuous of it.[145]

139. *South Carolina Gazette*, 22 October 1763.
140. *South Carolina Gazette*, 26 November 1772.
141. On this point, Lawrence McDonnell writes: "Master and slave confronted each other at the moment of exchange as bearers of commodities, stripped of social dimensions. . . . In this realm each knew perfect freedom and perfect dependence." McDonnell, "Money Knows No Master," 34. While McDonnell's idea is important and illuminating, I nonetheless have some significant reservations. Most important, I would argue that the market can never be entirely removed from its social context and that therefore market slaves cannot achieve "perfect freedom" (if such a thing ever exists for anyone). The equality of the market is necessarily one of degree, perception, and comparison; it is surrounded by limitations, as the following examples illustrate.
142. *South Carolina Gazette*, 1 February 1768.
143. *South Carolina Gazette*, 24 September 1772.
144. *JCHA*, 21 May 1741, 18; *South Carolina Gazette*, 22 October 1763.
145. *JCHA*, 5 February 1747, 154–55; *South Carolina Gazette*, 26 November 1772.

Such descriptions of women's actions by male authorities were not confined to slave societies. Natalie Zemon Davis has noted that language and imagery representing women as "disorderly" was common in early modern Europe. Market women in England were portrayed in the same way. A description of bread riots in England in 1807 observed: "Women are more disposed to be mutinous; they stand less in fear of law, partly from ignorance, partly because they presume upon the privileges of their sex, and therefore in all public tumults they are foremost in violence and ferocity."[146]

As long as the actions of slave marketeers could be read as a female challenge to male authority, rather than as a challenge by blacks or slaves to the authority of whites or masters, they could be fit into this tradition of "unruly women" and contained within the parameters of what constituted acceptable manifestations of social conflict. To some degree, therefore, the female market slaves may have been "hiding behind their sex" in their defiance of laws and statutes.[147]

The behavior of slave marketeers provides an example, in microcosm, of how gender differences in a patriarchal society may have shaped slave resistance. The descriptions of the complainants indicate that the resistance of the market women largely took the form of verbal aggression and "impudence." Ridicule, bluster, and wit were the market women's strongest weapons. In 1741, the clerk of the market complained that the "insolent abusive Manner" of slave marketeers rendered him "afraid to say or do Anything in the Market" and left him to be made "a Game of."[148]

Female slave marketeers may have chosen to express resistance in these forms precisely because they felt confident that such verbal insolence from "disorderly" women was unlikely to provoke a violent response. A visitor to the market wrote in 1772, "I have known those black women to be so insolent as even to *wrest* things out of the hands of white people, pretending they had been bought before, for their masters or mistresses, yet expose *the same* for sale again within an hour after, for their own benefit."[149] It is unlikely that a black *man* could have committed

146. Natalie Zemon Davis, *Society and Culture in Early Modern France* (Palo Alto, Calif., 1975), 124–51; and Thompson, "The Moral Economy of the English Crowd," 115–16.

147. Davis, *Society and Culture in Early Modern France*, 146. Wole Soyinka vividly describes the social "power" of contemporary West African market women (who, among other things, led a successful protest against unpopular legislation) in the Nigeria of his childhood; Wole Soyinka, *Aké: The Years of Childhood* (New York, 1983), 199–223. For the same phenomenon in present-day Peru, see Linda J. Seligmann, "To Be In Between: The *Cholas* as Market Women," *Comparative Studies in Society and History* 33 (October 1989).

148. *JCHA*, 21 May 1741, 18.

149. *South Carolina Gazette*, 24 September 1772.

such an overt and physical affront without provoking retaliation. Perhaps the continuing subordination of the slave marketeers as *women* allowed them momentarily to escape the limitations imposed by race and caste.

Occasional public punishments of slave offenders provided another outlet for the anxieties and resentments that the slaves' domination of the market engendered among masters. The laws against slaves' trading "on their own accounts" in the market were never strictly enforced, partly because of the effort required to do so, but largely because whites had no ready alternative through which the city could gain a regular supply of fresh food. In the ordinary course of events, the black market was permitted to continue and whites merely complained, doubtless largely in conversation but also through the presentments of grand juries of the market slaves' defiant behavior and galling presumption.

Every few years, however, whether sparked by a temporary shortage in which the market slaves' monopoly power became painfully evident, or merely by a general feeling among whites that slave marketeers were taking their "liberty" too much for granted, the Negro Act's prohibitions against slave trading would suddenly be enforced. In May 1773, for example, the *Gazette* reported that "a large quantity of Earthen ware, &c. was seized from Negro Hawkers in Meeting Street, notwithstanding the many examples lately made by forfeitures for this atrocious offense."[150]

Continued complaints of grand juries indicate that these sporadic efforts to enforce the law had little real effect in limiting slave marketeering, but the momentary and public enforcement of the law asserted the authority of the slave society over the slave market women and may have placated white anxieties and resentments.[151] By threatening the marketeers with the loss of what they had so painstakingly gained and punishing them with twenty lashes if they stepped too far, such tactics might also have served as a means of keeping prices down.

A similar process may have taken place much more often on an individual and personal level. In the market, whites could at any time add their social superiority into the balance to gain an unfair advantage or to remove the humiliation of trading with a slave; worse still, whites could arbitrarily renege upon a contract with a slave. Slaves engaged in marketplace exchange, but they were still fettered by their inferior social

---

150. *South Carolina Gazette*, 17 May 1773.
151. For instance, the "many examples" of slaves' goods being seized for violation of the law in the spring of 1773 did not prevent the Grand Jury of complaining on May 21 "that the Huckstering and selling dry goods, cook'd rice and other victuals is still practised about the Markets and streets of Charles Town by Negroes"; Journal of the Court of General Sessions [Charles Town], 1769–1776, SCDAH, 241.

status. They were constantly aware of their lack of any legal right to property and knew that their white "customers" could at any time void a contract simply by moving the relationship from one between buyer and seller to one between white and black or master and slave. Although masters constantly complained of the "profiteering" of the slave marketeers, it seems more likely that, with such a constant threat hanging over them, slave women accepted a smaller margin of profit than genuinely free traders would have done.

Through occasional demonstrations of their power, masters could draw a line around the ordinary "disorder" of the market house and remind the slaves and perhaps reassure themselves that the black market continued only upon their sufferance.[152] Given their very real dependence upon the slave marketeers to gather and distribute the city's food supply, this construction was based largely on wishful thinking. By periodic punishments, however, authorities could make the point that the dependency was at least mutual. If whites were forced to rely upon the market women for their basic necessities, slave marketeers were just as reliant upon white forbearance for their *de facto* "liberty." More importantly, the occasional enforcement of otherwise dormant laws served to remind all members of the slave society where authority lay. By such actions, masters contained the independence of the slaves marketeers within the realm of tolerated illegalities.

The Law of the Market

At most, several hundred slave women were regularly engaged in selling "sundry sorts of wares" in the mid-eighteenth-century Charles Town marketplace. Therefore, in numerical terms, the threat that slave marketeers posed to the slave society was of small consequence. But the location of the market house in the center of the city gave it a significance beyond mere numbers. Although the black marketeers were few, they "played" to a large audience. Along with the urban population, thousands of country residents, white and black, visited the city every day and came into contact with the black market. The ability of slave

152. It is impossible to ascertain, given the lack of evidence, how often (or how seldom) the laws against slaves' market trading were enforced. The presentments generally were directed as much at white law officers as at slaves; for example, a presentment published in the *South Carolina Gazette* on 8 June 1765 complained of "the magistrates and constables of Charles Town ... not carrying into execution the laws ... particularly those against ... negroes hawking and selling. . . ." Such language indicates that the laws were rarely enforced. This inference is also supported by the "surprised" tone adopted in the account of slaves being punished for illicit trading in 1773.

women to dominate the proceedings at the market in the center of the slave society's metropolis and to escape the limitations of their condition in such a public way challenged white authority and served as an example to other slaves.

But the black market may have also had a two-edged effect on the low-country black community. On one hand, by allowing slaves to hold property and accumulate wealth within slavery, the market may have acted to lessen overt slave rebelliousness in the short term. In the longer term, however, the slave marketeers remained a focus of dissent and a challenge to the notions of white supremacy and patriarchal authority in the slave society. In the market, buyer and seller negotiated over more than the price of food. The collisions, collusions, and conflicts that took place each day in the Charles Town marketplace helped to construct and reckon relations among slaves and masters, blacks and whites, women and men, property and power. The transactions and encounters that took place each day in the Charles Town marketplace provide a glimpse in microcosm of the complex power contests that shaped the social order of the colonial slave society.

At the same time, at the public vendue house a few blocks away, a far grimmer struggle was under way each day. On the auction block, slaves came to the market not as traders and agents but as commodities and objects. If, in the marketplace, slaves could turn market relations to their own advantage, in the vendue house their masters' need for liquid capital to satisfy creditors or heirs could weigh every slave and every slave family in the scales of the market.

For many slaves, the prospect of being sold and separated from loved ones precipitated a desperate decision. Runaway slave advertisements frequently made reference to the fact that the fugitives had acted to escape the auction block as much as the lash. One family, "Boston, his wife Sue, and child Sib," ran away "immediately" after they were sold at auction in October 1753 and were still at large six months later.[153] Similarly, the nine slaves of Thomas Gaillard, who "were mortgaged to Mrs. Stoutenburgh," ran off in the spring of 1761 after they heard they were to be "exposed to open and public vendue . . . to discharge the said mortgage."[154]

In the long run, the "disorders" of the marketplace could do little to deter the proceedings at the Exchange house or the vendue. It might even be said that the food sold at the marketplace appeased the grosser appetites of the planters, merchants, auctioneers, and bidders who gathered

153. *South Carolina Gazette,* 16 April 1754.
154. *South Carolina Gazette,* 4 July 1761.

each day at the Exchange house and the vendue. (Perhaps it would be harder to keep up with the bidding if one was distracted by an empty stomach.) Through the produce of their gardens, the sale of their labor, or their activities as traders in the marketplace, slaves may have employed the "law of the market," and their masters' respect for property, to assert their economic equality and their humanity, but they could neither escape nor forget the threat posed by the larger market forces in which both they and the colonial slave society were entangled.

[5]

Little Kingdoms:
The Political Economy
of the Plantations

T welve miles northwest of Charleston, on the west bank of the Ashley River, lies the plantation great house of Drayton Hall. The mansion, completed in 1742, testifies to the wealth and ambition of colonial South Carolina's planter elite. The house is a remarkable survivor. Despite the passage of two-and-a-half centuries, it has never been altered to accommodate electricity, central heating, or plumbing. Drayton Hall's two-story portico looks down upon a broad empty lawn and a long, oak-lined drive. Apart from a small brick privy off to one side, the great house stands empty and alone.[1]

The quiet solitude of Drayton Hall, like that of most other "historic" plantation mansions, is not apt to surprise late-twentieth-century visitors. The setting of the "great house" resembles that of the mansions built by nineteenth-century industrialists or modern millionaires. Like them, the plantation great house seems to embody tasteful consumption and leisurely refinement, "a world that only . . . wants to be graceful and beautiful," as a character in *Gone With the Wind* sighs.[2] Similarly, in tourist literature, the "magnificent mansions" and "formal gardens" of lowcountry plantations are described as if they were the creation (and residence) of their owners alone.[3]

1. Since 1974, Drayton Hall has been owned and maintained by the National Trust for Historic Preservation and is open to the public.
2. Edward D. C. Campbell, Jr., "*Gone With the Wind*: The Old South as National Epic," in Richard Harwell, ed., "*Gone With the Wind*" as *Book and Film* (Columbia, 1983), 179.
3. Consider the following description of Magnolia Plantation and Gardens (a few miles

Drayton Hall (photograph by author)

In the late-twentieth-century low country, the image of the plantation has itself become a commodity. Resort developments in the Charleston suburbs and on the sea islands have adopted the names of real or imagined "plantations," turning the grace, privilege, and tradition that the term evokes into a selling feature.[4] These real estate brochures ignore the fact

---

north of Drayton Hall): "[The present owner's] family has owned Magnolia Plantation since the late 1600s, when Thomas Drayton, Jr., the son of a British Plantation Owner in Barbados, [and the grandfather of Drayton Hall's builder] married Ann Fox, daughter of a sea captain who owned a tract of Indian-controlled wilderness ten miles from Charleston. In that wilderness Drayton and his wife built a magnificent mansion reminiscent of the Drayton ancestral home in Northamptonshire, England, and immediately began to cultivate a formal garden near the house." Derek Fell, "Magnolia," *Americana*, January–February 1988, 34.

4. In May 1995, one such development, "The Plantation at Stono Ferry," offered prospective residents "relaxed luxury living" on lots priced from $20,000 to $160,000. The developer's brochure noted that "the first homesite to grace the sweeping acreage of Stono Ferry dates back to 1682 when James Beamer and his family of 13 from Barbados settled on the land

that in the "old South," the meaning of "plantation" depended upon where one stood. The view from the porch of the great house was quite different from that gained from the slave quarters. The current revival of the term seems painful proof of Ralph Ellison's remark "that Americans are notoriously selective in the exercise of historical memory."[5] Low-country blacks, at least, have not forgotten. Referring to the gates around the "new plantations," one local resident remarked with bitter humor, "it used to be you couldn't get off the plantations, now you can't get on."[6]

The plantation great house was not always so isolated, innocent, and serene. Left stranded by the tides of history, Drayton Hall, like many other surviving plantation great houses, stands bereft of its original social, economic, and political context. The combined effects of hurricanes, earthquake, revolution, and civil war have swept away the rice fields, outbuildings, and slave quarters that once occupied the site. At the time that it was built, and for the next six generations, John Drayton's "Palace" was the busy center of a populous and purposeful domain.[7] The plantation was created as a place of production—of rice, money, and power.

In the mid-eighteenth century, "plantation" signified not just a house but an entire community. On plat maps, great houses were drawn surrounded by a host of smaller structures, evocatively called "dependencies."[8] To one observer, the resulting scene was not unlike an English village; the "planters houses resemble Mannour houses" and the slave's housing resembled the "wooden cottages" of "poor villagers."[9] On plats, the great house and the cluster of buildings that surrounded it were often designated "the Settlement."[10]

---

to become planters." Given that a 50-acre headright was offered for every settler, regardless of status, it is very likely that Beamer's large "family" included several slaves.

5. See Mark Pinsky, "Hilton Head Report—Sea Island Plantations Revisited," *Southern Exposure* 10 (May–June 1982), 33; and "South Carolina—The New Plantations," *Economist*, 16 October 1993, 33; Ralph Ellison, *Going to the Territory* (New York, 1987), 124.

6. Peter Applebome, "Tourism Enriches an Island but Hilton Head's Blacks Feel Left Out," *New York Times*, 2 September 1994; see also "South Carolina—The New Plantations," 33; and Pinsky, "Hilton Head Report—Sea Island Plantations Revisited," 33.

7. *South Carolina Gazette*, 22 December 1758.

8. On seven plantation plat maps drawn between 1773 and 1786, an average of fourteen structures were depicted, including the great house; see "Plan of a Plantation belonging to Richard Waring," 21 December 1773, SCHS, 33–39; Estate of Jeremiah Savage (1782), SCDAH, Forfeited Estates Plats; Estate of Joseph Seabrook (1782), SCDAH; " 'Matanza' Plantation, belonging to John Holmes, Esqr." (1784), SCHS, 32–55–4; "Lands Belonging to Arthur Middleton, Esqr." (1785), SCHS, 32–30–14; " 'Skinking' Plantation belonging to Ralph Izard, Esqr." (1785), SCHS, 32–29–3; and "Turkey Hill Tract" (1786), SCHS, 32–30–8.

9. Quoted in John Donald Duncan, "Servitude and Slavery in Colonial South Carolina" (Ph.D. diss., University of Virginia, 1971), 249.

10. See, for example, "Plan of a Plantation belonging to Richard Waring"; " 'Skinking' Plantation belonging to Ralph Izard, Esqr."; and "Turkey Hill Tract."

In style, Drayton Hall and other great houses of the mid-eighteenth-century low country commonly sought to mimic the Georgian architecture then in vogue in Britain. In some cases, the builders made little or no allowance for the vast difference in climate between the English countryside and the low country.[11] Plantation names were also inspired by the metropolis and its adjacent palaces and parks. On the banks of the Cooper River in the mid-eighteenth century, slaves were hard at work in the rice fields of "Hyde Park," "Kensington," "Windsor," and "Richmond."[12] The desire of the low-country elite to Anglicize their plantations paralleled larger processes at work in the slave society. As with the country houses of the eighteenth-century English gentry, Drayton Hall and other plantation mansions were designed to serve as "power houses," the seats of a newly confident ruling class.[13]

Like Drayton Hall itself, the word "plantation" is a survivor. The experience of colonization not only engendered adaptations in English customs and institutions but it also altered the English language. Originally, plantation simply meant "planting."[14] In the late sixteenth century, when England's colonial ambitions began to take root, the word began to be used to denote "plantings" of people as well as of crops. In 1671, Lord Ashley wrote in this way of "the Plantation" of Carolina which had just begun.[15]

Soon, however, colonists' pursuit of private gain forced writers to distinguish between the "particular plantations" that settlers had staked out for themselves and the larger colony as a whole.[16] In early Carolina,

11. Compare, for example, Fenwick Hall, completed in South Carolina in 1730, and Delbridge House, built in the same decade in Wingham, Kent; Mills Lane, *Architecture of the Old South-South Carolina*, (Savannah, 1984), 29; and Daniel D. Rieff, *Small Georgian Houses in England and Virginia: Origins and Development through the 1750s* (Cranbury, N.J., 1986), 152.
12. From a map of Cooper River plantations in 1749 printed in Philip D. Morgan and George D. Terry, "Slavery in Microcosm: A Conspiracy Scare in Colonial South Carolina," *Southern Studies* 11 (Summer 1982), 133. Plantations along the Ashley River included "Windsor Hill," "Chatsworth," and "Runnymede"; Henry A. M. Smith, "The Ashley River, Its Seats and Settlements," *SCHM* 20 (1919), 11.
13. See Mark Girouard, *Life in the English Country House: A Social and Architectural History* (New Haven, 1978), 2; and also Philip Jenkins, *The Making of a Ruling Class: The Glamorganshire Gentry, 1640–1790* (Cambridge, 1983), 198.
14. *Oxford English Dictionary*, 2nd ed. (Oxford, 1989), 11, 976–77. For example, John Smith employed the word in this way in his 1612 *Map of Virginia*: "In April they [the Indians] begin to plant, but their chief plantation is in May"; reprinted in Karen Ordahl Kupperman, ed., *Captain John Smith. A Select Edition of His Writings* (Chapel Hill, 1988), 138.
15. Quoted in Peter H. Wood, *Black Majority: Negroes in Colonial South Carolina from 1670 to the Stono Rebellion* (New York, 1974), 26–27 and note. Similarly, seventeenth-century Englishmen wrote of "Plymouth Plantation," the "Plantation in Ulster," and the "Plantation begun in Virginia." The official name of the smallest state remains the "State of the Rhode Island and Providence Plantations."
16. The directors of the Virginia company were making this distinction as early as 1619; see Edmund S. Morgan, *American Slavery, American Freedom: The Ordeal of Colonial Virginia* (New York, 1975), 94.

"plantation" usually denoted private property and was often closely linked to slavery. In 1676, for example, a Virginia widow wrote that her late husband "did formerly Transport Severall Negros . . . into Carolina and did there Settle them upon a Plantacon."[17]

By the early eighteenth century, the diverse meanings of plantation on both sides of the Atlantic could cause confusion. In John Lawson's account of his travels through "Carolina," for instance, the word variously denoted the planting of crops, the fields cultivated by Indians, or entire colonies ("the plantations of *America*"), or, in the new "colonial" mode, the private estate of a colonist ("Mr. *Southwell's* Plantation").[18]

A fictive dialogue between "a West-Country Farmer" and "a Carolina Planter" shows not only that colonists were aware of the discrepancy between the colonial and metropolitan definitions of plantation but also that they expected to have the last word on the matter. When the farmer inquired about the "English Plantations in America," the planter corrected his terminology, describing the colonies as "Dominions." Later the planter instructed the farmer as to the proper, colonial usage. By the end of the pamphlet, the Englishman also used plantation in its new, "American" sense, asking if immigrants could "enter forthwith on a Plantation of their own, and in Business . . . for themselves."[19]

The colloquial and colonial redefinition of the plantation as a private enterprise first gained wide circulation in England with the publication of Daniel Defoe's *Life and Adventures of Robinson Crusoe* in 1719. Before being shipwrecked, Defoe's hero traveled to America, "purchased as much Land . . . as my Money could reach," "bought me a Negro slave," and enjoyed "the happy view . . . of being a rich and thriving man in my new Plantation."[20] Once marooned, Crusoe enacted colonization in miniature. He set about to transform his island into a recognizable English landscape. "I had . . . two Plantations in the Island," he declared after establishing a seashore camp and an inland garden; "besides this [beach hut], I had my Country Seat."[21] The appearance of the obedient and faithful Friday provided Crusoe with a slave for his "plantations." The

17. Quoted in Wood, *Black Majority*, 31.

18. John Lawson, *A New Voyage to Carolina*, ed. Hugh Talmage Lefler (London, 1709; Chapel Hill, 1967), 195, 66, 81, 226.

19. John Norris, *Profitable Advice for Rich and Poor in a Dialogue, or Discourse Between James Freeman, a Carolina Planter, and Simon Question, a West-Country Farmer* (London, 1712), reprinted in Jack P. Greene, ed., *Selling a New World: Two Colonial South Carolina Promotional Pamphlets* (Columbia, 1989), 87, 91, 107.

20. Daniel Defoe, *The Life and Adventures of Robinson Crusoe* (London, 1719), 39, 42, 43. The shipwreck that began the hero's more famous adventures occurred while Crusoe was en route to "Guinea" to obtain additional slaves.

21. Ibid., 179.

addition of a group of stranded Spaniards to his labor force moved the castaway to rhapsody:

> My Island was now peopled, and I thought myself very rich in Subjects. And it was a merry reflection which I frequently made, how like a King I look'd. First of all, the whole country was my own mere property; so that I had an undoubted right of dominion. Secondly, my people were perfectly subjected; I was absolute Lord & Lawgiver.[22]

Crusoe's reverie reveals that while plantation denoted a private estate, the word retained connotations beyond that of "mere property." A plantation was also a small "country" in which the owner, as absolute "King," could exercise "an undoubted right of dominion" over his "Subjects." A plantation denoted a set of social relations as well as a form of property; a true plantation must be "peopled."[23]

Like Crusoe's island, Drayton Hall (and every other low-country plantation) was a small world unto itself, with its own internal social, political, and economic relations. Each plantation was a microcosm of the larger society, a little kingdom within *the* kingdom. The doctrines of obedience and hierarchy that were exalted in the established church, the justice, mercy, and violence of the law, and the negotiated relations of the market all found expression within the gates of every plantation and in the relations between every master and his slaves. The plantation was the colonial slave society writ small; and equally, the colonial slave society was the plantation writ large. Ultimately, the entire social order rested upon the culture of power on every individual plantation. Before John Drayton could play a leading place in the church, the assembly, the magistrates' court, or the Govenor's Council, he first had to establish and maintain his dominion within his own plantation and over his "people."

Unlike Robinson Crusoe, however, low-country plantations did not exist in isolation. Masters needed the collective power of the slave society to impose and enforce their rule. Slaves had to know, quite literally, that there was nowhere to run. In the institutions of the law, the church, the slave patrol, and the militia, masters acted together to shore up their individual power on their own plantations. Each plantation, like

---

22. Ibid., 286.
23. In his sequel to *Robinson Crusoe*, published in the same year to take advantage of the enormous success of the first book, Defoe expressed the same idea even more explicitly: "I pleased my self with being the Patron of those People I placed there, and doing for them in a kind of haughty Majestick way, like an old Patriarchal Monarch; providing for them, as if I had been father of the whole Family, as well as of the Plantation." Defoe, *Farther Adventures of Robinson Crusoe* (London, 1719), 216–17.

the colony itself, was embedded in a much larger world. By definition, plantation societies are located on the "hinterland," "frontier," or "periphery" of larger social, political, and economic systems.[24] Drayton Hall was also a colonial institution.

To white Carolinians, the mansion at Drayton Hall may have proclaimed the wealth, confidence, and sophistication of a mature colonial ruling class. But the great house had a quite different meaning to the slaves who lived and worked in its shadow. To the slaves who made its bricks, built its walls, and whose work in the plantation's rice fields paid for its lavish appointments, Drayton Hall represented in a very literal sense the fruits of their labor. They may well have felt a justifiable pride in what they had made. At the same time, the arrogance, ambition, and power embodied in the great house spoke loudly to the slave quarters of John Drayton's determination to be the "absolute Lord & Lawgiver" to all who lived within the plantation's gates.

The Profits of Patriarchy

The plantations of the colonial low country were peripheral institutions in still another way. They stood on the boundary between early modern concepts of property and contemporaneous concepts of authority, and between the impersonal cash nexus of the market on the one hand and the personal, hierarchical social relations of a patriarchal society on the other. To a large extent, the success of the plantation as a political and as an economic institution depended upon masters' ability to traffic across this ambiguous frontier. The political economy of colonial low-country plantations was based upon a continued paradox: the cultivation of a stark conceptual distinction between property and authority so as to profit (both politically and economically) through the mitigation of this distinction in everyday practice.[25]

The preamble to the Negro Act highlighted the duality of the colonial slave society. On one hand, by reducing slaves to the status of commodities, the act seemed to deny their humanity. As "subjects of property,"

24. For discussions of plantations as peripheral institutions, see P. P. Courtenay, *Plantation Agriculture* (Boulder, Colo., 1980), 7–21; Edgar T. Thompson, "Introduction: The Plantation—A World-wide Institution," and Thompson, "The Institution of the Plantation Comparatively Considered," both in Sue Eakin and John Tarver, eds., *Plantations around the World* (Baton Rouge, 1986), 1–8 and 10–16; and Ann Laura Stoler, *Capitalism and Confrontation in Sumatra's Plantation Belt, 1870–1979* (New Haven, 1985), 6–13.
25. I use "political economy" according to the definition provided by Drew McCoy: "a dynamic interdependence among polity, economy, and society"; Drew McCoy, *Elusive Republic: Political Economy in Jeffersonian America* (New York, 1980), 6.

slaves were chattel that could be bought and sold, borrowed against, mortgaged, and reduced to cash equivalents like any other commodity. On the other hand, when the act proclaimed that slaves were to be kept "in due subjection and obedience," the opinions and actions of the slaves as human beings became the law's main object.[26] In this respect, the statute was concerned not with the slaves' value as commodities but with the expropriation of the labor of slaves as subject persons. Although these two definitions of the slave, as property and person, may seem at odds, they were closely related. Slaves were valued as property largely because of their masters' ability to extract their labor as subject persons.

The prosperity of the low country in the colonial period was based upon crops raised through the labor of the colony's slaves in rice and indigo fields. If the swamps of the low country were "the golden mines of Carolina," the colony's slaves were the miners.[27] Masters knew that their ability to command the labor of their slaves was the essential source of their wealth. After deducting the small costs of the slaves' maintenance, masters could expect a handsome profit from the product of their slaves' labor. In 1750, Johann Bolzius reported: "Intelligent planters say that an industrious Negro may earn [his master] 10 pounds [sterling] . . . apart from his food and clothing, in one year."[28] Twenty years later, James Grant was slightly more cautious in his projection of the possible profits of slavery to the master: "A Planter makes a great deal if he makes at the rate of eight pounds a year of his Negroes, clear of all expenses. To do that a plantation must be well established, and the Slaves must all be seasoned able working hands."[29]

The process of extracting this profit from the labor of the colony's slaves took place every day on the plantations and in the colonial metropolis of Charles Town. To describe colonial South Carolina as a slave society is to say much more than the obvious fact that the colony's labor force, and indeed a majority of its population, was comprised of slaves.

---

26. *Statutes*, 7, 397.
27. George Milligen-Johnston, *A Short Description of the Province of South Carolina* (London, 1770), reprinted in Chapman J. Milling, ed., *Colonial South Carolina: Two Contemporary Descriptions by Governor James Glen and Dr. George Milligen-Johnston* (Columbia, 1951), 119.
28. Klaus Gloewald, Beverly Starika, and Paul S. Taylor, trans. and eds., "Johann Martin Bolzius Answers a Questionaire on Carolina and Georgia," *William and Mary Quarterly*, 3rd ser., 14 (April 1957), 245. While Bolzius boasted of the potential profits of slave labor, the human "cost" of such wealth did not entirely escape him; he wrote that he could not help "marvelling that one feeds these poor creatures so miserably and keeps them in eternal slavery."
29. James Grant to the Earl of Egmont, 9 February 1769, Ballindalloch Castle Muniments, Ballindalloch, Scotland. Grant added a significant qualification: "I mean of produce to go to Market, so as to remit the Money to Europe, many things are consumed in a plantation which are of great utility in point of Living, tho' they cannot be converted into Cash."

It also indicates that the central relation of domination in this society, the foundation on which the social and economic relations of the entire society turned, was masters' daily assertion of authority over their slaves.[30] Every aspect of the society was shaped by masters' need to gain the labor they required to maintain the orderly and profitable production of rice and indigo for export.

The daily evocation of "due subjection and obedience" lay at the heart of the slave-master relation and, indeed, of all personal relations of domination.[31] The slaves' routine compliance could never be taken for granted. Each time slaves refused to play the part of dutiful subordinates, masters were reminded that their authority (as well as their prosperity) depended upon gaining their slaves' assent in the rituals of obedience. A slave who would not obey contradicted the very definition of slavery. In 1770, the Virginia planter Landon Carter was faced with one such refusal to comply. "My man Toney," Carter wrote, "is determined to struggle whether he shall not do as he pleases." After reviewing how his slave had ignored, deliberately misunderstood, and altogether frustrated his commands, Carter reflected in exasperation, "I might as well give up every Negroe if I submit to this impudence."[32]

Of course, in this constant "struggle" with their slaves, masters held the whip hand in a very literal sense. Masters advocated "smart flogging" and other forms of overt violence as a vital tool for keeping slaves at their labor. Because whipping was considered such a routine part of slave management, it was seldom thought worthy of mention by either overseers or masters. Thus, the figurative silence of the lash in the documentary record must not be taken literally. Rather, between every line of every letter that masters and overseers exchanged, the crack of the whip upon slaves' backs should be heard.[33] Slaves knew that direct disobedience would bring the whip as certainly as thunderstorms brought rain. More dangerous forms of rebelliousness would be met with increasingly harsh punishments and ultimately death. The market provided masters with another powerful

30. Of colonial Brazil, Stuart B. Schwartz writes that "no action could be taken, no decision made, no thought expressed without at least tacit recognition of the dominant labor form and the servile population it had created"; Stuart B. Schwartz, *Sugar Plantations in the Formation of Brazilian Society, Bahia, 1550–1835* (Cambridge, 1985), 258.
31. On the reciprocal nature of domination, see David Warren Sabean, *Power in the Blood: Popular Culture and Village Discourse in Early Modern Germany* (Cambridge, 1984), 24.
32. Entries of 15 and 31 March, 1770, in Jack P. Greene, ed., *The Diary of Landon Carter, of Sabine Hall, 1752–1778*, 2 vols., (Charlottesville, 1965), 1, 369, 378.
33. In 1766, Henry Laurens wrote to one of his overseers concerning a slave whom he ordered to be sold, "I think him the Laziest Rascal that ever was in my service & that he will require some smart flogging before he grows better." Henry Laurens to Joseph Brown, 21 August 1766, *PHL*, 5, 171. On this point see Winthrop D. Jordan, *Tumult and Silence at Second Creek: An Inquiry into a Civil War Slave Conspiracy* (Baton Rouge, 1993), 93–98.

and coercive weapon. Slaves who repeatedly refused to obey could be sold and forever separated from their loved ones and relations. Planters exalted their independence, but the individual authority of every master and the internal order of every plantation rested upon the collective and public foundations of the gallows (representing the state) and the auctioneer's gavel (representing the market).

While such measures served admirably to restore order and crush rebellion, they could not, by themselves, bring the crop in. If every perceived offense or affront (however minor) were punished with the sale or death of the offender (or provoked the offender to become a fugitive in order to avoid these consequences), masters would have destroyed the very relationship that they needed to exploit. No obedience could be extracted from slaves who had been sold, executed, or driven off. Moreover, like other subaltern groups, slaves learned to couch their resistance in forms that were not likely to provoke a massive retaliation. Subtle forms of resistance required subtle forms of control. The example of the gallows and auction block was a terrifying threat (and last resort) on every plantation. But the everyday exercise of plantation government was based upon more "economical," and less final, modes of domination.[34]

Hence, masters sought to extract obedience not only through the whip, gallows, and gavel but also through the power of words. The fact that all forms of domination are expressed in language is, on one level, a banality. Before orders can be obeyed, they must first be articulated and understood. But language and discourse are far more than passive telegraphs through which power can be quickly and unambiguously relayed. Language and the discursive process constitute fields of contention in themselves and are a primary locus of struggle between rulers and the ruled.

To speak of domination as discourse implies a degree of exchange. Orders from above require a response from below. Even if, as in most cases, the only response that masters sought was the silent assent of full comprehension and prompt obedience, they soon discovered that the clearest commands were apt to fall upon deaf ears. As masters learned when they employed slaves to carry messages, dialogue was inevitably two-sided. Made to listen or called to speak, slaves could turn the power of words to their advantage. A tiny but illuminating example of the po-

34. Pierre Bourdieu notes: "In a society in which overt violence, the violence of . . . the merciless master, meets with collective reprobation and is liable to provoke a violent riposte from the victim or to force him to flee (that is to say, in either case, in *the absence of any other recourse*, to provoke the annihilation of the very relationship which was intended to be exploited), . . . the violence of credit, confidence, personal loyalty, hospitality, gifts, gratitude, piety . . . cannot fail to be seen as the most economical mode of domination, i.e., the mode which best corresponds to the economy of the system." Bourdieu, *Outline of a Theory of Practice*, trans. Richard Nice (Cambridge, 1977), 191–92.

tential for inversion that language offered can be found in Eliza Pinckney's effort to interrogate a slave messenger about a report that her son-in-law lay gravely injured at her plantation. "I asked him many questions," she wrote in exasperation, "but I could not get anything out of him more than it was a scratch."[35]

The letters, journals, and accounts of low-country planters are a catalogue of masters' continued inability to transform their wishes into their slaves' commands. If slaves had understood every command perfectly and had obeyed without hesitation, planters would have had small reason to correspond with their overseers and agents and consequently, little evidence of the internal social relations of plantations would have survived. Instances of orders gone awry provide a good source for investigating how power was imposed and masked on low-country plantations. Examples of miscommunications and imperfect, incomplete dialogues between masters and slaves document the processes of domination. Careful scrutiny of the language and metaphors within which masters sought to rule and of the shifting and multiple interpretations of these encounters reveals the ongoing struggle between masters and slaves and the gap between the total obedience masters claimed and the limited compliance slaves grudgingly provided.

Patriarchy was the dominant cultural metaphor used to express and naturalize unequal social relations of every kind in the early modern period.[36] In this specific historical context, patriarchy extended the familial model and the ideal of paternal authority beyond the household to encompass all forms of authority. As a historian of early modern England has noted, "virtually all social relationships—not merely fathers and children or magistrates and subjects—were regarded as patriarchal or familial in essence."[37] Political society was akin to a large family; the

---

35. Eliza Pinckney to Daniel Horry, 9 March 1768, Pinckney Papers, SCHS.
36. Following Rhys Isaac, I have chosen "metaphors" to describe what Pierre Bourdieu terms "taxonomies." See Isaac, "Discourse on the Method," in Isaac, *The Transformation of Virginia, 1740–1790* (Chapel Hill, 1982), 323–57, and Isaac, "Communication and Control: Authority Metaphors and Power Contests on Colonel Landon Carter's Virginia Plantation, 1752–1778," in Sean Wilentz, ed., *Rites of Power: Symbolism, Ritual, and Politics Since the Middle Ages* (Philadelphia, 1985), 275–302.
37. Gordon J. Schochet, *Patriarchalism in Political Thought: The Authoritarian Family and Political Speculation and Attitudes Especially in Seventeenth-Century England* (New York, 1975), 165; for the presence of patriarchal ideology in eighteenth-century America, see Jay Fliegelman, *Prodigals and Pilgrims: The American Revolution against Patriarchal Authority, 1750–1800* (New York, 1982); and Gordon S. Wood, *The Radicalism of the American Revolution* (New York, 1992), 11–92; for planters as patriarchs, see Philip D. Morgan, "Three Planters and Their Slaves: Perspectives on Slavery in Virginia, South Carolina, and Jamaica, 1750–1790," in Winthrop Jordan and Sheila Skemp, eds., *Race and Family in the Colonial South* (Jackson, Miss., 1987), 54–68; Allan Kulikoff, *Tobacco and Slaves: The Development of Southern Cultures in the Chesapeake, 1680–1800* (Chapel Hill, 1986), 165–204; Kenneth A. Lockridge, *On the*

king was described as "the common father of all those that are under his authority."[38] Patriarchal metaphors were used to describe not only human relations but also the hierarchies that were perceived to exist in nature. A tract published in England in 1757, for example, confidently asserted that "the Universe resembles a large and well regulated Family, in which all the officers and servants, and even the domestic animals, are subservient to each other in a proper subordination."[39]

This conflation of the family and the state worked both ways; if politics was familial, the family was likewise political. The early modern family was a small kingdom, and every father and husband was the monarch of his household. Whether they were wives, servants, or slaves, all subordinates who murdered their lord and master were judged to be guilty of "petty treason" and suffered the death of a regicide: burning at the stake.[40] The Negro Act similarly indicated the political character of the master-slave relationship when it placed slaves "under the government" of their masters.[41]

In 1785, Henry Laurens penned a portrait of himself as a slave master. At the time, Laurens held extensive plantations in the South Carolina and Georgia low country and was the owner of over three hundred slaves. But plantation pursuits had come late to Laurens; he was nearly forty when he first became master of a plantation in 1762. In his younger life, he had devoted his considerable energy and abilities to acquiring a fortune as a Charles Town merchant. According to a contemporary, Laurens was "a sober arbitrator . . . in little differences of accounts and reckonings, . . . skilled in the rate of exchange . . . and in the price of commodities."[42]

Yet, while he was undoubtedly well versed in the vocabulary of the counting house and the law of the market, Laurens chose to portray his relations with his slaves in quite another language. "My Negroes," he wrote,

---

Sources of Patriarchal Rage: The Commonplace Books of William Byrd and Thomas Jefferson and the Gendering of Power in the Eighteenth Century (New York, 1992); and Kathleen M. Brown, *Good Wives, Nasty Wenches, and Anxious Patriarchs: Gender, Race, and Power in Colonial Virginia* (Chapel Hill, 1996), 319–66.

38. *The Whole Duty of Man* (London, 1735), 288.

39. Soame Jenyns, *A Free Inquiry Into the Nature and Origin of Evil* (London, 1757), quoted in John Dunn, "The Politics of Locke in England and America in the Eighteenth Century," in J. W. Yolton, ed., *John Locke: Problems and Perspectives* (Cambridge, 1969), 65.

40. J. M. Beattie, *Crime and the Courts in England, 1660–1800* (Princeton, 1986), 78–79.

41. *Statutes*, 7, 397, 403, 411. For a recent debate on the character and meaning of "household government" in early America, see "Anglo-American Household Government in Comparative Perspective," Carole Shammas, and the comments of Daniel Scott Smith, Richard White, and Patricia Seed, *William and Mary Quarterly*, 3rd ser., 52 (January 1995), 104–66.

42. This description of Laurens is taken from Egerton Leigh, "The Man Unmasked" (Charles Town, 1769), printed in *PHL*, 6, 457.

are in more comfortable circumstances than any equal number of Peas-
antry in Europe, there is not a Beggar among them nor one unprovided
with food, raiment & good Lodging, they also enjoy property; the Lash is
forbidden; they all understand this declaration as a Substitute—"If you
deserve whipping I shall conclude you don't love me & will sell you. . . ."

. . . Yet I believe no man gets more work from his Negroes than I do,
at the same time they are my Watchmen and my friends; never was an
absolute Monarch more happy in his Subjects than at the present time
I am.[43]

Like Robinson Crusoe, Laurens imagined his plantations as a world,
where he reigned as an "absolute Monarch" over his "Subjects." He
depicted the slaves' provision of labor and his provision of food, clothing, and shelter as part of a reciprocal relationship of obligations and
duties. Disobedience and misbehavior, on the other hand, were portrayed by Laurens as evidence that the slaves concerned " 'don't love
me.' " While claiming to shun "the Lash," he menaced slaves with the
prospect of sale and separation from their homes and families. Both in
threatening his slaves with harsh punishments and in promising to provide for their basic needs, Laurens echoed Defoe's castaway in celebrating his role as the "Patriarchal Monarch" of his plantations.[44]

Ideally, each plantation household was constructed as a miniature version of the larger social order, as a little kingdom. Likewise, every individual plantation was both agent and subject of the larger economic,
political, and cultural structures of the early modern Anglo-American
world. Masters sought to foster a vision of authority and a system of
social relations that would enable them to achieve their economic and
political goals. Masters, magistrates, and Anglican ministers readily appropriated the patriarchal metaphor to explain masters' rule over slaves.
They asserted that the obedience slaves owed to their masters was the
same as that which all social inferiors owed to their superiors. In 1773,
Laurens described his slaves as "poor Creatures who look up to their
Master as their Father, their Guardian, & Protector, & to whom their is
a reciprocal obligation upon the Master."[45]

43. Laurens to Alexander Hamilton, 19 April 1785, in Harold C. Syrett et al., eds., *The Papers
of Alexander Hamilton*, 27 vols. (New York, 1961–87), 3, 605–8.
44. Even more evocative of Crusoe were the words of George Oglivie in a letter to his sister
in 1774: "It is not worth mentioning—but having no overseer here just now, I slept last
night for the first time in my life at least four miles distant from any white person—like
the Tyrant of some Asiatick Isle the only free Man in an island of slaves." George Oglivie
to Margaret Oglivie, 25 June 1774, Oglivie-Forbes of Boyndlie Mss., Aberdeen University
Library, Aberdeen, Scotland, 2740/10/5/1.
45. Henry Laurens to Lachlan McIntosh, 13 March 1773, *PHL*, 8, 618.

From the time Laurens purchased his first plantation and assembled his first slave workers, he began to take on the role and language of a patriarch. For many slaves, the first lesson was to acknowledge their master's power. Describing one slave as "a Cunning, Quarrelsome, Young fellow," Laurens instructed the overseer to "take him down early but don't drive him away."[46] Laurens described another slave in a similar vein: "She is a sullen Slut but easily kept down if you exert your Authority."[47] However, two slave women who were "with Child & near their time" received different treatment; "Mrs. Laurens has given Baby Clothes to one & will send some for the other next Week," Laurens noted.[48]

The distribution of clothes and commodities to the slaves provides an example of the way in which everyday events and practical necessities could be shaped and interpreted through the metaphors of patriarchy. Masters interpreted these transactions as unequal exchanges in which slaves' acceptance of these gifts tacitly acknowledged their subjection. Slaves could see through their master's patriarchal pose and were aware that the goods their master so "graciously" provided had been bought with their labor. They also knew that to stand at the foot of the steps of the great house and openly reject the master's patriarchal script was fraught with dangerous consequences. Therefore, slaves were usually content to take the blankets and bacon they needed (and had earned) and to give their master the symbolic gratitude that he demanded. In the public transcript, at least, slaves acquired their sustenance with their thanks rather than with their labor. In 1759, for instance, Robert Raper, a plantation agent, wrote his absentee employer in London "that your Negroes were all well pleased to receive their cloathes & desired me to thank you for the same."[49] Nine years later, Raper wrote that he had distributed "the Hatts you sent for which your negroes thank you much."[50]

Masters could also use the plantation store and cellars of the great house as the source of special commodities to mark extraordinary occasions in the slave quarters. At Christmas, and whenever there was a wedding, a birth, or a death among their slaves, masters commonly provided rum, sugar, and often some of the food, especially meat, that played a large part in the slaves' festivities.[51] Through these gestures, a

46. Henry Laurens to James Lawrence, 1 January 1763, *PHL*, 3, 203.
47. Henry Laurens to James Lawrence, 7 January 1763, *PHL*, 3, 205.
48. Henry Laurens to James Lawrence, 1 January 1763, *PHL*, 3, 203. But pregnant women could also receive another sort of treatment. In 1766, for example, Frederick Wiggins, overseer of Laurens's Ashepoo plantation, was denounced by a neighboring planter as "an impudent Saucy fellow . . . [who] must whip Wenches till they misscarry"; John Jackson to Frederick Wiggins, 20 March 1766, *PHL*, 5, 97.
49. Robert Raper to John Colleton, 6 December 1759, Robert Raper Letterbook, WSCRO.
50. Robert Raper to Margaret Colleton, 15 November 1768, WSCRO.
51. For examples of slaves being provided with rum and sugar to commemorate births and

master could intrude into the social life of the slave quarters and play the part of a benevolent patriarch providing for the needs of his subjects.

Patriarchal discourse framed the provision of sustenance and protection as a gift from the master, which slaves as grateful subjects repaid through their obedience and labor. Masters could then apply a portion of the profit from the slaves' labor to provide the slaves with new "gifts," thus forging new obligations, which required more labor, and so on in an endless cycle of unequal reciprocity. The relationships, obligations, and duties within the patriarchal social order were meant to be both perpetual and inescapable. In one sense, patriarchal metaphors functioned as an etiquette of socially approved behavior. Each individual within the social order was called upon to understand and live up to the responsibilities and obligations of his or her station.

The master or manager could dictate not only the place but also the time that such necessities would be distributed. Masters often waited until periods when a high degree of resistance to their commands was anticipated. In 1768, for example, Laurens sought to transfer some of his slaves from South Carolina to a new plantation in Georgia. He informed his overseer that to prevent the chosen slaves from running away, "I have been oblig'd to keep them constantly on board my Schooner . . . [and] I have also given a few Cloths amongst the whole to encourage them to go away chearfully as well as because such was necessary to them."[52]

The early summer, when the rice fields had to be constantly hoed, was also the peak period of the year for slaves to take refuge from the driver's whip by running away.[53] Many masters chose this period to provide slaves with their summer clothing. Josiah Smith, for example, wrote in the summer of 1773, "that to encourage . . . [the slaves] perseverance in duty, [I] have treated them with a suit of oznaburgs each with a Beef and some Liquor to be given after hoeing is all over."[54] Planters provided other goods beside clothing to "encourage" their slaves not to flee during the intense stoop labor that the rice crop required during the weeks of "dry cultivation" in early summer.[55] Smith portrayed the distribution of

deaths, see Charles Pinckney Account Book, 1753–1757, Pinckney Family Papers, LC, and also Plantation Book (1773), William Wragg Papers, SCHS. For an example of slaves being given "a hog or two to entertain the company" at a wedding, see James Barclay, *The Voyages and Travels of James Barclay* (London, 1777), 27.

52. Henry Laurens to William Stork, 28 January 1768, *PHL*, 5, 573.

53. See Philip D. Morgan, "The Development of Slave Culture in Eighteenth-Century Plantation America" (Ph.D. diss., University of London, 1977), Graph 2–1, 71.

54. Josiah Smith to George Austin, 22 July 1773, Josiah Smith, Jr., Letterbook, SHC-UNC.

55. According to Charles Joyner: "For the slaves, the three weeks of dry cultivation were excruciating. They worked under intense heat and humidity on muddy ground with short narrow hoes. They had to complete two or three complete hoeings with the small hoes

these items as a "treat" from the master to his slaves, for which the latter were expected to be dutifully thankful. Smith noted in 1772: "I have desired that the Howers . . . may be properly encouraged to stand firm to that heavy part of their work by a present of Meat & Liquor which I hope has had the good effect of keeping them at home, not having heard that so much as one hath run away."[56] The timely presentation of such valued commodities could have an impact far beyond their cost. As one plantation agent wrote to his employer a few years later, "such presents are only a small charge, but [are] a great service to the poor slaves."[57]

In this context, ingratitude and rebellion were thought to be synonymous. The Virginia master Landon Carter thought " 'Ingratitude' . . . to be no less than 'the Devil.' " It was, he wrote, "the basis of every species of evil."[58] Similarly, low-country masters commonly described slaves who resisted or rejected their authority as "ungrateful rascals" or "ungrateful villains."[59]

Masters portrayed their recourse to physical punishment or sale as a response to the slave's social ingratitude, of which the particular disobedient act was but a symptom. In 1767, the colony's chief justice, William Simpson, wrote: "Mr. Dunnett about three years ago purchased of me a Negro fellow and his Son; the fellow writes to his wife frequently, and appears by his letters to be in great distress for want of her, he disobliged me, otherwise I would not have parted with him."[60]

In 1777, one of Laurens's slaves "dropd a hint" that he was dissatisfied with working in the field and threatened to run away. Laurens claimed to have "expostulated with him in the kindest Terms" until the slave "made fair Promises" to remain at work. "If [after these promises] he sh[oul]d elope and you can recover him," Laurens instructed his overseer, "after due Correction, cause Irons to be put upon him which he cannot disengage." Laurens concluded, "it will be the first Instance of any Negro of mine put in Irons, but his Ingratitude will deserve the punishment."[61]

By speaking to the slave personally, Laurens responded to a challenge to his authority by attempting to bind the slave with affective ties. When confronted face to face, the slave was compelled to give Laurens his

during this period—the last very lightly and carefully." Charles Joyner, *Down by the Riverside: A South Carolina Slave Community* (Chicago, 1982), 47.

56. Josiah Smith to George Austin, 30 July 1772, Josiah Smith, Jr., Letterbook, UNC-SHC.

57. Robert Raper to Thomas Boone, 13 May 1768, Robert Raper Letterbook, WSCRO.

58. Greene, ed., *The Diary of Colonel Landon Carter*, 1, 52.

59. John Lewis Gervais to Henry Laurens, 8 May 1778, Henry Laurens Papers, SCL-USC; Henry Laurens to John Lewis Gervais, 5 September 1777, *PHL*, 11, 492.

60. William Simpson to James Grant, 15 June 1767, Ballindalloch Castle Muniments, Ballindalloch, Scotland, 0771–243.

61. Henry Laurens to John Loveday, 21 June 1777, *PHL*, 11, 386–87.

pledge that he would obey. To have rebuffed his master in this context would doubtless have been an act of "impudence" itself deserving of punishment. Laurens felt the slave was now bound to his word. A breach of this coerced promise would justify harsh measures. The blame for any resulting punishment, Laurens concluded, would lie upon the slave for his ingratitude.

Masters could solicit promises upon almost any occasion. When James Akin learned in 1749 that his slaves had been conspiring to rebel and "kill the white people" in South Carolina before escaping to St. Augustine, one of his slaves testified that Akin responded by calling "his Negroes together and talked to them so much that they promised they would attempt no such thing."[62] Such practices may have served to mark the limits of acceptable dissent. Slaves who crossed the line after giving their word could expect to be harshly dealt with.

Slaves' desire to secure greater autonomy *in the short term* often led them to negotiate within and therefore tacitly accept the patriarchal metaphor that their masters proferred.[63] Slaves who spoke in the language of the dominant class and exhibited deference were far more likely to be successful in their appeal for redress than were slaves who sought to negotiate on their own terms and in their own language.[64] Slaves often chose to speak within the metaphors of patriarchy in order to make use of them in their own interests. If they performed their assigned duties, these slaves also sought to claim their reciprocal due. By calling on their owner to live up to the precepts of the patriarchal ideal, such slaves may have accommodated themselves to their servitude but they also tried to secure the best bargain that they could for their compliance. The struggle undertaken by these slaves was from *within* slavery and from *within* the metaphors of domination put forward by the masters.

In some cases, slaves could turn masters' use of verbal agreements to

62. JGC, 24 January 1749, microfilm, LC, 50.
63. As Bourdieu notes: "[Those] disadvantaged by the symbolic order . . . [inadvertently] recognize the legitimacy of the dominant [metaphors] . . . in the very fact that their only chance of neutralizing those of its effects most contrary to their own interests lies in submitting to them in order to make use of them." Bourdieu, *Outline of a Theory of Practice*, 165.
64. An interesting example of this phenomenon can be found in the diary of Philip Fithian, tutor to the children of Virginia planter Robert Carter from 1773 to 1774: "About ten [o'clock] an old Negro Man came with a complaint to Mr. Carter of the Overseer that he does not allow him his Peck of corn a Week . . . We were sitting in the passage, he sat himself down on the Floor clasp'd his Hands together, with his face directly to Mr. *Carter*, & then began his Narration." Although Carter's slave is calling on his master to overrule the decision of the white overseer, his challenge to the authority of the overseer is couched in terms of extreme outward deference to Carter. Quoted in Isaac, *The Transformation of Virginia*, 75.

their own advantage and demand that their voice be heard with respect to decisions affecting their lives. In this way, spoken promises and personal ties created a discourse that allowed slaves some room to negotiate in their own interest. Promises given *after* a transgression could be used to repay the debt of ingratitude and thereby avoid a whipping or worse punishment. When four of Laurens's slaves ran away in 1777, the plantation manager thought it "best to over look this fault, as they came in of their own Accord, & promise to behave better for the future."[65]

That slaves could negotiate within the metaphors of patriarchy did not mean that they had internalized the metaphor's depiction of social reality. Slaves were capable of seeing the reality of their exploitation through the facade of patriarchy. The metaphors of the market offered slaves an alternative language in which to contain encounters with their masters. While they were seldom able to speak their minds directly in the face of power, slaves sought to gain whatever concessions they could for their compliance.

Ordinarily, masters' ability to induce slaves to negotiate in the language of patriarchy allowed them to confine slave resistance to less threatening channels. However, if the master somehow failed to live up to the duties or character of a true patriarch, slaves could, without departing from the "rules" and challenging the slave society directly, make a bid to withdraw their labor and subordination altogether. While seeming to acknowledge their acceptance of the social order, slaves could deny their obedience by claiming that their master was not a genuine patriarch and therefore did not deserve their submission.

The experience of women slave owners illustrates the way that social weakness allowed slaves to take advantage of a suspect claim to patriarchal authority. The metaphors of patriarchy called for women's subordination to their husbands and fathers as much as for slaves' subordination to their masters. For a woman to be master of herself and sole master of others went against patriarchal conventions about who were considered rightful holders of authority. In this world, the words "female master" were a contradiction in terms.[66] White male neighbors often expressed doubts about the authority of female masters, and women slave owners may have faced an increased level of challenge from their slaves. In 1769,

65. John Lewis Gervais to Henry Laurens, 29 July 1777, *PHL*, 11, 412.
66. For more on the gender-specific nature of patriarchy and the unease created by women whose independence seemed to subvert the established order, see Julie Hardwick, *The Practice of Patriarchy: Gender and the Politics of Household Authority in Early Modern France* (State College, Pa., 1998), and Natalie Zemon Davis, *Society and Culture in Early Modern France* (Palo Alto, Calif., 1975), 124–51. For a discussion of the social suspicion that fell upon women of property in colonial society, see Carol F. Karlsen, *The Devil in the Shape of a Woman: Witchcraft in Colonial New England* (New York, 1987).

for example, Robert Raper remarked that one woman's slaves "have been very troublesome lately having had too much of their own way for a long time."[67] Some empirical evidence suggests that female masters did in fact confront a greater degree of slave resistance than did their male counterparts. A comparison of the sex-ratio among those masters who placed advertisements for runaways with the distribution of all slaves between male and female masters reveals that female masters were far more likely than male masters to advertise for a runaway.[68]

But successful patriarchy was about more than gender hierarchies. Patriarchs also had to have the economic and social resources that were expected of their station. A poor man was also a poor master. One incident exemplifies the way in which patriarchy and property were linked in the minds of slaves and masters alike. In 1777, Henry Laurens was acting as the manager of absentee Ralph Izard's South Carolina plantations. In a letter written to Izard in April, Laurens informed his friend that

> A report has been whispered here that you had taken lodgings in the King's Bench . . . [and] it had reached the Ears of your Negroes, I could not contradict the Story, but recommended Strongly to them to work you out again—upon some, this has had a good effect—others, who think themselves more judicious than their fellows—say tis your own fault—you don't deserve Negroes.[69]

Some of Izard's slaves, it appears, having heard (or created) rumors that their master had been thrown into debtor's prison, reasoned that since he was no longer capable of governing himself, Izard did not have the right (or, more concretely, the power) to exercise "government" over others. A patriarch who failed to live up to his own obligations and the responsibilities of his station might not "deserve Negroes" or, more to the point, might not have the support of the social order necessary to keep his people in order.

A second letter, written two months later, described the slow disintegra-

67. Robert Raper to Thomas Boone, 8 April 1769, Robert Raper Letterbook, WSCRO.
68. In a census of all males slaves between sixteen and sixty years of age kept by the road commissioners of St. John Berkeley Parish between 1762 and 1788, women held 5.1 percent (912) of the total of 17,949 slaves. But women placed 7.6 percent (59) of 778 runaway slave advertisements placed in the *South Carolina Gazette* between 1740 and 1759. Although I believe these figures do indicate an actual difference in the occurrence of runaways on male- and female-headed plantations, it could also be the case that female masters were more inclined to advertise for runaways from their estates. Minute Book of the Commissioners of the Roads, St. John's, Berkeley County, SCDAH; and Lathan A. Windley, ed., *Runaway Slave Advertisements* [*South Carolina Gazette*] (Westport, Conn., 1983), 39–178.
69. Henry Laurens to Ralph Izard, 2 April 1777, *PHL*, 11, 331–32.

tion of this doubtful patriarch's authority. While reflecting that the most "troublesome . . . Branch of Plantation Business" was "restrain[ing the] . . . vicious Designs" of the slaves, Laurens complained that "I have had more of it fall to my Lot from your Negroes . . . than I had experienced in twenty Years with my own." "Your Negroes," Laurens wrote, "are continually deserting the plantations and going [to Charles Town]." Laurens reported that Izard's plantation residence "had been plunder'd by the Negro Woman in whose Care you left the house, and by her Companions" and that "the greatest part" of Izard's wine cellar had been stolen or consumed by slaves of the vicinity. In conclusion, Laurens advised his friend that to silence "the Voice[s] . . . against you" and for "the Amendment of your Estate," Izard should "attempt to appear" before his slaves in person.[70]

The metaphors of patriarchy had a larger social context than the bounds of each individual plantation. A master who was not accorded respect among other masters risked losing the respect of his slaves. Izard's slaves were shrewd judges of their master's authority and of his potential ability to call upon the collective power of the slave society. A master who was socially or geographically isolated might have difficulty in engaging other slaveholders in the vicinity for support in the day-to-day maintenance of patriarchal authority. In 1766, for example, Laurens based his opposition to the establishment of plantations in the wilderness of East Florida by saying that "if you have no neighbours or no good ones your Negroes will be exposed to the arbitrary power of an overseer & perhaps sometimes [be] tempted to knock him in the head & file off in a body."[71] The vaunted autonomy of each plantation existed within a social context. Robinson Crusoe notwithstanding, no plantation could exist as an island complete unto itself.

The Ties That Bind

Masters may have hoped that their slaves would internalize a sense of their obligations and dependency, but cash and credit were so closely intertwined in the words and minds of slaveholders themselves that such a selfless slave was difficult for masters themselves to imagine. In a letter to one of his overseers, for example, Laurens wrote: "I send

70. Henry Laurens to Ralph Izard, 9 June 1777, *PHL*, 11, 349–54.
71. Henry Laurens to Richard Oswald, 12 August 1766, *PHL*, 5, 156–57. Similarly, in 1769 Laurens warned a ship captain: "If he should Ship Negroes on board your Sloop, be very careful to guard against insurrection. Never put your Life in their power a moment. For a moment is sufficient to deprive you of it . . . & yet you may treat such Negroes with great humanity"; Henry Laurens to Hinson Todd, 14 April 1769, *PHL*, 6, 438.

old Stepney to s[t]ay three or four Weeks to assist in turning and watching the new Indigo. He is very honest & if you will speak to him he will not allow anybody within his sight to rob you. . . . [G]ive him a dram & a Little Toddy every day but not too much."[72] Apparently, even the obedience of a favored slave could not be reliably secured without the creation of a personal, verbal tie and the provision of a material reward. Personal interest and economic calculations were woven into the fabric of the slave system by a patriarchal language that constantly equated love with labor and coercion with correction.[73]

Slaves' ability to produce for themselves in their gardens and to engage in market relations in the evenings and on Sundays stood in marked contrast to the equation of labor with love and duty which, according to the metaphors of patriarchy, was to govern their work the remainder of the week. Cash transactions and commodity exchange had no part in the master's extraction of the "due subjection and obedience" that he needed to cultivate his fields. But, as the "law of the market" gained a foothold in the slave quarters, slaves were provided with a language through which they could escape the smothering confines of patriarchy and express their grievances in terms which their masters would understand and respect.

When interpreted through market metaphors, the masters' unrequited appropriation of the product of slaves' toil was little more than theft. Market relations exposed the extent of slaves' economic exploitation and revealed the hollowness of patriarchy and the arbitrary basis of the masters' authority. For slaves, the realization that they were denied "the just reward of . . . their labor" gave moral justification for retribution in the form of theft, sabotage, and flight.[74] At least some worried masters agreed. For example, Thomas Jefferson excused slave theft on the grounds that "the slave may . . . justifiably take a little from one who has taken all from him."[75]

---

72. Laurens concluded the letter by saying that as "the Old Man Stepney does not seem very willing to be from home . . . you must send him down" as soon as he can be spared; Henry Laurens to John Smith, 15 August 1765, *PHL*, 4, 661–62.

73. In 1765, Laurens instructed a new overseer on how to deal with his slaves: "Use gentle means mixed with easy authority first. If that does not succeed make choice of the most stubborn one or two & chastize them severely but properly & with mercy that they may be convinced that the end of correction is to be amendment." Henry Laurens to John Smith, 30 May 1765, *PHL*, 4, 633.

74. Frederick Douglass, "The Slaves' Right to Steal," excerpted from *My Bondage, My Freedom*, reprinted in *Frederick Douglass: The Narrative and Selected Writings*, ed. Michael Meyer (New York, 1984), 137. For an interesting discussion of these issues see Alex Lichtenstein, " 'That Disposition to Theft, With Which They have been Branded': Moral Economy, Slave Management, and the Law," *Journal of Social History* 21 (Spring 1988), 413–40.

75. Thomas Jefferson, *Notes on the State of Virginia*, ed. William Pended (Chapel Hill, 1954), 142.

Ultimately, such interpretations threatened to reduce master-slave relations to little more than a brutal power struggle in which each side took what it could and recognized no obligations of reciprocity. While this might have been a closer approximation of reality than the fictionalized metaphors of patriarchy, such a perpetual state of war between masters and slaves could not serve as the foundation for a stable labor regime. If patriarchy could never be fully implemented, a new if more contingent "economy" of master-slave relations had to be constructed. Market relations offered one alternative.

Slaves' economic initiative was founded above all upon the determination of slaves themselves to gain some control of the product of their labor. Masters reacted to these hard-won initiatives and sought to limit the damage done both to their practical authority and to their ideology of complete subordination. If slaves primarily sought individual ends—to eat better, to hold wealth as families, and to acquire some few "creature comforts"—and acquired these "privileges" incrementally, the long-term effect could nonetheless result in significant concessions from masters and transform the "rules" of the slave society.

An illuminating example of such a transformation is the long struggle between slaves and masters over the produce of the slaves' provision grounds and masters' responsibility for slaves' subsistence needs. The practice that predominated at the beginning of the eighteenth century required slaves to devote their free time and the produce of their provision grounds to meeting their basic requirements of food and clothing. For example, the colony's ministers noted in 1712 that "to free themselves from the trouble of feeding and cloathing their slaves [planters] allow them one day in the week to . . . plant for themselves."[76] Similarly, in 1742, Johann Bolzius wrote: "These Negroes, like many others, receive no clothes from their master but must work on Sunday too, and afterwards they turn their crops into money and buy themselves some old rags."[77] As this practice relieved the master of the expense of providing for his slaves' subsistence, slaves were, in effect, working for the master on their own time as well as his.

The practice of growing their own provisions and trading their surplus for clothes had the side effect of teaching slaves the commodity value of their labor. By acting in the market, even if it were only to acquire "some old rags" and other badly needed necessities, slaves learned that the product of their work had a material value and could be exchanged for

76. "The Instructions of the clergy of South Carolina given to Mr. Johnston [1712]," SPG records, microfilm, LC, A8 429.
77. George Fenwick Jones, trans., "John Martin Boltzius' [Johann Bolzius] Trip to Charleston, October 1742," SCHM 82 (April 1981), 104.

an equivalency of goods. Accustomed to producing for themselves part of every day and aware that through the agency of the market surplus foodstuffs could be exchanged for other commodities, slaves may have begun to expect that the product of labor rightly belonged to the laborer.

As contact with the market slowly furthered this belief among the slaves, masters may have begun to feel that their authority was being undermined. Gradually, the increasing disequilibrium between the slaves' concept of what was "just" and the practice of the plantations may have led masters to begin to bear a larger share of the costs of the slaves' daily subsistence needs. By the mid-eighteenth century, planta- tion record books show that masters had come to perceive the feeding and clothing of their slaves as part of their responsibility as plantation patriarchs. A visitor to the low country in 1773 described the "custom" as it had evolved by that time. Slaves, he wrote, "do not plant in their fields for subsistence, but for amusement, pleasure, and profit, their mas- ters giving them clothes, and sufficient provisions from their granaries."[78]

In this way, the labor of slaves in plantation fields could be said to be "exchanged" (in keeping with the idea that the slaves' labor had a "com- modity" value that had to be acknowledged) with their master in return for their basic food and clothing. Accordingly, slaves could now feel that their labor was in some way compensated and the plantation equilibrium could be restored. If slaves were denied this "customary" right, they could, as in their defense of property right, give their master "a hard time."

A rare, because explicit, illustration of how masters and slaves might bargain over the terms of labor is contained in a newspaper advertise- ment of 1778. A North Carolina correspondent informed Charles Town readers that Tom, "a negroe fellow," had lately turned up on his door- step. Tom claimed that he had run away from his master in South Car- olina seven years earlier, "that he had lived two years in the woods" and had eventually arrived in Wilmington, where "he was taken up by one Nathaniel Williams . . . [and that] Tom agreed to go home with the said Williams and to work for him [in return] for victuals and cloths." After five years of working for Williams, however, Tom decided to try to return to his original master. Tom reached this drastic decision, the paper reported, "on his being obliged by Williams to pay for his own cloaths out of his Sundays work."[79]

Through an almost imperceptible process of negotiation, slaves gained

78. ["Scotus Americanus"], *Information Concerning the Province of North Carolina*, in William K. Boyd, ed., "Some North Carolina Tracts of the Eighteenth Century," *North Carolina Historical Review* 3 (1926), 616.
79. *South Carolina and American General Gazette*, 2 April 1778.

the ability to use the product of their free time, not for their subsistence, but instead as a source of "profit" with which they could purchase goods to supplement the clothes and rations provided by their master. By the end of the eighteenth century, masters themselves had accepted this transformation of the "rules" governing slaves' labor as the natural and even "traditional" method. In 1802, for example, a South Carolina master asserted that slaves "are encouraged to plant for their own emolument; raise poultry for their own use, or for sale; and are protected in the property they thus acquire."[80]

Like most masters, Henry Laurens continued to depict the provision of necessities as the embodiment of his patriarchal responsibilities. Such reassuring reasoning however, served only to mask that what masters regarded as an exchange of protection for obedience had become, in the eyes of slaves, a far more tangible and worthwhile exchange of goods for labor. Masters attempted to salvage the guise of patriarchal benevolence by defining the clothing and foodstuffs they provided as given in compensation for their slaves' good behavior rather than for their labor *per se*. In 1771, for example, Laurens instructed one of his overseers to "Tell them I intend to send the best Cloth next year that ever they wore, together with several additional Articles of use to them, for such as shall have behaved well."[81] Three years later, Laurens again wrote: "tell the Negroes that I hope to meet them when they are beginning to Thrash Rice, & to find at least as many in number of my Cattle, Sheep, & Hogs as I left, & that I Shall be provided with proper rewards for Such of them as have behaved well."[82] The concept of reward occupied a middle ground between the unrequited gift and ensuing obligation of patriarchy and the transitory and impersonal character of market relations. A reward could be both freely given and well earned.

Runaway slaves also posed a challenge to the foundations of authority on a patriarchal plantation. Every such act was not only an expression of self-mastery on the part of the slave but also a withdrawal of labor and a denial of obligation. Runaway slaves obliterated the master-slave relationship and rejected the metaphors of patriarchy by removing themselves from the confines of the plantation. In some cases, fugitive slaves sought a permanent escape from slavery, and their actions were evidence of a complete rejection of their master's claim to dominion. More often, however, runaways recognized the risks that weighed against such a drastic choice, and sought to gain only a brief refuge from the master and the whip.

80. John Drayton, *A View of South Carolina as Respects Her Natural and Civil Concerns* (Charleston, 1802), 145.
81. Henry Laurens to Peter Nephew, 20 December 1771, *PHL*, 8, 111.
82. Henry Laurens to John McCullough, 2 February 1774, *PHL*, 9, 262.

The practice of temporary truancy followed by an eventual return to the plantation has been termed *petit-marronage* and was common in all new world slave societies.[83] Through their actions, such truant slaves sought to renegotiate the terms of the master-slave relationship. Examples of *petit-marronage* contained in runaway advertisements reveal an unspoken dialogue in which masters and slaves could contend within and about the dictates of patriarchy. An extreme and exceptionally clear example of this sort of negotiation is provided by the case of a runaway slave who was brought to the Charles Town workhouse in June 1768. "Jemmy," the paper reported, "was sold to William Lyford of Savannah . . . but not liking him, was coming to Charlestown to look for a [new] Master."[84]

The act of *petit-marronage* itself was an opening gambit in a protracted process of negotiation. Occasionally, masters' advertisements made explicit reference to this bargaining process. In 1778, one master advertised that he had recently purchased Tom, a slave carpenter, who had "absented himself ever since [his sale], without any reason whatever except that he does not chuse to live in the country." Seeking to recoup his losses, the slave-less master attempted to contact Tom through the press. "In order . . . that the said fellow may be satisfied," he wrote, "I do hereby promise that the said Tom may . . . have a ticket to look for a new master and no notice taken of his past conduct."[85]

Slaves could become fugitive in an effort to defend their own interests against their master's inclinations. Each slave's decision to run away was a personal, self-interested act, but it also contributed to a larger resistance against the masters' authority. When hundreds of such individual acts were compounded, the net effect could convey a distinct message and have a significant impact. James Scott has noted that when such personal acts by a subordinate group "become a persistent pattern (even though uncoordinated, let alone unorganized) we are dealing with resistance."[86]

Analysis of runaway advertisements in the Charles Town newspaper reveals the possible motivations and inducements that led slaves to con-

---

83. According to Richard Price, "throughout the Americas, planters seem to have accepted as part of the system the common practice of *petit marronage*—repetitive or periodic truancy with temporary goals such as visiting a relative or lover on a neighboring plantation"; Richard Price, ed., *Maroon Societies: Rebel Slave Communities in the Americas* (Baltimore, 1979), 3.
84. *South Carolina Gazette*, 14 June 1768.
85. If Tom failed to accept this olive branch, however, his owner offered a reward to whoever could capture him and bring him to the workhouse for punishment; *South Carolina and American General Gazette*, 6 August 1778.
86. Scott concludes that, although such "forms of resistance will win no set piece battles[,] . . . [they] are admirably adopted to long-run campaigns of attrition." Jim Scott, "Everyday Forms of Peasant Resistance," *Journal of Peasant Studies* 13 (January, 1986), 26–27.

sider such a desperate act—at least as these motives were perceived by the runaways' owners. Many slaves apparently decided to become fugitive when the forces of the marketplace threatened the survival of their families. In the two decades between 1740 and 1759, 40 percent of all runaway advertisements placed in the *South Carolina Gazette* made reference to the fact that the escaped slaves had changed owners in the recent past or were faced with sale in the near future.[87] When advertisers speculated on where their escaped slaves might be heading, they put the restoration of family ties high on the list of the fugitives' possible priorities and destinations. Over 70 percent of South Carolina runaways in the years 1760–1790 were thought by their owners to be " 'visiting' either friends, acquaintances, or relatives."[88] Advertisements commonly reported that slaves were motivated to run away through a desire to reestablish family ties sundered through sale or the division of estates. "Paul, a tall likely black Barbados born fellow, about 40 years of age" became a fugitive in 1752; his master "supposed . . . [he would] be harbored either at Mrs. Bennet's, where he hath a wife, or at Henry Middleton, Esq.'s Savannah plantation, where his mother and sister are."[89] Eight years later, another master wrote that an escaped slave, whom he had purchased from the estate of Sir Alexander Nisbet, "may be harbored by SOMERSET her father."[90] When Richard Wade's slave, Phillis, ran off in 1775, he "supposed [her] to be gone . . . to her husband" at the plantation of "Thomas Adams of Wasmesaw," where Wade had "lately" acquired her.[91]

Planters were certainly aware that their slaves desired to live as families. In 1764, for example, Henry Laurens purchased "a Stout young Woman to be a Wife to whom she shall like best amongst the single men." He told his overseer to inform "the rest of the Gentlemen" that "I do not forget their request" and that they "shall be served as I have

---

87. This figure was calculated from an analysis of all advertisements for the period 1740–1759 contained in Windley, ed., *Runaway Slave Advertisements*, vol. 3. The total number of runaways (excluding the 49 described as "new negroes") contained in advertisements between 1740 and 1759 is 778. Of this number 319 (or 41 percent) were described by one of the following terms (with numbers): "formerly belonged to" (172); "formerly belonged to . . . deceased" (54); "lately belonged to" (41); otherwise described as recently sold or bought (25); "lately belonged to . . . deceased" (16); "formerly belonged to the estate of" (10); and "to be sold" (1). I assume that all runaways described by these terms had recently been sold or were faced with imminent sale.
88. Philip D. Morgan, "Black Society in the Lowcountry, 1760–1810," in Ira Berlin and Ronald Hoffman, eds., *Slavery and Freedom in the American Revolution* (Charlottesville, 1983), 128–29 and 130 (Table 18).
89. *South Carolina Gazette*, 10 August 1752, in Windley, ed., *Runaway Slave Advertisements*, 3, 113.
90. *South Carolina Gazette*, 9 February 1760, in ibid., 3, 180.
91. *South Carolina and American General Gazette*, 12 May 1775, ibid., 3, 471.

opertunity."[92] A Florida planter reported that his male slaves constantly took leave of his plantation "after the wenches in town." When he confronted the slaves on their behavior, they justified their actions by asking him, "what must they do for a wife?"[93]

In the summer of 1764, the death of Henry Laurens's brother-in-law, John Coming Ball, compelled a division of a plantation of three thousand acres and nearly eighty slaves, in which Henry Laurens held a half-share.[94] Before the final settlement of the estate the following spring, Laurens informed the executor of a "design . . . to avoid that inconvenience & I will say inhumanity of seperating & tareing assunder my Negroes' several families." Apparently, Laurens wrote that he would agree to purchase the other half of the estate's slaves or "to part with the whole in preference to an Act which has always shocked me too much to submit to it." Despite this offer, Laurens found that in the settlement of the estate "no less than seven or eight families & some of them my best Negroes will be torn to pieces." On a practical level, Laurens worried that a failure "to keep the families together" would "probably cause great disruption amongst the whole" of the slaves and "embarrass my plantation."[95]

More abstractly, denying the patriarchal principles that he used to justify his own authority made Laurens uneasy. "I don't know anything," he wrote,

> that could have been contrived to distress me . . . more than this unnecessary division of Fathers, Mothers, Husbands, Wives, & Children who tho Slaves are still human Creatures & I cannot be deaf to their cries least a time should come when I should cry & there shall be none to pity me.

Had Laurens wanted to protect his slaves' families, he certainly had the financial wherewithal to do so. In this circumstance, however, Laurens was torn by other patriarchal "obligations," to both his wife and to himself as a reputable and respected member of the larger society. In the early modern era, the economic and personal meanings of credit were still closely intertwined. Laurens's dilemma is a reminder that patriarchy

92. Henry Laurens to Timothy Creamer, 26 January 1764, *PHL*, 4, 148.
93. David Yeats to James Grant, 3 February 1781, Ballindalloch Castle Muniments, Ballindalloch, Scotland, 0771–250.
94. Laurens purchased a half-interest in Wambaw plantation in the parish of St. James Santee, northwest of Charles Town, from John Coming Ball in May 1756 for about 400 pounds sterling. This was Laurens's first plantation venture. Ball continued to manage the estate until his death in August 1764. In an account book of 1766, Laurens notes that there were 79 slaves on Wambaw at that time; *PHL*, 2, 180 and note; 6, 611.
95. Henry Laurens to Elias Ball, 1 April 1765, *PHL*, 4, 595.

had gendered and familial as well as political contexts. Forced to choose, Laurens preferred to shed his slaves rather than his pride.[96]

This affair is also a reminder that blacks' efforts to defend their families did not always succeed. Indeed, in some instances, a determination to take temporary leave of their masters in order to visit loved ones could provoke a permanent estrangement. In 1740, Robert Pringle sent a young slave woman to Portugal with directions to his Lisbon factor "to sell her to good advantage." Explaining his action, he wrote:

> The only reason of my sending her off the Province is that she had a practice of going frequently to her father and Mother, who live at a Plantation I am concerned in about twenty miles from Town from whence there was no restraining her from running away there, & staying every now & then, which determined me to send her off.[97]

For masters to have respected slaves' family ties in all situations would have contradicted the economic rationale that saw slaves as commodities as well as persons, but the prospects for black families would have been far worse if the slaves had done nothing to assert their right to family life. When slaves threatened to withdraw their labor if their kinship ties were violated, they made patriarchy economically prudent for their masters. While a few masters may have been moved to respect slaves' family ties through a desire to live up to their patriarchal responsibilities, the actions of slaves themselves were the primary reason why some slave families were protected from the market. Masters rightly worried about the "great disruption" that might ensue if they failed to respect the domestic lives of their slaves. To the extent that masters lived up to their patriarchal responsibilities and allowed their slaves to maintain families, they did so because the slaves themselves, through their actions, compelled them to do so.

Masters who acknowledged family ties among slaves had their own interests at heart. They recognized the possible consequences if they did otherwise. In 1767, for instance, the plantation agent Robert Raper in-

96. The division of John Coming Ball's estate was clouded by an earlier dispute over the estate of Laurens's father-in-law. Laurens felt that his wife had been denied her share of the inheritance on that occasion and now believed that he "had a right to expect some little indulgence in the division of the Wambaw Negroes and effects." Thus, Laurens's offer to purchase the other half of the Wambaw slaves may have been pitched at a price somewhat below market value. He may even have argued that he (or his wife) should inherit *all* of the Wambaw slaves. In any case, the executor of the estate told Laurens that his "proposal concerning the Negroes at Wambaw is not at all liked of by the other part concerned."
97. Robert Pringle to John Mayne, 19 September 1740, in Walter Edgar, ed., *The Letterbook of Robert Pringle*, 2 vols. (Columbia, 1972), 1, 247.

formed an absentee planter that her slaves were "all now quiet & well" but warned that "if an alteration is made with regard to the Negroes being divided or otherwise it will occation uneasiness & trouble amongst them."[98] Such calculation meant that even in the public vendue, where the law of the market reigned supreme, slaves' families were occasionally respected. In 1761, Raper attempted to buy a single slave at an auction in Charleston but discovered that "they put 'em up in familys." To acquire the thirteen-year-old boy whom he wanted, Raper "was obliged to take his Father" as well.[99]

In allowing slaves to live as families, masters conceded to the blacks' demands in matters that came at little or no cost and may have furthered plantation stability by giving slaves a stake in the status quo. One planter noted in this regard, "it is most beneficial for the seller to sell in gangs & it is attended with beneficial effects to the purchaser also, because the people are more satisfied when sold in Families & with their connections."[100] But masters also used slaves' strong family ties to bind slaves to obedience. As one master wrote: "by selling a few, who proved obstinately bad, [I have] taught the others to consider their being sold as the greatest punishment I can inflict & the hopes of living and dying my property, without being separated from their families, connexions, and friends, the greatest incitement to their duty."[101]

The long negotiation and contestation between slaves and masters on the issue of slave families gradually altered the political economy of the plantations and won some room for the protection of black family ties. Between 1740 and 1775, the proportion of inventoried estates whose records recognized some slave families by listing husbands and wives together or parents with their children increased from 17 percent to 41 percent.[102] Nonetheless, these figures also indicate the continued threat to all slave kinship ties and the slim thread upon which such ties depended.

Blacks' efforts to maintain their family and kinship ties in the face of the market provide one instance in which slaves could employ the meta-

98. Robert Raper to Margaret Colleton, 20 October 1767, Robert Raper Letterbook, WSCRO.
99. Putting the best face on his bargain, Raper described the older slave as "a very honest Fellow & willing & I dare say will make a gardiner for many years." Evidently the father was not thought to be capable of field labor. Robert Raper to Thomas Boone, February 24, 1761, Robert Raper Letterbook, WSCRO.
100. Edward Rutledge to Mrs. Nathanael Greene, 12 March 1789, Edward Rutledge Papers, SCL-USC.
101. George Oglivie to Alexander Oglivie, 25 April 1778, Oglivie-Forbes of Boyndlie Mss., 2640/10/5/3, Aberdeen University Library, Aberdeen, Scotland.
102. Morgan, "The Evolution of Slave Culture in Eighteenth-Century Plantation America," Table 4–9, 315. Since these figures include only those inventories which clearly recognized slave families, they are only minimum estimates of the true figures.

phors of patriarchy in their own interest. Through their own actions, blacks could lay claim to a share of the family values of patriarchy and assert their right to a stable domestic life. By running away to escape the auction block, slaves exposed the hypocrisy of would-be patriarchs who would convert their subjects into cash in the marketplace.

Slaves who ran away to visit relations or to protect their families from sale disrupted the orderly function of the plantation and thereby exacted an economic cost upon owners who violated family ties and who reneged upon the promises of patriarchy. In the long run, many slaveholders came to feel that it was incumbent upon a good master to preserve the families of his slaves except in the case of death or dire economic necessity.

Masters' accumulative ends and commercial requirements demanded that slaves be readily convertible into cash or credit, but such actions destroyed much of their credibility as the patriarchs of their plantations. While masters' desire to play the part of a patriarchal monarch could, to some degree, become an end in itself, in the larger world social status was closely related to economic success. To maximize their economic return, masters needed to secure their slaves' labor as regularly and as economically as possible, which required them to make withdrawals from the patriarchal ideal.

In 1768, for instance, an advertisement for the sale of a plantation and its thirty-four slaves crystalized the complex relationship between patriarchy and profit. "If any person inclines to purchase the above settlement and the negroes together," the seller promised, "out of compassion to the slaves, I will sell . . . [at] a great bargain, and will give [the buyer] a small flock of cattle, sheep and hogs, and two or three hundred bushels of corn."[103] Presumably, the "bargain" was not such that the seller was willing to forego all considerations of profit. Moreover, the advertisement implied that, although the owner preferred to sell "the negroes together," he was willing to sell them individually if no offers for the entire lot were forthcoming.

While the intersection of patriarchal and market relations usually served masters' interests in terms of cash and credit, slaves could also attempt to turn the collision and collusion of these metaphors to their benefit. In 1775, for example, Levinus Clarkson "let . . . his house, [and] sold his furniture" and slaves in Charles Town and moved to New York.

---

103. *South Carolina Gazette and Country Journal*, 8 March 1768. The *South Carolina Gazette*, 28 April 1767, contained the following advertisement: "a healthy, likely, Negro wench, born in Charles Town, about 15 years old . . . [who was] very unwilling to leave this province being strongly attached to her mother and family, the owner would gladly exchange her for a Negro boy, that would make no objection to his residence in any other part of the continent; both to be valued and the over cash to be paid down on either side."

He claimed that he "could have got £300 more" for "Dina & [her] Children. But she chose her Master who could give me no more." Clarkson wrote that, despite "all that I could do or say," Dina persisted in her choice. In the end, he consented "as there we are all pleased."[104] By responding to the dictates of their pocketbooks as well as to those of the patriarchal ideal, masters balanced the demands of patriarchy and the market.

Plantation Justice

On most low-country plantations, the everyday direction and supervision of labor as well as the routine administration of corporal punishment came at the hands of a white overseer or black driver and not the slaves' actual owner.[105] By law, masters were obliged to hire one white man to reside on any plantation with ten or more male slaves.[106] Masters often did not think highly of those whites who were eligible for such employment. A society that placed great value upon landed independence and in which property ownership was so readily achieved regarded white men who were reduced to the necessity of placing themselves in the employ of others with suspicion and a degree of contempt. In 1766, for example, the few whites available for this labor were disparaged by one master as "unskillful, idle and disorderly."[107] In the same year, the plantation agent, Robert Raper, wrote to his employer that "with respect to New Overseers, some years there is no help for it as they are in general an odd sort of men & we must do the best we can with them."[108] Some masters did without, leaving their plantations entirely under the direction of black drivers and preferring to risk the fine rather than to risk their estates in the hands of someone they did not trust.[109]

Although masters constructed their own dominion over their slaves within the metaphors of patriarchy, they placed no such constructions

---

104. Levinus Clarkson to Anonymous, June 1775, Levinus Clarkson Papers, LC, 129–131.
105. According to Philip D. Morgan, during the period 1750 to 1770, three-fourths of the slaves in the low country lived on plantations of 20 slaves or more, and two-fifths on plantations of 50 or more; Morgan, "The Development of Slave Culture in Eighteenth-Century Plantation America," Table 1–1, 2. Plantations of this size were likely to contain an overseer.
106. JCHA, 26 February 1755, 125.
107. JGC, 28 April 1766, microfilm, LC.
108. Robert Raper to Margaret Colleton, 18 November 1766, Robert Raper Letterbook, WSCRO.
109. See, for example, JCHA, 16 May 1744, 147.

upon the rule of their overseer. As a hired hand, the overseer was no master, and consequently he could never wield true patriarchal authority. In the eighteenth century the terms "power" and "authority" carried very different meanings. While authority rested on "trust and opinion . . . strengthened and confirmed by custom and habit" and deserved "willing obedience," power was synonymous with brute force.[110] When masters talked of "the arbitrary power of an Overseer" or warned their overseers "not to make an ill use of your power," they were suggesting the tenuous, and violent, basis of the overseers' rule.[111] When a plantation agent complained that "every inhuman Overseer [was apt] to cut & slash and drive the Negroes away," he contrasted the overseers' need to resort to the whip with his own more distant authority.[112]

However, for all their complaints, masters found the office of the overseer a most useful resource. The presence of the overseer permitted planters to be "master" of multiple plantations while living in a "great house" in Charles Town. More important to the political economy of the plantations, it allowed masters to distance themselves from the day-to-day management and discipline of the plantation. That masters disdained cracking the whip themselves did not mean that they were prepared to do without it. Someone had to do their dirty work. White overseers and black drivers relieved most masters of the task of administering corporal punishment. (For city masters, the Charles Town workhouse came to serve the same purpose.) Masters could thereby evade the overt confrontation and antagonisms that were engendered by the resort to coercion.

For slaves, the existence of a supervisor between themselves and their master permitted them to appeal to their master for redress against their overseer. Although the overseer was merely the agent of the master's domination, slaves could create space for negotiation between the day-to-day demands of the overseer and the patriarchal metaphors of the master. On the other side, by placing themselves above the actions of the overseer, masters could engage in negotiation with their slaves without retreating from, and even enhancing, their metaphorical claims to absolute authority. In this way, the overseer's office became an intermediate ground upon which slaves could contest with their masters without the danger of a direct confrontation. By looking to the master for redress

---

110. Sir William Temple, "An essay upon the Original and Nature of Government" (London, 1680), quoted in Jack P. Greene, "Independence, Improvement, and Authority: Toward a Framework for the Histories of the Southern Backcountry during the Era of the American Revolution," in Ronald Hoffman et al., eds., *An Uncivil War: The Southern Backcountry during the American Revolution* (Charlottesville, 1985), 21.

111. Henry Laurens to Richard Oswald, 12 August 1766, *PHL*, 5, 156–57; Henry Laurens to Frederick Wiggins, 20 March 1766, *PHL*, 5, 92.

112. Robert Raper to Mr. Swainston, 25 February 1764, Robert Raper Letterbook, WSCRO.

against the overseer, slaves appealed to the master's patriarchal pretensions. The language and roles that were employed in the resulting encounters might fairly be termed the "judicial metaphor."[113]

Particular cases reveal these relationships in action. One such incident occurred in 1767, when an overseer on Charles Hutson's plantation informed his employer that several slaves had run away. Within a few days, the runaways arrived at Hutson's Charles Town house. Hutson wrote that he "had them all carried to the Workhouse, intending to flog them first & then hear them afterwards, but when we came to the door of the Workhouse they begged to have a hearing first." Hutson's letter to the overseer describing what ensued is worth quoting at length:

> They said they had nothing against you, but that Paul [the black driver] had a spight against them and endeavoured to set you against them, as we found all their complaints was against Paul & he was in Town, we tho't proper to examine them first. We should not have much regarded what they said but Paul acknowledged the greater part of it. In the first place they said that on Monday and Tuesday last, which were the days that Jimmy Owen and Harry failed in their Tasks, they had scarcely any victuals, & this had great weight with us, for I think it is unreasonable to expect Negroes to work without victuals. I asked them why they could not do their Tasks as well as the rest, they answered that their tasks are harder, now I know there is sometimes a great difference in tasks, and Paul told he remembered that Jimmy had a bad task that Day. I was sorry to see poor Caesar amongst them for I knew him to be an honest inoffensive fellow & tho't if any will do without severity, he will. I inquired his fault, & Paul told me that he complained to you that he had been 2 days in a Task.[114]

Read carefully, this account suggests an element of collusion between the fugitives and Paul, the black driver, as well as an effort by the slaves to mask their challenge against the overseer. Although the fugitives claimed that they "had nothing against" their overseer and charged Paul with having "a spight against them," Paul did not react as if he were the one being accused. Instead, Paul "acknowledged the greater part" of the fugitives' claims and provided further evidence in support of their case. Despite the fugitives' protestations to the contrary, the bulk of their complaints were directed at the overseer who, they argued, had failed

---

113. For another image of the "judicial metaphor" on an eighteenth-century plantation, see Isaac, *The Transformation of Virginia*, 342–43.
114. Charles Woodward Hutson to "Mr. Croll," 22 August 1767, Charles Woodward Hutson Papers, SHC-UNC.

to provide sufficient food and to adjust unequal tasks even after (as Paul corroborated) the discrepancies had been brought to his attention.

In Hutson's account, it was the slaves who first asked him to be judge when they arrived at the door of the workhouse and pleaded for a "hearing." Hutson could not resist the role of patriarchal protector that the slaves offered him. Although he somewhat self-consciously admitted that "we should not have much regarded what they said," Hutson's use of the royal "we" indicates that he saw the affair as an opportunity to enhance his own authority. While the final result of this episode is unknown, the slaves at least evaded a whipping and were able to air their grievances against their overseer.

In other cases, the slaves' challenge to an overseer could be far more overt. In 1764, for instance, a group of slaves "full of complaints" against their overseer, "Mr. Swainston," traveled from their plantation to the home of Robert Raper who, as a plantation agent for the absentee planter Margaret Colleton, was acting as their *de facto* master. Once before Raper, the slaves persuaded him to take on the role of impartial judge. In later explaining his actions to Swainston, Raper wrote that "I cannot, nor is it justice to punish a person before he hath account of the matter from both parties." Raper sought to "enquire more fully about the matter" and convened an informal examination. When the slaves and the overseer were brought before him to tell their sides of the matter, the agent found the slaves' "complaints to be reasonable," and Swainston "could not nor did not deny" them. In the end, Raper countermanded Swainston's orders, rebuking the overseer for his part in the "most silly affair as ever was heard."[115]

Even when the master did not side with the slaves against the overseer, the result might not turn out badly. In 1774, for example, George Oglivie was summoned from Charles Town to his plantation "Myrtle Grove" on the Santee River "on account of some misunderstanding between my negroes and overseer a very common and the most disagreeable circumstance attending planting." When Oglivie arrived, he found

> no less than ten of the best say most useful hands were runaway but they all returned to their duty on hearing that I was at home which induced me to pardon them much more easily than they deserved as running away is one of the faults I am angriest at that Negroes have and I do not find that the Overseer had asked anything unreasonable of them.[116]

115. Robert Raper to "Mr. Swainston," 25 February 1764, Robert Raper Letterbook, WSCRO.
116. George Oglivie to Margaret Oglivie, 22 November 1774, Oglivie-Forbes of Boyndlie Mss., Aberdeen University Library, Aberdeen, Scotland, 2740/10/5/2.

In this case, the calculated deference of the slaves induced Oglivie to issue the plantation equivalent of a royal pardon, asserting his own supreme authority (and expressing his benevolence) at the overseer's expense.

Of course, slaves' efforts to gain the support of their master could backfire. Slaves who gained a reputation as troublesome might well be sold; appeals to the master might only add to the slaves' punishment. Henry Laurens returned one slave petitioner to his overseer with the remark: "He says that you are too hard upon him, tho' his back does not shew anything like it. Don't fail to give him his full deserts."[117]

All parties concerned in these negotiations could recognize that the practice by which the master agreed to arbitrate conflicts arising between the slaves and the overseer resulted in a gradual erosion of the overseers' ability to control the slaves. Some overseers attempted to assert a "professional" standard, which denied the slaves any such recourse. James Postell, overseer on several of Ralph Izard's plantations in 1770, quit when Izard's agent intervened on behalf of a slave who complained of ill treatment. In his angry letter of resignation, Postell wrote:

> The Steps you have taken with Respect to Mr. Izards Slaves . . . is by no means agreeable to me, as it will prove of great Disadvantage to the Plantations this Way, one expecting the same Indulgence as another. . . . I dont imagine after this, it will be in my Power to carry that command over the Negroes I have hitherto done, and which I've an undoubted Right to.[118]

Most masters privately acknowledged, as Henry Laurens wrote, "that it is very ill consequence to receive all the complaints that the Negroes shall make of an Overseer's conduct," and they promised their overseers that "none of . . . [the slaves] shall meet with improper encouragement from me" in seeking such redress.[119] In practice, however, the chance to play the part of the patriarchal judge (and more importantly, their desire to protect their slave property) often induced masters to take the part of the slaves against the overseer.

Unless slaves succeeded in getting an unpopular overseer discharged,

---

117. Henry Laurens to Abraham Schad, 23 August 1765, *PHL*, 4, 665–66.
118. James Postell to Peter Manigault, 2 February 1770, "Letterbook of Peter Manigault, 1763–1773," *SCHM* 70 (1969), 181.
119. Henry Laurens to John Jackson, 19 March 1766, *PHL*, 5, 90; Henry Laurens to Frederick Wiggins, 19 March 1766, *PHL*, 5, 91. Interestingly, in this last instance Laurens prefaced this declaration with an example of the very thing he averred he would not do: "Adam came down to me with a trifling complaint for which I was gong to send him to the work house & to order proper chastisement but upon further consideration I pardoned him for this once & desire you will after a severe reprimand excuse him."

which was seldom the case, they returned to the plantation at the mercy of the overseer's anger and vengeance. In some cases, slaves paid for their victory over the overseer when before the master by the overseer's later resort to the whip. For example, a few days following the "trial" held in Raper's house in Charles Town, Raper discovered that the overseer afterwards "whipt one of . . . [the slaves involved] severely[,] who has, I believe, not worked since."[120]

In the end, the slaves were the master's property and were themselves a valuable portion of his estate, while the overseer was only a hired hand. In the triangular relations among slaves, masters, and overseer, it was the overseer who was the stranger. Distant masters commonly solicited their slaves' opinion on the overseer's performance. When Josiah Smith visited the plantations in his charge, for example, he recorded that "not one of . . . [the slaves] offered the least complaint against their new overseer Brown."[121]

If the overseer hoped to keep his job very long, he had to reach something of a *modus vivendi* with the slaves under his charge. The overseer's primary aims were to keep slaves healthy and to produce a large crop. These goals were not always compatible. Slaves knew that, by repeatedly withdrawing their labor and otherwise disrupting plantation productivity, they could put any overseer's position in jeopardy. Whippings that drove the slaves to seek refuge in the forest or in town could be counterproductive. Henry Laurens criticized the severity of one of his overseers by saying, "what signifies his knowledge of Planting if . . . he drives away the People without whose aid he can neither Plant nor beat out his Crop[?]"[122]

The need to elicit a degree of cooperation from the slave quarters or at the very least to silence slaves' complaints may have led some overseers to make concessions. In 1772, for instance, John Lewis Gervais inspected one of Laurens's Georgia plantations and found that the "pole" the overseer used to mark out the daily tasks of each slave was two feet shorter than "the rule."[123] This short measure led to a deficiency in

---

120. Robert Raper to "Mr. Swainston," 25 February 1764, Robert Raper Letterbook, WSCRO.
121. Josiah Smith to George Austin, 22 July 1773, Josiah Smith, Jr., Letterbook, SHC-UNC.
122. Henry Laurens to Lachlan McIntosh, 13 March 1773, *PHL*, 8, 617–18. Laurens's letter continued: "signify to him that it is my particular desire & order to treat the Negroes with more humanity, Temper, & discretion & that I am persuaded he will find it contribute to his own Ease . . . & that I have no doubt of making more Rice by gentle and discreet Authority than by perseverance in a contrary conduct. I am not unaware of advantages which maybe taken of such an Order, by flying to the opposite extreme, 'Mr. Laurens won't allow his Overseers even to speak roughly to a Negro, how can he expect any work to be done?' But if Mr. Gambrell is really an honest Man he will Aim at a Medium."
123. In plantation rice cultivation, a task was the area of the rice field that an individual slave was assigned to cultivate in a given day. Generally, a task was about a quarter-acre

the tasks of ten feet on each side, which resulted in a 20 percent reduction in the slaves' daily work load. "What Views . . . [the overseer] could have in [doing] this I cannot guess," Gervais concluded, "except to make Friends with the Negroes."[124]

To a large extent, the overseer was a screen through which slaves and masters could contend in a way that did not involve direct and dangerous confrontation. Masters' willingness to overrule the overseer meant that over time the overseer's ability to control or coerce slaves was gradually bargained away. Masters' concessions came, not at the expense of their own authority, but from the power of the overseer. Sooner or later, the overseer would no longer have the ability to command the slaves' labor. In 1777, Henry Laurens wrote that one of his Georgia overseers "seems to be held in contempt by the Negroes & I am afraid of some fatal accident."[125] This gradual process of attrition meant that few overseers were employed at any one plantation for more than a few years. Using a piquant simile, Virginia planter Landon Carter noted that "overseers tire as cornfields do."[126]

Overseers served as lightning rods that drew the focus of the slaves' resistance away from the dominant class itself and absorbed the antagonisms arising out of the slaves' exploitation. In fact, by acting as arbiters between slaves and overseers, masters were able to separate themselves to some degree from the process of labor extraction and to pose as the patriarchal protectors of slaves against the harsh demands of the overseer. The presence of the overseer between masters and slaves allowed masters to negotiate with their slaves without putting their own authority on the bargaining table. By making concessions from the "arbitrary power" of the overseer, masters could appear to recognize and address slave grievances while continuing to assert that their own authority remained absolute and non-negotiable. The uses and abuses of the overseer's office required that the post have a relatively high rate of turnover. If an overseer remained too long he would cease to be an outsider and would inevitably become identified by the slaves with the master's interest. Moreover, in order to support a long-term overseer a master would have to avoid contravening his commands and thus would have to accept a diminution of his own patriarchal pretensions and authority in the slave quarters. The operation of the judicial metaphor and the

in area. See Philip D. Morgan, "Work and Culture: The Task System and the World of Lowcountry Blacks, 1700–1880," *William and Mary Quarterly*, 3rd series, 39, (October 1982), 575.

124. John Lewis Gervais to Henry Laurens, 5 May 1772, *PHL*, 8, 287–91.

125. Henry Laurens to John Lewis Gervais, 5 September 1777, *PHL*, 11, 487.

126. Entry of 26 May 1766, in Greene, ed., *Diary of Colonel Landon Carter*, 1, 302.

masters' desire to be seen as a protector of their slaves required that withdrawals be made from the overseers' power. When, after a few years, the overseer could no longer extract the labor that plantation operations required, masters knew that it was time to hire another overseer and start again.

"A Reckoning of Accounts"

Both masters and slaves could recognize that their relationship was to some extent based upon reciprocal (although involuntary) exchange. Each side struggled over the metaphors and languages that would be applied to the encounters which took place at the steps of the great house and over what exactly was being exchanged for what. This contentious bargaining between masters and slaves extended to the meanings that would be given (or taken) from public events and actions. In some cases, as in the distribution of cloth and foodstuffs on the steps of the great house, slaves and masters might cooperate in the act itself without agreeing on its meaning. For masters, the provision of such "gifts" was a mark of their dominion and slaves' acceptance of these goods an acknowledgment of their subordination, dependency, and "gratitude." For slaves, interactions with masters were better understood as the product of mutual "exchanges," whether of goods for labor or of spoken agreements and overt negotiation. From the slaves' point of view, no lasting dependency or gratitude was either implied or created by such transactions. Nonetheless, the slaves' desire to achieve immediate ends and a degree of control over their lives *within* slavery led them to negotiate within the metaphors of the dominant class when it suited their interests. Slaves accepted the metaphor proffered by their masters in an effort to trade their cooperation for concessions that would further their short-term goals of petty property rights and autonomy.

Slaves could also invoke patriarchal ideas in support of their own goals. By threatening to run away (as well as actually doing so) if they were separated from loved ones, slaves asserted their right to a stable family life. Taking masters at their word, slaves demanded that patriarchal masters preserve the slave families under their "protection." Because this "resistance" was expressed within the dominant discourse, masters could concede somewhat to slaves' interest in maintaining kin ties without undermining their claim to be the "patriarchal monarchs" of their plantations.

If slaves thus secured a mode of appeal and a language through which dissent and resistance could be phrased in non-confrontational and therefore safe ways, masters were able to play the part of patriarchal protectors of their slaves and to enhance their authority in the slave quarters. Through this perpetual discursive tug-of-war, masters collectively and individually imposed their dominion and forged slaves' "subjection and obedience" into labor.

The presence of the market in the slave quarters offered an alternative discourse for master-slave relations. Alongside the personal and affective ties that were to bind slaves to masters according to the metaphors of patriarchy, there was a market-based interpretation of the relation as one of an exchange of goods for labor. In practice, the two often co-existed. In 1771, Laurens described his relationship with his slaves in a mode quite removed from the patriarchal ideal he expressed in 1785:

> Such Negroes as behave well in my Absence, I shall remember with Gratitude. Those who behave ill, I shall only lose Money by. And there's an End of that matter, until they and I come to a reckoning of Accounts. And perhaps a Consciousness of their Error, or some other means may prompt or oblige them to make up all Deficiencies.[127]

The vocabulary of the counting house that Laurens carefully avoided in his idealized depiction of himself in 1785 surfaced here. Yet the passage was not couched entirely in market metaphors. If patriarchy had no place for "a reckoning of Accounts" between master and slave, neither did market relations allow for the existence of "Gratitude" and "obligation." Although in theory, the two concepts were implacably opposed, in everyday practice, masters and slaves negotiated and reconciled the conflicting metaphors of patriarchy and the market. If masters were motivated by a desire to exercise a profitable control of their plantations, slaves likewise sought a measure of control over their daily lives.

127. Henry Laurens to James Laurens, 5 December 1771, *PHL*, 8, 66–67.

The ruins of Sheldon Church, Prince William Parish, at the end of the eighteenth century. Sheldon Church was built in 1753. In terms of size, brick construction, and style, it was typical of the Anglican chapels that were being built throughout the low country in the mid-eighteenth century. Apparently, it also conformed to established doctrine in terms of ceremony. Local tradition long remembered the custom of Colonel Stephen Bull, who "usually invited as his guests on the Sabbath, the more respectable part of the Congregation who attended divine service; while his overseer, by his direction, and at his expense, liberally entertained the rest." The church was burned in 1779 during the first British invasion of the low country. This painting, by Charles Fraser, captures the desolation of the war and evokes the end of the colonial regime. Rebuilt in 1826, the church was again destroyed by invaders in 1864. Source: Carolina Art Association, Charleston, South Carolina. Gift of Miss Alice Ravenel Huger Smith.

[6]

Revolutions Achieved and Denied: Charles Town and the Low Country, 1775–1782

In Charleston harbor, as any of the city's horse-and-carriage drivers will tell you, the Ashley and the Cooper Rivers meet to form the Atlantic Ocean. This old saw tells several truths about the city and its past. Most obviously, the remark refers to Charleston's location at the end of a peninsula between two rivers. At the same time, the joke plays upon the considerable pride of local residents, which as early as 1778 one visitor thought "great beyond description."[1] Finally, the saying may also reflect a once-boundless confidence in the city's future. As the last quarter of the eighteenth century began, the Charles Town waterfront may indeed have seemed to look upon a vast sea of wealth and power.

For the last 137 years, however, the view from Charleston's waterfront has been dominated by a small, fortified island that stands astride the harbor mouth. Fort Sumter is Historic Charleston's best-known attraction. Each day, boats ferry visitors from the city docks to the place "where the Civil War began."[2] From the southern tip of the city, cannon point toward the fort in a pantomime of defiance. Conquered by the Yankees in 1865, Charleston is today occupied by an army of tourists. To entertain this host the city is doomed forever to recall its ancient folly

---

1. H. Roy Merrens, ed., "A View of Coastal South Carolina in 1778: The Journal of Ebenezer Hazard," *SCHM* (October 1972), 192.
2. *Charleston Area Visitor's Guide* (Charleston, 1994), 43.

and downfall. Do the descendants of the Trojans sell toy wooden horses beside the ruins of Troy?

In the late-colonial era, before Fort Sumter was built or bombarded, Charles Town's prospects were still unbounded. As they walked along Bay Street and counted the ships laying at anchor in the Cooper, or climbed to the top of St. Michael's belfry to see the "charming Prospect . . . [of] Ships, at a Distance, sailing towards the Port," the inhabitants of Charles Town might well have had a somewhat inflated sense of their city's importance.[3]

Charles Town harbor was the threshold of the colonial slave society. If the Ashley and Cooper did not single-handedly form the Atlantic, the two rivers did form colonial South Carolina's gateway to the Atlantic world. It was here that most visitors arrived and that news of the cultural and political affairs of the metropolis was first received. Over the harbor bar sailed ships from "every Quarter of the Globe" (or at least the Atlantic), their holds filled with British goods or African slaves to be exchanged for cargoes of the colony's rice and indigo. In 1743, 206 ocean-going ships called at the port.[4] Twenty years later, this number had swelled to "above three Hundred Top-sail Vessels."[5] When he sailed into the harbor in 1773, Josiah Quincy was impressed by all the bustle; "the number of shipping," he wrote, "far surpassed all I had ever seen in Boston."[6]

Slaves were one of the most important commodities traded in colonial Charles Town. The port was the largest entrepot for slaves on the British-American mainland. In all, almost one-fourth of the Africans brought to America during the entire duration of the Atlantic slave trade came into Charles Town harbor.[7] Those Africans who survived the rigors of the "middle passage" first touched American soil (or sand) at Sullivan's Island, at the mouth of Charles Town harbor, where a "pest house" or quarantine stood ready to receive them. In June of 1765, a curious visitor from Philadelphia rowed out to the island, which he described as "very

---

3. George Milligen-Johnston, *A Short Description of the Province of South-Carolina* (London, 1770), 34, reprinted in Chapman J. Milling, ed., *Colonial South Carolina: Two Contemporary Descriptions* (Columbia, 1951).
4. James Glen, *A Description of South Carolina* (London, 1761), 40–41, reprinted in Milling, ed., *Colonial South Carolina.*
5. Milligen-Johnston, *A Short Description of the Province of South Carolina*, 35.
6. Quincy claimed that "about 350 sail lay off the town," but the majority of these were doubtless local rather than trans-Atlantic craft; Mark DeWolfe Howe, ed., "Journal of Josiah Quincy, Junior, 1773," in Massachusetts Historical Society *Proceedings* 49 (Boston, 1916), 441.
7. W. Robert Higgins, "Charleston: Terminus and Entrepot of the Colonial Slave Trade," in Martin L. Kilson and Robert I. Rotberg, eds., *The African Diaspora: Interpretive Essays* (Cambridge, Mass., 1976), 118.

sandy, hot, and barren," and observed "2[oo] or 300 Negroes performing quarantine."[8]

Two issues of the newspaper provide a glimpse of Charles Town harbor during the height of the slave trade. On June 1, 1769, an anonymous correspondent to the *Gazette* reported that "the marsh opposite to the town, from the number of dead bodies there, had the appearance of a field of battle where they had not had time to bury their dead."[9] The next week, a proclamation from the royal governor solved the gruesome mystery:

> Whereas . . . a large number of dead negroes, whose bodies have been thrown into the river, are drove upon the marsh opposite to Charles-Town, and the noisome smell arising from their putrefaction may become dangerous to the health of the inhabitants of this province . . . I do hereby offer a reward . . . to any person that will inform against any one . . . guilty of such practice.[10]

In the same issue, and with far less fanfare, the paper printed several other notices of a sort that were all too common. One serves as an example of them all:

TO BE SOLD
On Wednesday, the 14th Instant
A Cargo of 157 Choice
SLAVES
Imported in the Brigantine HARRIOT, Thomas Rymer, Master, from the
Windward Coast of Africa, by Thomas L. & Roger Smith.

In this and other such advertisements in the same week, Carolina planters were promised their pick of nearly nine hundred "Choice Healthy Negroes" who were "just arrived" from Africa. Presumably, those Africans who perished before they could be disembarked or who did not survive their quarantine on Sullivan's Island were cast without ceremony into the harbor to be swept out to sea or driven upon the Cooper River marshes according to the dictates of the tide.

The white residents of colonial Charles Town may have regarded the "noisome smell" wafting from the harbor as the price of their prosperity,

8. "Journal of a Visit to Charleston, 1765," in H. Roy Merrens, ed., *The Colonial South Carolina Scene: Contemporary Views, 1697–1774* (Columbia, 1977), 224.
9. *South Carolina Gazette*, 1 June 1769.
10. *South Carolina Gazette*, 8 June 1769.

but it may also have served to remind them of the larger economic and political currents on which they and the colony depended. The rise and fall of the harbor tide was like the ebb and flow of the larger Atlantic world. The low country's reliance upon the sea also shaped the language in which locals expressed themselves. In January 1775, for instance, at the first meeting of the South Carolina Provincial Congress, Henry Laurens referred to himself and his fellow delegates as "fellow Adventurers in the Same perilous Voyage."[11]

Laurens's analogy, although conventional, was particularly apt, for the colony was indeed like a small vessel adrift upon a vast and furious sea.[12] Aboard their tiny ship of state, masters could employ the institutions of the church and the law and the relations of patriarchy and the market to impose a measure of order and discipline, but they could do nothing to calm the waters of the wider world. If, as Laurens declaimed, the assembled delegates hoped to "Steer safely" through the "raging Sea" of contingency upon which the colonial ship was cast, "Skilful Pilotage" would surely be required.[13]

Between 1740 and 1775, a nearly constant series of political storms clouded relations between the colonial Commons House of Assembly and a succession of royal governors.[14] In part, the members of the assembly regarded their willingness to contest with the king's governor as a marker of their Englishness. Participation in politics offered low-country masters an outlet for their ambition and a measure of prestige. As one governor astutely remarked, every assemblyman could be expected to be "a zealous stickler for the rights and privileges, real or imaginary, of the body of which he is a member, because he derives his own importance from it."[15] Another, less charitable Englishman described the members of the Commons House sourly as "sordid legislators . . . that no King can govern nor no God . . . please."[16]

11. Henry Laurens to John Laurens, 22 January 1775, *PHL*, 10, 40.
12. The analogy was especially concrete for Laurens himself. Just a month earlier, returning to the colony from England, his ship momentarily "struck Ground" off the Charles Town harbor bar in the middle of a stormy night, an accident Laurens later attributed to "an unskilful . . . Pilot." Henry Laurens to John Laurens, 12 December 1774, *PHL*, 10, 1–2.
13. Henry Laurens to John Laurens, 22 January 1775, *PHL*, 10, 40–41.
14. For a detailed treatment of colonial South Carolina politics, see M. Eugene Sirmans, *Colonial South Carolina: A Political History, 1663–1763* (Chapel Hill, 1966); Robert M. Weir, " 'The Harmony We Were Famous For': An Interpretation of Pre-Revolutionary South Carolina Politics," *William and Mary Quarterly*, 3d series, 26 (October 1969), offers a perceptive analysis of late-colonial South Carolina political culture.
15. Governor Henry Lyttleton to the Board of Trade, 6 December, 1756, quoted in Weir, " 'The Harmony We Were Famous For,' " 489.
16. William Knox to Governor Henry Lyttleton, 5 March 1760, quoted in Sirmans, *Colonial South Carolina*, 320.

For the most part, these political squalls took place behind the closed doors of the assembly hall and council chamber.[17] As long as low-country masters and royal governors confined their conflicts to the corridors of power and restricted themselves to rhetorical bombast, their political struggles posed little threat to the domestic social order. If, however, contests between provincial and imperial rulers spilled into the street, they could become far more dangerous. When political disagreements entered the public sphere, slaves might be tempted (or invited) to take sides in the dispute, or they could seek to turn the division of authority to their own advantage.

In the winter of 1765, for example, a group of Charles Town slaves, in imitation (or inversion) of the public demonstrations that Charles Town's "Sons of Liberty" had held against the Stamp Act, paraded through the city's streets "crying out 'Liberty.' " Shouted from black mouths, the word took on a meaning quite different from that which the original demonstrators had intended.[18] Masters responded to the blacks' parade with an outburst of fear and violence. The result was the most serious slave conspiracy scare in the colony in sixteen years. Given the slave population's ability to perceive and respond to political divisions among whites, it is perhaps not surprising that Henry Laurens thought "domestic broils . . . more awful & distressing than Fire, Pestilence, or Foreign Wars."[19]

The sudden and unexpected outbreak of war with Britain in the spring of 1775 struck the colony like a political hurricane. Both during the initial blast and through the next seven-and-a-half years, masters, slaves, and royal officials confronted new and unprecedented choices, unknown dangers, and alluring but uncertain opportunities. The decisions and actions that each of these groups (and the individuals within them) made in this crisis revealed a great deal about the social order's strengths and weaknesses, even as their choices helped bring the colonial regime to its end.

The low country's experience of the American Revolution can be divided into three distinct parts, defined both by chronology and by opportunity. In the first year of the war, roughly from May 1775 through March 1776, the struggle was largely a domestic one between masters and slaves. In this initial phase of the crisis, South Carolina masters faced a double challenge; they had not only to make a revolution against their

17. Sirmans writes that "the frequently violent constitutional struggles in the assembly stood in marked contrast to the general political calm that prevailed outside the legislature," Sirmans, *Colonial South Carolina*, 223–24.
18. Henry Laurens to John Lewis Gervais, 29 January 1766, *PHL*, 5, 53.
19. Henry Laurens to Christopher Rowe, 8 February 1764, *PHL*, 4, 165.

king but also, far more important, to suppress any revolutionary designs of their slaves.

The Revolution entered a new phase with the arrival of large British military forces in the low country in December 1778 and the conquest of Charles Town and occupation of much of the region in the spring of 1780. The royal army and the imposition of martial law offered a challenge (or at least an alternative) to the prewar social order. The experience of those slaves who sought refuge beneath the Union Jack revealed the possibilities and the limitations of "Liberty" for slaves in the revolutionary era. With the British defeat and evacuation from Charles Town in December 1782, this phase of the low country's revolution came to a close.

In these same years, those slaves who chose to stay upon their home plantations during the chaos of the war experienced another kind of freedom. Temporarily free from their masters and the culture of power, these slaves were able to live according to their own vision of the social order. On these "abandoned" plantations in the eye of the revolutionary hurricane, the dream that one day "the Negro's should live happily & have Laws of their own" came true, at least for a brief and fleeting moment.

Things Fall Apart, 1775–1776

On January 11, 1775, the South Carolina Provincial Congress convened on the second floor of the Exchange house in Charles Town. The Congress's purpose was to enact and enforce the "Continental Association," a non-importation agreement that the Continental Congress, an assembly of representatives drawn from all of the mainland British-American colonies (except Georgia), had drawn up the preceding fall. Because its authority was not recognized by the royal government, the Provincial Congress was an illegal, or at least extra-legal, assembly, but it was not otherwise very radical. Many of the delegates to the Congress were also members of the colonial assembly, which continued to meet a few blocks away in the Statehouse. After selecting February 1 as the day to begin enacting non-importation and appointing February 17 as a day of public fasting and prayer, the Congress adjourned until May. The actual enforcement of the non-importation agreement was left to a committee of Charles Town members.[20]

20. John Drayton, *Memoirs of the American Revolution Relating to South Carolina* (Charleston, 1821), 168–80.

This was hardly the first time that South Carolina's political leaders had opposed British policy. As always, the low-country elite were determined to defend their accustomed control over the internal affairs of the colony, but they were not bent upon revolution. That spring, Henry Laurens explained to an English friend that " 'Reasonable Liberty' is all we pray for—Independence is not the view of America not a Sober Sensible Man wishes for it."[21]

From previous experience, the colony's leaders had reason to believe that they could achieve their objective peacefully. On January 1, before the Congress had even met, the South Carolina Gazette published a letter from London that informed readers that while the royal ministers "are loath to give up their tyrannical power . . . they must if the colonies are steadfast. . . . if the colonies are firm for one year, and neither import nor export, it would establish American freedom."[22] David Ramsay, a Charles Town resident, later recalled the prevailing mood:

> This was the third time that a scheme of non-importation had been adopted, from its success on two former occasions and an apprehension that the trade of America was necessary to the inhabitants of Great Britain it was generally hoped the obnoxious acts would soon be repealed. . . . During the first months of the year 1775, hopes were entertained that Great Britain would follow the same line of policy that had led her to repeal the Stamp Act.[23]

For South Carolina's leaders, non-importation appeared to offer a potent, yet safe, mode through which to challenge imperial policy. A voluntary boycott of British manufactures broke no laws and need not result in the "domestic broils" that low-country masters had good cause to fear. Yet the economic boycott, if continued, might exert considerable pressure on Parliament through the complaints of the British merchants who were threatened with financial ruin by a prolonged closure of the American market.

Therefore, in the early spring of 1775, low-country masters steeled themselves, not for battle, but to do without the "good things from En-

---

21. Laurens's letter continued: "We pray for King George 3d. for the protestant Succession in the line of Bruns[w]ick—[and] we desire to continue in that State of Subordination in which His present Majesty found us at his accession to the Crown"; Henry Laurens to Johann Rudolph Von Valltravers, 22 May 1775, PHL, 10, 134.
22. South Carolina Gazette, 1 January 1775.
23. David Ramsay, A History of South Carolina, From Its First Settlement in 1670 to the Year 1808, 2 vols. (Charleston, 1808), 2, 132.

gland" that they craved. This "bloodless, self-denying opposition," as David Ramsay later described it, "was all that South Carolina designed, and was all the sacrifice, which as she supposed, would be required at her hands."[24]

Having closed their purses, the colony's leaders waited for word from London. News was eagerly asked of every ship that arrived in the harbor, and hopes and fears rose and fell according to the latest rumor. In the *Gazette* of April 15, Charles Town was informed that "the latest accounts from England, by way of New York, are of a few days later date, and seem somewhat more favorable than those we had by the Eagle Packet boat."[25]

Then, without warning, the hurricane blew in. On May 3, a ship entered Charles Town harbor from England carrying an alarming report that the British government was considering a proposal "to grant freedom to such Slaves as should desert their Masters and join the King's troops."[26] Five days later, as low-country masters were still debating the reliability and repercussions of this rumor, another ship, the *Industry*, arrived from Massachusetts, bringing word that the first battle in the war between Britain and America had already taken place three weeks earlier outside of Boston.[27]

Perhaps it was the coincidental arrival of these two bombshells that caused them to be linked in the minds of low-country masters. Henry Laurens, who once described Charles Town as "a Town where the Inhabitants are as suddenly blown up by apprehensions as Gun powder is by Fire," described the ruling emotion in their wake as a mixture of "Fear, & Zeal in a delirium."[28] "Upon the news of the affair at Lexington," another resident testified, "the people of Carolina were thrown into a great Ferment." "An Opinion prevailed," he added, that the ministry planned "to Employ the Indians and to Arm the Negroes for

24. Ibid.
25. *South Carolina Gazette*, 15 April 1775.
26. Alexander Innes to Lord Dartmouth, 16 May 1775, in B. D. Bargar, ed., "Charlestown Loyalism in 1775: The Secret Reports of Alexander Innes," *SCHM* 63 (July 1962), 128.
27. *South Carolina General Gazette*, 12 May 1775; and also entry of 8 May 1775, Diary of Oliver Hart, Oliver Hart Papers, SCL-USC; the following account of events in South Carolina in 1775–1776 expands on material first presented in Robert A. Olwell, " 'Domestick Enemies': Slavery and Political Independence in South Carolina, May 1775–March 1776," *Journal of Southern History* 55 (February 1989), 21–48. Other studies of the subject include Peter H. Wood, " 'Liberty Is Sweet': African-American Freedom Struggles in the Years before White Independence," in Alfred F. Young, ed., *Beyond the American Revolution: Explorations in the History of American Radicalism* (DeKalb, Ill., 1993), 149–84; and Sylvia R. Frey, *Water from the Rock: Black Resistance in a Revolutionary Age* (Princeton, 1991), 55–67.
28. Henry Laurens to John Laurens, 23 June 1775, *PHL*, 10, 191; Henry Laurens to John Laurens, 8 June 1775, in *PHL*, 10, 166 and note.

the service of the Government."[29] Another witness wrote of "the fears of the people . . . that His Majesty's ministers and other servants instigated their slaves to rebel against their masters and to cut their throats."[30]

In the weeks to come, fresh rumors rocked the colony. On May 29, for example, the *Gazette* printed a purported letter from London claiming that "there is gone down to Sheerness, seventy-eight thousand guns and bayonets, to be sent to America, to put into the hands of N*****s [Negroes], the Roman Catholics, the Indians and Canadians; and all the . . . means on earth used to subdue the Colonies."[31] Soon, as a result of these and other reports, "massacres and insurrections were words in the mouth of every child."[32]

When South Carolina's new royal governor, Lord William Campbell, arrived in Charles Town on June 19, he found that "it was . . . reported and universally believed that to effect [a slave insurrection] . . . 14,000 stands of arms were actually on board the *Scorpion*, the sloop of war I came out in." In a letter to Lord Dartmouth, Campbell wrote: "Words cannot express the flame that this [belief] occasioned amongst all ranks and degrees; the cruelty and savage barbarity of the scheme was the conversation of all companies."[33]

While masters may have genuinely worried that royal ministers were scheming to provoke a slave uprising, in the summer of 1775 there were, in fact, few British officials and no British military forces present to implement such a design. Of far more immediate danger was the impact that rumors that the British "have it view to liberate the slaves and encourage them to attack their masters" might have on the low-country black community.[34] Some masters may have hoped to quarantine their slaves from the news. Thus the *Gazette's* feeble attempt to disguise the report that slaves might receive British arms by rendering "Negroes" as "N****s." But most masters realized that, whether from reading the newspaper or from overhearing "imprudent conversations," the crisis that beset the colony "could not escape the notice" of their slaves.[35] Masters also knew that any news would soon be spread via the black community's grapevine. "Negroes have wonderfull art of communicating Intelligence among themselves," two low-country planters reported

29. John R. Alden, ed., "John Stuart Accuses William Bull," *William and Mary Quarterly*, 3d series, 2 (July 1945), 318.
30. George Milligen to Lord Dartmouth, 15 September 1775, in *DAR*, 11, 110.
31. *South Carolina Gazette*, 29 May 1775.
32. Alden, ed., "John Stuart Accuses William Bull," 320.
33. Governor William Campbell to Lord Dartmouth, 31 August 1775, in *DAR*, 11, 94.
34. James Wright [Governor of Georgia] to Lord Dartmouth, 25 May 1775, in *DAR*, 9, 144.
35. Governor William Campbell to Lord Dartmouth, 31 August 1775, in *DAR*, 11, 95.

gloomily; news could "run several hundreds of miles in a week or a fortnight."[36]

Masters were right. Low-country slaves did discover what was happening. But slaves were not merely passive receivers and transmitters of information. In their whispered conversations, slaves interpreted the news of the war in the context of their own lives and circumstances. Consequently, slaves not only intercepted and passed on rumors; they also altered the meaning and message to suit and reflect their own objectives and desires. In clandestine meetings, low-country blacks asserted that they were themselves the central issue of the struggle. In May, for example, one Charles Town resident wrote that the city's slaves "entertained ideas that the present contest [with Britain] was for obliging us to give them liberty."[37] Similarly, a plantation agent reported that the colony's slaves "believe they will all be sett free on the arrival of our new governor."[38] A few weeks later, the same correspondent described this notion as "common talk throughout the Province" among the slaves.[39]

Masters feared that low-country slaves might not await the arrival of the British but might take steps to liberate themselves. Rumors of slave insubordination and insurrection soon fanned across the colony. Soon after war was announced in Charles Town, for example, "reports were daily circulated that the Negroes of this plantation had refused to work, that in another they had obtained arms and were gone into the woods, that others had actually murdered their masters and their families."[40] Likewise, when "a schooner . . . loaded with goods . . . was robbed by some Negroes" outside of the city, it was noted grimly that the thieves "took Nothing else but [gun] Powder."[41]

Many masters also thought they could also detect a more subtle challenge. One man reported that the slaves' "deluded . . . notion of being all set free on the arrival of our . . . new Gov[erno]r . . . has occasioned impertinent behaviour in many of them."[42] In a face-to-face society, such "impertinence" might take a thousand forms. Slaves might have hesitated a moment longer than usual before obeying, have held their masters' gaze for another second before looking away, or have talked under their breath while walking past. Suddenly, the sort of "insolence" and

36. Entry of 24 September 1775, in L. H. Butterfield, ed., *Diary and Autobiography of John Adams*, 4 vols. (Cambridge, Mass., 1961), 2, 182–83.
37. Drayton, *Memoirs of the American Revolution*, 179–80.
38. Josiah Smith to James Poyas, 18 May 1775, Josiah Smith, Jr., Letterbook, SHC-UNC.
39. Josiah Smith to George Appleby, 16 June 1775, Josiah Smith, Jr., Letterbook, SHC-UNC.
40. George Milligen to Lord Dartmouth, 15 September 1775, in *DAR*, 11, 110.
41. Joseph Manigault to Gabriel Manigault, 4 June 1775, Manigault Family Papers, SCL-USC.
42. Josiah Smith to George Appleby, 16 June 1775, Josiah Smith, Jr., Letterbook, SHC-UNC.

"contempt of government" that masters had long, if grudgingly, accepted from slaves in the marketplace may have begun to appear elsewhere in the society. Both masters and slaves knew that the boundaries of authority were being put to the test.

As one planter noted, a colonial slave society wherein slaves could believe (or hope) that the distant king had become their champion in the struggle against their masters was indeed "in a ticklish situation."[43] The specter of divided authority placed the colonial establishment in an extremely awkward posture. When masters were themselves defying their acknowledged superiors, by what logic could they call upon their slaves to obey? Moreover, in this crisis of authority, many of the officers and institutions, and even the languages and metaphors, through which masters had long exercised their collective dominion were either suspect or severely compromised.

The Anglican church, for example, whose ministers, ceremonies, and liturgy had traditionally exalted civil obedience and submission to worldly authority, was particularly unsuited to the occasion. Although divine right ideology had long been dismissed by most political theorists, for many ordinary eighteenth-century Anglo-Americans (and especially Anglican clergy) the notion that earthly power was divinely sanctioned remained both persuasive and comforting.[44] Ministers sympathetic to these ideas, or others only recently arrived from England, either found the events of 1775–76 impossible to comprehend or perceived the actions of the low-country leaders as a sin against both God and king.

In August 1774, the Reverend John Bullman entered the pulpit of St. Michael's Church to preach on "the Christian Duty of Peaceableness."[45] In his sermon, the minister called upon "every Man to keep his own Rank, and to do his Duty in his own Station" lest there be "Schisms in the Church, and sedition and Rebellion in the State." On previous Sundays, a sermon on the subject of passive obedience would hardly have roused the parishioners from their slumber. But with South Carolina's delegation to the Continental Congress having just departed for Philadelphia, the parson's message took on another meaning and had a very different impact. As Bullman went on and on in the same vein, the audience became more and more indignant. When the minister decried "every Silly Clown" who sought "to censure his superiors" and meddle "in Matter[s] wherein he is not . . . concerned," the congregation erupted in outrage. Within days, the parish vestry had voted to remove Bullman

43. Ibid.
44. See J. C. D. Clark, *English Society, 1688–1832* (Cambridge, 1985), 119–76.
45. S. Charles Bolton, *Southern Anglicanism: The Church of England in Colonial South Carolina* (Westport, Conn., 1982), 77–78.

from his office. The haste of Bullman's dismissal was surpassed two years later, when the next minister of St. Michael's dared to offer public prayers for the king in the midst of the royal navy's attack on the city.[46]

But such public "schisms" between parson and parishioners were rare. Most other loyalist ministers bit their tongues and quietly left their posts. The majority of the Anglican clergy, moreover chose to side with their planter neighbors and employers against their distant king and bishop.[47] Ultimately, the established church and its ministers were enlisted in the rebel cause. On February 17, 1775, the day which the Provincial Congress had set aside for fasting and prayer, Eliza Pinckney attended at St. Philip's and saw the members of Congress enter "in a body with their speaker at their head and the mace carryed before him." The minister, she wrote, offered a "prayer suited to the occation."[48]

These events offered black Anglicans a political education. From the furor that their masters directed at Bullman and his successor, as well as from the quiet but sudden resignation of other ministers who felt unable to forswear their oath to the king, slaves could perceive the rift between their local and their imperial (and perhaps spiritual) lords. Even when the church and its ministers sought to serve the slave society's new rulers, the result was hardly less informative to attentive slaves. After all, the same biblical references that ministers deployed to defend the colonists' right to resist a tyrannical monarch might well be applied by the slaves to their own masters. Given these pernicious possibilities, many slaveholders felt that the less contact the church had with their slaves in these troubled times, the better. One ex-slave later remembered, for example, that when the "war was coming on . . . Ministers were not allowed to come amongst us lest they should furnish us with too much knowledge."[49]

But the conflation of the sacred and secular and the habit of reasoning from the heavens to the earth that Anglican ministers had long preached to slaves and masters alike could not abruptly be revoked or recalled. Like many low-country whites, black Christians may also have reasoned that the present crisis was evidence of a divine judgment against the colony. Slaves thought they knew the cause of God's wrath. In early May

46. This was Robert Cooper, Bullman's replacement in the St. Michael's pulpit; Ibid., 78.
47. Ibid., 79. For example, Paul Turquand, who in 1767 had called upon his St. Matthew's congregation to obey "every ordinance of man for the Lord's sake," became a member of the Provincial Congress.
48. Eliza Pinckney to Harriet [Horry], 17 February 1775, Charles Cotesworth Pinckney Papers, LC.
49. "An Account of the Life of Mr. David George from Sierra Leone in Africa; Given by Himself," in John Rippon, ed., The Baptist Annual Register, 4 vols. (London, 1793–1802), 1, 473–84.

1775, for example, a slave was overheard telling a gathering of Charles Town blacks that "God would send Deliverance to the Negroes, from the power of their Masters, as He freed the Children of Israel from Egyptian Bondage."[50]

Two months later, a slave court in St. Bartholomew Parish gathered evidence that illustrates how slave converts could interpret the crisis in terms that were at once political, religious, and rebellious. The court was called after a local justice received "Information . . . that Several of the Slaves in the neighborhood were exciting & endeavouring to bring ab[ou]t a General Insurrection."[51] The chief witness for the prosecution was "Jemmy, a Slave belonging to John Wells," who testified to the court that "for two Years last past," several slaves had "been preaching . . . to Great crouds of Negroes in the neighbourhood of Chyhaw [Chehaw] which he himself has attended. . . . [and] that at these assemblies he had heard of an Insurrection intended & to take the Country by Killing the Whites."

The testimony as to what was said at these gatherings reveals how slaves could intertwine the sacred and the profane in their response to the revolutionary crisis. The court was told

That he Jemmy, had heard the Prisoner George Say that the old King had rec[eive]d a Book from our Lord by which he was to Alter the World (meaning to set the Negroes free) but for his not doing so, was now gone to Hell, & in Punishm[en]t—That the Young King, meaning our Present One, came up with the Book, & was about to alter the World, & set the Negroes Free.

In their summation of the case, the freeholders and magistrates placed the blame for the affair upon John Burnet, a local white man, who "had often appointed Nocturnal Meetings of the Slaves under the Sanction of Religion" and was "extremely Obnoxious to the People" of the parish. After placing Burnet at the service (or mercy) of the Charles Town Council of Safety, the court ordered the "Exemplary" execution of George and the whipping of several other slaves judged to be "Principal leaders of their Infernal designs."

At the gallows, George declared that Burnet had convinced him and the other Chehaw slaves that "they were equally entitled to the Good Things of this Life in common with the Whites." Not surprisingly, Burnet told another story when he appeared before the Council of

50. James Habersham to Robert Keen, 11 May 1775, in Georgia Historical Society *Collections* 6, (Savannah, 1904), 243–44.
51. Thomas Hutchinson to the Council of Safety, 5 July 1775, *PHL*, 10, 206–8; unless otherwise noted, all subsequent references to this incident are taken from this source.

Safety on July 18.[52] Burnet "utterly denied having any Knowledge of the pretended Book" and claimed that he "had never a thought of exciting . . . [the slaves] to Insurrection." On the contrary, Burnet swore that "he had endeavoured to reconcile them to the Lot in Life in which God had placed them." More significantly, he insisted that he had not preached to slaves since he was "admonished" against the practice in August 1773.

Given the limits and contradictions of the surviving evidence, it is impossible to get to the bottom of this intriguiging affair. Perhaps the likeliest explanation is that a religious spark that Burnet had planted among the slaves of Chehaw smoldered quietly until, fanned by the political winds of 1775, it suddenly burst into flame. In the interval, and in the novel situation that confronted them, the slave preachers had drastically reinterpreted Burnet's message of redemption and equality, changing its focus from a distant and heavenly future to an immediate and earthly present and transforming its its implications from patient submission to expectant rebellion.

Because the offices and institution of the slave court were firmly in the hands of local masters, the law and the gallows offered more reliable support in the crisis of 1775 than did the unsteady pillar of the church (as the events in St. Bartholomew amply demonstrated). Throughout the low country during that summer and fall, slave courts were hastily convened to sit upon the trial of slaves arrested "on Accusation of being Concerned in an Insurrection."[53]

In the hands of the masters the law, as always, proved to be a pliable instrument for administering punishment. In the prevailing mood of crisis and vulnerability, magistrates and freeholders may have felt a need for "example[s] of justice" to remind the slave population of their coercive power. In their deliberations, justices may have set legal technicalities aside in order to secure convictions and executions. For example, although the law specified that no slave could be found guilty of conspiracy in the absence of physical evidence, the apparent lack of such "proofs" in St. Bartholomew did nothing to save George's life.

But the operations of the slave court could not be entirely detached from entanglements with the law's colonial character and parentage. In mid-June 1775, a Charles Town slave court was called to sit upon the "Trials of Several Negroes Suspected & charged of plotting an Insurrection."[54] Among those thought to be "the most Criminal" was Thomas Jeremiah (more commonly known as Jerry), a free black fisherman and harbor pilot.

52. Council of Safety to St. Bartholomew Committee, 18 July 1775, *PHL*, 10, 231; all quotations from Burnet's testimony are taken from this source.
53. Little River Committee to the Council of Safety, 23 October 1775, *PHL*, 10, 499.
54. Henry Laurens to John Laurens, 18 June 1775, *PHL*, 10, 184.

At Jerry's trial, a slave named Sambo testified that, two months earlier, he had been approached by Jerry while working at the waterfront. According to Sambo, Jerry had asked him, "Sambo, do you know anything of the war that is coming?" Sambo claimed that he answered no, and then asked, "what shall we poor Negroes do?" To which Jerry had answered, "Jump on shore, and join the [British] soldiers," for, Jerry added, "the war was come to help the poor negroes."[55]

Jemmy, a city slave who was Jerry's wife's brother, was persuaded to testify against Jerry in return for the promise of a pardon. Jemmy reported that, one month before the news of war reached Charles Town, Jerry had "asked him to take a few Guns to . . . Dewar [a runaway slave], to be placed in Negroes hands to fight against the Inhabitants of this Province." Jemmy also declared that Jerry had claimed "to have the chief command of the said Negroes; [and] that . . . [Jerry had] said he believed he had Powder enough already, but that he wanted more arms" and that "he would try to get as many as he could."[56]

Although "every argument, [and] every art was employed to draw him to a confession," Jerry continued to insist upon his innocence.[57] The justices postponed their verdict and returned Jerry to the workhouse in hope either that he might confess or that "further proof could be got against him."[58] Neither was forthcoming. After two months, and with no new evidence, the court reconvened, returned a verdict of guilty, and sentenced Jerry to "be hanged and afterwards burned."[59]

When Governor Campbell, a newcomer both to the colony and to slave court proceedings, reviewed the trial transcripts, he wrote that "my blood run cold when I read on what grounds they had doomed a fellow creature to death."[60] As the provincial representative of the king, South Carolina's governor had long exercised a discretionary power to offer convicted criminals a colonial version of the royal pardon. But Campbell's fledgling efforts to do so on Jerry's behalf provoked a storm. "My attempting to interfere in the matter raised such a clamour amongst the people as is incredible," he reported; "they openly and loudly declared [that] if I granted the man a pardon they would hang him at my door."

55. Quoted in Peter H. Wood, " 'Taking Care of Business' in Revolutionary South Carolina: Republicanism and the Slave Society" in Jeffrey J. Crow and Larry G. Tise, eds., *The Southern Experience in the Amerian Revolution* (Chapel Hill, 1978). 284.
56. Ibid.
57. Governor William Campbell to Lord Dartmouth, 31 August 1775, in *DAR*, 11, 96.
58. George Milligen to Lord Dartmouth, 15 September 1775, in *DAR*, 11, 111.
59. Ibid., 95.
60. William Campbell to Lord Dartmouth, 18 August 1775, in *DAR*, 10, 93–98; unless otherwise noted, all references to this affair are taken from this source.

A royal pardon, Henry Laurens warned the governor, "would raise a flame all the water in Cooper River would not extinguish."

Frightened and startled by these threats, the governor desisted, and the gruesome sentence was carried out on August 18. At the gallows, Jerry "asserted his innocence to the last, behaved with the greatest intrepidity as well as decency, and told . . . [the watching crowd and the attendant executioners that] God's judgment would one day overtake them for shedding his innocent blood." For Governor Campbell, the proceedings at the execution proved that "the man was murdered." To Henry Laurens, the flames of Jerry's pyre declared that "Justice is satisfied!"[61] What message the "many . . . people of his own Colour" who witnessed Jerry's death took away from the ceremony is left unrecorded.

Given that South Carolina's slave masters were busily taking up arms against their monarch, the metaphors of patriarchy and obedience might seem to offer dubious ideological support in exercising dominion over slaves during the revolutionary crisis. But without the oil of patriarchy to grease its exploitative gears, a slave society could scarcely function. Absent patriarchal metaphors, master-slave relations would likely soon be interpreted through the language of war and conquest. Such, at least, seems to have been the case with Joshua Eden and his slave Limus. On November 4, Limus confronted his master and, as Eden later wrote, "though he is my Property, he has the audacity to tell me, he will be free, that he will serve no Man, and that he will be conquered or governed by no Man." After issuing this personal declaration of independence, Limus disappeared.[62]

In the chaos that followed the outbreak of the Revolution, few slaves were able either to see as clearly or act as boldly as Limus. But as the revolutionary disorders continued to bring established patriarchal ideas and institutions into question and weakened plantation patriarchs' ability to punish or recapture those who sought to deny their subordination, acts of individual or collective enlightenment and liberation became both more common and more dangerous to the social order.

The intemperate reaction that followed the governor's consideration of a pardon in Jerry's case indicates how sensitive low-country whites were to any exercise of the royal prerogative in this crisis. But low-country masters were nonetheless reluctant to break openly with the old regime. Many slaveholders would have preferred that the king or his governor, like the established church, be present but passive, seen but not heard. Accordingly, when in September 1775 Governor Campbell

---

61. Henry Laurens to Alexander Innes, 18 August 1775, *PHL*, 10, 333–34.
62. *South Carolina Gazette*, 7 November 1775.

fled his Charles Town house for the security of a royal navy ship in the harbor, the General Committee entreated him to "return to Charles-Town," promising that "whilst . . . your Excellency shall take no active part against the good people of this Colony, in the present arduous struggle for the preservation of their civil liberties, we will . . . secure to your Excellency that safety and respect . . . which the inhabitants of Carolina have ever wished to show the representative of their Sovereign."[63]

Such an awkward posture of loyal rebellion was hardly tenable, as the governor's reply made clear. "I never will return to Charles-Town," Campbell declared, "till I can support the King's authority and protect his faithful and Loyal Subjects." But in the revolutionary crisis, with the slaveholders in "actual and open Rebellion," where could such people be found? The testimony gathered against George at Chehaw and Jerry in Charles Town provides evidence that low-country blacks were as able as anyone in the colony to see and grasp the possibility of a coalition between the distant king and his "faithful and Loyal" slave "Subjects."[64]

In the summer and fall of 1775, the social order of the colonial slave society threatened to collapse into disorder and anarchy. Throughout the previous thirty-five years, low-country masters had become accustomed to proclaiming and legitimating their own authority by emphasizing the close ties between the local regime and the prestige and power of the metropolitan culture. Slaves who participated or witnessed the ceremonies of the law or church had long heard the British monarch described as "the fountain of authority," who deserved "reverence & obedience by a right that cannot be dispensed with."[65] Local power and authority had commonly been depicted as descending from the king through his governors and justices down to the dominion that each master wielded on his plantation. Masters who now refused to obey their own superiors naturally worried that their slaves might be inspired to do likewise. Moreover, by taking up arms against their king, masters had broken the chain of descending authority and raised uncomfortable questions about the legitimacy of their own rule.

Some masters met the challenge head on. Henry Laurens called together the slaves under his charge in Charles Town one Saturday evening during the first week in June and "admonished them to behave with great circumspection in this dangerous times [and] set before them the great risque of exposing themselves to the treachery of pretended friends." "Poor Creatures," Laurens added, "they were sensibly affected,

63. General Committee to Lord William Campbell, 29 September 1775, *PHL*, 10, 435.
64. William Campbell to the General Committee, 30 September 1775, *PHL*, 10, 442.
65. *The New Whole Duty of Man* (London, 1744), cited in Clark, *English Society*, 126–27.

& with many thanks promised to follow my advice & to accept the offer of my Protection."[66] By bringing the matter out into the open and forcing his slaves publicly to choose between the master who stood before them and more distant "pretended friends," Laurens felt that he had faced down the challenge, at least in his own household.

Attempts to censor the newspaper indicate that not all masters were as confident as Laurens on the question of how their slaves would respond to such knowledge or such an appeal. Moreover, slaves who voiced their obedience to the master's face might well have other thoughts in their minds and act differently when opportunity arose. With the ordinary institutions and discourses through which they had long exercised their domination paralyzed or suspect in the revolutionary crisis, masters resorted to more naked expressions of their power. Slave trials and public executions served this purpose, as did public displays of the slaveholders' military strength. Accordingly, in mid-May, the General Committee directed that "the Inhabitants" of the colony "do Patrole Duty and to Mount Guard every night" and ordered that "the militia thro'out The Province . . . [be] armed and drawn out."[67] Soon, according to one resident, the city was filled with "the daily & nightly sound of Drums and Fifes."[68]

It was obvious to all who the intended audience for this martial display was. Josiah Smith reported on May 18 that "our militia . . . perform duty . . . principally to guard against any hostile attempts that might be made by our domesticks."[69] When the Provincial Congress reconvened at the beginning of June and called for the "immediate raising of two thousand men horse & foot," Smith thought the measure designed "to keep those mistaken creatures [the slaves] in awe."[70] At the same time, in a rare burst of confidence, the newspaper reported that since the imposition of martial law "the nightly Meetings and Riots of the Negroes are entirely suppressed."[71]

The sight of the colonial militia on guard and well armed, as well as the executions of Jerry and George, may have scotched any plans for overt rebellion that low-country slaves were entertaining. Moreover, none of the hoped-for British aid had as yet arrived. In fact, colonial governments were so ill equipped to cope with the crisis that by October the royal governors of both South Carolina and Georgia were forced to

66. Henry Laurens to James Laurens, 7 June 1775, *PHL*, 10, 162–63.
67. Alden, ed., "John Stuart Accuses William Bull," 318.
68. Henry Laurens to John Laurens, 15 May 1775, *PHL*, 10, 119.
69. Josiah Smith to James Poyas, 18 May 1775, Josiah Smith, Jr., Letterbook, SHC-UNC.
70. Josiah Smith to George Appleby, 16 June 1775, Josiah Smith, Jr., Letterbook, SHC-UNC.
71. Wood, " 'Taking Care of Business,' " 282.

seek refuge aboard royal navy ships in Charles Town harbor and the Savannah River respectively.

But while slaves were not foolhardy enough to rise up unassisted against a well-prepared and better-armed foe, neither did they quietly submit. With the royal governments of South Carolina and Georgia quite literally adrift, the only places in the two colonies still under the crown's effective control were two small islands: Sullivan's Island in Charles Town harbor, and Tybee Island in the mouth of the Savannah. Soon both islands became "den[s] for runaway slaves," as blacks in the vicinity sought asylum from their masters under the guns of the king's ships.[72]

It is possible that these refugees may have been moved to act by news that on November 7, Lord Dunmore, the royal governor of Virginia, had promised freedom to slaves of rebel masters who joined him to fight for the king.[73] Or perhaps the runaways were merely reacting to what they could see with their own eyes, and sought to turn the confused political situation in the colonies to their advantage. Whatever their inspiration, hundreds of fugitive slaves were soon encamped on the two islands where, as one account of Sullivan's Island reported, "huts were building for them in the woods."[74]

Throughout December, reports vividly demonstrated the impact that the British naval presence in Charles Town harbor and the growing fugitive camp on Sullivan's Island were having upon the black population of the vicinity. In Christ Church Parish, opposite to Sullivan's Island, a black man was brought before a slave court charged with "inticing other slaves to desert on board the man of war."[75] In Charles Town itself, the militia intercepted five slaves attempting to escape in canoes to the royal navy sloop *Cherokee*, and one white resident overheard an evening conversation "between a mulatto fellow and some slaves belonging to the inhabitants of this town; one of which [slaves]," he added, "is since missing."[76] Perhaps most frightening of all to the slaveholder revolutionaries,

72. "Extract of a letter to a Gentleman in Philadelphia, dated Charlestown, February 7, 1776," in Peter Force, ed., *American Archives*, series 4, 9 vols. (Washington, D.C., 1840), 3, 950.

73. For more on Dunmore's proclamation, see Benjamin Quarles, *The Negro in the American Revolution* (Chapel Hill, 1961), 18.

74. Testimony of Jacob Milligan to the Council of Safety, 6 December 1775, "Journal of the Council of Safety Appointed by the Provincial Congress, November 1775," *Collections of the South Carolina Historical Society* 3 (Charleston, 1859), 63. William Moultrie estimated that nearly five hundred fugitive slaves were encamped on Sullivan's Island by December 1775; William Moultrie, *Memoirs of the American Revolution*, 2 vols. (New York, 1802), 1, 113. In March 1776, Stephen Bull reported that two hundred fugitives were on Tybee Island; Stephen Bull to Henry Laurens, 13 March 1776, *PHL*, 11, 155.

75. "Journal of the Council of Safety," 3, 233.

76. Ibid., 88, 103, 63.

a free black fisherman, Scipio Handley, was discovered to be carrying messages across the harbor between the governor and the city. After his capture, Handley was sentenced to death "for acting against the Congress."[77]

Nor were the British averse to cooperating with fugitive slaves in more active measures. In mid-December, Henry Laurens, now the president of the South Carolina Council of Safety, wrote bitterly to Captain Edward Thornborough of the *Tamar* that "we have daily complaints from the inhabitants on the sea-coast, of robberies and depredations committed on them by white and black armed men, from on board some of the ships under your command."[78] In a similar vein, Laurens wrote that "Lord William Campbell had gone great lengths in harbouring & protecting Negroes on Sullivants Island from whence those Villains made nightly Sallies and committed robberies & depredations on the Sea Coast of Christ Church."[79]

South Carolina masters may not have been surprised that their slaves had taken advantage of the possibility of escape that the British forces in Charles Town harbor and the Savannah River seemed to offer them. However, the realization that the British were "protecting negroes who fly from their masters" was deeply shocking.[80] "Humanity must revolt," John Rutledge declared, at the ministry's scheme "to make the ignorant domesticks subservient to the most wicked purposes."[81] That "Captains of British Ships of War & Noble Lords" should engage in such perfidious deeds "disgrace[d] . . . their Master and . . . their Cause," thought Henry Laurens.[82] To many colonial slaveholders it may have seemed as if the empire had turned upside-down. They had always seen the officers and culture of the metropolis as the embodiment of order and rightful authority. But now the forces of the king seemed a font of lawlessness and anarchy. Virginia masters scornfully christened Governor Dunmore "King of the Blacks," as befit his

---

77. While awaiting execution, Handley was smuggled a file by a friend, broke his irons, jumped two stories to the ground from his cell window, and escaped to find refuge with the British fleet. He later joined the British army and served in the ranks in Georgia. In 1783 Handley appeared before a board of loyalist commissioners in London and applied for compensation for one hundred pounds' worth of goods that were lost when he fled Charleston in 1775; "Memorial of Scipio Handley, a black," Loyalists, microfilm, SCDAH, vol. 53, 166–68.
78. "Journal of the Council of Safety," 3, 94–95.
79. Henry Laurens to Richard Richardson, 19 December 1775, *PHL*, 10, 576.
80. "Journal of the Council of Safety," 3, 94–95.
81. John Rutledge, "Address to the General Assembly of South Carolina, April 11, 1776," in William Edwin Hemphill et al., eds., *Journals of the General Assembly and House of Representatives, 1776–1780* (Columbia, 1973), 53.
82. Henry Laurens to John Laurens, 14 August 1776, *PHL*, 11, 224.

new role as lord of misrule.[83] In the same manner, Laurens characterized the policy that Britain seemed to have adopted toward the slaves:
"What meanness! what complicated wickedness!...O England, how
changed! how fallen!"[84]

While low-country leaders hesitated to cross the revolutionary Rubicon by directly attacking the British ships in the harbor, they deemed it
"absolutely necessary" that an example be made of slaves who had
"gone over to the enemy."[85] A party of soldiers drawn from South Carolina's newly raised infantry regiments was ordered to cross over to
Sullivan's Island under cover of darkness. "Disguised as Indians," the
soldiers attacked the fugitives' camp "early in the morning" of December
18.[86] Laurens described the result:

> The Company of Foot Rangers or 54 of them under the command of
> Lieut[enant] Withers made a descent on that Island burnt the House in
> which the Banditti were often lodged brought off four Negroes killed three
> or four . . . destroyed many things which had been useful to those wretches
> in the Houses—many of the Men of Wars Water Casks, a great loss to
> them, exchanged a few Shot with Some of the Men of Wars Men & came
> off unhurt.[87]

Laurens hoped that the attack would "mortify his Lordship [Governor
Campbell] not a little" and "serve to humble our Negroes in general."[88]
Thus, the first bloodshed in the low country's Revolution occurred in a
struggle between white and black Carolinians.[89]

As the year ended, the low-country leadership decided to risk the consequences of refusing any future demands to supply the governor's flo-
tilla with fresh water and food. At the same time, South Carolina's
soldiers began to build fortifications on the east shore of the harbor from
which cannon could threaten the warships at their anchorage. Faced with

---

83. *Virginia Gazette*, 16 November 1776.
84. Henry Laurens to John Laurens, 14 August 1776, *PHL*, 11, 224.
85. Moultrie, *Memoirs of the American Revolution*, 1, 113.
86. *South Carolina and American General Gazette*, 22 December 1775; and Josiah Smith to
James Poyas, 10 January 1776, Josiah Smith, Jr., Letterbook, SHC-UNC.
87. Henry Laurens to Richard Richardson, 19 December 1775, *PHL*, 10, 576.
88. Ibid.
89. This was not, however, the first bloodshed in South Carolina, nor were these the first
shots fired in the low country. On 11–12 November, two of the British warships in Charles
Town harbor briefly exchanged cannon shots with the *Defence*, an armed schooner that the
colony had outfitted. The range was too great for the shots to be effective and no one was
injured. On 19–22 November, a clash between republican and royalist militia took place in
the backcountry in which two men were killed and two dozen wounded. See *PHL*, 10, 509
(note), and 536 (note).

this prospect, the governor and his little fleet sailed out to sea on the morning of January 6, 1776. Campbell took with him the official seal of the government and also, according to Henry Laurens, "no inconsiderable number" of the colony's slaves.[90]

Three months after the raid on Sullivan's Island, a similar scene was played out to the south. In mid-March, Laurens authorized the militia commander in the southern part of the colony "to seize & if nothing else will do to destroy all those Rebellious Negroes upon Tybee Island."[91] Earlier, Colonel Stephen Bull had sent a letter to Laurens and the General Committee that included a confidential passage, which Bull urged them to keep "a profound Secret": "People ought not to know anything of the following matter." He continued: "The matter is that it is far better for the Public . . . [that] the deserted Negroes on Tybee Island . . . be shot" than be allowed to escape with the British.[92] As on Sullivan's Island, a terrifying demonstration of violence might send a powerful message to the slaves of the low country. Laurens and Bull justified the admittedly "awful business" of putting "fugitive & Rebellious Slaves to death" on the grounds that "it perhaps may deter other Negroes from deserting."[93]

On March 25, 1776, seventy militiamen, again "painted and dressed like Indians," along with thirty actual Native Americans, launched an assault upon Tybee Island. According to a British report, the attackers exhibited a "most savage barbarity, in which . . . the white people exceeded the ferocity of the Indians." The report noted that two British marines had been killed and "scalped" but said nothing of the fate of the fugitive slaves who had sought refuge on the island.[94]

The next day, eighty miles northeast of Tybee Island, the members of the Provincial Congress convened at the Exchange house in Charles Town and declared South Carolina's independence from Great Britain. But if this was a revolution, it was an oddly conservative one. In the preamble to the new constitution, the members claimed that they had acted to maintain "peace and good order" in the colony in response to

90. Henry Laurens to Stephen Bull, 6 and 20 January 1776, *PHL*, 11, 1–2, 49–50. In November 1783, a census was taken of the three thousand ex-slaves who were to be evacuated with the British army from New York City. Included in the register was "Sam[ue]l Drayton [age] 40, stout fellow . . . formerly slave to Geo[rge] Ancrum [in] Charles Town left him with Lord W[illia]m Campbell in 1775"; British Headquarters Papers [Carleton Papers], BPRO, 301/55/100/19427 (microfilm), SCDAH.
91. Minutes of the Council of Safety, 17 March 1776, original and microfilm at SCDAH.
92. Stephen Bull to Henry Laurens, 14 March 1776, in *PHL*, 11, 163.
93. Henry Laurens to Stephen Bull, 16 March 1776, *PHL*, 11, 172; Stephen Bull to Henry Laurens, 14 March 1776, *PHL*, 11, 163–64.
94. Patrick Tonyn to David Taitt, 20 April 1776, *DAR*, 12, 108–9.

actions of the royal government that threatened to "loosen the bands of government and create anarchy and confusion."[95] Henry Laurens, the newly appointed vice president of South Carolina, cautiously approved of the measure. "In our present situation with respect to England," he wrote, "it is certainly a good Act, it can work no Evil & will be productive of much good—Men will be brought into more order & will be better tempered for receiving terms for a happy reconciliation."[96]

Although they accepted it as a "necessary expedient," low-country leaders did not regard their declaration of independence as irrevocable.[97] In his first address to the new government, South Carolina's first president, John Rutledge, declared: "Let it be known that this Constitution is but temporary, till an accommodation of the unhappy differences between Great Britain and America can be obtained; and that such an event is still desired by men who yet remember former friendships and intimate connections, though for defending their persons and properties they are stigmatized and treated as rebels."[98] South Carolina's low-country masters were revolutionaries by necessity rather than choice. As he cast his vote, Henry Laurens claimed that he felt like a "dutiful son, thrust by the hand of violence out of a father's house into a cruel world."[99]

"The King's people are coming!"

Two months after South Carolina's leaders declared their provisional independence, a British fleet of eleven warships and thirty transport ships carrying twenty-five hundred soldiers arrived off the Charles Town bar. Also on board was Lord William Campbell, who was determined to regain his governorship and restore his majesty's government to South Carolina.[100] The previous September, two low-country planters had predicted glumly that if a British military force arrived in the colony and an appeal were made to the slaves of the low country, "20,000 Negroes" would flock into the royal army's camp "in a fort-

95. The text of the 1776 constitution is reprinted in Drayton, *Memoirs of the American Revolution*, 2, 186–97.
96. Henry Laurens to John Laurens, 28 March 1776, *PHL*, 11, 194.
97. Ibid.
98. Quoted in Edward McCrady, *The History of South Carolina in the Revolution, 1775–1780* (New York, 1901), 116.
99. Quoted in David Duncan Wallace, *The Life of Henry Laurens with a Sketch of the Life of Lieutenant-Colonel John Laurens* (New York, 1915), 10.
100. This description of the battle of Sullivan's Island is based on Christopher Ward, *The War of the Revolution* (New York, 1952), 665–78.

night."[101] But the commander of the fleet, Admiral Peter Parker, had no intention of resorting to such unorthodox tactics. Instead, in a southern version of the battle of Bunker Hill, Parker decided to make a frontal attack upon Charles Town's improved harbor defenses.

On the morning of June 28, 1776, anxious spectators, black and white, lined the Charles Town waterfront as the British squadron closed in to bombard the unfinished fort on Sullivan's Island. By day's end, the British had lost the battle, Admiral Parker had lost his britches, and South Carolina's new government had gained a hero, a holiday, and a new flag.[102]

Far more important, South Carolina's new government had gained valuable breathing space. In fact, two-and-a-half years passed before British military forces again threatened the slave society's domestic peace. In the interval, the new regime had ample time to establish itself. In March 1778, the legislature finally acknowledged the impossibility of a reconciliation with Britain and declared a permanent and unconditional independence. South Carolina ceased to be a colony and became a state, and Charles Town was made the capital of a new republic. Consequently, when British military forces at last arrived in the low country, they came less as the army of the rightful king, back to enjoy his own, than as an invading enemy. Likewise, after so long a pause, the ensuing military conflict had less the character of a civil war than it did of the invasion, conquest, and occupation of the state of South Carolina by an outside aggressor.

While the military conflict offered low-country slaves new opportunities and options, the choices were quite different from those of the Revolution's first year. In 1775–76, slaves' talk of the "Young King" represented their own dreams of deliverance more than it did a tangible reality. In contrast, between December 1778 and December 1782, slaves could see that the king's army was real and usually victorious but, upon close inspection, they could also see that their hopes for a royal liberator were illusory. While the war for the low country raged, neither the royalist nor the republican combatants expressed much interest in slaves'

101. Entry of 24 September 1775, in Butterfield, ed., *Diary and Autobiography of John Adams*, 2, 182 89.

102. That Admiral Parker "had his britches blown off" in the battle is from John S. Pancake, *This Destructive War: The British Campaign in the Carolinas, 1780–1782* (University, Alabama, 1985), 24. The hero of the day was a "Sergeant Jasper," who in the midst of the fight leapt upon the parapet of the fort to replace a fallen flag. The anniversary of the battle became a day of celebration, in many ways a substitute for earlier royal holidays; see, for example, *Gazette of the State of South Carolina*, 30 June 1778. The flag that flew over Fort Sullivan, with a white crescent and the word "liberty" upon a blue field, became the new flag of the colony/state.

hearts and minds. Rather, they fought for control of slaves' bodies to use as laborers, soldiers, or merely as confiscated property.

The low country's war began in earnest with the British invasion and conquest of Georgia in the closing days of 1778.[103] For the next year, the region between Charles Town and Savannah became the focus of the revolutionary war in the south. Across this area, royalist and republican forces marched and counter-marched, engaged in numerous skirmishes, and met in three pitched battles. As the rival armies traveled along low-country roads and rivers, thousands of slaves had their first encounter with war and with the dangers and the possibilities that followed in its train. The campaigns of 1779 wreaked unprecedented destruction and disorder among the plantations of the region, but neither side was able to gain a clear advantage.

The military stalemate was abruptly shattered in the spring of 1780, when a British fleet arrived off the South Carolina coast carrying General Henry Clinton and ten thousand royalist soldiers. Clinton landed his army on John's Island south of Charles Town and, in a methodical three-month campaign, surrounded and laid siege to the city. Trapped within the city's fortifications were General Benjamin Lincoln and the entire southern republican army of five thousand troops, including all of South Carolina's own continental regiments, as well as many members of the state legislature. Given Clinton's great superiority in ships, cannon, and troops, the result was not in doubt. On May 12, 1780, after a six-week siege, Lincoln surrendered both his army and the city.

With the capture of Charles Town and the establishment of small military garrisons near Beaufort and Georgetown and to the west, the South Carolina low country effectively became conquered territory. For the next fifteen months, while a bitter guerrilla war raged in the backcountry, the coastal district from Georgetown to Savannah remained largely pacified. Recognizing the futility of further resistance and fearful as always that continued disorder might inspire slave revolt, hundreds of low-country masters (including a former president of the state and a former president of the Continental Congress) came forward to make their peace with the king. The British commandant of Charles Town established a civilian "Board of Police" comprised of leading loyalist citizens and former royal officials to serve as an interim occupation government.[104]

It was not until the summer of 1781 that republican military forces returned to the low country. Georgetown was retaken in July, and

103. For a recent examination of the military aspects of the revolution in the low country, see Pancake, *This Destructive War*; for slaves' role, see Frey, *Water from the Rock*, 108–42.
104. For a detailed treatment of the occupation, see George Smith McCowen, Jr., *The British Occupation of Charleston, 1780–82* (Columbia, 1972).

Monck's Corner at the head of the Cooper River was captured in August. After a final, bloody battle at Eutaw Springs on the Santee River in September, the royalist forces were withdrawn to a cordon a few miles outside of Charles Town. The next month the surrender of Cornwallis's army at Yorktown, Virginia, ended any British hopes of resuming the offensive in the low country. For a year the royalist forces in Charles Town merely stood their ground while peace negotiations began. In the fall of 1782, the British command ordered that the city itself be abandoned. In mid-December, the British evacuation of the city brought both the low country's war and the colonial regime to an end.

During the four years that the conflict lasted, both masters and slaves recognized that the vortex of the wartime disorders lay in the camp of the British army. Within the camp, the writ of the slave code and slave patrol were moot. By displacing, destroying, or merely disregarding the ordinary authority of the slave regime, each body of the royalist army was like a mobile hole in the fabric of the slave society at least as large as its outermost pickets.

In one sense, the events of the revolutionary war in the low country can be seen as a meeting of two cultures: the British military establishment and the low-country slave community. More than an ocean divided these two worlds. Even communication was often difficult. After an encounter with a group of slaves speaking Gullah in 1780, for example, a royalist officer remarked that "none of us could manage to talk with these people because of their bad dialect."[105]

But cooperation across this cultural divide was possible. At the very least, the invading British army and low-country blacks shared a common foe in the republican slave masters of the low country. The simple logic that "the enemy of my enemy is my friend" was the basis for much of the mutual understanding that occurred between slaves and the royal soldiery. Ultimately, however, the redcoats and the slaves sought quite different ends. The hostility of the royal army was aimed at rebellious slaveholders and not at slavery itself. Slaves as always, were merely tools to be used to accomplish this objective. But low-country blacks had their own agendas. Slaves sought to turn the British army's campaign against their masters into a larger war against slavery, or to use the fog of war as an opportunity to secure their own independence and liberty.

An eighteenth-century British army camp was hardly an egalitarian commune, but the military code placed far more emphasis on rank than on race. Moreover, a stark contrast often existed between the soldiery's

---

105. Captain Johann Ewald, *Diary of the American War: A Hessian Journal*, trans. and ed. Joseph P. Tustin (New Haven, 1979), 23.

brutal subjection to martial discipline and military order and their casual breach of, if not outright contempt for, civil laws regarding private property, including slavery. Slaves who visited the army or whose plantations the army visited saw in the royal army's camp a small-scale version of an alternate world.[106]

The sheer spectacle of an eighteenth-century army on the march, drums beating, fifes playing, silk banners flying, and thousands of soldiers marching past in brightly colored uniforms, must have made a profound impression on people who had lived out their lives in what were, in essence, small rural villages. A glimpse of slaves' excitement and fascination when they first saw the royal army appears in Eliza Wilkinson's account of the redcoats' arrival at her Yonge's Island plantation in June of 1779. News of the soldiers' approach was first brought by one of Wilkinson's slaves, who was out "visiting" at a nearby plantation. The slave woman ran toward the great house exclaiming: "O! the King's people are coming! it must be them, for they are all in red!" A few minutes later, Wilkinson and her slaves watched as "the whole British army" went past along the road. The sight put an end to work, at least temporarily. "In a little time," Wilkinson recalled, "the Negroes in the field came running up to the house with a hundred stories of what they had seen."[107]

Masters anticipated the attraction that a royal army would have for their slaves. Before the redcoats even set foot in the state, one writer predicted that "numerous domesticks . . . would undoubtedly flock in multitudes to the banners of the enemy whenever an opportunity arrived."[108] Masters also dreaded the political import of the royal army's intrusion into the plantation districts. Nothing, masters feared, would so quickly undermine slaves' obedience and deference as the sight of their own defeat by, or retreat before, a more powerful outside enemy. "In Slave Counties," the general commanding South Carolina's military forces remarked in the spring of 1776, "so much depends upon opinion, and the opinion which the slave will entertain of our superiority or inferiority will naturally keep pace with our maintaining or giving ground."[109]

For the slaves on many plantations, the challenge that the British army posed to their masters' authority was far more than theoretical. Often, a

106. For eighteenth-century British military culture, see Sylvia R. Frey, *The British Soldier in America: A Social History of Military Life in the Revolutionary Period* (Austin, Texas, 1981).

107. Caroline Gilman, ed., *Letters of Eliza Wilkinson, During the Invasion and Possession of Charleston, S.C., By the British In the Revolutionary War* (New York, 1839), 28–29, 47–49.

108. General Robert Howe to Congress, February 1777, in Quarles, *The Negro in the American Revolution*, 125.

109. Charles Lee, "Instructions to Brigadier General Armstrong," 10 April 1776, quoted in ibid., 122.

passing royalist patrol dramatically demonstrated the hollowness of their masters' power in the midst of the war. In May 1780, for example, a "party of the Enemy" descended upon Henry Laurens's Mepkin plantation ten miles north of Charles Town. Laurens's agent traveled to the plantation and heard the overseer's story of what ensued:

> [The soldiers] broke open the trunks in the house . . . carried off all they could carry . . . & robbed . . . him [the overseer] of what money he had, his watch, shirts, stockings, & took his wifes shoes from her feet. . . . [They] told him they were informed . . . [that] Colonel Laurens . . . was a grand rebel, that he was an unhappy man to live at . . . [Laurens's] plantation [and] that everything he had would soon be taken.

As he related this tale, the agent noted, the overseer still "seemed much frightened."[110]

Similar experiences at other scattered plantations suggest the net effect of such episodes, repeated throughout the low country and retold by onlooking slaves to others. At Ashepoo plantation in May 1779, "the overseer concealed himself in the swamp" while the redcoats "burnt the dwelling house & books destroyed all the furniture, china &ca. . . . and drank the liquors." When he returned to the plantation after the British soldiers had departed, the overseer found that "the Negroes [would] pay no attention to his orders."[111] Perhaps the most vivid surviving record of how the British army could turn the prewar world upside down occurred at Silk Hope plantation in April 1780 when, in full view of the plantation slaves, a passing British patrol "bound the overseer . . . & whipped him most unmercifully."[112]

Given such sights and experiences, slaves might easily believe that not only their masters but slavery itself had been swept away by the arrival of the redcoats. "Upon the approach of any detachment of the King's troops," a British officer wrote, "all negroes, men, women, and children . . . thought themselves absolved from all respect to their American masters, and entirely released from servitude. Influenced by this idea, they quitted the plantations and followed the army."[113]

But slaves who saw the King's forces as an army of "jubilee" were led by false hopes. The British army's attitude toward the slaves and toward

110. John Lewis Gervais to Henry Laurens, 13 May 1780, Henry Laurens Papers, SCL-USC.
111. Thomas Pinckney to Eliza Lucas Pinckney, 17 May 1779, Pinckney Family Papers, SCHS, 38-3-5.
112. John Lewis Gervais to Henry Laurens, 30 April 1780, Henry Laurens Papers, SCL-USC.
113. Banastre Tarleton, *History of the Campaigns of 1780 and 1781 in the Southern Provinces of North America* (London, 1787), 89–90.

the institution of slavery was based upon convenience rather than conviction. The closest the British ever came to issuing an emancipation proclamation was General Clinton's "Philipsburg Proclamation" of June 1779, in which Clinton offered "every NEGRO who shall desert the Rebel Standard, full security to follow within these Lines, any Occupation which he shall think proper."[114] But the freedom tendered by the Philipsburg Proclamation was limited to rebels' slaves and was contingent upon the continuation of the war. Clinton carefully made no mention of what the status of slave refugees might be after the cessation of hostilities.

Ultimately, Britain's political objectives in the revolutionary war were conservative, to restore the colonial status quo before independence. Plans for a colonial "reconstruction" to follow the successful quashing of the American Rebellion were never explicitly formulated, but the institution of slavery would have had an important place in any future British North America. After all, as many slaves lived in the loyal colonies of the Caribbean as in the rebellious colonies of the mainland. Moreover, the sugar islands were considered a far more valuable part of the mercantilist imperial economy than were the colonies of the continent. Destroying slavery to save America would therefore cost Britain more than it might gain.

In the absence of any explicit anti-slavery program or ideology, the British response to the slaves who flocked to their flag was always guided by short-term tactics rather than deeply felt principle. In this sense, the Philipsburg Proclamation closely paralleled the policy later followed by the federal government in the first year of the American Civil War: fugitive slaves were sheltered under the guise that they constituted contraband enemy property, rather than recognized as liberated persons.

Like their federal counterparts eighty years later, the British did not turn the fugitives away, for while the war continued slave refugees could serve multiple purposes. Runaways provided valuable intelligence of enemy troop strength and movements. On several occasions, slaves guided royal troops via secret routes to surprise attacks on American positions.[115] Fugitives were also a source of labor that could be put to the king's use

114. Quoted in James W. St. George Walker, *The Black Loyalists: The Search for a Promised Land in Sierra Leone and Nova Scotia, 1783–1870* (New York, 1976), 2.
115. For example, before the British attack on Savannah in December 1778, Quamino Dolly, "an aged Negro," came to the tent of the British commander, Archibald Campbell, and offered to guide the British along a "private way" through the swamps to a position behind the American lines. Dolly's intelligence allowed the British to surprise the Americans and gain an easy and decisive victory. See Quarles, *The Negro in the American Revolution*, 144.

and denied to his enemies. Moreover, every newly arrived refugee represented a *de facto* confiscation of rebel property. Slaves who ran away
to the royal army may have "stolen themselves," but it was the British
who claimed the plunder. Finally, the need to deter slave desertion could
be expected to distract rebel authorities and deplete rebel resources. As
one British officer put it, the "Negroes who flock to the conquerors . . .
do ten thousand times more Mischief than the whole Army put together."[116]

If the redcoats were not the liberators that the slaves hoped for, they
were at least allied with the slaves as enemies of the slaves' rebel masters.
As limited and conditional as the freedom of the royal army camp was,
it was nonetheless a *kind* of freedom, and first hundreds, and eventually
thousands, of slaves rushed to experience it. Slaves came to the army
singly, in families, or as entire plantation communities. "Today came
thirteen Negroes fleeing from Young's plantation on Wadmalaw Island,"
a British officer noted in March 1780. Three weeks later, John Lewis Gervais noted that "thirty-four of Mr. Lowndes's Negroes have joined the
enemy" and predicted sourly that "this will be the fate of many." After
the war, David George, an ex-slave become Baptist missionary, remembered that "my master was an anti-loyalist" who, "being afraid" at the
approach of the British army, "retired from home and left the slaves
behind." Thereupon George, his wife and two children, "and fifty or
more of my master's people" left the plantation and walked "about
twenty miles . . . [to] where the King's forces were."[117]

Slaves who went to the British were not necessarily motivated by revolutionary fervor. Boston King fled to the royal army to escape an anticipated beating from his master.[118] Other slaves may have gone to the
camp of the British army to satisfy their curiosity as much as from any
other motive. Slaves could place a visit to a nearby encampment into
their prevailing custom of *petit marronage* and casual visiting. Nor, upon
arrival at the camp, did slaves necessarily feel that they had burned their

116. Archibald Campbell to Unknown, 9 January 1779, quoted in Philip D. Morgan, "Black
Society in the Lowcountry, 1760–1810," in Ira Berlin and Ronald Hoffman, eds., *Slavery and
Freedom in the Age of the American Revolution* (Charlottesville, Va., 1983), 109.
117. "Diary of Captain Hinrichs," in Bernard A. Uhlendorf, ed., *The Siege of Charleston* (Ann
Arbor, Mich., 1938), 199; John Lewis Gervais to Henry Laurens, 29 March 1780, Henry
Laurens Papers, SCL-USC; David George, "An Account of the Life of Mr. David George,
from Sierra Leone in Africa; Given by Himself," in John Rippon, ed., *The Baptist Annual
Register* (London, 1794), 473–84.
118. "Memoirs of the Life of Boston King, a Black Preacher, Written by Himself, during his
Residence at Kingswood-School," *The Methodist Magazine for March, 1798* (London, 1798),
reprinted in Vincent Carretta, ed., *Unchained Voices: An Anthology of Black Authors in the
English-Speaking World of the 18th Century* (Lexington, Ky., 1996), 353.

bridges. They could simply walk home. The existence of a two-way traffic between nearby slave quarters and the army camp is indicated by a "list of the Negroes that is gone from Kensington [plantation] to the British Army in 1780" kept by Cooper River planter John Ball. In his record, Ball noted several instances of slaves having "gone to the Camp" and later returning to their work.[119]

Slaves who first tested the waters of the army camp with a temporary visit could later decide to seek a permanent refuge with the redcoats. Ball noted that "Tanner Charles" first went to the camp on May 11, and afterwards "came home & went away again"; the second time he did not return. [120] Similarly, Samuel Mathis noted that his slave woman, Esther, first visited the royal army outpost near Camden on Sunday and came back the following Monday afternoon.[121] Upon her return, Mathis "threatened her and set her to work," but the threats did not have the desired effect. Two days later, Mathis awoke to discover that Esther had "run off in the night." As evidence of her intentions, this time Esther "[had] taken her child and cloaths."[122] Mathis soon discovered that she was with the army.

The large numbers of slaves who sought refuge beneath the Union Jack meant that an irregular "army" of refugees soon adjoined any British encampment or followed in the train of the king's army as it marched. David Ramsay wrote that refugee slaves "collected in great crowds, near the royal army" and estimated that when the king's army first invaded the state in the spring of 1779 (in a march from Savannah to Charles Town and back) it was trailed by three thousand slaves, a number approximately equal to the army itself.[123]

But slaves who risked their lives in escaping to the royal army found themselves in perhaps even greater danger upon their arrival. Eighteenth-century army camps were notoriously filthy and unhealthy places. In 1781, for example, a visitor to the American army outside of Charles Town wrote that "on our near approach, the air was so infected with the stench of the camp, that we could scarce bare the smell."[124] Sickness was so prevalent in the vicinity of the camp that a distinct illness, "camp fever," was diagnosed. In keeping with eighteenth-century medical theory, the "bad air" was thought responsible, but a more likely culprit was drinking water contaminated with raw sewage. The informal

119. "John Ball's Planting Book for the Year 1780," Ball Family Papers, WPL-DU.
120. Ibid.
121. Journal of Samuel Mathis, 26 March 1781, SCL-USC.
122. Ibid., 28 March 1781.
123. David Ramsay, *History of South Carolina*, 1, 312–14.
124. Moultrie, *Memoirs of the American Revolution*, 2, 356.

camps of slaves who lived near the army shared this foul environment. Because the fugitives were lacking in almost everything, from tents and blankets to the tools and discipline that compelled soldiers to dig and use latrines, the situation in the refugees' makeshift camps soon became desperate and deadly.

On top of this, in 1780, the low country suffered its worst smallpox epidemic in seventeen years. The filth and contagion of the camps wrought a terrible toll on the refugees. David Ramsay chronicled with a grim satisfaction the fate of many: "the slaves . . . being crowded together were visited by camp fever. [Then] the small-pox . . . broke out among them, and spread rapidly, from these two diseases and the impossibility of their being provided with proper accommodations and attendance in the British encampment, great numbers of them died and were left unburied in the woods."[125] In September 1780, Eliza Pinckney described "the death of slaves . . . [from] the small pox . . . in the British camp. Thousands of Negroes dyed miserably with it," she wrote, "for it became quite a plague."[126]

Boston King came down with smallpox soon after escaping to the army and "suffered great hardships." He later recalled that "all the Blacks afflicted with that disease, were ordered to be carried a mile off from camp, lest the soldiers should be infected . . . [where] we lay sometimes for a whole day without anything to eat or drink."[127]

Threatened by the outbreak of disease among the refugees and impeded in their movements by the "crowds" of slaves who followed them, British officers soon began to complain of the "very great Inconveniences . . . found from Negroes leaving the service of their masters and coming to the British Army."[128] Moreover, when the British undertook to create a registry of all slave refugees within their lines, they made the embarrassing discovery that, despite the Philipsburg Proclamation's attempt to limit its offer of protection to the slaves of rebels, many slaves of loyalists had also found shelter in the army. Before returning to his headquarters in New York, Clinton directed that loyalists' slaves be restored to their owners, and instructed his replacement to the Carolina command, General Charles Cornwallis, "to make such arrangements as will discourage . . . [slaves from] joining us."[129]

125. Ramsay, *History of South Carolina*, 1, 334.
126. Eliza Lucas Pinckney to Unknown, 25 September 1780, Charles Cotesworth Pinckney Papers, LC.
127. "Memoirs of the Life of Boston King," 353.
128. General James Patterson to the Board of Police, 13 June 1780, Proceedings of the Board of Police, BPRO records, microfilm, SCDAH, C05/520, 2.
129. Frey, *Water from the Rock*, 119; Henry Clinton to Charles Cornwallis, 20 May 1780, quoted in Ibid.

In practice, however, the British were reluctant to act as slave catchers, even for loyalist masters. Officers were loath to detach their troops to serve as armed escorts for such a disagreeable and unsoldierly duty. Moreover, to return slaves to their owners by force, soldiers would have to be withdrawn from other assignments that seemed far more vital to the royalist war effort. Thus, although the British may have wished to halt, or at least limit, the flight of refugee slaves to the army, it was thought better for all concerned "if the slave could be persuaded to return voluntarily to the service of his master."[130]

Refugee slaves would hardly have returned willingly to their masters if they knew that they faced certain and severe punishment. To placate such fears, the British ordered that "care must be taken to prevent the Negroes being punished . . . for any offense which the master might think was committed by the slaves in leaving his service to join the king's troops."[131] The logical culmination of this policy was reached in February 1781, when the commandant of Charles Town declared that in order that "the Negroes [may] be freed from the apprehensions, which many of them are under, of ill-treatment, if speedily returned to their respective masters, . . . no Negro . . . shall be restored to his Owner, without . . . his own, free consent."[132]

A labor system based upon obtaining the workers' "free consent" was something other than slavery, but it also fell far short of freedom. Throughout the duration of the occupation, British policy followed the path of least resistance (or least inconvenience) concerning the slaves. If the army offered masters small aid, the troops were also quick to act if the slaves themselves sought to make trouble. In July 1780, for example, word was received in Charles Town of "the ill-behaviour and insurrectious conduct of Mr Isard's Negroes toward their Overseer."[133] In response, Colonel Nisbet Balfour "order[ed] a party of soldiers under a sergeant to be sent to Mr. Isard's plantation to inflict such punishment upon the principle offenders in the insurrection as may be adequate to their Crimes."[134] The following January, soldiers quashed a similar "insurrection" among slaves on a James Island plantation and executed one of the slaves concerned.[135]

The soldiers' apparent willingness to shield slave refugees from their

130. General James Patterson to the Board of Police, 13 June 1780, Proceedings of the Board of Police, BPRO records, microfilm SCDAH, C05/520, 2.
131. Ibid.
132. *South Carolina and American General Gazette*, 14 February 1781.
133. Proceedings of the Board of Police, 14 July 1780, BPRO records, microfilm, SCDAH, CO5/520, 7.
134. Ibid.
135. *South Carolina and American General Gazette*, 20 January 1781.

masters did not mean that they sought to destroy slavery or to undermine notions of black subordination. For instance, a report that a slave refugee who had been recaptured by his master "was rescued . . . by Capt. Alex. Campbell of the South Carolina Royalists [regiment], who threatened to split down the head [of] any person who should again take hold of the said Negroe," might suggest anti-slavery motives. But Campbell's subsequent claim that the slave in question "was his property" casts the affair in a different light.[136]

The British remained convinced that it was the slaves' lot to labor; the only question was at what tasks and for whose benefit they would work. One month after the fall of Charles Town, the newly created Board of Police proclaimed that "Negroes would be very apt to contract bad habits, . . . such as might be dangerous to the community . . . if they were suffered to remain in a state of idleness."[137] From the British perspective, there was certainly no lack of hard work to be done. In March 1781, the *Royal Gazette* published a list of 652 refugee slaves who had "joined the army" and were employed in occupations such as "Labourers," "Artificers," "Drivers," and "Nurses."[138] The warship *Providence*, on duty in Charles Town harbor, likewise put blacks to work as caulkers, carpenters, and blacksmiths.[139]

The British soon realized that the surest way to secure the labor they needed was to engage the refugees' self-interest. When the British withdrew to Charles Town in November 1781, the commandant of the city advertised in the *Royal Gazette* for workers to labor on the fortifications then hurriedly being built. Any interested slaves were asked to report "to the barrier" every morning, "where an overseer from the engineer department will attend to employ them."[140] The refugees were promised that "they will be allowed to go home in the evening" and were offered wages that were similar to those paid hired slaves before the war and twice the daily pay of a British private.[141]

Similar bargains were struck between individual refugees and officers or groups of soldiers. Boston King, for example, served for some time as

136. Testimony of Samuel Gruber, 23 October 1781, Proceedings of the Board of Police, BPRO records, microfilm, SCDAH, CO5/523, 2–3.
137. Proceedings of the Board of Police, 13 June 1780, BPRO records, microfilm, SCDAH, Co5/520, 2.
138. *Royal Gazette* (Charles Town), 14 March 1781.
139. Proceedings of the Board of Police, 29 August 1780, BPRO records, microfilm, SCDAH.
140. *Royal Gazette* (Charles Town), 7 November 1781.
141. The army offered to pay slave workers (or their masters) "at the rate of one shilling sterling per day," while a British private received six pence (or one half of one shilling per day); Frey, *The British Soldier in America*, 54.

the body servant to an English captain, and David George's wife served as a washerwoman for a company of loyalist troops.[142] In one case, a master bargained for his own slave's labor. When Thomas Pinckney, a republican captain, was recovering in a British field hospital after being wounded and captured, his mother informed him that one of the family's slaves had "join[ed] the British camp" and urged him to "employ her." She "will be of great service to you, if you can prevail with her to be with you," Pinckney's mother wrote, suggesting that she realized that in the upside-down world of the camp the slave woman was free to refuse.[143]

Some female refugees secured the protection of the army by forming sexual relationships with soldiers. The resulting arrangements may have been based on consent or coercion, calculation or commerce (and perhaps all of these at once). One Charles Town royalist reported that "it was not uncommon for persons to let out the Negro girls to British Officers"; another wrote that her "Negro woman went away with a British regiment with her own consent," adding that "she went off with the officers."[144] Similarly, Samuel Mathis's efforts to recover his slave Esther from the British camp at Camden in 1781 were finally defeated when he learned that "she was hid in an Officers room."[145]

In and of itself, interracial sex was neither novel nor particularly subversive to the slave society's social order, but an episode that took place in February 1782 suggests how British-slave liaisons could become, for both the British and the slave women involved, a means of subverting and ridiculing the prewar regime. An indignant letter written from the headquarters of the republican army described "an Ethiopian Ball" held in occupied Charles Town in which

> [the guests were] the Officers of the [British] Army and our female Slaves ... who these shameless tyrants had dressed up in taste, with the richest silks, and false rolls on their heads, powder'd up in the most pompous manner. These chaps, who call themselves Gentlemen, waited on these ... [women] in carriages to convey them to the Ball, ... many ... were taken out of houses before their mistresses faces, and escorted ... by these British [officers].

142. "Memoir of the Life of Boston King," 353; "An Account of the Life of Mr. David George," 473–84.
143. Eliza Lucas Pinckney to Thomas Pinckney, 13 September 1780, Pinckney Family Papers, SCHS.
144. Testimony of John Pearson, 11 November 1783, in Loyalists, microfilm, SCDAH, vol. 52, 132; Testimony of Elizabeth Thompson, 11 November 1783, ibid., 127–28.
145. Journal of Samuel Mathis, 3 April 1781, SCL-USC.

The outraged reporter had also acquired an invitation to the affair, which revealed that the "managers . . . were three Negro wenches, [that] this Ball was held at a very capital private House[,] . . . and the Supper cost not less than . . . [eighty pounds] sterling."[146]

The "Ethiopian Ball" both encapsulates the challenge that the king's army posed to the slave society and reveals its limitations. The event illustrates in an exaggerated fashion how the army could embody an alternate, almost inverted vision of the slave society. In the ceremony of the "Ethiopian Ball," royalist officers and slave women flaunted their ability to trespass upon the ordinary rules regarding gender and race. For a moment, an evening, slaves experienced a world turned upside down. At the same time, however, the dance was, like the army itself, transitory and ultimately superficial. The morning after the ball, Charles Town's slaves returned, Cinderella-like, to their kitchens and wash-houses. Similarly, the army eventually folded its tents and moved on.

The royal army might have served as the catalyst for more permanent change if royalist officials had allowed the slave refugees to bear arms against the society that had enslaved them. Several British officials did advocate such a policy, most notably Lord Dunmore, last royal governor of Virginia, who arrived in Charles Town in January 1781 with a plan to raise an army of 10,000 slaves who were to be promised freedom in exchange for faithful service.[147] But the political objectives of the British, as well as the aristocratic backgrounds of the British officer corps, made the adoption of such a radical policy unthinkable. Most British army officers could not see the logic in instigating one rebellion to suppress another.

Nevertheless, behind the "official" prohibition against putting slaves in the ranks, immediate wartime necessity and local circumstances meant that a considerable number of blacks did put on red coats. Among a group of 155 black refugees in Nova Scotia after the war, 61 claimed to

146. David Stevens to John Wendell, 20 February 1782, in "Boyd-Stephens Letters," Massachusetts Historical Society *Proceedings*, 48 (Boston, 1915), 342–43. The invitation (which was enclosed in the letter) read as follows:

My Lord,
    Your'e invited to a Ball on Thursday Evening at No. 99 Meeting Street, The Ball to be opened at Eight O'Clock.
HAGAR ROUSSELL
IZABELLA PINCKNEY } Managers
MARY FRASER
Jan'y 1st, 1782, Charlestown.
    To Lord Fitzgerald, Pres't.
147. Quarles, *Negro in the American Revolution*, 150–51.

have served in the British army, three as non-commissioned officers.[148] Some slaves fought and died beside British masters. In April 1782, for example, the *Royal Gazette* commended the conduct of "a negro man, servant to Capt. Alex. Campbell" for his part in a skirmish with American cavalry; the *Gazette* reported that "the Negro was killed after making a most gallant defence."[149]

When a large Franco-American army besieged Savannah in October 1779, the British enlisted a body of several hundred fugitive slaves. This battalion of "armed Negroes" subsequently played an active part in the city's successful defense. A royalist noted on October 16 that "our armed Negroes [were] skirmishing with the Rebels the whole afternoon," and two days later that "the armed Negroes brought in two Rebel Dragoons and eight Horses, and killed two Rebels who were in a foraging party."[150] This black battalion thereafter formed a permanent part of the city's garrison.[151]

The experience of four slaves of former royal governor Thomas Boone illustrates in miniature the enormous diversity of the black experience in the armed forces on both sides. In detailing the slaves he lost in the war, Boone wrote that, among others, "Joe a shoemaker died [in battle] in the service of the British army, Bacchus was blown up in the American frigate Randolph, Isaac a bricklayer was hanged by the Americans [as a spy] . . . [and] Anthony was drowned by a Capt. of a British vessel in Cooper River."[152]

Along with the ordinary hazards of the camp and the battlefield, the black redcoats faced extra risks. When captured in arms, they were not always treated according to the rules of war. The royalists were liable to treat captured blacks as booty, and republicans often regarded them as rebellious slaves. A "negro fellow of Mr. Odum's" was included among a list of "persons. . . . taken in arms against the united states" in 1779. When, shortly after his capture, this prisoner "broke custody insulted the centry & carried off his hat & gun," he was turned over to the civil court to "be tried as the law directs in such cases," that is, according to the dictates of the Negro Act.[153] The British were also inclined to vindictive-

---

148. Walker, *Black Loyalists*, 6.
149. *Royal Gazette* (Charles Town), 24 April 1782.
150. Benjamin Franklin Hough, *The Siege of Savannah, By the Combined American and French Forces Under the Command of Gen. Lincoln and the Count D'Estaing in the Autumn on 1779* (Albany, N.Y., 1866), 78.
151. In April 1780, a report reached Charles Town that "Col. Pickens had been down with a party within 5 miles of Savannah, [and] had killed about 60 Negroes in Arms"; John Lewis Gervais to Henry Laurens, 28 April 1780, Henry Laurens Papers, SCL-USC.
152. Memorial of Governor Thomas Boone, Loyalists, microfilm, SCDAH, vol. 53, 444–56.
153. "South Carolina Prisoners of War," LC.

ness when dealing with black prisoners. After the battle of Camden in August 1780, a British officer wrote to General Cornwallis that "twelve Negroes taken in arms ... are now prisoners of war." "Will it not be worthwhile," the letter continued, in order "to convince *Blackie* that he must not fight against us, to sell them and buy shoes for your corps?"[154]

While the sight of slaves in arms for the king infuriated their rebel masters, the black redcoats were still under the command of white officers and subject to military discipline, including the lash. Far more dangerous and revolutionary in potential were the independent parties of armed blacks that formed between the lines and carried on a private war against the slaveholders. Even if these bands were little more than brigands, the racial inversion and challenge they represented was obvious to all. In 1779, for instance, Eliza Wilkinson's isolated plantation was plundered "of everything ... worth taking" by a gang that included "several armed Negroes" who, she remembered, "threatened and abused us greatly."[155]

The crowd of slave refugees that followed behind the royal army could also operate as an independent "army," spreading out along the road to wreak destruction and vengeance on the slave society. The refugees did not distinguish between rebel and loyalist masters, indicating that their war was against slavery itself. William Bull, the colony's last lieutenant governor and a staunch royalist, retired to his plantation at the outbreak of the Revolution in 1775. Despite his political sympathies, he stood by helplessly as his "plantation at Ashley Hall ... [was] plundered and greatly damaged by the irregular and great swarm of Negroes that followed ... [the British] Army."[156]

In the last year of the low country's war, as the British bitterly contemplated defeat and prepared for the evacuation of Charles Town, they created military units comprised entirely of refugee slaves. It was a gesture made more of pique than policy, and it was too little and too late, either to save Britain's colonial regime or to destroy slavery.

The best known or most notorious of these refugee battalions was a cavalry troop that patrolled the region between the two armies in the last year of the war. In January 1782, William Matthews described a visit made by these "Negroe Dragoons" to his plantation:

> On the night of the 17th Janr. a Party of armed Negroes ... surrounded the House & endeavoured to get me out by stratagem—failing in their

154. Nisbet Balfour to Charles Cornwallis, 22 September 1780, Cornwallis Papers, BPRO, 30/11/64/97.
155. Gilman, ed., *Letters of Eliza Wilkinson*, 29.
156. Henry DeSaussure Bull, "Ashley Hall Plantation," *SCHM* 3 (Summer 1952), 63.

first attempt they threaten'd to break in by force—but I was not to be intimidated or cajoled into their Power—after having demanded and obtained some refreshment they departed—swearing . . . that had I not been an Invalid they would have fired the House and cut me in pieces.

. . . their pilot went from this neighborhood where he has large connexions & as the surrounding Plantations are People[d] with large Gangs of unruly Negroes . . . [whose masters are] absent from them I cannot think myself safe a single night.[157]

In April, a republican cavalry captain reported that he and his men had clashed "with one of ye British negro Captains and his Troop."[158] In August, Charles Cotesworth Pinckney complained that "the black Dragoons . . . are daily committing the most horrible depradations and murder."[159] Later the same month, in a battle at Wadboo Plantation, General Francis Marion's republican brigade beat off an attack made by several hundred British troops and "some Coloured Dragoons."[160] Less than a week before the final British departure from Charles Town, the "black dragoons" were reported still to be out on patrol.[161]

Both royalist and republican masters were inclined to regard blacks in arms not as soldiers but as rebellious slaves. According to the republican general, Thomas Sumter, the sight of independent units of black soldiers provoked "the resentment and detestation of every American who possesses common feelings."[162] Royalist William Bull likewise opposed the arming of slaves because of "the indiscriminate outrages . . . to which their savage nature prompts them," and more importantly, "the danger of the[ir] example to the rest of that class of people."[163] In the last months

157. William Matthews to Gideon White, 26 April 1782, White Collection, Public Archives of Nova Scotia, Halifax, Nova Scotia, No. 130.
158. "Extracts from the Journal of Lt. John Bell Tilden, Second Pennsylvania Line, 1781–1782," *Pennsylvania Magazine of History and Biography* 29 (1895), 225.
159. Colonel Charles Cotesworth Pinckney to Arthur Middleton, 13 August 1782, in Joseph W. Barnwell, ed., "Correspondence of Hon, Arthur Middleton," *SCHM* 28 (1926), 64.
160. Francis Marion to John Matthews, 30 August 1782, quoted in Frey, *Water from the Rock*, 138.
161. The report read: "the black dragoons . . . have been out four times within the last ten days plundering & robbing between the Quarter house and this place—last night they came as high as Mrs. Godins, where they continued from 11 o'clock till 4 this morning & carried off everything they could, except what was in the house which they did not enter—all her cattle, sheep, hogs, horses, & half the provisions she had was moved away. She thinks the number·at least one hundred all Blacks . . . at going off they said they would return this evening or tomorrow night & pay a visit to Mr. Parker and Mr. Smith, which they may possibly do." Thomas Bee to Governor Benjamin Matthews, 9 December 1782, Thomas Bee Papers, SCL-USC.
162. Thomas Sumter to Francis Marion, 20 February 1781, quoted in Jerome J. Nadelhaft, *The Disorders of War: The Revolution in South Carolina* (Orono, Me., 1981), 63.
163. William Bull to George Germain, 25 March 1782, in *DAR*, 21, 50–51.

before the final British evacuation, royalist militiamen accepted paroles from the republican government and joined in combating the "black dragoons."[164] Despite seven years of war, for low-country whites a man's skin color still took precedence over his politics.

The Slaves' Home Front

While the British army may have been the focal point of wartime disorder, the chaos that the army left in its wake had important effects, not only on those slaves who escaped to enjoy the *de facto* freedoms of the camp, but also on the slaves who remained behind. In the absence of masters and the ordinary institutions of power, slaves were free to reshape the social order of the plantations according to their own desires. In these places, and among these people, we can gain a tantalizingly brief and fragmentary glimpse of a world that colonial South Carolina's slaves made by and for themselves.

On many plantations, masters fled in advance of the royal army's arrival, leaving their slaves to fend for themselves. A British officer who visited a "large plantation" on James Island in February 1780 found that the master "who lived here is runaway," leaving "near 100 Negroes— young and old" behind.[165] Two weeks later, the same officer remarked that "all the white men have left this Island and gone into town."[166] Even on plantations where white masters or overseers stayed, the hostile, or at least contemptuous, attitude of the British toward them made such men unlikely to put their authority over their slaves to the test and allowed the slaves to disregard their orders.

Such islands of anarchy, where ordinary government, the slave code, and plantation discipline were displaced, must have existed in the near vicinity of every royalist army camp and on every plantation that the redcoats visited. Yet, as with the alternative world of the army itself, such lawless moments were usually transitory. In a short time, the army marched on, and authority in the guise of the master, overseer, or slave patrol returned to restore law and order. In these instances, blacks' moment of "liberation" was so brief that they could take little advantage of it except, of course, to follow the army when it marched on.

In some areas, however, the circumstances of the war developed so as to disable or destroy the masters' authority for far longer periods. The

164. Nadelhaft, *Disorders of War*, 72.
165. Diary of John Peebles, 12 February 1780, SCL-USC.
166. Ibid., 25 February 1780.

fall of Charles Town in May 1780 led to a complete collapse of civil authority. For the next eighteen months, the government of South Carolina was little more than the person of Governor John Rutledge. Rutledge escaped from the city prior to the surrender, but was largely a governor without a government. For most of this period he did not even reside within the borders of his state. In the backcountry and in the low country north of the Santee River, the war against the British occupation forces was continued by partisan leaders who operated as independent, and largely self-sufficient, warlords.[167]

Although the British imposed martial law within the occupied territories, they had neither the ability nor the inclination to enforce the slave code with much vigor. On many of the plantations of the low country, particularly those at some remove from Charles Town, martial law was little different from no law at all. As a result, during the interval between the British conquest of Charles Town in May of 1780 and their withdrawal to the environs of the city in September of 1781 (and the restoration of civil government), the slaves on many low-country plantations were effectively left to govern themselves.

Of course, the degree of isolation varied markedly from plantation to plantation, according to whether the master or overseer had fled, if or when the royal army had visited, or if the slaves themselves had visited or left with the army. For most slaves, these fifteen months may have been little different from, although perhaps more difficult than, their previous and later lives. But for the slaves on at least a few plantations, this brief period in the midst of the revolution was like the eye of a hurricane; suddenly, after decades of leaning against the prevailing wind of their masters' power, low-country blacks awoke to a strange calm and a deafening silence.

In a letter written from Charles Town in the spring of 1781, William Bull, the former lieutenant governor in the colonial regime, undertook to describe "the disadvantages that the planting interest of this province is subject [to] at present from the rebellion." Bull's narrative provides a portrait of the slow unraveling of the social order. Bull began by noting that with the outbreak of the war "many men were drawn from their plantations to be in arms . . . whereby all attention to the care of . . . their Negroes was relaxed." Consequently, Bull continued, "the slaves became ungovernable, absenting themselves often from the service of their masters." Finally, he concluded, "the code of laws calculated for the government of that class of people could not be carried into execution."[168] The

---

167. See Nadelhaft, *Disorders of War*, 71–74; and Pancake, *This Destructive War*, 83–90.
168. William Bull to George Germain, 22 March 1781, in *DAR*, 20, 94–95.

preceding fall, Eliza Pinckney described the same process, or at least its result, when she noted that the slaves who "remained at home" following the conquest of Charles Town became "quite their own masters."[169]

Rare surviving accounts of low-country plantations during this period suggest how the authority of the slave society eroded. Masters, for example, had a great deal of difficulty in securing the labor of their slaves in the plantation fields during the summer and fall following the British conquest of the low country. On her Ashepoo plantation, Eliza Pinckney wrote in September 1780, that "the [rice] crop made this year must be very small by the desertion of the negroes in planting and hoeing time."[170] Similarly, the entire 1780 rice crop at Margaret Colleton's Watboo plantation was described as "lost."[171]

The events of this remarkable period on a single plantation illustrate the progress of this "general strike" in the rice fields. When the plantation agent Josiah Smith traveled to a plantation on the Peedee River at "the latter end of June" (a month after the fall of Charles Town), he "had the pleasure of seeing a very fine [rice] crop on the ground." At the same time, however, Smith remarked ominously that "the Negroes were very far from being in a good temper," and he noted that "several of them went off soon after my return to town." By December, Smith was forced to report that "the convulsions in Carolina" since the spring, including the British arrest of the plantation overseer, which had left "no white person . . . on the plantation to see after the Negroes," had destroyed any ability to command the slaves' labor; consequently, "60 acres of rice were lying rotting in the fields."[172]

Accounts suggest that in the spring of 1781 many planters simply chose to forego any large-scale effort to cultivate their plantation fields. Smith, for example, after his bad experience with the 1780 harvest, noted in the spring of 1781 that "all things respecting the crop were at a stand."[173] The blacks' deliberate departure from the fields the previous year forced many masters to realize that in the absence of civil government they simply lacked the coercive power to obtain the degree of obedience that large-scale cultivation demanded. Further, many planters may have feared that any effort to secure labor through

---

169. Eliza Lucas Pinckney to Unknown, 25 September 1780, Charles Cotesworth Pinckney Papers, LC.

170. Ibid.

171. Robert Muncrief to Allen Swainton, 17 February 1781, Margaret Colleton Papers, SCL-USC.

172. Josiah Smith to George Appleby, 2 December 1780, Josiah Smith, Jr., Letterbook, SHC-UNC.

173. Josiah Smith to George Appleby, 15 March 1781, Josiah Smith, Jr., Letterbook, SHC-UNC.

threats might only hasten the erosion of authority when the blacks called their bluff.

Given this possibility, many masters chose simply to lie low, tacitly conceding to their slaves' refusal to grow rice and seeking to "persuade" them not to run away to the British—all the while, as one of them phrased it, "hoping for better times."[174] John Lewis Gervais's report of his 1781 visit to Henry Laurens's Mount Tacitus Plantation encapsulated this pragmatism. Gervais began by noting that "there was no [white] overseer" at the plantation and that "Montezuma [the black driver] was Commander in Chief." Gervais described the "situation" as "very unsettled" and remarked that "some of the Negroes had emigrated" to another of Laurens's plantations nearer to Charles Town without his permission. Gervais acknowledged that he "did not expect any great crops could be made this year." Yet, despite all the apparent insubordination, Gervais concluded that "take it upon the whole, I think they have behaved very well."[175] At this point, good behavior was apparently anything short of overt rebellion, mass desertion, or the outright destruction of the plantation.

The absence of white overseers forced many planters to a greater reliance upon black drivers and may have enhanced the authority of the driver in the slave quarters. Of course, the drivers had their own motivations for their actions, independent of their master's designs. At Mount Tacitus, for example, Montezuma may have been following a conservative course that dissuaded the slave community from choosing the risky path of fleeing to the British while also rejecting "business as usual" upon the plantation. As "Commander in Chief" of what was, in effect, a rural village, Montezuma may have felt that his first priority was to keep the plantation settlement intact as a viable community.

The black drivers' interest in preserving and protecting the plantation community and the masters' desire to secure the slaves as property were different agendas that could be pursued through similar means. After the war, for example, one driver was advertised as particularly valuable because "during the invasion of the country, [he] never went with the British, and had the address to prevent any going who were under his care."[176] Of course, as another postwar advertisement shows, conflict was also possible: "driver Andrew when the British were in possession of Savannah . . . [led] all Mrs. Graeme's Negroes that were then in Prince

174. Memorial of Elias Ball, 24 July 1786, Loyalists, microfilm, SCDAH, 55, 98.

175. John Lewis Gervais to Henry Laurens, 27 September 1781, John Lewis Gervais Papers, SCL-USC.

176. *South Carolina Gazette and General Advertiser*, 10 June 1783, quoted in Morgan, "Black Society in the Lowcountry," 109.

William's Parish; and Mrs. Graeme could not get them back until she made terms with Andrew."[177]

The records left by masters, agents, and overseers provide a glimpse of the plantations from the perspective of the dominant group. In this era, these authors were primarily concerned with what slaves *were not* doing. If white observers were frustrated that slaves were not laboring in the plantation rice fields, they were relieved that blacks were not engaged in overt rebellion or mass desertion. Evidence concerning what slaves *were* doing and of the blacks' perspective on events is far more difficult to obtain. Unfortunately, least of all is known of the "desolate" plantations, where no whites were resident and black independence and initiative in this extraordinary period may have been most pronounced. Given the nature of slave societies, the historical record says least about the situations in which slaves were most autonomous.

By examining what low-country slaves did with the "petty liberties" and "free time" that they had won from the plantation regime before the war, we can begin to approach the question of what blacks would choose to do when free to do whatever they chose. Many low-country slaves used their afternoons (after they had finished their assigned task in the plantation fields) and their Sundays to cultivate their garden plots and tend their poultry flocks. They used the produce of these activities to supplement the meager rations provided by the master or as the basis of trade both within and off the plantation.[178]

Such activities and practices had a political as well as an economic import. Anthropologist Sidney Mintz has compared the mode of life based upon "small-scale, self-sufficient agriculture" that was adopted by many new world slave communities both during and after slavery to that of third-world or premodern "peasants." For Mintz, the widespread emergence of *"reconstituted* peasantries" among diverse slave populations suggests that these practices represented both *"a mode of response* to the plantation system . . . and *a mode of resistance* to imposed styles of life." The peasant ethos, with its primary emphasis upon the worker's autonomy and self-control, was in many ways, he concludes, "the ideal anti-thesis to the plantation."[179] Faced with the collapse of the authority of the master class, and perhaps the absence of any resident representative of it, blacks may simply have taken the opportunity to expand upon the hours and acres they already devoted to working for them-

177. *City Gazette*, 30 November 1796, quoted in ibid.
178. See Philip D. Morgan, "Work and Culture: The Task System and the World of Low-country Blacks, 1700–1880," *William and Mary Quarterly*, 3d Series, 39 (October 1982), 563–99.
179. Sidney W. Mintz, *Caribbean Transformations* (Baltimore, 1974), 132–33.

selves in their own gardens. Freedom for such people was not an intangible "right" but a practical ability to do for themselves. Eliza Pinckney, for example, wrote that the slaves at Ashepoo plantation considered themselves to be "perfectly free"; they "pay no attention to . . . [the] orders" of their overseer, and "live upon the best produce of the plantation."[180]

With something tangible (their small property holdings) to lose by leaving the plantation, and something tangible (the "peasant" ideal of independent, small-scale land ownership) to gain by staying, many blacks chose to protect and enlarge upon the kind of freedoms they already knew rather than trade them for an uncertain future as a fugitive with the royal army.

The disorders of war reveal the powerful affective ties that bound many low-country blacks to their plantations and to the communities and kinship of the quarters. When, in the face of a British army's incursion, Eliza Pinckney attempted to persuade her slaves to leave her plantation for the security of Charles Town in 1779, she found them too "attached to their homes and the little they have there" to consent to leave.[181] Similarly, when John Faucheraud Grimke learned that "for the sake of security" an effort was made to relocate his slaves across the Santee River, he protested on the grounds that "it would be impossible to prevent the Negroes from running away . . . [and] that they should be much more satisfied to remain at their own plantation homes."[182] Boston King later recalled that while he began to "feel the happiness of liberty" when he found refuge in the camp of the royal army, he was "also much grieved at first, to be obliged to leave my friends, and reside among strangers."[183]

While the war offered slaves unprecedented opportunities for autonomy and self-control, it also left few plantations unscathed. The appetite for pillage and destruction the war inspired put both slaves' belongings and their communities at unprecedented risk. In February 1781, for example, the agent for Watboo Plantation wrote that "the Negroes . . . [were exposed] to a sett of Plunderers who go about in parties and distress the different plantations."[184] Both armies sent out parties to forage for food at plantations in the vicinity of their camps,

180. Thomas Pinckney to Eliza Lucas Pinckney, 17 May 1779, Pinckney Family Papers, microfiche, MEL-JHU, 38–3–5.
181. Eliza Lucas Pinckney to Thomas Pinckney, 17 May 1779, Pinckney Family Papers, microfiche, MEL-JHU, 38–3–6.
182. John Faucheraud Grimke to Colonel Starke, 2 May 1782, Grimke Family Papers, SCHS.
183. "Memoir of the Life of Boston King," 353.
184. Robert Muncrief to Allen Swainton, 17 February 1781, Margaret Colleton Papers, SCL-USC.

and did not exempt slaves' gardens, poultry, or livestock from their depredations.

Low-country blacks were soon caught in the middle of a spiral of destructive revenge and retaliation. Josiah Smith wrote that "parties of American light troops . . . are continually upon the visit . . . [at his Peedee plantation] taking off Rice & killing Hoggs &ca."[185] Another observer wrote that the British army besieging Charles Town had "taken all the provisions [from nearby plantations] even the poultry."[186] Following the fall of the city, Henrietta Wragg received special permission from the British commandant to carry provisions to her slaves after "the Crops and everything upon the estate had been destroyed by the rebels."[187] The ultimate result of such activities was reported by a British officer encamped on James Island, who reported that "the poor negroes [were reduced] to a starving condition in many places hereabout."[188]

A far more serious threat to the survival of plantation communities than privation, which low-country blacks had endured before, was the fact that they were themselves considered property and therefore subject to confiscation. The "American light troops" who visited Josiah Smith's Peedee plantation in 1781, for example, not only seized rice and hogs but also "took away four of the estates Negroes."[189]

The wholesale seizure of slaves and the breakup of plantation communities became an established policy of the republican military forces in the last two years of the war. Lacking any funds with which to compensate soldiers, the South Carolina state government resorted to paying recruits in captured slaves. One loyalist slaveholder, who fled his plantation for Charles Town, later "heard [that his slaves] were distributed by the American General Sumpter in bounties for raising soldiers."[190] The bounties increased with rank; privates were to receive "one grown negro," while colonels were promised "three grown Negroes and a small one."[191] Such an egalitarian distribution ensured that few if any slaves from a single plantation would be given to the same master. Confiscation therefore dealt a death blow to the plantation community. When "a party

185. Josiah Smith to George Appleby, 15 March 1781, Josiah Smith, Jr., Letterbook, SHC-UNC.
186. John Lewis Gervais to Henry Laurens, 30 April 1780, Henry Laurens Papers, SCL-USC.
187. Robert McCullough on behalf on Mrs. William Wragg, widow, Loyalists, microfilm, SCDAH, 55, 84.
188. Diary of John Peebles, 25 May 1780, SCL-USC.
189. Josiah Smith to George Appleby, 15 March 1781, Josiah Smith, Jr., Letterbook, SHC-UNC.
190. Memorial of John Hopton, 1786, Loyalists, microfilm, SCDAH, 54, 513.
191. Quarles, *The Negro in the American Revolution*, 108–9.

of the Americans under General Marion" descended upon James Cassells's plantation in the summer of 1781, they left nothing behind: "After
burning and destroying the Crop and other articles thereupon they carried away 48 Slaves together with Horses, Oxen, [and] Cattle."[192]

When threatened with confiscation, few slaves went willingly. Francis
Peyre, for instance, witnessed "50 or 52" of Elias Ball's slaves march past
"under a guard" after they were taken from Ball's estate by American
troops in 1782. Other blacks did what they could to avoid being seized
by the raiding parties. Of Henry Mills's fifty-two slaves, thirty-five were
confiscated and sold while the remainder, "who concealed themselves
in a swamp near the House," escaped.[193]

Even after confiscation, some blacks attempted to reconstitute their
communities by escaping from their new owners and making their way
back to their home plantations. Four of the fifty-two slaves of Elias Ball
confiscated in 1782 were granted in payment to John Taylor. After the
war, Taylor took his bounty home to North Carolina. However, "some
time after [arriving in North Carolina] . . . the said Negroes quitted Mr.
Taylor and returned to Mr. Ball."[194] Likewise, "many of" the slaves of
John Orde who were "carried off by the Americans . . . [later] made their
escape and returned to the plantation."[195]

Low-country blacks were torn between the strong desire to stay on the
plantation and be "their own masters" and the equally important imperative to preserve their plantation community and family ties regardless of where they might be forced to relocate. The experience of the
slaves of the former royal lieutenant governor, William Bull, suggests
these conflicting goals and the different strategies that blacks employed
to secure them. In the spring of 1781, an American force raided Bull's
"Congaree Plantation" and, Bull later recalled, "leaving the old, took
away 160 of my best Negroes."[196] Twenty of these confiscated slaves later
escaped their captors and "with difficulty got through the woods to the
King's army." In the fall of 1781, when "all the outposts garrisoned by
the King's troops were taken or drawn in . . . my old Negroes left . . . [at
Congaree Plantation] followed the army where they were kindly treated
by the General's orders and forwarded down to me."

192. Memorial of James Cassells, Loyalists, microfilm, SCDAH, 55, 109.
193. Memorial of Francis Peyre on behalf of Elias Ball, Loyalists, microfilm, SCDAH, 55,
106; Memorial of Henry Mills, January 1788, ibid., 57, 89.
194. Lark Emerson Adams, ed., *Journals of the House of Representatives, 1785–1786* (Columbia,
1979), 22 March 1785, 281.
195. Memorial of Mary Ann Gibbes on Behalf of John Orde, Loyalists, microfilm, SCDAH,
52, 25.
196. Memorial of William Bull, Jr., February 1788, Loyalists, microfilm, SCDAH, 57, 178–
79; all the following references to Bull's slaves are taken from this source.

The black community at Bull's Wappoo Plantation remained in place all this time, presumably living by and for themselves, until the fall of 1781 when they too were visited by "small parties" of American cavalry. This, Bull continued: "so much alarmed my Negroes there (being about 120 [in number]) lest they should all be carried off as those at Congaree had been that they all except a few old ones [crossed] Ashley River in the night and threw themselves under the protection of the King's troops then making lines upon Ashley & Cooper River." With the evacuation of Charles Town, the majority of Bull's slaves sailed with him, choosing to remain together as slaves in East Florida and Jamaica rather than remaining behind on the plantation and risking the prospect of being divided among victorious rebel masters as spoils of war. The incongruous sight of slaves fleeing *toward* their master indicates both the complexities and the limits of the choices that the low country's revolution offered blacks. Because neither side's promise of freedom could be relied upon, many black communities, like that of William Bull's Wappoo Plantation, may have chosen to make self-preservation their first priority. If they could not escape from slavery, at least they would endure it together.

End of Empire

$\mathbf{B}$y the summer of 1782, it had become obvious to all that the low country's war was ending and that the British had lost. In the fall, as the British began preparing to evacuate Charles Town, the question arose of what was to be done with the thousands of slaves who had been given refuge behind their lines. Defeated and embittered, the British were in no mood to be conciliatory. For several months, republican and royalist commissioners wrangled over the issue of the fugitives. Republicans threatened to repudiate debts owed to British merchants if the slaves were not returned to their owners. When the British commandant of the city, Lieutenant General Alexander Leslie, wrote to his superiors for instructions on what was to be done with the refugees, he was told that any slaves who had received a specific promise of freedom or who feared reprisals if they returned to their master should at least be given a choice as to whether or not they wished to leave with the British.[197]

In October, a compromise was achieved. Leslie agreed to return all the refugees except those who had already been promised their freedom or

197. See McCowen, *The British Occupation of Charleston*, 106–10; and Frey, *Water from the Rock*, 174–79.

who feared for their lives. For these, the British offered to provide compensation.[198] It quickly became apparent, however, that the bargain contained an enormous loophole. The only basis for determining whether or not any individual refugee had been promised freedom or had legitimate fears of reprisal was the refugee's own word. In the first week of November, a committee of British officers and loyalist civilians convened at the Statehouse to examine the refugees' claims.[199]

A strange scene ensued. As hundreds of black refugees lined up in the street outside the Statehouse awaiting their turn to testify, low-country masters who had acquired permission to enter the city sought to persuade them to return to their duty. One master wrote that "I spoke to several of them that I knew, who told me with an air of insolence [that] they were not going back."[200] Republicans claimed that the refugees had been coached by sympathetic British officers so that when they stood before the board they would know what to say. As the examinations went on, however, this seemed hardly necessary. The British members of the board were so inclined to accept without question every refugee's testimony that the civilians on the committee resigned in disgust.[201]

But not all of the blacks in Charles Town were eager to secure a berth aboard one of the ships loading in the harbor. Slaves with loyalist masters in the city often did not welcome the prospect of separation from their families and low-country connections. In the last days before the evacuation fleet sailed, such slaves endeavored to miss the boat. One loyalist master later reported that his slave woman "got out of the way on the evacuation and remains there," adding that "she was secreted by her friends."[202] Another loyalist testified that a slave man "ranaway overnight when they were to embark the next morning."[203]

On December 14, 1782, the last British troops, loyalists, and refugees in the city were embarked. A few days later, the fleet weighed anchor and the last remnant of the royal government sailed out of Charles Town harbor and out of South Carolina's history. According to British records, the evacuation fleet took with it over five thousand blacks. Few of these

---

198. Frey, *Water from the Rock*, 177.
199. Letter of 8 November 1782, "Marion-Gadsden Correspondence," *SCHM* 41 (1940), 54; Frey, *Water from the Rock*, 177–78.
200. Letter of 8 November 1782, in "Marion-Gadsden Correspondence," 54. The writer claimed that he had "used every argument I was master of to get them to return, but to no effect"; Letter of 2 November 1782, 48–49.
201. Letter of 8 November 1782, in "Marion-Gadsden Correspondence," 54; see also Frey, *Water from the Rock*, 178.
202. Memorial of John Chambers, 19 October 1787, Loyalists, microfilm, SCDAH, 56, 497.
203. Testimony of James Alexander on behalf of Leonard Askew, 28 April 1787, Loyalists, microfilm, SCDAH, 56, 150–51.

were actually free, however; the great majority were the slaves of loyalist refugees and were taken to establish plantations in Jamaica or British Florida.[204]

The total number of low-country slaves who were "lost" in the war was much larger. If those slaves smuggled out of the colony clandestinely, those evacuated prior to the fall of 1782, those who were taken as spoils of war by republican soldiers, and the thousands who died of disease or privation while fugitive are all added together, the contemporary estimate of twenty-five thousand missing slaves may not be much of an exaggeration.[205]

For a fortunate few of these people, the revolutionary storm allowed them to gain their freedom. Others only drifted to continued slavery on a different shore, and for many the currents of war led but to the grave. Whatever their fate, between 1775 and 1782, the tides of revolution and war had swept more than one-fourth of the low country's slaves out of the region forever. When the storm at last abated, those who remained stepped out into the calm and prepared to resume their lives.

204. Joseph W. Barnwell, "The Evacuation of Charleston by the British in 1782," *SCHM* 11 (1910), 26. Barnwell gives the total number of blacks evacuated as 5,327, of whom nearly 80 percent were taken to Jamaica or East Florida where they probably remained enslaved.
205. Moultrie, *Memoirs of the American Revolution*, 2, 356; see also Frey, *Water from the Rock*, 179; and Morgan, "Black Society in the Lowcountry," 111 (and note).

Conclusion:
Restorations

Perhaps the strangest relic of South Carolina's colonial regime is today on display in the lobby of the Charleston Museum. Between the entry doors and the admissions counter stands a weather-worn, larger-than-life statue of a one-armed man in classical costume. Most likely, few of the museum's visitors could identify the subject of the statue as William Pitt, the Earl of Chatham. Fewer still would know why an English parliamentarian is depicted in the garb of an ancient Roman. And probably no one would be able to explain how a statue of an eighteenth-century English lord dressed in a toga came to rest in Charleston. Those who engraved upon the pedestal the solemn pledge that "Time shall sooner destroy" the statue than it would "erase . . . the grateful memory" of South Carolinians had not reckoned upon the permanence of marble or the transience of all human institutions and intentions. To follow the strange career of Pitt's statue is to trace in microcosm the transformation of the low-country from a colonial to a republican social order.

The statue's origins reflect the character of South Carolina as a colonial society, but they also indicate the complexity of the colony's relationship to the metropolis. In the summer of 1766, the South Carolina Assembly resolved to "make provision for defraying the cost of procuring, from England, a marble statue of the Right Honourable William Pitt" as a mark of gratitude for his "generous assistance towards

obtaining the REPEAL of the STAMP ACT."[1] The legislators allotted one
thousand pounds sterling for this purpose, and directed South Carolina's agent in London, Charles Garth, to commission an English sculp-
tor for the project. Garth selected Joseph Wilton, in part because
Wilton had just completed a statue of Pitt for the Irish city of Cork. In
light of the classicism then in vogue in Britain and the ideas of classical republicanism that were invoked in eighteenth-century Anglo-
American political discourse, it was decided to portray Pitt as an
ancient Roman senator "in speaking attitude." Alluding to his role as
the defender of English liberty, the romanized Pitt would carry in one
hand "a roll . . . inscribed Magna Charta." The design of the statue testifies to the colonials' desire to consume metropolitan culture, but as
every member of the South Carolina Commons knew, Pitt was a leader
of the Parliamentary opposition. When William Wragg, a contentious
member of the assembly, proposed that the subject of the statue, and
the object of the colony's gratitude, should rightly be King George III,
he was overwhelmingly out-voted.[2]

Four years later, when the statue finally arrived in Charles Town harbor, the assembly decided that it should be "fixed in the most public
part of our town," and indeed should have the post of highest honor in
the entire colony: in the center of the intersection of Broad and Meeting
"between the State House, Guard House, St. Michael's Church and the
Public Market."[3]

On July 5, 1770, a large crowd gathered at the four corners for the
ceremonial unveiling of the statue. Beneath a banner declaring "Pitt and
Liberty," Peter Manigault, the speaker of the Commons, did the honors.
After a speech, Manigault "was pleased to condescend to the request of
the people" that he read aloud the inscription engraved upon the pedestal.[4] When the speaker finished, the crowd gave three "huzzas," St.
Michael's bells pealed, and cannon boomed from the city batteries. "Joy
sat on every countenance," the *Gazette* reported. That evening, "a great
body of the principal inhabitants" of Charles Town celebrated at a city

1. *South Carolina Gazette*, 13 May 1766.
2. Charles Garth to the Assembly, 9 July 1766, "Garth Correspondence," *SCHM* 31 (1930),
60, 235, 241–44. D. E. Huger Smith, "Wilton's Statue of Pitt," *SCHM* 15 (1914), 18–38, *PHL*,
5, 128–29, notes 1 and 2.
3. *South Carolina Gazette*, 6 January 1767 and 17 May 1770.
4. The inscription reads: "In grateful memory of his services to his country in general, and
to America in particular, the Commons House of Assembly of South Carolina unanimously
voted this statue of The Right Honourable William Pitt, Esq., who gloriously exerted himself
in defending the freedom of Americans, the true sons of England, by promoting a repeal
of the Stamp Act in the year 1766. Time shall sooner destroy this mark of their esteem, than
erase from their minds their just sense of his patriotic virtues."

tavern where "they drank forty-five toasts," the first two to the king and queen.[5]

The statue and pedestal, surrounded by an iron railing with lamp posts at each corner, completed the development of the four corners as the formal civic center of the colonial state. Visitors differed in their opinions. William Dillwyn, who visited Charles Town in 1772, described the statue as "an elegant piece of workmanship," but Josiah Quincy, while conceding that "the drapery was exquisitely well done," thought that "the attitude, air and expression of the piece was bad."[6]

For almost twenty-five years, the marble minister stood amid and above the bustle and chaos of the four corners. The declaration of American independence that came almost six years to the day following of the statue's triumphal dedication may have made a monument to an English lord seem out of place, and the pedestal's description of Americans as "the true sons of England" may have grated a bit, but the petrified Pitt endured.[7] As with the rest of Charles Town, the harsh realities of war finally touched the statue in the spring of 1780. During the siege that ended in the city's surrender, a royal army cannonball tore off the statue's right arm.

After the war, as Charleston continued to grow, the statue, standing in the center of two of the city's busiest streets, was increasingly seen as a hindrance to traffic and a public nuisance. In 1794, it was ordered to be removed. In the years of the French Revolution and the amid the emerging domestic political tensions between nascent Republicans and Federalists, it was perhaps inevitable that the downfall of Lord Chatham would be read as a political allegory. In the words of the *Gazette*:

> Yesterday, the marble statue of the late Earl of Chatham, which had been standing for a number of years, in Broad and Meeting Streets, was pulled down. . . . It is somewhat ominous to the *aristocrats* that in removing this effigy, the *head* was literally severed from the body, though without the assistance from the *guillotine*. A correspondent observes that the *executioners* showed no kind of contrition on this melancholy occasion; not even a *basket* was provided to receive the *head*; not a single person was observed to dip a handkerchief in the blood; nor will it be at all surprising

5. *South Carolina Gazette*, 5 July 1770. Among the other toasts were: "The men who will part with life before liberty"; "All honest, resolute and disinterested patriots"; "Property to the Lovers of Liberty only"; and "Our Land's free, our Men honest, our Women fruitful."
6. Alexander S. Salley, Jr., ed., "Diary of William Dillwyn During a visit to Charlestown in 1772," *SCHM* 36 (1935), 6; Mark DeWolfe Howe, ed., "Journal of Josiah Quincy, Junior, 1773," in Massachusetts Historical Society *Proceedings* (Boston, 1916), 456.
7. Its survival may be due in part to Pitt's well-known opposition to the American war.

if the body should remain without *internment* till the sound of the last *trump*. SIC TRANSIT GLORIA MUNDI.[8]

While Charleston's republican rulers may have hoped that the sight of a headless aristocrat biting the dust would serve to validate their revolutionary credentials, the bloodless character of Lord Chatham's demise (as well perhaps as the fact that he has been restored to his pedestal) more accurately reflects their conservatism. In reality, the collapse of South Carolina's *ancien regime* was far less dramatic and far less complete than the toppling of Pitt suggests. From the perspective of South Carolina's black population in particular, the events of the postwar years were more a restoration than a revolution.

"Welcome the War Home"

In September 1781, William Moultrie, a republican general who had been taken prisoner at the fall of Charles Town and recently paroled, returned with several companions to his low-country plantation for the first time in over fifteen months. He found the low-country landscape through which he passed "destitute of all." Royalist and republican armies and freebooters had taken "all of the horses, cattle, hogs" of the neighborhood. Here and there, Moultrie observed "the bones of some unfortunate fellows, who had been shot or cut down" and left unburied. At last, after "the most dull, melancholy, dreary ride that any one could possibly take," Moultrie arrived at his own plantation. In his memoirs he described what followed:

> as soon as the negroes discovered that I was of the party, there was immediately a general alarm, and an outcry through the plantation, that "Massa was come! Massa was come!" and they were running from every part with great joy to see me. I stood in the piazza to receive them: they gazed at me with astonishment, and every one came and took me by the

8. *South Carolina Gazette*, 14 March 1794, quoted in *The Southern Literary Journal* 1 (January 1836), 329. After this dramatic moment, the statue's subsequent history is something of an anticlimax. For almost a century the statue lay forgotten on the grounds of the city orphanage, while the stones of the dismantled pedestal were built into the wall of a Charleston garden. In May 1882, the Charleston city fathers rescued Pitt from his prolonged exile and placed the statue upon a brick pedestal, containing the original inscription plaque, in Washington Park (the site of the old Charles Town marketplace), less than a hundred feet from its original location. A century later, in order to rescue the statue from acid rain, it was relocated one last time to its present, and one hopes, final resting place, preserved but not remembered, like an artifact excavated from a buried city.

hand saying, "God bless you, massa! we glad for see you massa!" and every now and then some one or other would come out with a "ky!" And the old Africans joined in a war-song in their own language, of "welcome the war home."[9]

Nostalgia might well have clouded Moultrie's twenty-year-old memory of this "affecting meeting between the slaves and the master." For example, Moultrie also remembered his slaves as entirely faithful in his absence; "not of them left me during the war, although they had great offers," he wrote.[10] Yet the names of twenty of Moultrie's slaves appeared on a list of "Negroes . . . that joined the [royal] army since the landing under Sir Henry Clinton in 1780" published in the spring of 1781.[11]

Nevertheless, Moultrie's depiction of his homecoming offers a rare glimpse of a meeting that must have taken place on many plantations throughout the low country as the British withdrew and absent masters, agents, and overseers returned. Although several thousand blacks departed with the British, the majority of the fugitives who had found shelter with the royal army, and all of those who had stayed on their home plantations, were left to make their own peace with their masters and with the restored slave society on whatever terms they could get.

In this light, the actions of Moultrie's slaves might be seen as an opening gambit in these negotiations. By the time that Moultrie arrived at the plantation gates, the ultimate outcome of the war was becoming increasingly apparent. In the face of these military realities, what would Moultrie's slaves have gained by greeting him with a public display of sullen contempt or hatred? For blacks, the restoration of slavery also meant the revival of their accustomed ways of dealing with their master's power. Moreover, for slaves who had been subject to wartime privation and diseases and who had lived under the constant threat of pillage and confiscation, the status quo ante bellum may have not appeared an unmitigated evil. At least they and their families had lived to fight another day.

According to the advertisements that filled Charleston's newspapers in 1783, the roads of the low country were filled with "masterless" people who were trying to locate family members, return to their plantation homes, or somehow preserve the *de facto* freedoms that they had enjoyed during the war years. Many of the fugitives had traveled quite widely;

9. William Moultrie, *Memoirs of the American Revolution*, 2 vols. (New York, 1802), 2, 355–56.
10. Ibid.
11. *Royal Gazette* (Charles Town), 14 March 1781; the list included eight men and twelve women, making it unlikely that they were drafted into British service.

some had even followed the royal army from South Carolina to Virginia or New York. Such people were understandably reluctant passively to accept the narrow horizons, harsh regimen, and strict discipline of their previous lives.

The stories that these "masterless" people told their captors reveal something of slaves' wartime experiences and of the low country's post-war state of confusion. Jemmy, for example, who was described as "about 21 years old, [and] about 6 foot high," claimed that his master had been killed at the Battle of Eutaw Springs in September 1781, and that since that time "he has been in the army of the United States." Jemmy was "going to the northward with some Continental soldiers" when he was spotted by a suspicious low-country master and pulled from the ranks.[12]

When they were challenged, some black people sought to reinvent themselves, taking advantage of the wartime chaos to rewrite their life histories so as to pass from slavery into freedom. When Jack was ac-costed on Wadmalaw island in May 1783, for example, he first claimed to be free. Only when questioned more closely did he reveal that "his master was killed at the siege of . . . [Savannah, in October 1779] after which he went with British Army to Charles Town."[13] Likewise, William Scott advertised that he had custody of "a negro wench of the Angola country, [who] says her name is Rose and that she is free." But, Scott added, "I am informed by one of my servants that he knew her once to be the property of David Strain, deceased."[14] Others fugitives may have been more successful in covering their tracks. Presumably, at least some of the 1,800 free people of color who were recorded in South Carolina's census of 1790 were self-liberated.

The pages of South Carolina newspapers in the year after the British evacuation had the character of a statewide lost-and-found. Individuals advertised slave "property" whom the tides of war had washed up on their plantation doorsteps. By law, before the "finder" of a slave could stake his or her own claim to the property, an advertisement describing the slave or slaves had to be placed in the newspaper. In most of these ads the copy is little different from what one might write about a stray horse or dog. But occasionally, the advertisements reveal the intelligent and human character of the property that had been lost or found. Joseph Turpin, for example, appealed to Rinah, whose decision to run away in the fall of 1781 he blamed on "the enticements of the British"; Turpin

12. *South Carolina Weekly Gazette*, 14 November 1783.
13. *South Carolina Gazette*, 17 May 1783.
14. *South Carolina Gazette and General Advertiser*, 16 August 1783.

promised Rinah that if she "will return . . . she shall be forgiven."[15] Some "found" slaves sought to prevent their being returned to their master by refusing to say his name.[16] But at least a few slaves were in search of their masters. In one ad, Catharine Ritfield declared that "a middle-aged wench, by the name of Betty came to me a few days past, and desired me to take care of her till she could hear from her master, whose name she says is Archy Smith."[17]

Even after their return to slavery, people who had been with the British often made renewed efforts at escape. Their masters assumed that camp life had taught their slaves lessons and skills that would make them more difficult to recapture. One such runaway, for example, was thought to be "very specious and knowing, having been sometime with the British, and will endeavor to deceive any one that apprehends him."[18] Similarly, Primus, who had joined the royal army in Port Royal in the fall of 1781, was described as "a sly, artful fellow," who could "speak very proper" when he had a mind to.[19]

In the immediate postwar years, what a slave had done in the war became itself an important descriptive attribute. One master wanted to sell a slave family of husband, wife, and infant. The ad described the couple's talents and admitted that "their behaviour when the British were in this state is the reason, and the sole reason, [for] their being sold."[20] At the opposite extreme, another master clearly expected to receive a premium price for "a stout, sensible, country-born Negro Man . . . who during the invasion of the country never went off to the British, and had the address to prevent any going who were under his care."[21]

But not all low-country blacks were reconciled to the return of their masters and the return of the prewar plantation regime. In the years immediately following the departure of the British, several bands of armed blacks attempted to establish maroon camps in the forests and swamps of the low country from whence they could carry on a guerrilla war against the slave society. In the spring of 1786, for example, the South Carolina Privy Council was informed that "Mr. Joseph Williams was murdered a few days ago by some Negroes in Christ Church par-

15. *South Carolina Weekly Gazette*, 31 May 1783.
16. See *South Carolina Weekly Gazette*, 17 May and 14 June 1783.
17. *South Carolina Weekly Gazette*, 15 March 1783.
18. *South Carolina Gazette and General Advertiser*, 12 April 1783; see also *South Carolina Gazette and General Advertiser*, 10 May 1783.
19. *South Carolina Weekly Gazette*, 21 June 1783.
20. *South Carolina Weekly Gazette*, 19 July 1783.
21. *South Carolina Weekly Gazette*, 10 June 1783; this slave proved more faithful than his master, who wrote that he "wishes to part with him, as the Overseer has appointed another driver, he no longer being useful in that capacity."

ish."[22] Faced with the prospect of armed and hostile blacks in the vicinity of the plantations, masters not only feared that they might be killed by these "Banditti of Negroes" but also worried that the presence of the maroons might well inspire an uprising "by our indoor domestics."[23]

In fact, the maroons were closer to bandits than rebels. By day, they hid out in the woods and swamps; at night they attacked isolated plantations, stealing provisions and seeking further recruits from the slave quarters. Despite their small numbers, the maroons posed a very real threat to masters' efforts to reestablish their authority. Banditry, if not suppressed, could eventually become rebellion. Consequently, when Governor Thomas Pinckney received word "that a party of runaway Negro men, many of them armed, are become very troublesome and dangerous to the plantations in the vicinity of Stono," he ordered the colonel of the local militia to call out his entire regiment "to apprehend or disperse" the band.[24]

By far the largest and longest lived of these maroon communities was located on an island in the Savannah River swamps from whence its inhabitants waged war on their ex-masters. Some of these men had first carried arms in the service of the king. The Savannah River maroons called themselves "the King of England's Soldiers," and their leaders, "Captain Cudjoe" and "Captain Lewis," were described as "the very fellows that fought and maintained their ground against the brave lancers at the siege of Savannah."[25]

In the fall of 1786, a concerted campaign was launched by the military forces of South Carolina and Georgia against the Savannah River maroons. In an episode that echoed a long series of armed clashes between low-country whites and blacks dating from Stono in 1739 and St. Augustine in 1740 through Sullivan's and Tybee Islands in 1775–76 and the "Black Dragoons" of 1782, the black maroons and white militia met in battle on October 11, 1786:

> A small party of Militia landed and attacked them, and killed three or four, but they were at last obliged to retire for want of ammunition, having four of their number wounded. The same evening, near to sunset, fifteen

22. Adele Stanton Edwards, ed., *Journals of the Privy Council, 1783–1789* (Columbia, 1971), 22 May 1786, 176.

23. Joachim Hartstone to Peter Porcher and William Fenwick, 15 March 1787, and J. L. Bourquin, Jr., to Joachim Hartstone, 14 March 1787, Governor's Messages, 1785–1830, SCDAH, 423.

24. This gang was thought to be "too numerous for the usual parties of patrol"; Edwards, ed., *Journals of the Privy Council, 1783–1789*, 6 August 1787, 203.

25. Sylvia R. Frey, *Water from the Rock: Black Resistance in a Revolutionary Age* (Princeton, 1991), 226–27.

of the Savannah Light Infantry and three or four others drove in one of their guards, but the Negroes came down in such numbers that it was judged advisable to return to their boats, from which the Negroes attempted to cut them off, but were prevented by Lieutenant Elfe of the artillery, who commanded a boat with 11 of the company, and had a field piece on board, which he discharged three times with a grape shot, and it is thought either killed or wounded some of them, as a good deal of blood was afterwards seen . . . [26]

Left in possession of the field, the maroons won this particular battle. But given their great disadvantages in numbers and firepower, as well as the impossibility of long concealing a large community of people in the relatively small confines of the low-country landscape, the maroons could not hope to win the war. Two days later, when the militia returned to the island, they found the settlement abandoned. The commander of the militia, General James Jackson of Georgia, did not attempt to pursue the maroons into the swamps. Instead, he ordered his men to lay the settlement to waste. According to Jackson, his men "destroyed as much rough rice as would have made 25 barrels or more if beat out, and brought off about 60 bushels of corn, and 14 or 15 boats and canoes from the landing. . . . [the militia] also burnt a number of their houses and huts, and destroyed about four acres of green rice."[27] In his report, Jackson claimed victory. "The loss of their provisions," he wrote, "will occasion them to disperse about the country, and it is hoped will be the means of most of them being soon taken up."[28] The General was half right. The low-country maroons were indeed dispersed and the threat they posed to the slave society was ended, but it would take a few more years before their attacks were entirely suppressed.[29]

26. *Charleston Morning Post*, 26 October 1786; quoted in Morgan, "Black Society in the Low-country, 1760–1810," 139 note.
27. Ibid.
28. Ibid.
29. One such attack was described in a letter that was sent to the Governor:

> I make no doubt but that you have already heard of the many depredations that have been committed by the run-away Negroes about here . . . they have in my hearing threatened the lives of many of the citizens amongst which I am included. Since your absence, they . . . paid a visit in our swamp plantation, & after some time they left us, with the loss of our driver fellow, ten barrels of clean rice & myself slightly wounded in the hip.

J. L. Bourquin, Jr., to Joachim Hartstone 14 March 1787, Governor's Messages, 1783–1830, SCDAH, 423. The state of South Carolina did not finally settle its accounts with "the militia who were employed in the service of suppressing the armed fugitive slaves in the southern

Neither the individual efforts of refugees to preserve the freedom they had enjoyed in the war years nor the collective courage and desperation of the maroon bands could alter the inescapable fact that the masters had returned. Amid the chaos and confusion of the immediate postwar period, "law and order" were restored to the low country. What was not yet clear, however, was what the character of the postwar slave regime, the plantations' post-revolutionary settlement, would be. The fact that low-country blacks were powerless to prevent the return of slavery did not mean that they had to accept the loss of all of their wartime gains and concede to a complete restoration of the prewar plantation regime.

Blacks entered into the renewed struggle armed with new weapons. After their wartime autonomy, many blacks may have acquired a greater confidence in themselves and their abilities. A small taste of freedom, as well as the memory of the masters' and the slave society's wartime weakness, may have altered the balance of power on the plantations. Masters who expected relations between the great house and the slave quarters quickly to return to the status quo antebellum often were in for a rude surprise. One loyalist exile commiserated with his low-country kin on "the Ill behaviour of the Negroes" in the postwar years.[30]

It was in the decade immediately following the revolution that low-country rice planters made the decisive shift from inland to tidal rice cultivation. Once the land was cleared and the dikes and ditches were constructed, tidal cultivation was decidedly less labor-intensive than inland cultivation. The more abundant and regular supply of water could be used to flood the fields, making it less necessary for slaves to spend hot summer days pulling weeds from the muddy soil. It was also in this decade that the use of rice pounding mills first became widespread. After the Revolution, these machines relieved slaves of the strenuous and time-consuming task of pounding the rice by hand with a wooden mortar and pestle.[31]

Joyce Chaplin has suggested that one possible explanation for the timing of this dramatic change may lie in a crisis of labor in the post-revolutionary low country. In other words, masters may have been drawn to tidal rice cultivation during these years because of its promise of reduced labor requirements. The new terms of labor might therefore have been based upon a slightly new equilibrium for the post-revolutionary culture of power. In Chaplin's words, "planters were . . .

---

part of the state" until the spring of 1788; Thomas Pinckney to the Assembly, 26 February 1788, Governor's Messages, 1785–1830, SCDAH, 439.

30. Elias Ball to Elias Ball, Jr., 29 April 1785, Ball Papers, SCL-USC.

31. Joyce E. Chaplin, *An Anxious Pursuit: Agricultural Innovation & Modernity in the Lower South, 1730–1815* (Chapel Hill, 1993), 227–76.

willing to consider relinquishing some power over slaves in order to remain . . . their masters."[32]

As time passed, the war was remembered and interpreted in stories told at night to appreciative audiences in both the great house and the slave quarters. (One can not help wondering, for example, how Moultrie's slaves remembered and retold the story of his return.) Like any veterans, blacks who were with the army may have told of what they saw on their travels. Men who bore arms may have relived past glories and regaled their audience with tales of the great battles and small skirmishes in which they had fought. (Because fighting was "man's work," old soldiers may have sought to use their claims to "martial glory" to alter gender relations in the slave quarters.) Those blacks who stayed "home" during the wartime troubles had their own memories and stories. They may have told their children and grandchildren of the day the "king's people" came, the masters fled, and the people, for a time at least, were free. For most low-country blacks, the events of 1775–1782 were remembered as but another campaign in their continual struggle for independence and autonomy.

"Slavery is our King"

The toppling of the statue of Lord Chatham from the center of the four corners symbolized for many in Charleston the end of the old regime. By the time Pitt lost his head, two other pillars of the colonial state had already toppled from their thrones. The established church was the first to go. In 1778, South Carolina's political leaders revised the state's constitution, making permanent the provisional independence that they had cautiously declared in March of 1776. Included in the new document was a clause that ended the Anglican church's monopoly as the official religion of the state. Again, however, the state's leaders moved cautiously. Rather than completely end the connection between church and state, they broadened the definition of the religious establishment to include any "Christian Protestant Religion." At the same time, it was also made a crime to say "anything, in . . . [a] religious assembly, irreverently, or seditiously, of the Government of this state." It was not until a third constitution was drafted in 1790 that the separation of church and state was made complete.[33]

32. Joyce E. Chaplin, "Tidal Rice Cultivation and the Problem of Slavery in South Carolina and Georgia, 1760–1815," *William and Mary Quarterly*, 3d series, 49 (January 1992), 29–61.
33. See Jerome J. Nadelhaft, *The Disorders of War: The Revolution in South Carolina* (Orono, Maine, 1981), 38–39, 206.

The Statehouse, where the colonial assembly and Governor's Council had met in the old regime, also did not long survive the collapse of the colonial government. In order to secure the support of a suspicious back-country during the Revolution, the South Carolina Provincial Congress had offered a significant number of seats to the backcountry. After the war, backcountry legislators used their new-found military prowess and political strength to wrest the state capital from Charleston. In 1786, the legislature voted to relocate the capital to a new city, Columbia, that was to be built at the confluence of the Broad and Saluda Rivers close to the geographical center of state. Low-country leaders sought to block or at least delay the move by refusing to appropriate the necessary funds. In February 1788, however, the old Statehouse was destroyed in a myste-rious fire. The foundations for the new capitol were laid in Columbia, and the state government left Charleston in January 1790.[34]

But even as some aspects of the old regime were pulled down and carted away, others were restored and revived. The Negro Act of 1740 was renewed and "made perpetual" in 1783.[35] The Town Watch contin-ued to police and punish slaves from its headquarters at the four corners. Likewise, the law of the market remained, although at the end of the century the public marketplace was removed to a new location and that corner of Broad and Meeting was chosen as the site for the new bank of the United States.

Patriarchal attitudes also survived the demise of the royal government and occasionally were expressed, somewhat awkwardly, alongside the new republican ideas. In 1784, for example, a contributor to the *Gazette* who described himself as a "steady open republican" depicted the proper relationship between the citizen and the republican state in pa-triarchal terms: "A respectable and fatherly government will commiser-ate with its subjects, overlook all it can, consistent with the safety of the state, punish with reluctance, and when obliged to punish, do it with spirit and alacrity."[36]

Patriarchal ideas also continued to influence relations between masters and slaves. But with the destruction of kingship, the links between po-litical and familial power were greatly weakened. Masters no longer de-scribed themselves as monarchs and their plantations as little kingdoms. Instead, they became masters of plantation "households." In their mas-ters' metaphors, slaves ceased to be subjects and became children. Grad-ually the distance, autonomy, and violence of patriarchy were replaced

34. Ibid., 201–2.
35. *Statutes*, 4, 540.
36. *Gazette of the State of South Carolina*, 6 May 1784.

with the closer and more controlling, if less overtly brutal, language of "paternalism."[37]

Eventually, the low country's white inhabitants would become accustomed to being citizens rather than subjects, but they never felt at ease with ideas of equality. As long as slavery and race continued to be the most important determinants of status, South Carolina remained fundamentally an *ancien regime*. In some ways, the shadow of the colonial slave society continued to linger over the low country. In the next century, South Carolina's political culture remained distinctly patriarchal and aristocratic. Although the actions and rhetoric of the state's leaders became increasingly detached from the prevailing opinion in the rest of the nation, it may not have been South Carolina that was moving apart.[38]

In the mid-eighteenth-century low country, masters had struggled to fit the new world innovation of slavery within old world ideas of rank, order, and kingship. Their great-grandchildren saw the situation completely differently. In the nineteenth century, low-country masters who sought to defend slavery from the attacks of abolitionists saw themselves as conservatives and slavery as a venerable and traditional way of life.

One hundred years after the laws of God, King, Masters, and Market were first seated upon the four corners of Broad and Meeting Streets, slavery had become the only rule that mattered. In the summer of 1860, in words that his ancestors would have found incomprehensible, J. S. Preston proudly declared to South Carolina's Democratic convention that "Slavery is our King—Slavery is our Truth—Slavery is our Divine Right."[39] When slavery was itself enthroned, slaves had nowhere to look for deliverance except to heaven and to themselves.

---

37. The literature on nineteenth-century slavery is vast. Two recent attempts to synthesize this mountain of material are Peter J. Parish, *Slavery: History and Historians* (New York, 1989); and James Walvin, *Questioning Slavery* (London, 1996). The classic formulation of paternalism as a mode of slave-master relations and domination is Eugene D. Genovese, *Roll, Jordan, Roll: The World the Slaves Made* (New York, 1974); Genovese's best-known critic is James B. Oakes, *The Ruling Race: A History of American Slaveholders* (New York, 1982).
38. See Robert M. Weir, "The South Carolinian as Extremist," *South Atlantic Quarterly* 74 (1975), 86–103. The political culture of antebellum South Carolina has attracted a good deal of attention from scholars. Among the most important works are William W. Freehling, *Prelude to Civil War: The Nullification Controversy in South Carolina, 1816–1836* (New York, 1966) and Freehling, *Road to Disunion, Volume One: The Secessionists at Bay, 1776–1854* (Oxford, 1990); Lacy Ford, *The Origins of Southern Radicalism: The South Carolina Upcountry, 1800–1860* (Oxford, 1988); J. William Harris, *Plain Folk and Gentry in a Slave Society: White Liberty and Black Slavery in Augusta's Hinterlands* (Middletown, Conn., 1985); Stephen Channing, *Crisis of Fear: Secession in South Carolina* (New York, 1970); John Barnwell, *Love of Order: South Carolina's First Secession Crisis* (Chapel Hill, 1982); and Stephanie McCurry, *Masters of Small Worlds: Yeoman Households, Gender Relations, and the Political Culture of the Antebellum South Carolina Low Country* (Oxford, 1995).
39. *Charleston Daily Courier*, 4 June 1860; I thank Manisha Sinha for alerting me to this reference.

Index

England, 3, 80, 97–98, 176
  influence of, 5, 10–11, 13, 38–42, 44, 51–
    52, 58, 60, 67, 183–84
  See also Anglicization; British empire;
    King; London
Englishness, 123, 224
Equiano, Olaudah, 126
Esther, 251, 255
Ethiopian ball, 255–56
Eutaw Springs, battle of, 246, 276
Everyday Resistance, 9–10, 48, 205–6, 229–
  31
Exchange House, 16, 144, 166–67, 179–80,
  226, 242
Executions (slave), 24, 60, 63–64, 74, 78,
  90, 134, 233–36
  crimes most likely to be punished by,
    79–80
  described, 96–99, 236

Federalist party (1790s), 273
Fielding, Henry, 97–98
Florida:
  British (post 1763), 75, 200, 207, 268,
    270
  slaves plan to escape to, 21–22, 85, 94,
    96
  Spanish (pre 1763), 21–22, 26–27, 85,
    87, 94, 96
  See also St. Augustine, Fla.
Fordyce, John, 119, 122
Fort Sumter, 221–22
Four Corners (of the law), 17–19, 38, 91,
  272–74, 283
  See also Broad and Meeting Streets
France:
  army of, 257
  war declared with, 27
Frank, 91
Fraser, Charles, 220
Free Negroes, 45, 51, 69, 87, 136–37, 174,
  234–40, 276
French Revolution, 273

Gaillard, Thomas, 179
Garden, Alexander, 8, 120–21, 137
Gardens, slaves', 145–47, 264–65
Garth, Charles, 272
Gender relations, 155, 165, 175–77, 198–
  99, 281

General Committee (of Charles Town),
  237–38, 242
General Court (of South Carolina), 18,
  62, 78
Gentlemen's Magazine, 33, 110
Gentry, 35, 39–41, 52, 54, 184
George (Henry Laurens's), 159, 163
George (preacher), 233–34, 237–38
George, David, 126, 250
  wife of, 255
Georgetown, S.C., 10, 34, 114, 245–46
Georgia, 26, 62, 77, 278–79
  Henry Laurens's plantations in, 192,
    195, 216–17
  revolutionary war in, 226, 238–39, 245
  See also Savannah; Tybee Island
Georgian architecture, 104, 184
Gervais, John Lewis, 216, 250, 263
Girardeau, Peter, 83, 87
Glen, James, 34, 41, 47–48, 59, 67–68, 94,
  111
Godin, David, 83, 87
Gone With the Wind, 17, 181
Gordon, Adam, 40, 50
Governors (Royal). See Campbell,
  William; Glen, James; Lyttleton,
  Henry
Governor's Council, 134, 137, 148
Graeme, Mrs., 263–64
Grand jury, presentments, 20, 147, 169
  against hired slaves, 161, 164, 166
  against slave marketeering, 150–52,
    173, 175, 177
Grant, James, 75, 188
Gratitude, meaning of, 196–97
Grimke, John Faucheraud, 265
Grimke, John Paul, 163
Gullah, 43–44, 246
Guy, William, 120, 122

Haiti, 172
Hale, Matthew, 65, 80
Hall, David, 115
Handley, Scipio, 239–40
Hannah (executed), 98
Hannah (Robert Wright's), 84
Harriot, 223
Harrison, James, 111, 116–17, 133
Harry (Charles Hutson's), 213
Harry (teacher), 121, 130
Hazard, Ebenezer, 48–50, 59, 221

Hired slaves, 158–66, 254–55
Hobcaw River, 49
Holman, Walter, 100
Horry, Elias, Jr., 44
Horry, Elias, Sr., 44
Horry family, 44
Horse-and-Carriages, 17–19, 221
Horses, slaves', 147, 153–54
Hutson, Charles, 213–14
Hyde Park Plantation, 184
Hyrne, Henry, 83

Indians. *See* Native Americans
Indigo, 27, 32, 166
Industry, 228
Inglis, Alexander, 123, 127
Inns of Court, 66, 70
Insurrections. *See* Rebellions
Isaac, 257
Isaac, Rhys, 7, 110
Ishmael, 159, 163, 165
Izard, Ralph, 199–200, 215, 253

Jack, 276
Jackson, James, 279
Jacksonboro, 57
Jamaica, 171–72, 268, 270
James Island, 253, 260, 266
Jefferson, Thomas, 201
Jemmy (at Jerry's trial), 235
Jemmy (runaway), 276
Jemmy (John Well's), 233
Jeremiah, Thomas (Jerry), 234–38
Jimmy, 213
Joe (James Akin's), 95, 147–48
Joe (Thomas Boone's), 257
John, 59–60, 83–88, 100
Johns (Jones), Philip, 136–37
John's Island, 149
Judicial metaphor, 212–13, 217–18
Jury, qualifications, 67–68
Justice of the Peace, 60, 63, 71–73, 81, 86–87
    See also Magistrates' court; Slave court

Kat, 91
Kensington Plantation, 184, 251
Kent, 92
King (of Britain), 1–4, 104, 272
    authority of, 19–20, 237
    invoked, 1, 72, 104, 231–35, 273

and slaves, 1, 231–35, 244, 278–79
    See also British empire; Royal Army
King, Boston, 250, 252, 254–55, 265
King of England's soldiers, 278–79
King's Bench Prison, 199

Lancaster, 162
Laurens, Henry:
    and market relations, 201–4, 206–8
    as master, 1, 148–49, 152, 155–57, 159–61, 163, 165
    as patriarch, 1, 192, 194, 200, 215–17
    during revolution, 224–28, 234–43, 248, 263
Laurens, James, 159, 163, 165
Law, rule of, 99–101
Law of the Market, 19, 144–45, 155, 173, 192, 201, 282
Laws:
    adopting English criminal code, 62
    compensating owners of executed slaves, 63–64
    controlling slave marketeering, 152–53
    See also Four Corners; Negro Act
Lawson, John, 185
Lawyers, 66, 70–71
Leander, 174
Leitch, Thomas, 16
LeJau, Francis, 124, 130, 135, 137
Leslie, Alexander, 268
Leslie, Andrew, 114
Lewis, Captain, 278
Lexington, battle of, 228
Limus, 236
Lincoln, Benjamin, 245
Lisbon (Portugal), 208
Literacy, slaves' possession of, 119–21, 129–30, 134–38
London, 38, 41, 109
    influence of, 18, 38, 41, 112
    news from, 228–29
    South Carolina colonists in, 66, 159, 194
    See also Bishop of London; *Gentlemen's Magazine*; Society for the Propagation of the Gospel
Low Country, definition of, 10–12
Lowndes, Rawlins, 250
Loyalists, 237, 252, 254–55
Lucrecia, 141
Lucy (Abba Camfill), 127